Innocence Lost

*A chronicle of carefree childhood days
and bitter years of a German war*

Else Elfriede Hopp

First published in 2011
by Else Elfriede Burt

ISBN 978-0-9570538-0-9

Printed in England by Blackwell Print & Marketing
Charles Street, Great Yarmouth, Norfolk NR30 3LA
01493 334600

Author Biography

Else Elfrieda Burt was born in Düsseldorf/Germany. She lived in this beautiful city during the early years of war, but was evacuated from her family twice, just like it also had happened to children in England. At the end of 1942, when her family was evacuated to Pomerania, near the Baltic Sea, Else, at thirteen years old, had to make the challenging journey alone from Oberwiesenthal near the Chechoslowakian Border, to join them.

Three untroubled years followed, far away from air raids, bombing, food shortages and other ravages of war. Being a member of the Hitler Youth Movement, as were most German children, Else believed, (with news of atrocities suppressed), that Hitler, her peacetime hero, could do no wrong. Then hints from her father about the army's lack of equipment and low morale; her wise mother's reservations, and grandmother's misgivings during her visits from Düsseldorf, all planted seeds of doubt into Else's mind.

That peaceful life came to an end, when in the winter of 1944 the Russian army invaded Pomerania. For Else, at fifteen years old, a difficult and dangerous time began. Her Alsatian dog, Senta, was killed by a Russian soldier; she herself was retained by them, interrogated many times, and finally incarcerated in the local prison with the threat of deportation to Russia hanging over her. Before this became reality, Else managed to escape during transportation and after harrowing days of walking, not knowing where she was going, she reached her village and was reunited with her mother at last.

Life became unbearable and after Else's escape in April 1945, her mother endeavoured to take her family home to the West of Germany. Arriving in Düsseldorf they found their home still standing when all around, the city lay in ruin.

Else returned to school in the autumn of 1945. After studying hard to obtain the German equivalent of 'A' level, she started work as a translator for the British Forces.

In May 1949, her Commanding Officer invited Else to go to England to work as an au pair for his two small boys. There she also met her future husband to whom she stayed happily married for almost fifty years.

After Else was widowed, she decided it was the right moment to face her suppressed traumas. This Autobiography "Innocence Lost" is the story of a normal family faced with the terrors of war whose fate is entirely decided by which side of a country's border one is born.

A sequel "Bridge of Love" will, in due course, follow-on.

Mrs Burt now lives in Norfolk, England. She loves to travel but is at her happiest at home with her small dog and surrounded by her loving family.

NORTH SEA

NETHERLANDS

Rhine

BELGIUM

LUXEMBOURG

SAARBRUCKEN
incorporated 1935

FRANCE

BA

Hamburg

Bremen

Osnabruck.

crossing
Point
Helmstedt

Münster

Honover

ALLIED
ZONE
1945

Weser

Dusseldorf
Cologne.

Rhine

che

oberwieser

GERMANY 193

Danube

Munich

Basle

SWITZERLAND

East
PRUSSIA
(GERMANY)

POLAND

Dresden

Oder

CZECHOSLOVAKIA.

A rough map of Germany
at the start of war
in 1939.
Dotted lines show
my journey from
Oberwiesenthal to
my Mother in Glowitz.
The dashed lines
show the rough route
of our return to Dusseldorf
Approx 1300 Km.

Gdor

Stettin

Stolp

Danzig

ostock

Lin

Küstrin

Bratislava

Vienn

Budapest

AUSTRIA
L1938

YUGOSLAVIA

HUNGARY

I dedicate this book to the memory of my dearly beloved mother Helena Hopp. Her family was her world and, when that world was threatened, she risked her life to fight for the survival of her four children.

Thank you mother.

Contents

AKNOWLEDGEMENT

My thanks and gratitude goes to my two sons for their
unwavering support during the four years it took me
to write this book.

A heartfelt thank you also to my many friends and
knowledgeable people who gave me guidance and
expert advice on how to transfer my memories
to paper in the form of a readable book

Introduction

Now that the autumn of my life has arrived I often think how carefree and full of joy my childhood was. My thoughts go back to a splendid German city, where I was born, and where I spent my early years. I have many treasured memories, all of them crystal clear.

I am talking of Dusseldorf, as it used to be before it was almost completely destroyed during the war. That wonderful city has stood on the banks of the river Rhine for centuries. Now I no longer live there but I remember my hometown with great affection, and thinking of her gives me overpowering feelings of homesickness, a longing to drop everything and go home.

Recently, I did just that. I went back.

I found that so much had changed since I was a child. As I leaned over the wall of the Rhine Promenade the beautiful river seemed just the same. But, all around me there was a new, modern, elegance. The street, once so busy and full of traffic, is now pedestrianised, and lined with two rows, not one, of Plane trees.

In my mind's eye I saw the harbour as it used to be. Barges spitting out gravel from Switzerland, or sand or coal from faraway places, whilst huge cranes swung around transferring cargoes to lorries and trains.

But that busy playground of my childhood, like my childhood itself, has gone. All the barges have disappeared from the harbour. It is now a Yacht Haven where exclusive pleasure boats are moored side by side. Barges, moving up and down river remain as they always have, but they are larger and more numerous and instead of towing a small rowing boat they now carry, for the convenience of the bargee, a small motor car on the stern. Somehow those little boats are anchored in my memory and conjure up visions of happy childhood days.

I looked around me and saw the tall, imposing radio tower with its revolving restaurant. On one side of the harbour the buildings are new and ultramodern. Most of them appear to be constructed mainly of glass. To me they seem alien but then I realise that time has not stood still while I had been away.

Over to my right the old flour mills and warehouses have been converted into apartments for the privileged and prosperous. There are new cafes, landscaped areas and small footbridges connecting both sides of the basins.

It was of course essential to rebuild the city after the destruction of the war. It is now beautiful and the people of Dusseldorf are rightly proud of their hometown and their magnificent achievement. But they have lived with the reconstruction and have seen it take shape over time. For me it is a sudden shock, and I can't stop the tears from running down my cheeks. I miss my old home.

I can see myself as a child being taken round my beautiful city. It has so much to offer: graceful old buildings hidden away in narrow cobbled streets. There is the old part of the town, the Altstadt, and nearby delightful parks where you can wander among the ancient trees and lovingly tended, beautifully coloured, flower beds.

1

The principal avenue, the Konigsallee, runs through the centre of the city. It is lined with elegant, fashionable shops .There are also luxurious cafes where, in the summer months, people sit outside to watch the world go by.

A waterway called the Stadtgraben flows through the middle of the Konigsallee. It is flanked by tall trees offering cool shade on hot summer days. Seats are positioned between the trees inviting people to enjoy the tranquillity away from the hubbub of the city. The Stadtgraben ends with Neptune's Fountain, the symbol of the Konigsallee.

Because of its many parks, Dusseldorf is called *'Gartenstadt',* the City of Gardens. The Hofgarten, near to the Cornelius Platz is just one of them and it was there that my best friend Marlies and I would often go after school. We loved to listen to the orchestra and Marlies would do a little dance. Then, we would walk along the Konigsallee looking at the fashionable clothes in shop windows, knowing that we couldn't afford them. It didn't bother me particularly if I owned a lace handkerchief or a pair of evening gloves. It always mattered to Marlies. She was pretty and proud of her blonde curls. I loved my nut-brown plaits, mainly because I could sit on them! We were both slim, but Marlies always seemed more dainty. In summer she would protect her sensitive skin with a large sunhat, whilst I was happy to be tanned.

Special places of beauty were the two small lakes, the Schwanenspiegel and the Kaiserteich. On Summer Sundays my mother would hire a canoe and she, my young brother Hans-Dieter and I would row across the lakes. Occasionally we were allowed to paddle. We had to take turns which could cause an argument between my brother and me. Then mother would intervene and there would be no treat of ice creams in our favourite café.

And when it was winter, the lakes froze and we slid across the ice. We loved every minute of it and when the early dusk fell we, like all the other tired and weary children made our way home. Our feet were frozen but mother had a remedy. From the balcony she would fetch a bucket of snow, which she would rub into our skin. She said it would stop us getting frostbite but I remember it hurting. Dieter and I nearly cried.

In September 1938 I was nine. It meant I was old enough to join the 'League of German Girls'. I was a member of the Hitler Youth. I had seen my older friends join, and had longed to be part of it.

Marlies would join a little later as I was two months older. I recall so clearly my mother taking me to buy my uniform. There were very precise instructions as to the details of badges and colours of lanyards, and my first one was red and white.

I was proud to be a Hitler Girl. The movement wasn't entirely political and we rambled through countryside, learning about flora and fauna. We sang around campfires and told each other scary stories. We were taught to be confident and fend for ourselves. I didn't know that I was learning skills that would in the not too distant future literally save my life. But life in 1938 was wonderful for us girls.

We loved every minute of it.

We were children and I remember the magic of Christmas time. I can savour the details such as the Advent wreaths, mother's cooking and my father playing carols on his guitar. As Christmas 1938 gave way to a new year none of us knew that the world was about to change.

For us, the first change of 1939 was the arrival of my baby brother, Ralf-Jurgen. Because my grandmother could not look after us my brother Hans-Dieter and I had to spend a brief time in a Children's Home while mother was in hospital with the baby. I remember not liking the idea, but it wasn't too bad, and even that spell didn't burst the bubble of happiness in which we seemed to live then.

There were the Carnivals, and Easter celebrations. We played in the streams in Summer and watched the barges on the Rhine. We made little theatres and put on plays for our friends.

And yet, there was something in the air. Even as 1939 played out its spring I kept going back in my mind to a night in the previous November. I will never forget the date. My father's birthday. November 10th 1938.

Mother and I had been into the city where, every week, she attended a Red Cross First Aid course. I also went as I wanted to learn how to deal with an emergency. I overheard a Red Cross Sister telling mother that 'ugly things were happening in the city' and that she should take me home straightaway. 'It would not be safe to be out this evening'.

We left. Outside it was already dusk and cold. But the sky was red; it looked like many fires burning.

Not far from the Red Cross Hall was a Synagogue. This imposing old building had stood in the Kasernenstrasse for centuries. But now it was burning, and no one was there to put out the flames. Many people had gathered to watch, but they did nothing. It was an extraordinary sight. I couldn't understand it. I asked my mother why nobody was putting out the fire, but she didn't explain. She took my hand and said .Come child, we must get home, it's your father's birthday'.

We pressed on and as we turned in to the Stromstrasse we saw another group of people, standing in stunned silence and looking towards the upper floor of a large apartment house. Mother and I stopped too. There was a deafening noise of smashing windows and we could see men, in brown uniforms, hurling furniture and other articles into the street. Even in that noise we could hear crying and screaming.

Again I asked mother what was happening. At first she tried to tell me to forget what I'd seen, but I wanted to know more.

She said that the men were SA men. Stormtoopers. Sometimes called Brownshirts. 'They are', she said, 'Hitler's special envoys, they're acting on his instructions. And this is happening not just here in Dusseldorf, but all over Germany'.

She went on, 'Child, you are too young to understand what is behind all this. Try not to dwell on it'.

We rushed home and I pleaded with my father to explain what we'd seen. He too said that I would find it difficult to understand. The people affected, he said, were Jews. They were not wanted and would be ordered to leave their houses, and this country to go and live in peace somewhere else. Anywhere, but not in Germany. I couldn't understand any of it. 'Vati', I said, 'do you know any Jews?'

'Yes Else', he said. 'Your mother and I do. They are people just like us, they have a different religion and way of life to us, but that is all. But now Else, please no more questions; time for bed. Perhaps one day when you are older you may realise what is happening tonight'.

Those events would go down in history as the beginning of the persecution of Jews in earnest, and it will forever be a blight on the German nation.

I'm not sure that my childhood ended that night. We still played and tried to be happy. But I know that the untroubled feeling of innocence was gone and that something had changed forever. I was soon to experience things that would take me from childhood to the adult world in ways I'd never imagined. Even I could see that November 10th 1938 was a turning point. Throughout history this night will always be called 'Die Kristall Nacht'.

But, we still played our games through 1939, even though those November memories had scratched the surface of our untarnished lives. As summer moved toward autumn it would become increasingly clear that momentous events were about to happen. When they reached their peak our world came to a standstill. It was September 3rd 1939 when we heard the radio broadcast that told us Germany was at war. It was just a few days before my tenth birthday. I was still allowed to celebrate, but in truth the party was over.

Memories, so many memories!

With a lump in my throat and tears running down my cheeks I think of all the years that have gone by since I last looked at my beloved river.

But now it is time to say farewell once more to my hometown, which forever will have a special place in my heart.

Shall I ever come back again?

I would like to think so.

But England is now my home....that's where my heart is and where my family is waiting for me to return.

Beneath the straw I lie asleep and dream of plums. Bottled plums, lined up on shelves where mother has stored them ready for winter. They look so inviting, succulent and delicious but I am not allowed to touch. Then I wake and freeze. I hear voices, which I cannot understand. Russian voices? The sound of something stabbing the straw. Bayonets? The stabbing comes closer, ever closer almost touching my face. I want to scream....

Innocence Lost

Chapter 1

War

3 September 1939

Soon after Hitler declared war, my father, like countless other German men, received his call-up papers. He had to travel to Koblenz to start his military training and my mother was allowed to go with him.

'For just a few days,' she said to me. 'And while I'm gone with father, grandma will come and look after you.'

I missed mother so much I became ill. Yet my dear grandma did her best, for she had no easy task with my two younger brothers and me. After all, the youngest, Ralf, was only a baby and needed a lot of attention.

Mother soon returned home, and then her troubles began. Like thousands of other women she had to learn to cope and look after her family without the support of a husband: a huge responsibility in time of war.

When father completed his military training in Koblenz, they posted him to Poland. But the campaign there was already over, for Poland had soon surrendered. Now Germany was in control.

Late spring, 1940

Every now and then sirens warned us an air raid was imminent. At first the older of my two younger brothers, Hans-Dieter, and I thought it was exciting to get up as fast as possible in the middle of the night, and rush downstairs to the air-raid shelter.

'Come, children. Quickly now! Don't dawdle,' mother would urge. 'Don't forget: our apartment on the top floor is nearest the enemy bombers!'

At first nothing much happened. The all-clear would sound and off we'd go, back upstairs, to our warm beds. But one night our routine changed.

The alarm sounded and all the tenants from our apartment house assembled in the shelter. However, there were no explosions; just anti-aircraft guns firing at what must have been enemy bombers. Then suddenly a banging on the door and there stood the air-raid warden.

'Get out! Get out quickly. Your house is on fire! Incendiary bombs have dropped and your roof's burning. Everyone out on the street!'

We looked up at the roof of our house and saw it ablaze. All I could think of was my shiny new bicycle in the attic. Now I'd never ride it. My longed-for Christmas present was gone, and only many years later would I again own a bicycle.

Early 1941

As time went by and air raids intensified, life in our western German city of Düsseldorf became more dangerous. The government decreed that all schoolchildren should be evacuated, and sent the girls from my school to Reichenbach in eastern Germany. I was very unhappy to leave home and thought to myself, *Why should I have to go, when Hans-Dieter and Ralf can stay behind with mother.* It made no sense. But my pleading did no good – I had to obey.

I hated it in Reichenbach. Our school was in the centre of town, and we had to sleep in bunk beds on straw mattresses. The whole affair was awful. I chose a top bunk, while another girl, also called Else, took the lower one. She and I soon became close friends, but I couldn't settle down, as everything was so unfamiliar and regimented. Our usual teachers had stayed behind in Düsseldorf, and the new staff and schoolmistresses were as strange to us as we were to them. The clock governed our days, and we had to obey the rules. I became dreadfully homesick and wouldn't eat. I cried much of the time and soon made myself ill. The school authorities discussed my case and, to my delight, sent me back home.

But not for long.

The bombing continued and became fiercer. Day and night sirens howled, bombs fell and blasted houses, and hundreds of people died or were injured. We had a strong shelter in the basement of our apartment house where all the residents (twelve families) fled for safety each time the alarm sounded. Mother had prepared for us to live there for long periods: we had food, drink, a mattress to sleep on, table and chairs where we could sit to play games and read, and, for Hans-Dieter and me, do our homework.

Late summer, 1941

They were tough times and the din of war was hard to bear – uninterrupted sleep was rare. The government again decided it was too dangerous for children between the ages of six and fourteen to remain in the cities. So again I had to say goodbye to my mother and brothers. This time we schoolgirls travelled to the elegant spa town of Karlsbad (now Karlovy Vary), where we stayed in the Grand Imperial Hotel. But we were not allowed out on our own. Our teachers escorted us, mostly on country walks through the peaceful fields and forest. If it weren't for the many soldiers everywhere, we could have believed the world was a peaceful place.

We stayed in Karlsbad for six weeks. Then, one morning before lessons began, our headmistress told us without explanation the good news that the time had come for us to return home.

We were excited and couldn't stop chattering, laughing and running around, eager to pack. We thought the sooner we packed, the sooner we'd be off.

Looking back at that time with adult eyes, I realise there must have been a lot of confusion, for in the spring of 1942 they told us to get ready for evacuation again. This time to Oberwiesenthal, a small village near the Czechoslovakian border.

Once more we assembled at the station, said our tearful farewells and left our families behind. While I was away, would mother and my little brothers be safe? Would they be hurt or killed by the ferocious bombing now going on with almost no respite? The thought that I might not see them again was almost too awful to bear. Kissing my dear mother and brothers goodbye, I burst into tears.

But what good was crying? I had to go and mother shouldn't see me upset. She had her own worries with father away on the Russian front. I tried to dry my tears and be brave and, as the train left the station, leant out of the window to wave to her.

'Don't be sad, mother!' I shouted. 'I'll only be away for three months, and then I'll come home again. The time will go quickly.'

How wrong I was. I had no inkling what the future held for us all.

Oberwiesenthal was a small but beautiful town, peaceful, without air raids, bombs or traces of war. It had hardly any traffic; just horses and carts leisurely trundling through the village street.

Situated on the outskirts of the village, our accommodation was, I believe, an old converted army barracks. We girls soon settled down, weary after our long journey.

This time I was much happier away from home. Our class mistress from Düsseldorf, Miss Beckhaus, had come with us. An elderly lady, she'd taught us from the day we'd started at the Flora School. We were fond of her, and she knew how to handle us. Kind and understanding, she was always there if we needed someone to talk to. We could go to her if we were troubled or homesick.

Our physical training mistress, Miss Cohen, had also come with us. Young and fun to be with, she insisted on daily gymnastics. We also played games and swam under supervision in the small lake nearby.

In autumn we wandered through fields and forests, picking mushrooms and blueberries, cranberries, wild strawberries and blackberries. Some mornings we saw ladies from the town walking to the woods with buckets in their hands. All day long they'd pick blueberries to sell at the market, and by the end of each day their backs must have ached dreadfully.

Chapter 2

The Telegram

October 1942

In the middle of the month we heard that all the girls and teachers had to return to Düsseldorf. But where was I to go? I couldn't return, for none of my family was there. Mother and the boys had been evacuated to the province of Pomerania, bordering on the southern shore of the Baltic Sea. Our apartment was empty.

I spoke to Miss Beckhaus, our teacher, and asked what would happen to me.

'Don't worry, Else,' she answered. 'I'll think of something. Just give me a day or two. I'll make enquiries and we'll see what we can do. First I have to find out how to get you to Pomerania.'

I had to be patient, but was confident she'd find a solution.

A few days later she called me to her study. 'Sit down, Else; I must talk to you. I fear you may not like what I have to say. At present there's no transport to Pomerania. Until such a day comes, you'll have to transfer to another camp and wait there. I'm truly sorry, Else. I really tried to find a way out for you. I know how important it is for you to join your mother.'

She was right – I didn't want to hear what she had to say. I was worried and unhappy, but couldn't change the situation.

At the end of October the other girls left for Düsseldorf. After a sad goodbye to all my friends and teachers, I was taken to another camp near Chemnitz, a town about 33 kilometres from Oberwiesenthal. My departure to Chemnitz was well organised. Someone soon arrived by car to pick me up and take me to my new and, I hoped, temporary home.

But while waiting to rejoin my mother I found it difficult to settle into the new surroundings. Although I soon made friends with girls and teachers, I was restless and wanted to be with my family. As a thirteen-year-old I thought I ought to be a grown-up, but in reality felt abandoned. I desperately needed my mother, yet she was far away.

I knew they lived in the small Pomeranian village of Glowitz, near the Baltic. But Pomerania was still a distant dream while I anxiously awaited a means to take me there. After waiting in Chemnitz for three weeks, I began to think the authorities had completely forgotten me. Without transport I was stuck.

I puzzled over the situation. How could I get to mother? There had to be a way. And then, out of the blue, an idea began to form in my mind. I'd approach my teacher with the request to send my mother a telegram, asking her to forward the money for me to travel by train to Glowitz.

The plan buzzing in my head, I went to my teacher's study. When she heard my suggestion, she was surprised, but to my relief didn't dismiss the idea.

Good, I thought. *I'm over the first hurdle.*

Now I had to convince her I was able to make the long journey on my own.

'Else,' my teacher said, 'do you realise what you're asking me? Do you really think your mother will allow you to travel all that way on your own? You've very far to go, and there's no one to accompany you.'

'Please don't be concerned,' was my answer. 'I'm not afraid. If I had to, I'd travel around the world to be back with my mother again.'

'Very well, Else, I'll do as you wish.'

And on 8 November 1942 she sent a telegram to mother. Now I had to sit and wait.

Please God, let mother do as I ask, I prayed, desperately hoping she'd answer favourably.

On 9 November, after breakfast, teacher called me into her study. 'Well, Else,' she greeted me, 'your mother did as you asked. I'm to give you fifty reichsmark for your journey to Pomerania, and once I've made travel arrangements and bought your ticket you'll be able to leave.'

For a moment or two I was speechless. I stared at my teacher, but my face must have shown what I felt. 'Thank you! Thank you! Oh, this is wonderful. When will I be able to travel? Will it be today? I've started packing already. How soon can I go?'

'Please Else, contain yourself! Calm down and listen to me. I'll go to the station now, buy your ticket and find out when the trains leave for Dresden. When you arrive there, a Red Cross nurse will meet you. She'll look after you and advise you what happens next. You may not be able to travel today: it depends on how often the trains are running to Dresden. Please be patient. Remember, there's a war on and timetables aren't always accurate. Go now and get everything ready. Spend the evening with your friends and I'll talk to you later.'

I didn't see teacher again that evening, but I knew I could rely on her to prepare everything for my departure.

With so many things going around my mind the excitement kept me awake for hours. But I must have dropped off, because the next thing I knew was a loud knock on my door and a voice telling me to wake up.

'Come on, Else. Get up. You'll start your journey today.'

Teacher had said the magical words and I was instantly awake.

'Your train leaves this afternoon at four-thirty. When you arrive in Dresden, the Red Cross will look after you, feed you and give you a bed for the night. Then in the morning, after breakfast, they'll take you to board a train to Berlin.'

'Thank you, Miss,' was all I could answer. If I'd said any more, I'd have cried.

I'll remember that day for the rest of my life. It was Tuesday, 10 November 1942, a damp, chilly day. But the weather couldn't stifle my happiness. I wrote in my diary:

Today I'm going home to mother! The day's passing so slowly, but as the time of departure comes nearer, I feel such excitement; I can't keep still for a minute. Butterflies in my stomach: is that a sign of fear? Of course I'm not afraid! I'm a German girl: German girls know no fear. And I'm one of them!

Chapter 3

Soldier Friends

The journey to Dresden was uneventful. There were no separate compartments on the train, only long wooden seats on either side of the carriage. Crowds of people had squeezed in, talking to each other, all very friendly. They were surprised I was travelling on my own and wanted to know where I'd come from and where I was going. 'A young girl like you, alone, going all the way to the Baltic? My, you're brave!' I just smiled, told them I was going to rejoin my mother, and enjoyed the fuss they made of me.

We soon reached Dresden. The journey hadn't taken long, but I was glad the first leg was behind me. Standing uncertainly on the platform, I heard my name called out: 'A message for Else Hopp! Please stay where you are. You'll be met shortly.'

I stayed and waited and, sure enough, a short while later a nurse found me and took me to the Red Cross station. All the nurses made me welcome. They offered me food and gave me a glass of milk; then they took me to a small room with a bed where I could spend the night.

After the day's excitement I was exhausted, and, with nourishment in my tummy and a warm bed to snuggle into, soon fell fast asleep.

When the nurse came to wake me, I thought I'd only just gone to bed. 'Else,' she said, 'you have to get up straight away. We mustn't waste time. Wash your face and come to breakfast, and then I'll take you back to the platform. The next train will take you to Berlin.'

My diary entry for that day says,

'I've been told Dresden's a beautiful city but, sadly, I've had no opportunity to see any of it. Perhaps one day, when the war's over and I'm a little older, my parents will bring me here and show me everything it has to offer.'

Little did I know what fate awaited Dresden.

Then on to Berlin. This time the train was much faster and didn't stop as often, and there were separate compartments. I gazed out of the window lost in my own thoughts as time flew by.

We arrived in Berlin in the early afternoon and I'll never forget my feeling of loneliness as I climbed down from the train. I didn't know what to do next, or where to go. So many people milling about, who seemed to know where they were going. And all the soldiers! I'd never seen so many before. *What's their destination?* I wondered, but there was no one to tell me. Luckily I didn't have long to wait, for again someone called my name on the loudspeaker and said someone would come to meet me. Everything seemed well organized.

I stayed where I was and waited patiently until a woman tapped me on the shoulder. 'Are you Else Hopp?'

'Yes, I am.'

'Good. Come quickly with me.'

Another Red Cross nurse had come to meet me, but she was impatient.

'Else, come on. We must hurry and can't hang about. We have to get to another platform where the train's already waiting. It won't be long before it leaves.'

I rushed as fast as I could but struggled to stay on my feet – so many people on the station, all running and pushing. In a frenzied hurry the nurse grabbed my hand and almost pulled me along.

We had to go down some stairs, and then along a corridor that seemed to run on for ever. And then up another flight of stairs. I was ready to collapse but thankfully right before me stood the train, hissing and puffing impatiently. I knew it would leave at any moment.

'Now, Else, you'll be all right until you get to Stolp. There you'll be met again.'

'Will my mother be there?' I asked.

'I don't know,' answered the nurse, 'but you mustn't worry. Someone will meet you, and you'll be put on the right train to your destination, Glowitz.'

But first I had to get on the train to Stolp.

Soldiers travelling east to the Russian front stood in corridors and leant out of windows, packed like herrings in a barrel. How could I get on a train that had no more room? But the soldiers were in high spirits, and my nurse was a resourceful woman.

'Here, you boys!' she shouted. 'Help me get this little girl onto the train. She has to get to Stolp and can't be left behind.'

Willing hands shot out.

'Come on, little girl. We'll lift you in. Nothing to it.'

The hands reached out and lifted me through a window into the compartment as if I were a feather, my case following behind! Standing there among all those strange soldiers, a feeling of shyness overcame me and I almost burst into tears. But the men soon cheered me up. They laughed and joked and sang army songs, some of which I knew. So I joined in and my shyness soon vanished. They also asked me where I'd come from and where I was going.

I told them my story and they were amazed to hear I'd travelled on my own from Chemnitz to Dresden, and then to Berlin, and now to Stolp. As they listened I felt most important.

When the soldiers asked me whether I was hungry, I had to admit I was starving, as the nurse hadn't given me anything to eat on the journey. They soon spread out their army sandwiches to share with me, together with a few treats from special rations.

Well meaning and warm hearted, many of those men and boys would never return home.

Yet here they were, laughing and joking as if they hadn't a care in the world.

I felt contented, surrounded by my soldier friends. They'd put me at ease and made me feel a part of them.

Outside lay a dark, cold world, but our compartment was warm and cosy. I wanted to look out of the window but couldn't. Blackout blinds meant not a chink of light could escape to betray us.

I should have been sleepy after my long, exciting day, but was edgy and had butterflies in my stomach. I longed to get to Stolp, where I hoped my mother would be waiting when the train pulled into the station.

One soldier told me snow had fallen and now a white blanket covered everything. Snow in November? I found that unusual, but in the remote part of Germany where I was going winter started early and lasted many months – sometimes to the end of April.

Eventually one after another of my companions settled down and closed his eyes. The sound of voices died down and soon silence surrounded us, broken only by the steady clickety-clack of the train as it sped through the darkness. Now and then I heard subdued conversation, and one soldier hummed a gentle, sad tune to himself. Perhaps he was homesick with thoughts of his family far away across the country.

I knew we'd soon arrive in Stolp and wanted to stay awake. I struggled against the sleep that tried to overpower me. *Not long now*, I told myself. *If you go to sleep you may miss your destination, and who knows where you'll end up.*

I must have dropped off, because suddenly someone shook me gently, and I was immediately awake.

'Else, we're approaching Stolp. Get ready: in a few minutes we'll be there.'

I was up instantly, hardly able to contain my excitement.

The train began to slow down and it was time to say goodbye to my soldiers. They'd been very good to me and I'd enjoyed their company. Now they were travelling further east to Russia and had no idea how their journey would end. I hoped God would look after them. Some were still almost boys, while others had told me of wives and children left behind. Yet they all had one wish – to survive the battlefields that lay ahead.

As the train came to a standstill and I stepped down onto the platform, cheerful voices echoed after me, 'Good luck, Else! Take care and stay safe. Have a good life.'

I waved a final farewell, the conductor blew his whistle and, slowly, the train pulled out of the station. Gathering speed, it soon disappeared into the night.

Standing on the platform, I realized I was the only person there. No mother, no one to meet me and I didn't know what to do or where to go. With the train gone, the deserted station felt eerie. A few scattered lamps glowed dimly here and there but, apart from them, darkness surrounded me.

'Hello, little girl. You must be Else Hopp.' I'd neither seen nor heard the conductor coming towards me. He greeted me with a friendly smile. 'I know all about you and will take you to your train, which soon leaves for Glowitz. Only another hour and you'll be at your destination. I'm sure your mother will be there to meet you; she couldn't come to Stolp, but asked me to tell you not to worry. She's not ill – just unable to meet you here.'

Never mind, I thought, *it won't be long and I'll be with her. My journey will be over at last.*

'Come, Else, we must hurry now: the train's about to leave.'

I glanced at the station clock – 8.30pm. It was 11 November 1942 and I'd travelled for nearly forty-eight hours. Admittedly I'd spent a night in Dresden, but it had nevertheless been a long journey and I was exhausted.

The train I boarded was almost empty and I had a compartment to myself. Huddling in a corner, I waited for the final stretch of the journey to start. Soon we'd be in Glowitz and I hoped mother would meet me there. Off we went and the little train stopped at station after station. Seeming to have plenty of time, passengers had no hurry to get on. But I was impatient and wanted to keep moving.

At last the train slowed and, hissing and gasping like an old gent out of breath, came to a standstill. The conductor opened my compartment door: 'Come on, girl. Time to get off. We're in Glowitz.'

As fast as I could, I jumped off the train. My suitcase was already waiting: someone must have unloaded it.

Glowitz station had only one platform, which looked like a ramp. There was a lot of snow on the ground and once more I stood alone, waiting.

Where's mother? I thought. *Why isn't she here to meet me?* By now I was starting to panic. But suddenly from the station entrance I saw running towards me a boy, waving his arms and shouting, 'Else, Else! Wait for me. I'm coming to take you home.'

It was my young brother Hans-Dieter. He had grown since last I had seen him and was almost as tall as me now. We hugged each other. 'Else', he said 'It's good to have you back'. 'Where are we going? I asked. 'Don't worry, Else,' he said. 'Just come with me to the station entrance and you'll see our amazing transport!'

I was intrigued. Whatever could he mean? But I didn't have long to wait: there before my eyes stood the most wonderful sleigh, pulled by two majestic horses with bells around their necks. And in front was a real sleigh driver, who looked at me in a kindly way and gave me a friendly smile, which made me feel much happier.

'Welcome to Pomerania, Else. Come, let me help you into the sleigh. You must be very cold and tired. Hans-Dieter, come on. Sit next to your sister. Take this rug and spread it over your knees.'

No sooner had the sleigh driver said this than he climbed into his front seat, and off we went, gliding over a white carpet of new-fallen snow.

How well I remember that crisp winter evening. A full moon shone in a cloudless sky, sending beams of silver light onto the frozen snow. The light made the snow sparkle, as if a billion stars had come to earth.

Silently, apart from the tinkle of the horse bells, the sleigh took us through the deserted main street of the village. Deep silence lay everywhere. Hans-Dieter, seeing I was nervous, tried to assure me: 'Not long now, Else. Soon we'll be home, where it's warm and cosy.'

As we reached the end of the village street the sleigh driver guided his horses through an old archway into a long, beautiful driveway flanked by graceful beeches. We passed a small lodge and in the distance I could make out farm buildings. The subdued lowing of animals snug in their stalls now and then broke the stillness of the winter night.

As we drove through a large ornate gate, I saw before me, surrounded by ancient trees, one of the most impressive buildings I'd ever seen. Thick snow covered everything and the moon's bright light reflected from many windows. They seemed to welcome me with their glinting and the whole scene looked magical. All these new impressions almost overwhelmed me, but overriding everything was the knowledge that within a few minutes I'd be back in the arms of my beloved mother.

The sleigh came to a halt below a portal in front of a large entrance door. Again I felt anxious, but no sooner had we stopped than the door opened and a tall, regal lady stood there.

She took my hand and introduced herself.

'I'm Baroness von Puttkamer. Welcome to my home, Else. We've waited for you, and I'm delighted to tell you that you've a little sister who was born yesterday. Your mother's waiting for you. Follow me and I'll take you to her.'

'Thank you, Baroness,' was all I could stammer, as I followed her in a daze, my brother in tow, through a vast hall and up a long flight of stairs.

There seemed so many corridors to walk through. Down a few steps, along another passage. At last she stopped outside a door and knocked. 'Frau Hopp, are you awake? I have someone here who's waiting to see you.'

She opened the door, and there was mother sitting up in bed with a tiny baby in her arms. 'Elslein, is it really you? At last, my child! I've waited so anxiously for you. Come here and let me see you. I can't believe you're here. This is a wonderful moment!'

I ran and flung my arms around her, laughing and crying at the same time. 'Mother, I've missed you so much,' I murmured over and over. 'I was so worried when you didn't come to meet me, but then I didn't know you had a baby.'

'Yes, Else, see, you now have a little sister – Marlene. Very soon she'll be christened here in the manor and I hope father can also be with us on that important day. All my family complete – what joy!'

My tiny sister opened her eyes for a second and glanced at me. Did she approve of what she saw?

With all the excitement I'd completely forgotten I also had another small brother. He sat in his cot, thumb in mouth, big blue eyes watching every move I made. To him I was a stranger, as he was only three years old.

I went to him and lifted him into my arms. 'I'm your big sister. Let me have a hug and a kiss, because I love you. He looked at me and then gave a hesitant smile. A pair of thin little arms went around my neck and he kissed me. 'Now let me tuck you into your nice warm bed. The sandman's just around the corner and he'll bring you happy dreams. A little fellow like you should have been asleep hours ago.'

Hans-Dieter also wanted to remind me he was there.

'Dieter,' I assured him, 'you're a big lad, mother's special helper. With father away, you're now the man of the house and there'll be many times when mother will have to rely on you.' My words had made him proud and happy, and he was content to go to bed.

I looked around our little family: mother, Hans-Dieter, Ralf and baby Marlene. If only father could have been here with us, how wonderful that would have been. But now I was home at last, my journey just a memory. *And*, I thought, *no matter what the future brings, one thing's certain: I'll never willingly leave my family again.*

Chapter 4

First Day

11 November 1942

'Else, it's so good to have you with us again. Now come, sit on the end of my bed and tell me, was your journey an adventure?'

'Mother, you won't believe all the things that happened to me.'

With the two boys settled for the night, and the baby also sleeping peacefully, I could sit with my mother and talk to her about my long journey and everything else that had happened to me since I'd left home. We had so much to tell each other, we could have talked all night.

But a gentle knock on the door interrupted our conversation. 'Frau Hopp, it's me, Trudi. I have a meal for your daughter and a drink for you.'

I ran to open the door, and there stood a young woman, the head parlourmaid, carrying a large tray of food and drink. Just to look at it made my mouth water and I suddenly realised how hungry I was.

The food was delicious and there were a few special treats I didn't even know existed. After all, it was 1942, and, with food rationing, treats were a rarity. There was freshly baked bread with butter, a smoked sausage, two boiled eggs, a large slice of ham, rice pudding with sugar and cinnamon, and a large mug of cocoa. What a feast! Never before had food tasted so good, and when I'd finished there was hardly a crumb left over.

Mother saw how tired I was – my eyelids kept drooping as I tried to concentrate on describing my school and journey. She smiled and asked me to leave the tray on a small table outside her door. 'It's time for bed, my child; we have plenty of opportunity to talk tomorrow. But first I must tell you where you'll be sleeping.

'Opposite my room's a door leading to our living room. There, behind a screen, is your bed. Hans-Dieter's bed is also in that room. He's asleep now. Don't worry – he won't wake up. At the end of the passage outside my room's a bathroom and toilet. That's all you need for now. Go to bed, Else. Tomorrow's another day. A nurse will come in the morning to see to baby and me. My breakfast will be sent up from the kitchen. The cook, whose name is Frau Krause, is very nice. They call cooks "Mamsell" here in Pomerania. As soon as you're ready tomorrow morning, go down and introduce yourself. You'll also meet Lotti. She's the scullery maid and does the menial tasks in the kitchen, helping Mamsell whenever necessary.

'So you see, Else, all's taken care of. You don't need to worry: we're well looked after.' Mother paused. 'But I'll tell you what, my child,' she added. 'Give it a day or two and I'll be up and about again. Even now I feel well and hate having to lie in bed when I so badly want everything back to normal.'

'Don't worry, mother. You have me now. I can do many things to help you, and to look after the boys and little baby will be my greatest pleasure.'

'Goodnight, child. Get to bed now. I thank God you're safely back with us.'

After I'd said goodnight to my mother, I looked again at our precious new baby and gently planted a kiss on my sleeping youngest brother's cheek. Then, wearily, I went to bed.

The thought of getting into that warm, inviting bed was heavenly. My day had started early and now it was almost midnight.

I slept solidly all night and when I awoke next morning felt completely refreshed. Opening my eyes, I made out the faint light of early dawn and wondered what time it was. I had no way of telling. The house was completely silent and I felt disorientated. Sitting up in bed, I looked around and quietly put my feet on the floor. Then I rubbed my eyes, which soon adjusted to the dim morning light.

It was a large room. Four steps led down to it and I was later told that it was the *Treppenzimmer* (room with steps).

I tried to accustom myself to its layout. The furniture was heavy oak and there was a lot of it. A large table surrounded by six chairs stood in the centre, yet there was still plenty of room for a family of children to have living space and move about with comfort.

To the left of the steps, behind the head of my bed, stood a wardrobe with drawers beneath. I assumed it was intended for my use.

In the right-hand corner was a stove, tiled from floor to ceiling. It gave out welcoming warmth and later I learned it was never allowed to go out. How lovely to wake up in a warm room. I remembered how cold it had been when I'd arrived, and that morning would be no different: snow, ice and a sharp frost during the night – such bitter cold was new to me.

Surrounding my bed was a beautiful screen, delicately embroidered with Chinese motifs. It gave me a privacy I appreciated.

Hans-Dieter's bed stood next to mine. I gazed at him as he slept soundly, and was amazed at how much he'd grown. He wasn't the little boy I'd last seen some months earlier: Now he was eight years old: an important little man of the house, taking the place of father.

At the end of the room were two large windows, both double-glazed to keep out icy winds that blew in from the east across the flatlands of Pomerania. I lifted one curtain and peeped out: before me was a beautifully laid-out garden, and beyond that a park, deeply covered with a thick white carpet of snow, untouched and magical, a winter wonderland in the early morning light.

Turning back, I inspected the room: everything was clear now daylight was getting stronger. The old, heavy, but beautiful, furniture gave a homely feel to the room.

Between the windows stood a large, comfortable settee, mother's favourite place I soon learned and room for us all to sit together. I could imagine her sitting there, telling the boys her stories. She was a wonderful storyteller with an endless supply of exciting tales that kept us spellbound.

To the right of the window mother had organised a tiny, but serviceable, kitchen. I tiptoed over to it and saw a small cooker with an oven beneath; a cupboard for crockery, pots and pans; and a table with a cutlery drawer that provided a useful surface for food preparation.

Mother also had a small but serviceable icebox, of which she was very proud. Ice from the kitchen coldstore was packed into a small compartment, where it kept perishable food cool and fresh for days. Very clever!

Mother told me that when they first arrived at the manor in Glowitz, the Baroness had suggested they take their meals with the Baroness's own Puttkamer family. Mother, however, had declined the offer. She preferred to cater for her own family, but expressed her gratitude to the Baroness for her kind proposal.

Next to mother's tiny kitchen stood a large, solid display cabinet. I tried a door. It was locked and I wondered what treasures it might contain, but I never found out. The next door was a small cupboard full of Hans-Dieter's and Ralf's toys, and one drawer mother had taken over for her own personal belongings. It creaked when I peeped inside, but Hans-Dieter didn't stir.

And then, in the corner, stood the handsomely tiled stove. I fingered the tiles, closely inspecting their raised patterns. Some were plain, but others, dotted here and there, illustrated life in a country-house kitchen.

Beside one window to my left stood an old but comfortable armchair with a large, solid-looking glass-fronted bookcase beside it, containing many fascinating books. Some were leather bound, and there was also a complete set of encyclopedias, old but in perfect condition. We'd always loved to look at pictures, but old books were informative as well and would answer our numerous questions. Mother might allow Hans-Dieter and me to look at them. They'd have to be handled carefully and treated with respect.

Beneath the bookcase was an intriguing writing desk with countless small drawers. Curious about these, I explored them but found them empty. If only mother would allow me to use the writing desk. There I could write letters to father, do my homework and keep my personal things, like my diary.

That then was our living room. Not really our home, but a temporary shelter until that wretched war was over. I liked what I saw. We were lucky, because our situation could have been much worse. Instead of a cramped space in a tiny cottage, we were living in what was almost a castle! *Yes, we have only a couple of rooms, but we're safe and must make the most of it – no one can hurt us here. We're comfortable and warm, and, most important of all, apart from dear father, we're together again*, I thought to myself.

Suddenly I heard mother's bedroom door open, followed by a gentle knock on my door. 'Else, are you awake?' She came in as I answered,

'Yes, mother. I've been up for ages, exploring the room. I love the big tiled stove, so cosy and warm. What do you burn on it? Coal, like we used in Düsseldorf?'

'No, Else,' she said, lowering herself into the armchair. 'The only form of fuel is peat, cut from local peat bogs. Each morning and evening Johann, the gardener, comes with a large basketful to stoke the fire, which burns day and night.'

'Does everyone in Glowitz use peat for heating?'

'I think so. Ask Johann when he comes. He'll answer all your questions. He's lived here all his life.'

'Yes, mother, but first can I have a quick bath? Then I can dress and help *you*.'

By now Hans-Dieter was also awake. He was old enough to see to himself and didn't need help from me. 'Good morning, Hans-Dieter. Did you sleep well?' I said in an older-sister tone. 'Go to the bathroom first and I'll follow. Be quick, so you can show me how to cook breakfast.'

Dieter looked at mother, resentful at this new bossy female. But mother merely nodded. 'Run along, Hans-Dieter. Do as Else tells you.'

And that's how my first day in Pomerania began. There was much to do and I was glad it had started early.

Entering mother's bedroom, I looked at my beautiful new baby sister, sound asleep in her basket. Then going across to little Ralf, I picked him up and gave him a big hug and a kiss. It was wonderful to feel his arms round my neck. He seemed such a frail little boy and to hear him laugh and feel him wriggle in my arms brought a lump to my throat.

'Mother, what's the matter with Ralf? Is he ill?'

'Yes, Else. For such a long time now he's not been well. The doctor has already seen him and given him medicine, but nothing seems to cure him. I've decided, as soon as I'm mobile, to take him to a specialist in Stolp hospital. Now you and your brother go down to the kitchen, introduce yourself to Frau Krause and ask her to please let you both have breakfast. Don't forget to address her as "Mamsell". That makes her happy. And, when you've eaten, at 10 a.m., I'd like you to go to the drawing room and introduce yourself to the Puttkamer family. In the meantime, nurse will see to baby, Ralf and me, and Trudi will bring us breakfast on a tray.'

I'd asked mother to let Hans-Dieter stay away from school for just one day. I wanted to see the park and walk through the village. Hans-Dieter would be my guide, as I longed to be with him, just the two of us. We had a great deal to tell each other and had been apart far too long. Reluctantly, but with a smile, mother agreed. 'But Else,' she said, 'whatever you do today, you must write to your father. He's worried about you. You have to tell him you've arrived safely here in Glowitz. Promise me you will.'

'Yes, mother. I promise.'

That settled, my brother and I ran down to the kitchen to ask for breakfast, he leading the way through a labyrinth of passages.

The kitchen was huge and a hive of activity. There was Mamsell, a big lady with a booming voice, who ruled her domain. Trudi, whom I'd met the evening before, was laying breakfast trays to take upstairs to the dining room. Lotti, the little kitchen maid, was busy washing pots and pans, and Maria, the under-parlourmaid, was collecting utensils needed for cleaning fireplaces and dusting rooms used by the family. There was so much to take in. I introduced myself to Frau Krause and, without our having to wait, she gave us a generous and delicious breakfast, which we ate on the corner of a table where places had already been laid for us.

While I ate, I surveyed the kitchen. It was fascinating. A huge cooking stove stood in the centre, and an enormous array of shiny copper pots and pans hung from the ceiling. A massive table, scrubbed almost white, stood below one window, and two large old stone sinks with draining boards stood against a wall. In one corner I noticed a lift. When I asked what it was for, I was told it was a dumb waiter, used for sending food upstairs to the dining room.

On one side of the kitchen was a large inglenook fireplace where a fire, never allowed to go out, burned brightly, warming the large draughty room and at the same time making it homely.

At the side of the fireplace stood Mamsell's rocking chair.

'After the day's work's done and the kitchen's clean and shiny,' whispered Trudi, 'she sits in her chair and then announces to us all, "I'll now take forty winks!" With that she settles down and the room vibrates with her snoring. It's her daily ritual, and not one of us dares disturb her!'

After breakfast, Hans-Dieter and I went upstairs to see if we could help mother, because shortly I had to meet the Puttkamer family. It frightened me a little. Mother expected me to be on my best behaviour, but I'd never before come face to face with people living in a huge fortified manor, which they called a castle even though it wasn't a real one. It must surely have meant that they were people of wealth. Mother told me they were 'aristocrats'. When I asked her what that meant, she said, 'People of noble birth who have great prosperity and are usually privileged to live in a large house like this where the family have lived for generations. They also own most of the village and the surrounding area.'

The thought of meeting such a family made me anxious. Mother shook her head and smiled when I told her of my nervousness.

'But Else, you're a well-travelled young lady. You managed the journey on your own across Germany without being scared, so tell me, why do you feel unsure now?'

'I don't know, mother. I'm just being foolish,' I replied. 'I expect I'll be fine.' But I didn't feel it.

Just then there was a knock on the door and Johann appeared with a large basket full of peat blocks. *Ah*, I thought, *here's my opportunity to ask him about this kind of fuel.* But first I introduced myself. 'Johann,' I said, 'I'm Else, mother's eldest daughter. I only arrived yesterday evening. But now I'm here, I'm not going away again.'

'Pleased to meet you, Fraulein Else,' answered Johann. 'Your mother told me how brave you were to take that long journey on your own across Germany.'

'Thank you, Johann. I know you must be busy, but may I ask you a question?'

'Of course. What do you want to ask me?'

'Johann might be in a hurry, Else,' Mother interrupted, but he shook his head.

'Johann, please tell me something about peat? Where does it come from? Does it grow?'

'Well, Else, that's easily explained. As I've lived in Pomerania all my life, I've learned all there is to know about peat. It's a kind of turf, a natural build-up of vegetable matter, which, after many, many years, becomes solid. It then has to be cut and shaped into blocks, and then dried before it can be used for fuel. One day, when I've more time, come downstairs where the fuel's kept, and I'll show you and tell you more. But that will have to do for now. I can't stop; got to go.'

I didn't want to be late for my appointment, so I hurried to the drawing room, which Hans-Dieter had pointed out to me earlier on the way to the kitchen.

I knocked, and the baroness, whom I'd met on my arrival, immediately opened the door.

'There you are, Else. Good morning. Come and meet my family. I've told them about your long journey to Pomerania, and you must tell us the adventures you had on the way. Meet my husband, Baron von Puttkamer. Come with me.'

She guided me towards an imposing, marble fireplace where flames burned brightly, trying to send warmth into that grand, but rather cool, drawing room. A large leather armchair was placed as close to the fire as possible and there, smoking his meerschaum (a clay pipe), sat an old gentleman, looking rather stern. But then I thought, *It's just like grandad looks at times. Perhaps all old men scowl like that.* His pipe fascinated me. I had never before seen one like it. I longed to ask him what it was made of, but it wasn't the right time so soon after meeting him. After all, he was the old Baron, head of the Puttkamer household.

'Come close, girl. Let me look at you. You've travelled far, but you're here safely.' He took a few puffs on his pipe. I waited. Then he continued, 'And now you have a little sister. How about that? A surprise for you, eh? Wonderful, wonderful! I trust she and your mother are both doing fine?'

'Thank you, sir; yes, sir,' was all I could think of to reply. 'I'm very happy to be here.'

In spite of his stern appearance, the baron looked at me and smiled. I offered him my hand and gave a small customary curtsy. Then, with a few kind words, he welcomed me into his home.

The Baroness beckoned me over to a settee on the other side of the fireplace. There she introduced me to two ladies in their early twenties: her granddaughters, Dorothea and Ottilia von Voeltheim. Their mother, Frau von Voeltheim, lived in Berlin, but the two young ladies spent most of their time, safe from the war, at Glowitz Manor, where they helped their grandfather – together with a trusted manager – to run the vast estate.

Ottilia, the younger of the two, was a happy-looking young woman, who liked to tell a good joke and then laugh heartily at it. She was mostly responsible for the horses – of which, it seemed, there were many. Miss Ottilia loved riding, apparently at tremendous speed, and no hurdle was too difficult for her to jump. She was a fun person and I liked her a lot.

'Else, can you ride?' she said.

'No, Miss Ottilia, I can't,' I answered. 'I lived in a city where it was impossible to ride horses: the traffic would frighten them. The countryside's so much better. It must be lovely to gallop through fields with nothing to worry them.'

'If you'd like to learn, Else, then, in spring, we'll see what we can do. My sister, Dorothea, is also a good rider. She won't object.'

'Thank you, Miss Ottilia,' was all I could say. I wasn't sure about those huge beasts.

Then I glanced at Miss Dorothea, who was smiling, and I felt immediately drawn to her. She was more ladylike: tall and slender with blonde wavy hair. I learned that her duties were looking after fields and extensive woodlands. She cared for the many estate workers, constantly keeping up to date with their reports. Also, she was accountable for the efficient general management of the farm. She loved forestland and her knowledge of flora and fauna was extensive. Later on I found it fascinating to watch her selecting a tree for felling, in order to give newly planted saplings plenty of light and room to grow.

'I also welcome you to our home, Else,' she greeted me. 'It can't be easy to be so far from your friends, but we can only hope it won't be too long before you can all return home again.'

'Soon, Else, you'll be able to meet our youngest sister, Sylvia,' added Ottilia. 'She's the same age as you and we hope you can be friends.'

'Where's Sylvia now, Miss Ottilia?'

'She's at boarding school in Berlin, but soon it will be holidays. She'll spend Christmas in Glowitz and then you can meet her.'

As I began talking to the family, I relaxed and felt more at ease. I told them how grateful we were for having been offered a home, away from the dangers of bombing raids that were now frequent in many cities both day and night. For us it was such a relief we could live in safety without fear. 'It seems so far away from the heart of Germany. Surely there's no danger here?'

'I fear nowhere in the world is truly safe in this war.' For a moment Dorothea looked haunted as if by a premonition, but, after a pause, smiled and changed the subject.

After a while I thought I'd better return to mother. I'd stayed longer than intended.

I approached the Baroness: 'Baroness, please excuse me. I must see if mother requires my help. Also I promised Hans-Dieter he could show me the park and village. I don't want to disappoint him.'

'Of course,' was her answer, 'But before you go, I've been thinking. While your mother's still confined to her bed, I'd like you and your brother to take your meals with us in the dining room. Mother and little Ralf will continue to have a tray brought up from the kitchen, but you and Hans-Dieter can eat with us. So much easier for you, dear, don't you agree?'

'Thank you, Baroness,' was my reply. 'I appreciate your generous offer. But I know how to cook and I'm looking forward to caring for mother and my young brothers. After all it will only be a few days and she'll be up and about again. Meanwhile, I'll try hard to look after us all as well as I can. If I need advice, mother can give it to me from her bedside. Thank you again, Baroness. I don't wish to appear ungrateful.'

'That's quite all right, Else. I understand. But I must say how astonished I am to learn what an independent young lady you are.'

'Thank you, Madam,' was my answer. And with those words I took my leave.

Chapter 5

Portraits in the Hall

As I closed the drawing-room door behind me, I stood awhile and looked down the grand staircase to the entrance hall below. The previous evening, when the Baroness had greeted me, I'd seen it only fleetingly. I'd been far too nervous to take note of my surroundings, but was now full of curiosity. Quietly I tiptoed down the stairs Later I wrote in my diary:

> The hall's spacious. A few small pieces of furniture are arranged tastefully against the walls: mostly glass-topped occasional tables filled with silver mementoes and war decorations, which the Baron earned for heroic deeds during the last war. One small table carries a vase, full of elegantly arranged winter greenery, pleasing to the eye and a friendly welcome to visitors.

> To the left of the entrance are two doors, one appears to lead to the estate office and behind the second door's a cloakroom for boots, walking sticks and all-weather garments.

> The centre of the hall's dominated by the grand staircase to the upper floor. Apart from the drawing room, where I'd come from, there's also a dining room and music room. Also on that landing's a long passageway leading to bedrooms for family members and guests.

> Underneath the window to the right of the front door's a small table with a silver tray for calling cards from friends and neighbours who wish to visit. Presumably the mail's placed there daily by the postman, collected later by Trudi, the head parlourmaid, who'd then distribute it among the household.

> Next to the window's a swing door. I have no idea why it's there, but I guess it leads to a long passage and steps to the kitchen and storage rooms.

> All walls in the entrance hall are wood-panelled from floor to ceiling. They're adorned with old portraits, showing ladies and gentlemen from past generations, probably ancestors of the Puttkamer family. Dotted here and there I find delightful little pictures depicting children who lived long ago. Their garments fascinate me: exquisite, yet so different from our present-day fashions.

> On the wall beside the staircase are more large paintings, mostly hunting scenes. One in particular attracts me – a painting of a boar hunt – for the Baroness mentioned that such a hunt takes place every year on New Year's Day, and a second hunt's arranged for the beginning of February.

> A brightly coloured carpet adorns the hall and covers the staircase to the upper floor. It's slightly worn in places, but still striking: its deep red complements the dark panelling.

But I'd dawdled long enough and it was time I found my way back to our family rooms.

I returned upstairs to the first floor; then climbed a second flight, which took me to the top landing. I knew I had to turn right, somewhere . . . along a corridor that seemed unending. Next down a few steps, along another passageway, and I was finally standing outside our two doors. When I told Hans-Dieter later how I got lost he laughed. Cheeky devil!

I knocked on mother's bedroom door. There was no answer. *She must be resting*, I thought, and decided not to disturb her. *But where's Hans-Dieter now? He must be in the sitting room.*

I'd soon find out.

I opened the door and there in front of me was a picture of total harmony, a scene so tranquil I felt reluctant to intrude. Mother sat in an armchair by the window, baby Marlene was asleep in her basket, Ralf, on a rug, played with his toys, and Hans-Dieter, sitting by mother, was listening with rapt attention to a story she was telling.

'Mother, you're up! Are you sure you feel well enough to be out of bed? Did nurse say you could?'

'Else, stop worrying so. I feel fine and happy to be sitting here. Hans-Dieter has made the beds and helped Maria tidy the rooms. The fire's been tended and everything's in perfect order. Now you and Hans-Dieter dress warmly and go out into the fresh air.'

'We'll do that, mother. Sorry I took so long: I got lost on the way back. But Hans-Dieter knows a quicker way to the basement, don't you Hans-Dieter?'

'Yes, Else. I'll show you on our way out.'

I looked out of the window. 'Mother, the weather's lovely today: blue sky and frozen snow glistening in the sunshine. It will be wonderful out of doors, but very cold.'

'You know, Else, when father came to Düsseldorf in September, the last time he was on leave, he advised me to take our warm winter clothing, yours included. He knew how cold winters are in the Baltic. I'm so glad I took his advice. Winters here can be so severe that the temperature often plummets to minus thirty or even minus forty. They say trees burst open in a bitter frost, and sound like guns going off. So if you hear bangs during the night, don't be alarmed. You'll now know what they are.' Mother shut the book she held. 'Right, you two. Get ready. Go through the park to the village. Just a quick walk today; there'll be plenty of opportunities later. When you've had your walk, come home and we'll think about lunch.'

Dressed like Eskimos, we looked at each other and burst out laughing. A colourful bobble hat, scarves and gloves in red and blue for me, green and brown for Hans-Dieter, thick woollen jumpers in bright colours, knitted by mother during long winter evenings, and heavy grey jackets, looking as if they were made from blankets.

'Laugh now,' mother said, 'but wait till you're outside. You'll be glad you're well wrapped up. Go! And as you run through the park, Ralf and I will watch from the window.'

'Please, mother, will you get back to bed after we've gone? It's only two days since you had baby, and you've been up for a while now.'

'Yes, Else, don't worry: I really can look after myself.'

It was exhilarating to be out in that white, frosty, winter world. It was all so new to me and I felt like a small child, excited and full of exuberance. Never in my life had I seen so much snow. I wanted to roll in it, make snowballs and have a snowball fight with my brother.

'Hans-Dieter, let's make a snowman when we come back from the village or perhaps after lunch. It'll be fun. We can ask Mamsell for a carrot for his nose; then we need two round stones for his eyes, and perhaps we'll find an old pipe we can put in his mouth. If not, we'll use a piece of branch that looks like one. What do you think?'

'Smashing, Else!' replied Hans-Dieter. 'But first you've got to see the village.'

The park looked unreal. Everything was thickly covered in deep snow, with trees and bushes hardly recognisable. The snow was almost untouched. No human foot had ruffled the white carpet, and there were just a few tracks from rabbits, birds or other small wild creatures. They were all hiding in their winter retreats, coming out only when they were hungry. The breathtakingly beautiful scene left me with a feeling of awe.

Before we left the park, I turned and looked up at our windows. 'Look, Hans-Dieter. There's mother, with Ralph in her arms, waving at us!'

We waved back and called out, 'See you soon!' knowing she might not hear us through the thick double-glazed windows.

On my arrival the evening before it had been too dark to notice the lovely house I was about to enter. Then I had been tired and just wanted to get to mother. But now, in daylight, I was spellbound, as the bright sun painted the grey stonework and reflected in numerous shiny windows.

'Dieter, how wonderful it all looks . . . so many windows. I wonder how many rooms there are? One day I'm going to count them,' I added, 'and you can help me. It'll be fun to find exactly how many there are. Perhaps tomorrow, Hans-Dieter, we'll investigate the house and then explore this lovely park. Mother told me last night that there's also a lake.'

'But, Else, it's got to be after school. Mother will not let me stay home another day.'

'I know that, Hans-Dieter, but now I'll race you to the drive. Let's see who gets there first!'

Out of breath, and together, we reached the wrought-iron entrance gates. Slowing down, we walked towards an archway at the end of the long drive. It looked so different from the previous evening. Then moonlight had greeted my arrival. But now the sun shone, and everything seemed friendlier in the daylight.

Seeing the avenue with its ancient trees either side, I suddenly realised what a long drive it had been to the house. Any visitor not knowing the estate would surely wonder what lay behind the gates of Glowitz Manor.

As we approached the arch, I noticed a small cottage to my right. 'Who lives there, Hans-Dieter?'

'That's the estate manager's home and office. He lives with his wife. Their names are Herr and Frau Lemke.'

I noted later in my diary:

> Herr Lemke's an efficient Manager. He's very kind to my brother and at weekends lets Hans-Dieter help him on the farm. He's also an important man in the National Party. We're allowed to call him Uncle, but have to greet him with 'Heil Hitler'.

> Mother has become very friendly with Frau Lemke, 'Aunt Gertrud'; politics are never discussed: mother's motto is, 'It's always a good thing to give the impression of being one of them.'

By now we'd reached the old archway, and as soon as we walked through we were at the edge of the village high street. I stood with my brother at the side of the road. Complete silence surrounded us: a strange emptiness. To me it seemed as if all the people and their animals were hiding behind locked doors, away from the deep snow, bitter frost and icy winds. No one wanted to venture out into such cold unless it was absolutely necessary. Indoors by the warm fireside was the best place to be . . .

In Pomerania, as in many parts of Germany, people and animals lived under the same roof. The stables were reached through a passageway from the family living quarters. Throughout cold winter days animals lived in such close proximity to the farmer and his family that they helped to heat the house until spring arrived. Then the animals were let out into the fields, where they remained throughout the summer months.

Two roads ran parallel to each other through Glowitz, one longer than the other. The longer road, the high street, started at the railway station, where I'd arrived. The road wound its way through the village and then down a gently sloping hill until it entered the next village, Klenzin.

Near the station, where the street began, stood a large building complex, which was the local dairy. Hans-Dieter started jumping up and down. I could see he was eager to tell me something.

'Else, do you want to know what happens here each morning? *I* know. Should I tell you?'

'Of course, Hans-Dieter. What is it?'

Then Hans-Dieter explained to me that, early each morning, farmers from many outlying villages came with horse-drawn carts and brought churns filled with rich, creamy milk. Some of the cream was used to make butter or cheese, which together with many churns of milk was sent by train to Stolp, about 30 kilometres from Glowitz.

'I changed trains at Stolp. How do you know all this, Hans-Dieter?' I asked.

'Karl told me.'

'Who's Karl?'

'My best friend. He lives near the post office and has a German Shepherd dog called Rex.

'Every morning the milkman calls, pulling his small handcart,' continued Hans-Dieter. 'You can't imagine the row he makes with his large bell – clang, clang, clang . . . and all the ladies rush out of their cottages, each carrying a milk can and they queue to get fresh milk for their early cups of coffee. He also sells butter and rich creamy cheese, fresh from the dairy. I once peeped into a farm dairy and watched how butter's made.' Hans-Dieter shuffled his feet through the snow. 'The milkman also sells big brown eggs, but they have to be ordered. Sometimes he brings vegetables. He's a very kind man.'

The high street was a busy thoroughfare with shops of many kinds. On one side were the butcher shop and bakery. There was also a cobbler, shoemaker and a haberdashery shop. One very important shop was the ironmonger's. The proprietor was eager to sell any item farmers or housewives needed. Nothing was too small or large, and if an item wasn't immediately available, it could be supplied in a short time.

On the left, just before reaching the estate entrance, were five or six small cottages, mostly occupied by workers and their families employed at Glowitz Manor. Each cottage had a tiny front garden, lovingly tended as soon as spring arrived after the long, hard winter.

Mother told me her friend Frau Ruch lived in one of the cottages. Her husband, once employed on the estate, had been killed on the Russian front. Her son was at school in Berlin and she needed a friend to help her through her bereavement and loneliness. She also had a small daughter called Ingrid, or Inge for short, who went to school with Hans-Dieter.

Also in the high street was a doctor's surgery, a village hall and a primary school.

'Look, Else. You see that building over there?' Hans-Dieter asked, pointing at the opposite side of the road. 'That's where I go to school.'

'I can see it, Hans-Dieter. Is it a nice school?'

'Oh yes, Else. I like it here. My teacher's very nice. It's a lady teacher. She can be funny sometimes and makes us laugh!'

As we walked down the high street, Hans-Dieter pointed out the bank on our left, and the residence and offices of the mayor on the opposite side.

The secondary road was almost all residential. There were a few farms, large houses and small cottages dotted here and there, as well as a pub and grocery store. At the end of the road, in a prominent position, stood the church and a meeting house; and the cemetery was there too.

My young brother had been a wonderful guide: he'd wanted to show me everything. But now we were both cold and had had enough.

'Come, Hans-Dieter, it's time to make our way home. Mother will be waiting, and we both need to thaw out before we turn into pillars of ice. We must leave the park until another day – it will still be there tomorrow. This afternoon we can explore the house. That's quite enough.'

We ran back, holding hands.

I could see Hans-Dieter was glad to return home. He was too proud to give in, but was only too happy to listen to me.

Chapter 6

Pink Blancmange

We returned from our outing, tired from walking through the deep snow, our cheeks rosy from the cold and our stomachs growling with hunger. Hans-Dieter suggested we take the back entrance. 'We can't go in through the front door, Else; that's reserved for the family and visitors.'

I didn't mind which way we went into the house, as long as we got out of the cold as quickly as possible.

We had to walk through a passage, past the kitchen where Frau Krause was busy preparing lunch. The aroma of her cooking surrounded us, making us hungrier than ever.

'Hello, Frau Krause,' we called out. 'Are we too late to have our lunch? Can we come down to eat in the kitchen?'

'Sure you can, but first go and tell your mother you're back from your walk.'

We hurried past larders and storerooms upstairs as fast as we could. But just as we approached the stairs, we met a lady whom I hadn't seen before. Hans-Dieter, wanting to be a gentleman, stopped to introduce me.

'Fraulein Elisabeth, you haven't met my sister. This is Else. She only arrived yesterday evening and didn't even know mother had a new baby.'

Fraulein Elisabeth shook my hand and explained to me that she used to be the governess of the two young ladies, Dorothea and Ottilia. But now that the ladies were grown up she'd taken the position of housekeeper here at Glowitz Manor.

'I'm very pleased to meet you, Else. I hope you'll be a great help to your mother. It's not easy for her to be without your father and also to have the responsibility of your young brothers and baby sister. But I can see you're a capable young lady and that your mother can rely on you.'

'I'll try to do my best, Fraulein Elisabeth, and I'll make every effort to help mother wherever I can.'

I gazed at her, but wasn't impressed. To me she looked like an old maid, so prim and proper, and without a smile. And yet I thought if she'd wanted to, she could have looked very pretty. Her dark hair was combed tightly away from her face, ending at the base of her neck in a thick bun held together by numerous metal pins.

I'd only met her a few minutes before, and already she'd given me a lecture. I knew my obligations to my family and took my responsibilities very seriously indeed. Fraulein Elisabeth might have meant well, but from that first moment she spoke to me, I took an instant dislike to her, and during the years I knew her that dislike never changed.

Later I spoke to mother about my feelings concerning Miss Elisabeth, but she could see only good qualities in everyone and reminded me to try to do the same.

As soon as Fraulein Elisabeth had disappeared around the corner to the kitchen, Hans-Dieter and I hurried upstairs to our rooms. We knocked on mother's bedroom door, but there was no answer. Gently we opened it just wide enough to peep inside, but all we could see was little Ralf, tucked up in his cot, sound asleep.

'She must be in the living room,' Hans-Dieter whispered. And, sure enough, there she was, resting on the settee with the baby asleep in a cradle by her side.

'There you are, children. Come to me. You've been out for a very long time and must be cold and hungry.'

'Yes, we are. But it was lovely outdoors in the snow. We've already spoken to Frau Krause and she told us our lunch is waiting for us in the kitchen.'

'Very well. Go and take off your outdoor clothes, and then hurry downstairs. You mustn't keep her waiting any longer.'

We didn't need telling twice. Like a flash we ran down the stairs eager to see what Frau Krause had prepared for us.

Of course, she wanted to know where we'd been and what we'd seen. She told us she'd lived in the village for many years, knew most of the people, young and old, who lived there and seemed to know all that was going on around her. She loved to talk about her time in Glowitz, and Hans-Dieter and I made a keen audience. I could see how busy she was and commented on it.

'Well, Else,' she answered, 'only a few years ago, before this war started, there were many members of staff employed here in the manor.' Frau Krause bustled away as she talked. 'Now, before I go on, I want you both to sit down and have your meal. It's ready and waiting for you.'

We had potatoes, stew and Brussels sprouts; and for pudding she served us pink blancmange.

While we were eating, she continued talking. 'There was a butler, a lady's maid for the Baroness and a valet for the Baron. There was also a housekeeper, and Ottilia and Dorothea's governess, Fraulein Elisabeth. She travelled with the family wherever they went, but much of her time was spent in Berlin. Trudi, our head parlourmaid has been with us since she left school at fourteen. She wanted to leave us to join the army, but wasn't accepted. As a child, she'd had polio, which, as you may have noticed, left her legs very deformed. With that deformity it was impossible for her to join the forces. But we're lucky to have her. She's a good worker, as are also Maria and Lotti, my two kitchen helpers. The three of us work well as a team and together manage to keep the house running smoothly.'

After a pause the cook continued. 'There was also a houseboy, a simple lad from the village. Not soldier material, but very handy round the house and yard. His favourite job was to clean the shoes for the baron. But when war broke out, he wanted to go to Stolp and work in a munitions factory. He was a nice lad, very pleasant . . . perhaps one day he'll come back to us.'

I could have chatted to Mamsell for hours, yet duty was calling. I had a pressing engagement upstairs: I had to write a letter to father.

Upstairs I stole a moment to look at my tiny, and beautiful baby sister sleeping peacefully in a delightful wooden cradle.

'Mother, where did this come from? Yesterday, when I arrived, baby was asleep in a basket, and now she's lying in that lovely old rocking cradle.'

'Yes, Else, isn't it perfect? While you and Hans-Dieter were out, Fraulein Dorothea brought it for the baby. It's an heirloom and has been hidden in the attic for over twenty years. She'd like me to use it and I'm most happy to do so.'

The cradle was indeed beautiful. It was carved by hand out of a single piece of wood and was smooth to the touch. It was hand-painted with hearts and flowers and, even after all these years tucked away in the attic, the colourful decorations hadn't faded. A rub with a small amount of polish and a soft cloth had made baby Marlene's little bed look like new. Mother was a picture of motherhood, sitting in her armchair, sometimes darning socks, and at other times knitting baby clothes or jumpers for my young brothers or me. Or she might be reading a book or quietly be wrapped in her own private thoughts, but all the time she'd gently rock the cradle and, consequently, our baby would sleep peacefully, rarely making a sound.

I felt so happy with life! There was mother and baby, both in good health; there was Hans-Dieter, a fine young boy, and beautiful little Ralf who, I hoped, would soon be in good health again. Only my beloved father wasn't with us. But now I wanted to write to him, for there was so much to tell him.

I opened the lovely old writing bureau, found paper and pen, sat down and began to write. But I'd hardly started when I heard mother's bedroom door open and a little voice calling, 'Mama! Mama!'

'Mother, stay where you are. I'll fetch Ralf, take him to the bathroom and bring you his clothes. Then you can dress him while I go on with my writing.'

But it was no good – I could no longer concentrate. Hans-Dieter and Ralf each needed a drink of milk and I'd promised mother to make her a cup of coffee, real coffee, almost impossible to obtain and very precious. Father had brought it the last time he'd been on leave in Düsseldorf, and mother had taken it with her to Pomerania. She guarded it and only allowed herself one cup daily. It couldn't last for ever but, until the day no more coffee was left, it was her most special treat.

I decided to go on with my writing after the boys were in bed and our baby was settled for the night. I suggested to mother that later we should both sit down and write a letter to father, and tell him the exciting news that now he had a beautiful second daughter and that both mother and baby were doing fine.

After we'd all had our drinks, it was playtime. By now it was getting dark and snow was falling again; a strong wind drove huge flakes that beat against our windows with muffled thuds. But we didn't mind how cold it was outside. Here, in our cosy room, it was warm and homely. Thick curtains were drawn to keep out the cold, and the soft light from small table-lamps positioned here and there created a cosy atmosphere.

'Mother, I'll run down to the kitchen to tell Frau Krause that this evening I'd like to prepare and serve a meal for us. No need for Trudi to bring a tray; tonight we'll be independent.'

'How lovely, Else. Are you sure you can manage?'

'Of course I can. Just wait and see – you may be surprised at what your grown-up daughter can conjure up! And Hans-Dieter will help me, won't you, big boy? And then, like magic, all will be revealed.'

Mother couldn't help smiling at our antics. I loved her dearly and vowed I'd do everything in my power to keep her happy. I always wanted to be there by her side and make life easier for her while father was fighting far away on the Russian front.

Just before I went down to the kitchen, there was a knock on the door. I went to open it and found Johann with a large basket of peat, sufficient to keep us warm until the morning. He was such a kind person, always cheerful, always a friendly word and a harmless joke for our two boys. As for me, I appreciated his help and good advice when I needed it, and as time went by, I came to like him more and more.

One day I met Johann at the back entrance leading to the kitchen. He was pulling a small handcart carrying a large block of ice.

'Johann, where do you get the ice?'

'Ah, young lady, that's made you curious, hasn't it? Just give me a minute to take this block of ice to Frau Krause. She's waiting for it and can be very impatient. In a few minutes you can come with me. I'll show you something I'm sure you've never seen before.'

He took me into the garden, to a corner where the sun never reached. There were sheets of metal and wood, neatly arranged and I immediately realised it was a lid of some sort. He moved some of the covering and I could see, what appeared to be a deep hole, full of large blocks of ice.

'There Else. This is our ice cellar.'

'But Johann, where does all that ice come from?'

'Let me tell you, Else. You know we have a small lake in the park, which completely freezes over in winter. The ice soon becomes so thick that horses can walk over it without breaking it. In the village there is also a pond, and from there families who occasionally need ice for some purpose go and get it. Also the landlord of the inn often uses it. Families here must build their own ice cellar, but the ice from the pond's free for all. It's an unusual type of harvest. Now you know, my girl. Today you've learned something you'll always remember.'

'But tell me, Johann, doesn't the ice soon melt away?'

'No, it lasts all winter – sometimes up to twelve months. It's so cold here there's no chance of the ice melting.'

Our evening meal was a great success. Hans-Dieter had helped to peel potatoes. Not perfectly, I confess, but he'd tried so hard that I couldn't possibly criticise him. I asked if I could help and I think he was relieved when I took over. So we had mashed potatoes and omelettes made with lots of eggs, as they were plentiful. I'd also found a swede in the cupboard, which I'd boiled and served with a lump of butter. Mother and Hans-Dieter enjoyed my first attempt at cooking and so did I. Little Ralf was more difficult, but that was nothing unusual. He ate a tiny piece of egg and a spoonful of potatoes, and we couldn't persuade him to eat any more than that. Yet that wasn't enough. Mother knew what to do. She had a roll left over from breakfast. I warmed some milk, broke the roll into small pieces and added a little sugar. Now our spoiled young pup was content. Giving us an angelic smile, he happily finished his meal without much persuasion. Mother and I looked at each other. She knew her little lad better than I did.

'Please, Else, don't think this happens all the time. I try to be firm, but Ralf's not well and because of this we must be a little more tolerant.'

That's what I also had to be. After all, I'd only been with my family for that one day. Who was I to disagree with my mother? I had much to learn.

'Mother, tell me, what would you like me to do next?'

'Will you and Hans-Dieter do the washing up? I'll take baby and Ralf to my bedroom. Nurse will come any minute now. She'll see to me and bathe the little ones. Hans-Dieter can stay up a while longer. He must pack his satchel ready for school tomorrow. When he's done that, take him to the bathroom and make sure he has a good wash, not forgetting his neck and behind his ears. And, Hans-Dieter, don't forget to clean your teeth.'

'Yes, mother. You tell me that every evening. I'm not a baby: I know what I must do!'

'Else, when all the work's done, nurse has gone and the children are settled for the night, then you and I will write to your father. After that I must talk to you.'

'Is it anything serious?' I couldn't help asking.

'No, child, not at all. But we haven't talked together for such a long time, and there are things I must discuss with you.'

The boys were in bed and soon asleep, and baby was tucked up snug in her beautiful cradle. The room was tidied and now, at last, mother and I were able to have some time to ourselves.

Apart from the icy north wind that occasionally rattled the windows, the house was silent as we both settled down to write to father.

I had much to write about. I tried to describe my long journey from Chemnitz to Glowitz and wanted to tell him how happy I was to be reunited with mother and the little ones. I spoke of our beautiful new baby girl and also my first impressions of life in that vast manor.

I told him how I missed him so very, very much and that we all loved and needed him to be with us again.

Mother seemed far away with her thoughts as she wrote her letter. I could imagine how much she was missing my father, not knowing where he was and even wondering sometimes if she'd ever see him again. Life was so uncertain.

When our letters were finished, she sealed them together in one special envelope. Every German soldier had a fieldpost number and no stamp was required.

Mother asked me to take the letter downstairs to the hall where the postman would collect it on the morrow.

'But mother, I don't mind walking to the village in the morning to post the letter. I'll enjoy the walk: it will give me a chance to meet people and have another look around.'

'No, Else, I'm afraid that won't be possible. Now come and sit down; I'd like to talk to you. Today, when Fraulein Dorothea brought the cradle to me, she told me that tomorrow she'd be travelling to Stolp to shop and also to sort out some estate business. I've asked if she'd let you travel with her. In Stolp she'll go with you to visit your new school, introduce and enroll you. I don't wish you to miss any more lessons. She'll take you to call on her doctor to request he come out to see little Ralf and me as soon as possible. Please stress the urgency.'

'But mother, I never thought I'd have to go to school so soon. I wanted to stay at home a little longer to look after you, baby and the boys.'

'I know how you feel, Else, but you can't miss school any longer. Soon it will be Christmas and you'll have a long holiday. There will be plenty for you to do and any help you're prepared to give me then will be most welcome.'

Chapter 7

Glowitz League of German Girls

I enjoyed my journey to Stolp with Fraulein Dorothea. It was all new to me, the country-side so flat, field upon field, with here and there a lonely farmhouse surrounded by barns and stables. Of course, everything was covered in a white blanket of deep snow, but I could imagine that in summer there would be acres of golden corn and the lush green of growing potatoes and turnips.

I don't know what I'd expected to find in Stolp, but was surprised at what a charming old town it was. From the station a wide avenue led to the centre, with shops on one side and hotels and private villas on the other. Mother had told me that as far away as Berlin, Stolp was called Little Paris. The people of Stolp were obviously proud of their town. Spotlessly clean, it looked prosperous and elegant. Fraulein Dorothea pointed out its charm and refinement. She assured me that, once I'd started school, it wouldn't be long for Stolp to become as familiar to me as was my hometown Düsseldorf.

'Not far from Stolp', Fraulein Dorothea said, 'is the well-known seaside resort of Stolpmünde. Beaches of golden sand stretch for kilometres and the gentle safe waters of the Baltic Sea have always made it a popular outing for local people and holidaymakers from other parts of Germany. This is where the river Stolpe flows into the Baltic Sea, and that's where the name Stolpmünde (mouth of the river Stolpe) originated. During the Middle Ages it was already a port of great importance and many Prussian ships lay at anchor in the wide bay.'

'I'd like to go to Stolpmünde and swim in the sea. I've never been to the seaside; it must be great fun. Do you think that it's possible to go there in the summer?'

'I'm sorry, Else, but now, while there's war, it's not permitted for the public to enter the harbour or walk on the beach. It's mined and strictly guarded by military personnel. There are no holiday visitors and it's out of bounds even for local people. Sometimes German battleships are anchored in the harbour and occasionally, on special days, the public are allowed to visit them. If I hear of such an open day, I'll let your mother know. Perhaps you can go there by train. Would you like that?'

'Oh yes, I'd love it, and so would Hans-Dieter. What a wonderful outing that would be.'

It didn't take long for Fraulein Dorothea to finish her business. She also called on the doctor to arrange a visit to Glowitz. He told her he'd already planned to call on mother and Ralf, and promised to get there that very day, as soon as he could.

'Now, Else, I've concluded all my business.' She took my hand as we walked towards the town centre. 'I'd love us to stop for a warm drink, but our first priority must be to visit the school and get your appointment over. Don't you think that's sensible?'

Glancing at me, Fraulein Dorothea could see I was very nervous. 'Come, don't look so worried – the interview will soon be over, and you have nothing to fear.'

The high school was in a side street near the town centre – easy to find. It was an old building that had stood there for many centuries, a school for girls only. As I looked at it for the first time, I wondered how many thousands of pupils must have entered that imposing establishment through the years.

I was nervous and my legs were shaking, yet I was determined to make a good impression. I carried all the necessary documents and my reports with me, which I'd brought all the way from Oberwiesenthal. I hoped the headmistress judged them good enough for me to gain entrance.

When we entered her study, I was surprised to be confronted by an elderly, very tiny, lady whose smile was so pleasant and friendly that my anxiety and fear immediately disappeared.

She was sitting behind a large, solid wooden desk, which made her look even smaller than she really was. I remember thinking she must be sitting on cushions. In my mind I could see her chin resting on the edge of the table. That vision nearly made me giggle and I had to pull myself together to keep a straight face!

The headmistress studied my reports and seemed pleasantly surprised at my previous educational achievements. She welcomed me and I was asked to report at 8.30 a.m. on Monday, 16 November 1942.

Soon it was time for us to return home. We had to wait awhile for our train to leave, which gave us sufficient time to have a longed-for drink in the station restaurant.

When we arrived back in Glowitz, mother was most excited. While we were in Stolp she'd received a letter from my father telling her he'd be coming home for a short visit at the end of February.

'Won't that be wonderful, Else? I've been thinking that, when father's home, we can have baby christened. The Baroness has already offered to have the christening here in the manor, and Baby's name will be Marlene. Father knows about that; it was his choice in case we had a little girl. He suggested the name last time he was on leave.'

'Yes, mother, and we can –'

'Else,' interrupted mother, 'there's still plenty of time for plans to be made. First I want to hear about your trip to Stolp, and most importantly about the interview with your new headmistress – I take it you've been accepted?'

'Of course I've been accepted, mother, and I'm looking forward to starting school on 16 November. It seems to be a nice school, very much like the one in Düsseldorf. I know I'll like it there. Has the doctor called yet? He said he'd come as soon as he could.'

'No, child, I'm still waiting. But meanwhile, you can sit here with Hans-Dieter and me and tell us about your day in Stolp.'

The words kept pouring out of my mouth, making mother smile and Hans-Dieter say, with a big sigh, 'Do be quiet, Else. You give me a headache. You sound like a gramophone record stuck in a crack.'

But there was no stopping me: I wanted to get everything off my chest.

'Mother, when I start school next Monday, I'll have to get up very early in order to catch the train at 6.05 a.m. Now it's winter, it will be dark when I leave, but if I take the footpath along the side of the field, it won't take me long to reach the station.'

'Do you know what time you'll come home in the afternoon, Else? Will it be very late? It gets dark early and I'll be waiting anxiously for you to come home.'

'My train will arrive in Glowitz at 4 p.m. But don't worry, mother. We have permission to stay in the classroom until it's time to leave for the station, and I'll have plenty of time to start my homework. Then, when I'm home, I'll be free to be with you.'

Towards the evening the doctor called to look at little Ralf.

'Frau Hopp, Ralf's a sick boy and ought to be in hospital. He ought to be admitted now, but I'd like to wait until after Christmas. Then we'll take him in immediately, so we can establish the cause of his being so very ill.' The doctor's face was grave. 'Meanwhile I'll send you more medication by train. It should arrive no later than tomorrow morning. Perhaps, Else, you could collect it from the station?' He looked at mother and, smiling happily, pronounced *her* to be in excellent health.

'Just take it easy, Frau Hopp. Another few days and you can be up and about. But you must take care: to have four children to look after is quite a responsibility.'

Mother looked at the doctor and smiled.

'You don't realize how lucky I am, Doctor: I have a wonderful daughter who helps as much as she can. I don't know what I'd do without her.'

Then she mentioned the news she'd had from father, that he was coming on leave at the end of February and that then we'd have our baby christened. 'She'll be called Marlene,' mother announced, 'and the christening will be held here in the manor.'

'That will be wonderful, Frau Hopp, and I'm delighted to hear you say your husband can also be present on your little daughter's most important day.'

Then, with a warming drink inside him, he left to return to Stolp.

Monday, 16 November 1942

The day arrived all too soon: the start of a new chapter in my life in Pomerania.

When I felt mother's hand on my shoulder and was told to get up, I felt as if I'd just gone to bed.

'What time is it, mother?' I asked, yawning.

'It's 5 a.m., Else. I expect you'd much prefer to turn over and go back to sleep, but this is your life from now on.' Mother bustled round checking my clothes. While she was busy, she was chatting away, but I was still half asleep and didn't want to listen. 'School's important and Stolp's the only town where you can get a good education. The only way there is by train and you mustn't miss it. So, get up and dress quickly now, my girl; time's running on.'

I had to catch a *very* early train every morning, Monday to Saturday. But on Saturdays my train left Stolp earlier, which meant I'd be in Glowitz while it was still daylight – so much better!

School was fun, however, and I enjoyed being a pupil there. I soon settled in. Our form mistress was very approachable and I made new friends easily. Many subjects were taught and I enjoyed most of them – except mathematics. I had difficulty getting to grips with algebra and geometry; arithmetic was a little better, but no matter how hard I tried, it was always a struggle.

We were given a choice of three languages to study: Latin, French or English. I didn't want to learn Latin: to me it was a dead language, which I felt I'd never use. French didn't appeal to me either, although mother spoke it well. Her mother, no longer alive, had been French, but that was irrelevant. I chose to learn English and, as time went on, it became one of my favourite subjects.

There were two grammar schools in Stolp: one for boys and the other for girls. But they were some distance apart and during schooltime we rarely met. On sportsdays or political celebration days we'd have a chance to be together, but such times were rare. To fraternize was frowned upon.

But my mother wasn't happy. She hated to see me getting up early and then returning so late in the afternoon. She wanted me to board during the week and come home only after school on Saturdays, returning Monday mornings. I hated the very thought of it. Mother tried to reason with me but the idea of staying away again was abhorrent to me. I cried and pleaded, but she wouldn't listen. She'd made up her mind and I had to abide by her decision. I knew she meant well, but I couldn't understand it. I felt angry and rebellious and, in my anger, felt I was in the way and she wanted to be rid of me.

Of course I was being unreasonable and realised that afterwards, but at the time I was extremely unhappy.

Suddenly, and unexpectedly, mother spoke. 'I don't like to see you upset, Else, but, believe me, I only have your best interest at heart. Yet I can understand how you feel. For too long you've been separated from us, and now you're getting used to a new sister and new surroundings – not to mention a new school. I'll make a suggestion. Very soon it will be Christmas and you'll have a holiday. While you're at home, I'll ask Miss Dorothea to make enquiries about finding a kind, respectable family with whom you can board during schooltime. You must promise to agree to this and be prepared to try it in the New Year until your Easter break. How does that sound?'

'Mother, does that mean I can travel daily between now and Christmas?'

'Yes, Else. There's no other way. First we'll have to find the right family for you to board with, but that can't be done quickly.'

'Thank you, mother, for being understanding.' To live with a family might not be so bad. I was prepared to give it a try. 'Sorry I've been difficult,' I said, hugging her.

I wanted to join the Glowitz League of German Girls but there was a problem: they had no leader. I visited our mayor in his office and suggested that, if he was willing to give me a try, I'd love to take charge. Of course, as it was winter we were limited in our activities, but we did have the village hall and met early evening once a week. I put a notice in the post office window, asking the village people for oddments of wool, as we wanted to knit warm garments for our soldiers on the Russian front. The response was incredible, for we received bag upon bag. Ladies from the village came to join us and together we started knitting socks and body warmers, gloves and balaclavas – items desperately needed to see our soldiers through that bitterly cold Russian winter. We were proud of our achievement. Then it was time to pack the parcels and send them to the front. As it would soon be Christmas, we decided to contribute something special to remind the soldiers, however far away they were, that they were not forgotten. Each parcel contained a note with good wishes for Christmas and the New Year and our hope and prayers for peace to come in 1943.

One day, when I came home from school, Frau Krause called me into the kitchen to meet two new young staff girls. They'd been sent to Germany from their home in the Ukraine and neither spoke a word of German. One of the girls, Dunja, was only sixteen or seventeen; the second girl, Anna, was a little older, about nineteen or twenty years old.

Dunja was very pretty. She had blonde hair and was tiny, fragile-looking and appeared more genteel than Anna, who was tall and big built. Anna had dark hair and gave the impression of being a girl used to hard work, most probably on a farm or in the fields. To me she seemed a little rough, but it was too early to judge. I felt sad to think they'd both been dragged from their homeland and sent to a country that must have seemed hostile and alien.

Mother felt sorry for them and took them under her wing. She taught them to speak German: a little at first, basic words to help them through the day. Anna must have come from a very poor environment. She had to be taught the basic principles of hygiene, and much of what mother tried to teach her, Anna thought totally unnecessary. Dunja was different. She must have had an easier life and, in contrast to Anna, was more refined. Dunja's brother was fighting with the Russian army. The German authorities got to hear of it and the family suffered incredible hardship. She clung to mother and a close friendship developed between the two., In the not-too-distant future that friendship would save our lives.

Soon the frosty days and nights heralded the end of November, and it snowed almost continously from a leaden grey sky.

Walking to the station each morning was hard going and I ought to have acknowledged mother was right to want me to board in Stolp. But I had time to think about it until after Christmas. Meanwhile it was best not to complain. I didn't want to admit that, in her wisdom, mother knew best.

November came to an end. Days were short and dark evenings so very long. When I arrived home from school, it was already dark and I had no chance to meet my friends. The only opportunity for us to get together was at weekends when we'd toboggan down any snow-covered slope we could find in the vicinity of our village. I loved the speed and sensation of flying downhill.

The land in Pomerania's very flat. Hills are few and far between and the only real slope available to us was a gentle incline that ran down from the top of the high street nearly to the railway line. But it was good enough for us!

By then the layout of the village meant little to me, but people *were* important. Young girls and boys with whom I travelled daily to school became good friends and constant companions. We lived a happy and carefree existence far removed from the horrors of war. To us the future looked bright, without a cloud on the horizon. It never entered our minds that before long our world, and with it our hopes and dreams, would be turned upside down.

3 December 1942

It was Hans-Dieter's eighth birthday. It was also the day – never to be forgotten – when we nearly lost him.

At the entrance to the kitchen stood a huge cast-iron baker's oven. To me it appeared to be enormous, with a heavy door in front and a chimney on top. Frau Krause would mix the dough ready to bake the bread for members of the family and staff. She'd bake up to ten loaves; sometimes more. Hard work forged good appetites and food was never in short supply, as larders and store cupboards were kept full. Frau Krause knew how to set an abundant table!

Early in the morning on baking day, Johann would light a fire in a box underneath the iron oven. Then, when it had reached a high temperature, he'd push the shaped loaves on a long-handled ladle deep into the interior of the oven.

There were oblong and round loaves, and often, when surplus dough had to be used up, Mamsell would form small rolls and add them to the baking bread. Oh, how I loved them! She'd often have one waiting for me when I came home from school. It was always spread thickly with creamy butter and topped with delicious home-made jam. Scrumptious!

All over the house was the wonderful aroma of freshly baked bread. Nothing could be better than that incredibly mouth-watering smell, which would linger in the air long after baking was done.

When the bread was baked, Johann would bring prepared fruit from the kitchen, to be dried slowly in the warm oven. Hans-Dieter saw him do that and an idea formed in his head. It was a great temptation that, once conceived, was quite impossible to resist.

Of course it took a while for the fruit to dry, but that didn't concern my brother. He wanted to get into the oven and help himself to as much fruit as he could lay his hands on.

There were sliced apples and pears, apricots and ripe, juicy figs from the greenhouse. Gifts from heaven!

He thought that, once in the oven, he could eat whatever fruit he fancied, and when he was full, he'd stuff his pockets and take the fruit to mother. He was certain she'd be delighted.

First he had to be sure Johann was out of the way. Once he'd gone home, it was safe for Hans-Dieter to act.

He waited a while until all was silent, and then, with difficulty, opened the heavy door and crawled into the oven, which was still warm but not hot. There before his eyes was all the tempting fruit within easy reach. Yet before he could put one slice of apple into his mouth, a gust of wind suddenly slammed the door, locking it from the outside. Hans-Dieter was left in total darkness, and he was terrified. Thinking Johann had gone home, the little lad was panic-stricken. He shouted and shouted for help but no one could hear him through the thick door. He was crying and calling for mother to rescue him.

By the greatest of luck, Johann hadn't gone home. He'd lingered in the kitchen, talking to Mamsell for a while. As he stepped outside the back door, he thought he heard a tiny voice shouting for help. At first he didn't know where it was coming from, but then realised it must be from the oven. Quickly he opened the door and into his arms tumbled my brother, almost hysterical and crying bitter tears. What good would it have done to be angry with him? He'd had his punishment and all he wanted was to be taken to mother and feel her arms around him. He'd learned a painful lesson and would relive the nightmare for many weeks. But how lucky he was – it could have turned out far worse, not only for him, but for all of us.

It wasn't the most successful birthday for my young brother. There was no party and now he was home, it was too late to have a birthday tea. Mother had baked a delicious cake for him with cream and jam, and sugar sprinkled over the top. But not today. Hans-Dieter had to be punished mildly, which meant waiting for his cake until the following day.

Chapter 8

Tree Angels

19ᵗʰ December 1942

My diary entry for that day reads:

> Today's the fourth Sunday in Advent: just a few days to Christmas Eve. This is a special day and we've been invited to come to the music room. Today the entire family's present: Baron and Baroness von Puttkamer; Frau von Voeltheim and her daughters, Dorothea, Ottilia and Sylvia; and Fraulein Elisabeth. Mother sits with baby Marlene in her arms, and I have little Ralf on my lap with Hans-Dieter standing at my side.
>
> In the corner by the window is a large tree, not yet decorated but standing tall and proud, waiting to be clothed in shiny Christmas splendour: on the branches many candles will give light and warmth to this lovely room on Christmas Eve. They'll be a symbol of peace on earth, and give us hope in these dark, uncertain times of unrest and war.
>
> The Baroness is giving a short speech, welcoming us all into her music room. 'And now Sylvia and Else,' she says, 'will you come to the table and light the last Advent candle to make the wreath complete. And you, Dorothea, come to the piano and play us some carols that we can sing together in anticipation of Christmas.'
>
> I put Ralfie on my chair and, together with Sylvia – home for the holidays – hold the lighted splint to the unburnt wick of the fourth candle. It catches uncertainly in the draft and threatens to go out. I continue to rest my wick's flame against it and whisper to myself, 'Light, candle, and end the war so father can come home to us!' It just hangs on to life and I blow out the splint.
>
> The Baron then hands a glass of Madeira wine to the adults, and we, the young ones – Sylvia, Hans-Dieter, Ralf and I – receive a tumbler of home-made lemonade.
>
> 'And now,' says the old gentleman, 'let's raise our glasses and drink a toast to absent friends, including Frau Hopp's husband, who's fighting on the Russian front. As our thoughts are with him, so his thoughts will be with his wife and children. Also we must pray from the heart and fervently hope that perhaps at this time next year this wretched war will be over and peace will reign once more in our beautiful country and the rest of the world.'
>
> Suddenly the undecided candle flame flares up strong. That proves it won't be long until there's peace again, I think. We've no need to worry.

As we leave the music room and enter the hall, we become aware of a wonderful aroma rising from the kitchen, filling the house with the spicy scent of Christmas baking. It brings back fond recollections of our Christmases in Düsseldorf with father, and I know I'll keep these memories with me for the rest of my life.

When we reached our room, there was evidence that mother had also been busy preparing for Christmas. The government had released special rations for everyone, and mother, with four children, had fared very well, considering the hard times. She was able to buy ingredients for typical German stollen bread and spices for biscuits and ginger nuts.

'You wait and see, Else. There may be a war on, but that won't stop us from having a wonderful Christmas. Father may not be with us, but we've written to him and I sent him a parcel, which I hope he's received by now. The socks and gloves we knitted and the thick body-warmer I was able to make for him will please him, and the bag of biscuits I included will remind him of home. Let's hope that next Christmas we'll all be together again. Meanwhile let's be strong and resolute. We must believe in our leader and also trust him when he tells us that Germany's certain to win this war. And soon.'

At last it was Christmas Eve. All over the house there was a lot of activity, and it was no different in our room. I asked mother if I could help her and, much to my surprise, she said yes.

On the farm, workers had finished early. They were all given a goose and, in high spirits, carried it home – a tradition repeated every year.

During the Christmas period, no work was done on the farm; only the animals had to be cared for, and the Russian prisoners were relied upon to carry out those duties.

After an early lunch, mother and I had to think about decorating our room. But what of the children? Ralf and baby Marlene were easy. They always had a nap after their midday meal and, once tucked up snug in their little beds, soon fell asleep. Dunja and Anna, the two Ukranian girls, had offered to entertain Hans-Dieter and it was good to know he was safely out of our way and well taken care of.

I enjoyed being allowed to help my mother with the Christmas preparations, the first time in my life I'd done so, and it made me feel grown up and very special.

Johann had brought up our tree and, even without any trimmings it looked beautiful, standing on a small table in the corner near the window.

From the hardware store mother had been able to obtain two packets of tinsel, delicate strands of silver paper, which in Germany were always part of Christmas tree decorations.

Also mother had managed somehow to get hold of a small tin of silver paint. A few days earlier she'd helped Hans-Dieter and me to cut many stars of different sizes from an old shoebox. We painted these silver, and with a small strand of white cotton threaded through a tiny hole, they were ready to hang on the tree. The silver stars looked perfect against the dark green of the fir tree, and after I'd added the shiny strands of tinsel, our Christmas tree looked truly wonderful. We used the largest star to adorn the top of the tree. It was lovely – just as good as the expensive glass star my parents always used in Düsseldorf.

Hans-Dieter, the dear lad, had trudged through deep snow in the park, trying to find fir cones. They were his contribution to our tree decorations, and when they too were painted silver they looked most impressive.

For each of us children the Russian prisoners had carved, out of a simple log of wood, a tiny angel to hang on our tree. I wondered where they'd managed to get the paint, but it must have come from somewhere local, because each little angel was decorated in beautiful bright colours. We loved them and hoped to treasure them for ever.

'What do you think, mother?' I asked. 'Are you happy with the way I've decorated our tree? I've tried to make it look pretty, but something important's missing.'

'Missing?' mother asked. 'What's that, Else?'

'Candles, mother. We can't have a tree without them, can we? It wouldn't look right.'

'Go to my drawer and in the corner you might find something to surprise you.'

I did as she said and found a box full of white Christmas tree candles.

'Oh, mother, where did you get them? Now we'll have a proper Christmas tree. I'm so excited. Wait till Hans-Dieter and Ralf see it; they'll be thrilled!'

Mother turned to me with a smile and tenderly planted a kiss on my forehead. 'Else, now *you* must leave this room. There are a few things *I* must do and for that I don't need your help. Go to my bedroom and see if the little ones are awake. If not, let them sleep a little longer – but if they're awake, bring baby to me and you see to Ralf. You know what to do.'

'All right, mother, I'll do that; then at 4 p.m. I'll go down and fetch Hans-Dieter.'

'Yes, Else, that would be a great help! Don't forget to thank Dunja and Anna for looking after him. I've cut two slices of stollen bread. Take them with you and wish both girls a very happy Christmas from us.'

Without interrupting her Christmas preparations, mother said to me, 'As you know, Else, just after four, all estate workers and their families have been invited to come to the manor, together with Mamsell, the cook, and the household staff, including Dunja and Anna. Everyone working on the estate has been invited, except the prisoners, who'll be well looked after by Uncle Kurt.'

I paused at the door. 'Mother, why are they all coming to the manor?' I asked.

'It's a tradition. The Puttkamer family is head of the village: most people living here are dependent on them for work and housing; so when they come on Christmas Eve, all the Puttkamer family will be present to show their gratitude to the workers for their loyalty. The men will receive a much-appreciated Christmas bonus, the ladies a basket of fruit from the gardens and each child a toy and bag of sweets.'

'But what of us, mother? What do we get?'

'We're not included, Else. You must understand we're not a part of the family; neither do we belong to the village. We're refugees: only through the kindness of the Puttkamer family are we able to live here away from the dangers and ravages of war. Does that satisfy your curiosity?'

As I went down to the basement to fetch my brother, I could hear many voices: presumably the first guests had arrived. I'd have loved to peep into the drawing room; how beautiful it must have looked with the Christmas tree decorated and candles burning! I doubted it was difficult for the baroness to obtain candles for *their* tree; but then, why should I have worried? We also had candles, and that evening our tree would be just as lovely as all the others in the manor.

Upstairs I knocked on our sitting-room door.

'Don't come in, Else,' called my mother. 'Go to my bedroom, please. See to little Ralf and, as soon as I've settled Baby, I'll join you.'

As I opened the bedroom door, I was amazed to see what mother had done in my absence. From the alcove on the landing she'd taken a small table, four chairs and Ralf's high chair from our sitting room. The table looked beautiful: candle in the centre, waiting to be lit, and dainty slices of stollen and the best china mother was able to acquire. Mother, a genius, always knew how to create the perfect atmosphere – she could have turned a cowshed into a palace, and I made a pledge that, when I grew up, I'd become just like her.

We sat in the bedroom waiting for her, all dressed in our Sunday best (after all, it was Christmas Eve), and very soon we'd be allowed to enter our sitting room. On the wireless they were playing well-known carols Hans-Dieter and I had heard so many times before. We knew most of them and sang along with the music with gusto while we waited for mother.

We didn't wait long, for soon, with baby Marlene in her arms, she came to join us.

'Now, children, let's eat and drink; and when that's done, we'll go to the sitting room and see what surprises are waiting for us.'

'Mother, do you think the Christ Child knows where we are?' asked Hans-Dieter.

'You don't have to ask that,' mother replied. 'Be assured Hans-Dieter, the Christ Child will know. Just wait a little longer: I'm certain your question will be answered.'

'Will the Christ Child also come to me, Mama?' piped up little Ralf.

'But, darling, of course. You've been such a good boy, how could you possibly be forgotten?'

After hearing those words, Ralf looked at mother with a big smile and eyes that shone like bright stars. We all knew how ill the little boy was, but today he was lively and cheerful. He'd been like it for a while now and mother was fervently hoping his new medicine would make his improvement permanent.

49

We began to eat and enjoy what mother had lovingly prepared earlier.

Something had been on my mind for some time, and I had to satisfy my curiosity. 'Mother,' I asked, 'what will you do with the goose Johann gave you this morning? Surely you can't cook it in your small oven; it looks far too big for that.'

That morning, when Johann came with the peat basket, he'd called out to mother, 'Where are you Frau Hopp? I have something for you, and if you wait a moment I'll fetch it.'

He disappeared and returned after a few minutes, carrying the huge goose, plucked and prepared for the oven.

'Frau Hopp, if you go to the kitchen and see Frau Krause, she'll tell you what she intends.'

'So, Else,' mother replied to my earlier question. 'I don't have to worry about that goose. Mamsell has offered to cook it for us, and not only that, she'll also make apple sauce and cook red cabbage. I only have to peel and cook the potatoes, and when it's all done, I'll fetch everything from the kitchen and we can eat here in our own cosy room.'

When we'd finally finished our meal, mother announced, 'Now, children, I think you've waited long enough. Let's see what the Christ Child has sent to surprise us . . .Wait here for just a few minutes; I won't be long. But please stay in this room.'

We waited impatiently: I could see excitement on my little brothers' faces. Suddenly we heard the faraway tinkling of a bell.

'It's coming from our sitting room,' whispered Hans-Dieter. Else, come on; I know mother's calling us into the Christmas room.'

With little Ralf on my arm and Hans-Dieter's hand held firmly, we all entered our beautifully decorated sitting room. There in the corner stood the tree I'd lovingly decorated with attention to every detail. The candles were alight, giving our room that festive and joyful effect that can only be created at Christmas time.

Next to the tree stood mother with baby Marlene in her arms. It was such a delightful picture: I ran to my wardrobe drawer and grabbed my precious box camera.

'Now when I take your photographs, give me your biggest smiles. We don't want father to think we're miserable. After all, it's Christmas Eve and the least we can do for him is to look happy.' So I took photographs: first of mother and baby, then of Ralf and Hans-Dieter, and last but not least, a special one for father of the four of them.

'I must now take a picture of you, Else. Stand by the tree with the boys and baby in *your* arms. Smile!' Click. 'That's perfect. How pleased father will be when he receives the photographs soon after Christmas.'

'Mother, do you think father will notice how much I've grown?' piped up Hans-Dieter. 'He hasn't seen us for such a long time; perhaps he won't know us any more?'

'Now, Hans-Dieter, that's silly. I know you miss him, but of course he will know his own children. No matter how much you all grow, he'll recognise you, wherever you are. And I know for certain that when he sees the photographs of you, he'll be really proud to think of what wonderful children are awaiting him on his return.'

Mother walked across the room to put the camera away in the drawer. 'Now, children, stand with me here by the tree. For one minute we'll be silent and think of father so far away; also, of the many, many soldiers who won't be able to spend Christmas at home with their families and loved ones. Then we'll sing our favourite Christmas carol. You all know it. What's it called?'

'I know, mother!' shouted Hans-Dieter. 'It's "Silent Night, Holy Night".'

'Right, let's sing with clear, joyful voices, and then we'll see what gifts await us. You can see them on the table: I'm sure you won't be disappointed.'

Had we ever been disappointed before? Never. And it would be no different that Christmas. The boys sang sweetly in clear high voices, like choirboys. Then, as mother walked to the table, I went to my drawer and took out a small parcel for her, wrapped in red tissue paper that Fraulein Elisabeth had given me. I wanted to give it to her before opening mine. It was a small book of German poetry I'd seen in a Stolp shop window. I'd saved up my pocket money because I was determined to buy it as a Christmas present for mother. I was also able to buy a bar of lavender soap for Ralf to give to mother. He was so excited when I gave it to him: his little eyes shone when he handed her his gift parcel.

And what did Hans-Dieter have for mother? He was very secretive as he went to his chest of drawers and took out a tiny parcel. 'Mother,' he said 'this is for you. One of the prisoners made it for me; it's beautiful: I hope you'll like it.'

'I'm sure I'll love it, darling,' answered mother. 'I want to wait until we open our gifts together. Let's do it now: I can't wait a minute longer.'

There were wonderful presents for us, and all made by mother while we were at school.

There were warm knitted balaclavas and scarves for Hans-Dieter and Ralf, also mittens and socks, and both boys were given a thick woollen pullover. For Hans-Dieter there was also a book about a Native American called Winnetoo, which he thought was absolutely wonderful.

'Oh mother, I've always wanted that book! I love all the books by Karl May, but this one you've given me is the best. Thank you, mother.' And with those words he ran and gave her a big hug.

For little Ralf there was a brightly coloured jumping jack carved out of wood. It had a string and when you pulled it, the little wooden jack bounced.

'Look mother! See what I can do: I can make the jumping jack dance.' And he pulled the string so vigorously that mother had to stop him. 'Steady on, my darling. If you go on like that, your poor jumping jack will soon be broken. Be gentle – you don't have to pull so hard.'

I was intrigued. 'Mother,' I asked, where did you manage to get Ralf's present?' But she wouldn't say; she just smiled and told me not to be so inquisitive.

For baby Marlene she'd knitted a delicate pink dress. Of course, baby was too small to wear it yet, but in springtime, when the weather was warmer, it would fit her perfectly.

For me there were also many presents: a white pullover; a shawl, bright red and very soft with a beret to match; gloves and socks to wear with my boots – all gifts mother had knitted when we were out of the way. I was deeply grateful. She also gave me a pretty petticoat. It was pink and I suspected she'd altered one of her own to make it suitable for me. I'll never forget that petticoat. It was made of silk, and utterly gorgeous. Mother must have been very fond of it, because it was a present from father. What she'd done was so typical of her; nothing was too good for us: it gave her immense pleasure to bestow happiness on her children.

I put my arms around her. 'Thank you, mother. The petticoat's lovely and I'll treasure it. It will always be special to me.'

The gifts we gave her were small and insignificant, but they made her happy. And when I tried to apologise, she would have none of it.

'Else,' she said, 'it means so much that you thought of me this Christmas. We're living in difficult times: it's not easy to buy things of good quality or value. But a kind thought is what matters and the three of you have shown me what wonderful children father and I have raised.'

It was a happy and peaceful Christmas Eve we celebrated that year. Candles on the tree were extinguished; they were precious and had to be used sparingly. They had to last two more days before new ones could replace them. Mother wanted them to last until Twelfth Night – still a number of days away.

Chapter 9

Letters to Father

Christmas Day 1942

The following morning, Christmas Day, at eleven o'clock, Hans-Dieter and I went to church. It would have been nice if Ralf could have come, but it was far too cold for that little fellow to be taken out of doors. He had to remain at home with mother. She wanted to put the final touches to our Christmas dinner and it was much easier with the two of us out of her way.

Hans-Dieter and I had to wrap up warm for our trip to the village. Not only for the snow, but how warm would the church be? Was there any heating? During the night fresh snow had fallen, which once again looked smooth and untouched. Although it was deep underfoot, it didn't prevent us from enjoying the walk. But it was *bitterly* cold and the tips of our noses were bright red, just like circus clowns, and to prevent frostbite we covered them with our scarves. Our breath produced millions of tiny diamonds glittering in the sunlight, a rainbow of colours. We grabbed at them, running and jumping about trying to capture them, together with occasional snowflakes. It made us forget the cold, and gave our cheeks a glow: four rosy red apples!

We appreciated our newly knitted Christmas presents. Not only did they look smart, but they kept us warm. I wore my bright red scarf, lovely new beret with pompom in the centre and warm knitted gloves. Hans-Dieter had his new dark-blue balaclava, scarf and mittens to match. We both felt proud of our new clothes.

When we arrived at the church, I was surprised to see so many people going the same way to join in the Christmas service. We walked up the path to where a beautiful tree stood tall and regal at the church porch. It had no decorations, except a few candles to light the winter day. Inside, the church was bright with a lot of lighting and many people. Never before had I seen it so crowded . . . Then I realised we all felt the need to pray for that dreadful war to end and for peace to come again. I also wanted to pray for harmony to be restored throughout the world, so people could live once more without fear, but with hope for a better future. I knelt to say my prayers and wondered if God heard me. I asked him to guard my beloved father and the many soldiers fighting on a far-off battleground, wherever that might be. Would God listen to me? Or did he have too many pleas? But I'd been told God could hear and see everything; perhaps if I prayed hard enough, he *would* be able to hear me and answer *my* prayers.

Looking up from my prayers, I saw to my amazement that every member of the Puttkamer family, including Fraulein Elisabeth, and from the household, Trudi and Maria, were present. I didn't see Frau Krause, but then perhaps she'd stayed behind to prepare and cook dinner for a large number of people.

I let my eyes wander: how meagre the decorations were. Not as elaborate as we were used to in our Düsseldorf church. But there, almost hidden in a corner before the altar, stood the crib. I could see it was old and worn from many years' use, but the lovely nativity figures were exquisite and just looking at them brought out the true meaning of Christmas.

As the service came to an end, Hans-Dieter and I approached the Baroness and Baron von Puttkamer. As was the custom in Germany, my brother bowed and I gave a small curtsy and both of us wished the family a very happy Christmas.

There was also my new girlfriend Gisela Krämer and her parents. Gisela attended the same school as I did and each morning we travelled together by train to Stolp. Her parents owned the village post office together with a small shop selling everything from groceries to odds and ends for household use. I liked Gisela and really wanted to be her friend. We'd known each other just a short time and up to now I hadn't met her parents, nor had she met my mother.

Gisela had also noticed me, and came over to wish me a happy Christmas.

'Else, come and meet my parents. I've often talked about you, and now's your chance to say hello to them.'

I shook hands with Herr and Frau Krämer and wished them both a happy Christmas and a peaceful New Year.

'Come and see us soon, Else,' Gisela's mother invited. 'We'd like to get to know you. Soon, I hope, I also would like the opportunity to meet your mother. I haven't seen her in church this morning; I hope she's well.'

'Yes, Frau Krämer, mother's well, thank you. But she has to stay at home to be with my small brother and baby sister. It's too cold for them to be out of doors.'

'Please give your mother our kind regards and perhaps, after Christmas, I'll see her in the post office. Tell her to make herself known to me; I look forward to meeting her.'

I hoped that as time went on, Gisela and I would become very close friends. Now I could only wish her and her family once more a happy time for Christmas and the New Year.

As Gisela's parents moved off, I noticed her father had difficulty walking and used a stick. Ah, I thought, that's why he's not in the army. Perhaps he's been wounded and is now on leave.

'Come, Hans-Dieter, before we go home, let's have one more look at the wonderful crib. I love it. Don't you?'

'It's just as nice as our Düsseldorf crib, Else. Don't you think?'

'Yes, Hans-Dieter, I agree, but just a few more minutes and then we must go home.'

Many people from the congregation surrounded the crib with oohs and ahs and 'Isn't it wonderful!' And it was. There were all the nativity figures: Mary, Joseph and the Baby in the manger. There were animals: sheep, donkey, cattle; also shepherds, looking in wonderment at the tiny Child before them. In the distance, not yet arrived, were the three holy kings from the Orient, bringing precious gifts from their faraway countries. They didn't reach the stables until 6 January, Twelfth Night.

The nativity scene was enchanting and I stood there lost in thought. I wanted to stay longer, but now my brother was impatient to get home.

'I'm hungry, Else. Come, let's get going; mother will be waiting and our dinner will be ready.'

What could I do? His tummy was grumbling; and when that happened, lingering wasn't allowed.

When Hans-Dieter and I walked in through the back door, a delicious aroma from the kitchen confronted us. It made our mouths water. After a quick 'Hello, Frau Krause. Hello, Trudi and Maria. A Merry Christmas to you all, and also to Dunja and Anna,' we rushed upstairs to find out what culinary delight was awaiting us.

'There you are, children,' mother greeted us. 'Quick, take off your coats; then I can start dishing up.'

Mother had been to the kitchen to collect our wonderful roasted goose. Mamsell had gone to a lot of trouble and it looked perfect – and, I hoped, would taste as good. It was filled with a chestnut stuffing, something I'd never heard of, and surrounding the goose were tiny roasted balls made of herbs, onions and breadcrumbs bound together with beaten egg. It made our mouths water and we couldn't wait to taste it.

But I couldn't take my eyes off the table. It looked stunning! Mother had worked hard while we were at church: she must have gone into the park to pick a handful of winter greenery.

'Mother, the ivy and small evergreen branches are perfect. You always know what to do to make a table look festive. I like the centrepiece. It's amazing what a few fir twigs and a red candle can do. It looks lovely, thank you . . . But where did the candle come from?'

'That, my child, was a present from Mamsell with her good wishes for Christmas.'

If only father could have been with us. We missed him and it was impossible to imagine how mother must have felt, yet she put on a brave face, laughing and joking, and for a while managed to make us forget one dearly beloved member of our family was absent and far away.

'Let's hope, children,' she said, 'that next Christmas, God willing, we'll all be together again, not here in Pomerania but in our own home in Düsseldorf.' We all nodded.

'Now, children, sit down. We don't want our dinner getting cold. Let's say grace, and then we can begin our meal.' Mother started to serve and soon we were eating. 'Before I forget, Else,' she said after a while, 'you and Sylvia have been invited to a party with friends in the next village. You haven't met them, but Sylvia will introduce you, and Fraulein Dorothea will take you. No need to worry, it will be very informal. Meeting other young girls will definitely be to your advantage.'

'Thanks, mother. I'll enjoy that, and when I next see Sylvia, we'll sort out the details.'

Our Christmas dinner was delicious, a meal fit for aristocracy. The goose was the most impressive centrepiece, accompanied by apple sauce, red and white cabbage, potatoes and a tasty gravy. The stuffing and little herb balls were unusual, but it all tasted so excellent that even our fussy little Ralf tried everything and – surprise, surprise – liked it all!

Last came mother's own creation: a semolina pudding made with milk and egg yolk, and, instead of sugar (strictly rationed even at Christmas), we all had a big spoonful of home-made strawberry jam. What a feast that was! We felt we didn't need to eat again for another week.

We really wanted to show mother how much we appreciated our special meal. I suggested that Hans-Dieter and I wash up and tidy the room whilst she and the little ones had a lie down. Hans-Dieter and I were also planning to write to father, which we could do when we were on our own. I said that perhaps, after she'd rested, mother could add a letter from her as well and that I would post them after Christmas.

Mother thanked me, and I could see how grateful she was. She said that she would tell father what a support I was to her, which pleased me.

With the room tidy and everything cleared away Hans-Dieter and I settled down to our letters. I wrote,

Dearest father,

Today's Christmas Day and Hans-Dieter and I are writing to you while mother's resting. What kind of day have you had? Surely, being Christmas there was no fighting? Did our parcel arrive in time, and if so, did you like what we sent you? It must be bitterly cold where you are, much colder than here.

We had a lovely Christmas dinner. Frau Krause cooked our goose in her large oven, mother's being so tiny, and it was truly scrumptious. It was a very large goose and we so wished you could have shared it with us.

At 4 p.m. we're invited to join the Puttkamer family in their drawing room for a little celebration. I'm looking forward to it, though mother feels sad because, without you, her family's incomplete. But she's very brave, a true German woman.

Tomorrow Baroness's granddaughter Sylvia and I have had an invitation to a party at the manor in the next village. Although I want to go, I'll feel out of place because, apart from Sylvia, everyone else will be a stranger to me. Miss Dorothea will take us there and has promised to introduce me.

We have deep snow and enjoy riding in a sleigh drawn by two strong horses with bells round their necks. It sounds beautiful when we glide along.

School's fine: I'm getting on well. I like almost all subjects, except I hate maths. Many girls find it easy and I try to understand, but it's hopeless. Why are sums so complicated? I'll never master them.

On 1 January there'll be a hunt. Hans-Dieter and I are allowed to take part. That's exciting: we've never been on a hunt before.

Father, will you really come on leave in February for Baby's christening? That would be wonderful! Then we can all be together again.

Now I must finish my letter. God bless you, father. I miss you.

Much love and hugs and kisses from us all, especially me.

Your daughter, Else

As I closed and folded my letter, I could see Hans-Dieter had also finished. 'Should I read your letter and correct any mistakes?' I asked.

'No, Else, my letter's private, and there aren't many mistakes! I've been very careful. Anyway, father won't mind. He'll be pleased to get a letter from me.'

Our letters folded and sealed into an envelope, I looked at the clock and saw it was after three. Time to wake mother and for us to get ready. I ran across the room and up the little steps, opened the door and there stood mother, already smartly dressed, holding Ralf's little hand. He smiled at me, like a small gentleman, proudly wearing his Sunday-best clothes.

'Goodness!' mother exclaimed. 'You and Hans-Dieter were a long time writing your letters. Didn't you hear us moving about? Now hurry. Hans-Dieter, have a good wash and don't forget behind your ears. Else, put on your dark-blue dress: you look nice in it.'

'With my new petticoat, mother?'

'Of course. That's what it's for.'

While mother watched Ralf and made Baby presentable for her first public appearance, Hans-Dieter and I changed. And when the clock struck four, everyone was ready to go downstairs.

Mother had little Marlene in her arms; Ralfie was with me and I carried a small basket of spicy home-made Christmas gingerbread cakes. For the Baroness mother had a pretty embroidered tray cloth, very old, but still a special gift.

We knocked and the Baron opened the door.

'Frau Hopp! Lovely to see you and your delightful family. Do come in. Merry Christmas!'

Every member of the family was present. Mother gave her Christmas greetings to them all and handed over her small gifts to Baroness von Puttkamer. Then, with a small curtsy from me and a bow from Hans-Dieter, we again wished everyone a happy Christmas.

I gave Sylvia a pretty pencil case mother had made for me to use in school (I already had one and didn't mind giving it as a present to my friend).

The Baroness went to a sideboard and picked up a tray.

'Frau Hopp, your gifts have given much pleasure. Please accept a few small tokens of our appreciation.

There were presents for all of us. Sylvia's gift was an exquisite handbag made of multicoloured beads. I was thrilled and treasured it.

Baby Marlene had a silver rattle and Ralf a box of building bricks. Mother and Hans-Dieter also had presents, though in all the excitement, I didn't see them.

I was also given an old brass bell. I decided I'd keep it as one of my most treasured belongings so that, when I had children of my own, every year at that time, I'd call them downstairs to the Christmas room as mother had done for us.

The atmosphere in the drawing room that evening was full of festive spirit. The room looked wonderful: it was huge and perfect for a celebration. At the end was a raised dais on which stood a majestic tree dressed in precious and glittering decorations; old and well used, handed down through many generations. Candles – on the tree and placed here and there throughout that large room – shone brightly and were more than sufficient to give us light. It created a wonderful homely atmosphere while we all celebrated a perfect Christmas.

The doors to the adjoining music room stood wide open, offering a glimpse of a grand piano, lid open, waiting to be played.

Everything was elegant, and the Baroness, ever watchful and responsive to the wishes of her guests, was a perfect hostess. She stood tall and dignified, dressed in dark colours, with white-laced edgings on neck and wrists, commanding respect without trying to, and I treated her with reverence.

The Baron, on the other hand, was the direct opposite: he was fond of the good life, stout, with rosy cheeks like two polished red apples, and a handlebar moustache, which he liked to twirl. His eyebrows were thick and bushy, giving the deceptive impression of an angry, grim despot. But he liked to sit in his comfortable armchair at the hearthside, smoking one of his precious meerschaums. It would have been fascinating to sit beside him and listen to tales of his younger years, which, for the most part, he'd spent in Glowitz Manor. I knew he'd fought in the 1914–18 Great War, and was told he'd also spent some time in India. I wasn't bold enough to ask him, because Trudi had told me these things about him, and I didn't know if she had her facts right. He and I understood each other. I was certain he liked me and that liking was mutual: he reminded me of an old, but well-preserved, toby jug.

That night I described the scene in my diary:

> Mother and the Baroness sit on a small settee, deep in conversation. I don't know what they're talking about, but most likely mother's telling the Baroness about our home in Düsseldorf and how she misses it.
>
> I can see little Ralf, sitting on the floor, playing with his new coloured bricks, and Hans-Dieter, on a small stool close to the baron, listening with rapt attention to a tale the elderly gentleman's telling him.

Sylvia and I are sitting on our own in a corner away from the adults and are discussing the forthcoming party. She tells me about the many Christmas presents she received from the family, and I tell her of mine. I mention my beautiful new pink petticoat and I believe Sylvia's just a tiny bit jealous.

Fraulein Dorothea has gone to the piano and plays wonderful background Christmas music.

Fraulein Elisabeth is on her own, knitting a woollen garment for someone.

I can't see Fraulein Otti. She must have left the room; most likely she went to the stables to check on her horses.

'We'll now have some refreshment,' announced the Baroness. 'No need to call Trudi. We'll help ourselves to whatever we like. Come Sylvia, Else, just take what you like. But first, Sylvia, please serve Frau Hopp, your grandfather and Fraulein Elisabeth . . . and call your sister from the piano.'

'Where's Otti, grandmother?' asked Sylvia.

'Don't worry about her, child. She'll come when she's ready.'

Sylvia and I handed round biscuits and slices of particularly delicious stollen, baked by Mamsell. There was real coffee for the grown-ups and, as usual, milk for the children. Sylvia and I were given the choice of milk or a coffee substitute made out of roasted rye. Horrible! How I envied the grown-ups. I loved the aroma of real coffee and had at times been permitted to taste it. But the general rule was no coffee for children: far too stimulating. 'It will stunt your growth,' mother said, and at that time, I still believed it might.

When we'd eaten, Fraulein Dorothea returned to the piano in the music room and we sang well-known Christmas carols. Afterwards Sylvia and I entertained the adults by playing charades. Of course, Hans-Dieter wanted to join in and nothing would prevent him trying. We all gave suggestions, which were not well received, and he became frustrated and angry. Mother had to pacify him: she said that for an eight-year-old boy, he'd done excellently.

In all we had great fun and, amid hilarity and laughter, earned a lot of applause and praise for our inventiveness.

While we were still laughing rather noisily, there came a knock on the door. 'Sylvia,' said the Baroness, 'please see who it is.'

Sylvia did so, and there stood Trudi and Maria carrying trays laden with a wide variety of supper snacks: ham and cold meats, cheese and fresh home-baked bread and dishes of tiny pickled onions and beetroot.

'My dear girls,' said the Baroness, 'you should be with your families: did Mamsell tell you to come back? Now leave the trays and off you go. Have a day off tomorrow; we can manage: we'll see you the day after Boxing Day.'

'Thank you, Madam,' the girls chorused and disappeared instantly.

The baroness told us to help ourselves, but mother insisted we eat seated at the table.

It was a wonderful end to a perfect Christmas Day, but once we'd finished our meal, it was time to take our leave. Baby Marlene had been very good all evening, but now started to cry heartily. She wanted to be fed, and wasn't prepared to wait! Everyone laughed.

Ralf was looking tired and on his cheeks were two bright red spots. He also felt hot to touch.

'I fear our little lad has a temperature.' I could see the worry on mother's face. 'Please, Else, take him upstairs and settle him for the night. I'll not be far behind, but must quickly talk to Fraulein Dorothea. She's found a family where you can board for the duration of the cold winter days.'

'But, mother –' I protested. I wanted to hear more.

'Please don't argue with me now, Else. I'm not talking about it this evening. Tomorrow we'll have plenty of time to discuss it further. At this moment I'm concerned about your little brother: he's our priority. Everything else must take second place and Fraulein Dorothea and Ottilia have promised to assist me wherever help is needed.'

Always, even to the last moment, formalities had to be observed. That meant, for Hans-Dieter and me, a thank you and a handshake all round, a curtsy and a bow to every person in the room . . . except Sylvia. For her there was a hug from me and a whisper in her ear, 'See you tomorrow when we go to the party.'

With Ralf on my arm, Hans-Dieter and I quickly left the room. Before mother returned, I wanted to get Ralf ready for bed, but was worried: the little lad was ill, no doubt about it. He was whimpering and felt even hotter. I was certain his temperature was high.

Come on, mother! I thought. *I don't know what to do.*

Ralf began crying, 'Mama, Mama!' Hans-Dieter also wanted attention. There was bedlam and I was on the verge of panicking.

Suddenly I heard mother running upstairs and, completely out of breath, she burst into the room with baby Marlene in her arms.

'Poor child,' she said to me. 'What was I thinking to let you go ahead on your own? See to your little sister while I tend to Ralf. I must try to get his fever down and tomorrow morning, Boxing Day or not, I'll have to contact the doctor: someone has to be on call for emergencies.'

Mother did her best to pacify my little brother, but it wasn't easy, as he was so distressed and restless. She washed down his hot little body with tepid water, gave him a small amount of medicine and when he was in his soft sleeping-suit and wrapped in a blanket, I took over, while mother nursed baby Marlene.

Hans-Dieter also wanted some attention but couldn't get it with little Ralf so ill. I told him I needed to rely on him. 'Please, Hans-Dieter, you must be grown-up and sensible; you and I are the only two people mother can depend on.'

'All right, Else. I know I can look after myself.' He had a good heart that young brother of mine. Only occasionally, as is common in boys of his age, a little devil would come to the surface to lead him astray.

Ralfie had gone to sleep in my arms and very gently I lay him in his cot.

Baby was also satisfied, clean and dry, and content with her little life.

With Hans-Dieter in bed and silence at last, mother and I realised we were also tired. 'Let's go to bed, Else. Who knows what tomorrow has in store.'

'Good night, mother, and thank you for everything,' I said, as I gave her a kiss and a hug.

'Good night to you too, my child. I'm the one who has to thank you for all the things you do.' Silence surrounded me. I let my thoughts wander wherever they wanted to go. To my beloved father so far away; to mother, who tried valiantly to cope without him. Did I really have to board with strangers? I'd hate it and how could mother possibly manage without my help?

But Ralfie, my little brother lying next door, worried me most. He was very sick. Of that I was certain. Sylvia told me her sister Dorothea had asked Baroness whether it could be tuberculosis? Surely not! I didn't know much about that illness, but knew it was very serious and that it was sometimes called 'consumption'. Would little Ralf get well again? I had to pray very hard for him. Surely God wouldn't let him die? I lay awake for a long time it seemed: sleep wouldn't come. But I must have dropped off, because I heard a creak and suddenly realised someone was quietly moving about in the room.

'Mother, is that you?'

'Yes, child. Go back to sleep. I've come for some warm milk for Ralf. He's very restless.'

'Mother, I can't go to the party tomorrow. I'll not leave you here with our little boy so sick. How could I possibly enjoy myself? Please don't say I have to go, because I'll not listen. I'll ask Fraulein Dorothea to make my apologies. Sylvia won't be alone: she knows many people there, and I'm only a stranger.'

'Let's wait until tomorrow, Else. it's much too late to talk about it now. Who knows, perhaps in the morning, Ralf may be much improved. Nights are always the worst time. Go back to sleep now. All will be well.'

Chapter 10

Sanatorium

26 December 1942

When at last it was morning, our little boy was no better.

Mother was terribly worried. 'Oh dear, why do we have to be in this godforsaken part of Germany. If we were at home, we'd have no difficulty getting a doctor: Boxing Day or no Boxing Day, I don't know what to do.' That wasn't like my mother: always so level-headed, she now seemed on the verge of panic.

It was my turn to take over. 'Mother,' I said, 'listen. I'll run quickly to the village and see if the doctor's at home. If he is, he *must* come immediately. If he's not there, then I'll talk to Baroness and ask her the best thing for us to do.'

The doctor wasn't at home, yet I had to find someone to help us. But we needn't have worried. The Puttkamer family rallied round and help was soon available. Fraulein Dorothea had to take Sylvia to the party, but Fraulein Ottilia was at home and offered to take mother and Ralf to the hospital in Stolp. What a relief! With everything settled, mother was once again in control of herself and able to make decisions.

'Else, is it still your intention not to attend the party this afternoon?' she asked me. 'Because I'll understand if you'd like to go.'

'No, mother, I told you last night I want to stay and help. Don't you want me here when you return from Stolp?'

'Of course I do. Thank you, child! Please look after Hans-Dieter. I don't know how long I'll be away. There's plenty to eat: please give him something if he gets hungry.'

Mother had been strong with father by her side, but now she was without him, she'd not yet acquired the strength to cope with adversity by herself. I had every faith in her, however. That courage would come later; it was buried deep within her, I was sure. In the future, when she really needed fortitude, it would surface. Then she'd become a lioness ready to defend her cubs; nothing would deter her from achieving her objective.

But here was something over which she had no control. She was beside herself with worry about her child. Fraulein Ottilia couldn't come quickly enough and when she did arrive, mother was waiting with Ralf, wrapped up like a little Eskimo child.

Luckily it hadn't snowed since Christmas night, which would make it easier to reach Stolp safely without hindrance.

I sat at home and waited, all the time trying to keep Hans-Dieter occupied. For a short while Sylvia came to be with me but was eager to go to the party: she couldn't stop talking about it. She wanted me to know what kind of dress she'd wear, and would I like to see her dance as Grandma Baroness had taught her? If she aimed to make me jealous, she wasn't succeeding;

my mind was with mother and my little brother. The party meant nothing to me.

Hans-Dieter and I waited a long time for mother to return. When I saw her, she was without little Ralf and I could tell she was very upset.

'Mother, tell me all about it. What's the matter with Ralfie? Why are they keeping him in hospital?'

'All I can say, child, is that Ralfie's very ill. The doctor fears it may be tuberculosis, but in order to be certain, tests have to be carried out. Our little boy cried bitterly when I left him. "Mama, Mama," he cried out over and over. I felt my heart would break. The worst thing was that they *told* me to go. Sister seemed to think it would only make matters worse if I stayed longer. How did she know what a mother feels? But it was no good; I've had to come home without him. Now we must wait till tomorrow when I can go back. It will have to be by train – I can't impose on the Puttkamers any more; as it is, they've been most kind and understanding.'

Next morning mother was up very early. She was restless and kept looking at the clock; I knew she was longing for the hours to pass until it was time to go to the station. She was very anxious. What would she find when she arrived at the hospital? What news would they have concerning her little boy? How I wished I could have gone to Stolp with her. She needed someone by her side, yet I had to stay behind and care for Baby and Hans-Dieter.

It had snowed again during the night; and when I looked out of the window, it was still snowing.

How was mother to get to the station? There were no taxis in the village and the street would be icy and treacherous. To walk through the field was out of the question. The snow lay very deep there and mother's footwear wasn't suited to that kind of walk.

'Don't worry, child. Have you ever known me to fail when I wanted to do something? To know that Hans-Dieter and Baby are well looked after takes a load off my mind. But I need to see our little boy and hear from the doctor how sick he really is. I'm still hoping we're worrying unnecessarily.'

Again help was at hand. As mother was talking to me, there was a knock on the door. I ran to open it and there stood Fraulein Ottilia.

'Come, Frau Hopp, I've harnessed the horses: they're waiting in the yard attached to the sleigh. We'll take you to meet your train and when you're ready to return, just ask someone to telephone the manor and you'll be picked up by either Dorothea or me.'

I could see utter relief on mother's face. I'd never seen her move so quickly and, with a little help from me, it didn't take long for her to be ready: hat and coat, gloves, boots and handbag; then a quick kiss for us all, and she was gone.

When mother left, I sat down for a moment to give thought to the coming day. Much had to be done to fill my hours. I wanted to keep busy, because to be idle would only encourage me to think, worry and wonder about what mother would find on her arrival at the hospital in Stolp.

Hans-Dieter was fine. He was a good lad and didn't need supervision all day long.

My first task was to bathe and feed baby Marlene and make her dry and comfortable. Then, after a cuddle, put her into her cradle when, I hoped, she'd fall into a peaceful sleep again.

Beds had to be made, and rooms to be tidied, dusted and polished. Keeping so busy, with no time to spare, I hadn't realised how fast the morning hours had moved on. It was time to think about what Hans-Dieter and I could have for lunch. I looked in mother's store cupboard and found no meat, but plenty of potatoes and vegetables.

That will make a wonderful soup, I thought. *Hans-Dieter's fond of soup and an extra lump of margarine and good variety of vegetables will warm and sustain him till mother returns bringing, I hope, little Ralf with her.*

Hans-Dieter was downstairs helping Johann brush away snow from the kitchen entrance. That little job kept my brother occupied and out of mischief. He loved being with Johann. Hans-Dieter called him old and wise but listened to him; and not having father there, Johann gave my young brother a lot of well-needed guidance.

But I knew that soon he'd come running upstairs, telling me he was starving and wanting to know what I was cooking.

'Soup it is, Hans-Dieter, a good wholesome vegetable soup,' I answered. 'And because you've been so good I made your favourite semolina pudding and with it you can have strawberry jam.'

'Oh, Else!' he shouted, dancing round the room, 'you're my best big sister. I'm so glad you're cooking today: I *love* semolina pudding!'

I had to smile at his antics. He was a dear little brother, and to please him wasn't difficult.

'Don't forget, Hans-Dieter, we eat at 12.30 p.m.; but be up here at noon. Now run along. Johann will tell you when it's lunchtime.'

'Righto, Else,' he called as he struggled back into his coat, 'I'll do as you say.' And like a whirlwind he was gone.

As soon as I'd cleared up after lunch, I went into the bedroom to look at my little sister. She'd been asleep all morning and I thought that surely by now she'd want another feed. I bent over her cradle and there she lay, eyes wide open, playing with her little hands.

Oh, you darling baby, I thought, *I love you: now you'll have all my attention.*

I laid her on my bed while I prepared her feed, and then, after changing her nappy and making her comfortable, it was time for a big cuddle. She was only six weeks old, yet when I tickled her chin and kissed her tiny hands I was certain she responded with a little smile. It was wonderful to have her in my arms; it made me feel very happy.

Just as I put Baby back into her cradle, there was a knock on the door and there stood Sylvia.

'Else, I'm sorry not to have seen you today, but I've been so busy. Otti made me brush and groom my horse. She said as I was at the party yesterday, I could work today. You don't realise how hard I've worked and the stables were bitterly cold.'

'Well, Sylvia, you're here now. Sit down and tell me about the party. Was it good? Were there many girls and handsome boys with whom you could dance? I wish I could have been there but, as you know, it wasn't possible.'

So we sat and chatted, and time flew by.

By 4 p.m. we were still waiting for mother to return. How I'd have liked to walk to the station to meet her off the last train. But how could I? I couldn't just leave the children. I hated the thought of her walking in the dark alone through the snow. However, as I was having a game with Hans-Dieter, there was a sudden knock and Fraulein Dorothea walked into the room.

'Else, I just want to let you know, your mother has telephoned. She's on her way back and I'm taking the sleigh to meet her at the station.'

'Can I go as well,' Hans-Dieter asked. But this time he received a firm no, and by my voice knew I meant it.

We waited and, to pass the time, I laid the small table and put the saucepan with the rest of the soup from lunch on our small stove – it would be ready by the time mother arrived.

After a while we heard sleigh bells coming nearer, until they stopped in front of the main entrance. Mother had returned and soon she'd be with us.

But immediately she entered our room, I knew something was wrong. She looked totally exhausted and very sad. All she said was, 'Hello, children,' and, without taking off her outdoor clothes, sat at the table, buried her head in her arms and burst into bitter tears.

Hans-Dieter and I were stunned. We didn't know what to do or say. Hans-Dieter wanted to go to mother, but I waved him away. 'Let her cry,' I whispered. 'She'll feel better afterwards and then she'll tell us what's making her so unhappy.'

After a while she composed herself and apologised.

'Come to me you two; in a moment or two I'll talk to you, but first I must know how the day went for you. Were you able to cope, Else? Was Hans-Dieter a good lad and did he listen to you? And little Marlene? Was she a well-behaved baby?'

So many questions from mother, yet all we wanted to hear was how she'd fared in Stolp.

'Mother, don't concern yourself. Everything's fine here; we coped very well. Now please tell us how our little brother is and why he didn't come home with you.'

After quickly peeking at baby, who was peacefully asleep, mother returned.

'Listen, I have sad news concerning your little brother. Ralfie's very ill. He has tuberculosis and will have to be admitted to a sanatorium somewhere near Swinemünde, on the Baltic coast. He may have to stay there for up to six months: he'll be in isolation and it won't be easy for me to visit him. But I'm determined to take him there. The doctors at Stolp hospital will arrange everything. They've given permission for me to accompany my little boy. But Else, now I want your answer. I'll be leaving the day after tomorrow and won't return till two days later. That'll be 30 December, a day before New Year's Eve. Tell me honestly, Else, do you think you'll be able to cope with baby and Hans-Dieter?'

'Mother, you don't need to worry about us. Honestly, we'll be fine. Anyway, there are plenty of people in this house willing to help if the need arises. But before we go on talking, you must have a taste of my delicious soup, which I cooked today. Hans-Dieter will agree it was scrumptious; now you must try it.'

'Yes, mother,' Hans-Dieter piped in, 'and I had semolina pudding with strawberry jam.'

In spite of mother's being so sad, Hans-Dieter and I managed to cheer her. I handed her a letter from father that had arrived during the day.

Mother tore it open and, joy of joy, inside were short notes for both Hans-Dieter and me:

> My dearest big Girl,
>
> Now Christmas is over and by the time you get this letter, the New Year may already have begun. Thank you so much for the wonderful gifts you sent me. Everything you and mother knitted is much appreciated. It's bitterly cold here and, no matter how many clothes we wear, we never seem to be warm. How I wish I could be with you, but I must wait until the beginning of February; then I hope I can be present for baby Marlene's christening.
>
> Please help mother whenever you can. You're a sensible girl and I know she can always rely on you.
>
> Give a kiss from me to your little brothers and sister. I miss you all and think of you very, very often.
>
> God bless you, my child; my love to you, father.

By the time I'd finished reading my letter, mother had also read hers. 'Does father say where he is?' I asked her.

'No, child, you know he's not allowed to give that information, but he talks of countryside being bleak and swampy. I have a feeling he may be somewhere near Stalingrad.'

I gave her my letter to read, after which she settled down to have her evening meal.

'Well done, Else,' she said. 'The soup you made is very good. I couldn't have done better.'

That was praise enough for me and I knew I could cope without her for a few days.

After mother had eaten, she went to tend to our baby; and after that was done, we settled down to answer father's letters.

The following day mother went downstairs to the kitchen to tell Mamsell of her impending journey to Swinemünde, and why she had to go. Mother asked if she'd kindly provide Hans-Dieter and me with a midday meal, and she was happy to oblige.

'Of course I'll do that, Frau Hopp. It will be a pleasure. Go with an easy mind; there's nothing to worry about here. We'll all keep an eye on your little family. Else will cope; of that I'm sure. Just go and settle your little lad. It will be very upsetting for you both but, with hope and our prayers, perhaps it won't be long before he's home again.'

Next morning, Tuesday, 28 December 1942, Johann called to take mother to the station. There she was to start her journey, first to Stolp, and from there on to Swinemünde.

At home everything was running smoothly. Hans-Dieter was helpful in every way and baby Marlene was no trouble at all.

Unless something prevented mother, she'd be home in the evening of the thirtieth, the night before New Year's Eve.

When we were in Düsseldorf, we used to celebrate New Year's Eve. That seemed a long time ago; yet here in Pomerania, it didn't seem to matter. There were many other things far more important to think about, and the thought of celebrating was totally insignificant.

Thursday, 30 December 1942

That was the day mother would return from Swinemünde. *How will she feel?* I wondered. Very upset and unhappy, of that I was sure.

My mind worked overtime thinking of what I could do to make her return special.

After I'd given Hans-Dieter his breakfast, I saw to our little sister, bathed and fed her and gave her the attention she needed to be a contented little baby.

Johann came with his usual basket of peat, so our room would be cosy and warm when mother arrived. I went down to the kitchen to ask Mamsell if she could provide a little extra food I could warm up for mother's return.

'Of course, I'll be only too pleased,' was Mamsell's answer. 'We must all look after your mother: life's not easy for her. By the way, Else, what are you doing tomorrow, as it's New Year's Eve?'

'I don't think we'll do anything in particular, Frau Krause. We might have gone for a walk through the village to visit a few of mother's friends. But it's too cold for little Marlene to be outside and that means we have to stay in.'

'Well,' answered Mamsell, 'if you all want to wish your mother's friends a happy New Year in the morning, leave your little sister with me. I'll enjoy looking after her.'

'Thank you, Frau Krause. That's so kind of you; I know it will please mother. But now I must run upstairs to start my housework. I want everything gleaming when mother comes home for the start of the New Year.

Hans-Dieter helped me, sometimes being a nuisance, but he was good company, and time flew by. Everything shone; and when I looked around, I was happy with our accomplishment and knew how pleased mother would be when she saw how hard we'd worked.

But there was a knock on the door and it brought great disappointment. It was Fraulein Elisabeth. She informed us mother wouldn't return until the following morning because she was delayed in Swinemünde.

'What will we do now?' asked Hans-Dieter, near to tears. 'Tomorrow's New Year's Eve and mother won't be here. And wanting to be brave, he tried hard not to cry.

'Come on, Hans-Dieter; don't be sad. I'm certain she'll come home as soon as she possibly can. By evening we'll all be together and you, mother and I can have a little New Year's Eve celebration. And don't forget, it's the boar hunt on New Year's Day. That's only the day after tomorrow, and you're looking forward to that, aren't you?'

'Of course I am, Else, but I didn't want to talk about it because Ralfie's so ill, and with mother not here I thought it wrong to feel happy.'

'Don't be silly, Hans-Dieter. No one wants you to be unhappy; if I can look forward to it, so can you. Now let's go to the kitchen to see what Frau Krause has prepared for our lunch.'

31 December 1942

Next morning Hans-Dieter and I were up and about very early. While he was in the bathroom washing and dressing, I attended to baby Marlene, who was demanding immediate attention. We realized mother couldn't possibly arrive home so early in the day, but there was much to be done before she returned: I wanted everything to be perfect.

That morning we didn't linger over breakfast.

'Come on, Hans-Dieter. Shift yourself. You said you wanted to help me; now *do* it!'

Poor lad – it wasn't fair to boss him about, and I could see his relief when I told him to dress warmly and find Johann, who would no doubt have something to keep him occupied. Hans-Dieter couldn't escape quickly enough, but as he opened the door he called out, 'Else, Johann has left a basket of peat by our door. Can you manage to bring it in or should I ask for his help?'

'No, Hans-Dieter, that's not necessary. Wait a moment; between us we can bring the basket in.'

It was the last day of the year 1942 and mother would soon be home. Johann had promised to meet her at the station and was expecting her to telephone with the time of her arrival.

Waiting for her here in our rooms was difficult and I desperately tried to find ways to pass the time, but couldn't concentrate.

Suddenly Hans-Dieter ran upstairs and burst into the room. 'Else, mother's coming! She spoke to Fraulein Dorothea just before her train left Stolp. Johann's harnessing the horses to the sleigh. Please Else, can I go with him? He said I could if you'd allow it.'

'Yes, of course you can. It will cheer her up to see you. Now hurry and dress in your warmest clothes: scarf, and a balaclava on your head, and don't forget your gloves. You can get icy cold riding in an open sleigh, even with rugs and on a short journey.'

Meanwhile the commotion had roused little Marlene. I lifted her out of her cradle and danced round the table with her, singing at the top of my voice, 'mother's coming home! Mother's coming home!' And my little sister, who didn't understand, burst into tears.

'Hush, Baby, no need to cry. Mother will soon be here and then we're going to have our very own New Year's celebration together.'

I didn't have long to wait. I strained my ears for the sound of sleigh bells, which I must have picked up from as far away as the park entrance. Then there was the sound of Hans-Dieter's boots stomping up the stairs with mother following wearily behind him. She'd arrived at last, and I threw myself into her arms.

I gazed into her face, trying to read her expression. She looked tired, drawn and sad. The previous few days had obviously not been easy. Concern about Ralfie was etched in worry lines on her forehead, but now was not the time for questions. It was enough to help her out of her boots and outdoor clothes, seat her in her favourite chair with a cup of good, strong, *real* coffee. That pleased her, as I knew it would, and, most importantly, it helped to cheer her up.

'Now, children,' she said, at last, 'sit beside me and I'll tell you where Ralfie is and where I've been.'

She then explained it was better for our little brother to be in a sanatorium than in a hospital. It was a small but beautiful building close to the sea, the care was excellent and Matron herself had given him special attention.

'Ralf may have to be there for six months – perhaps longer, depending on his progress. I'll be able to visit him, but not just yet. My fear is that, after so long away, he'll forget us; that's hard to bear.' As she talked, tears formed in her eyes and I could see how upset mother was.

Just then, at the right moment, Hans-Dieter answered a knock on our door. There stood a smiling Trudi, carrying a huge tray laden with goodies for our New Year's Eve supper: freshly baked bread, sausage, cheese and hard-boiled eggs, sweet and sour pickled pumpkin, slices of stollen, and, for each of us, a home-made doughnut filled with strawberry jam and lashings of freshly whipped cream!

'Frau Hopp, this is with compliments of Mamsell. She hopes you'll all enjoy what she's prepared and wants to be the first to wish you a very happy and peaceful New Year 1943.'

'Thank you, Trudi,' mother replied. 'Tell Mamsell how touched we are. Tomorrow morning early I'll thank her personally. I know she'll be busy catering for guests coming for the hunt. Perhaps she'd be glad of an extra pair of hands. But I'll talk to her myself about that. Goodnight, Trudi. Have a wonderful evening and enjoy yourself. Who knows what the New Year has in store for us. Let's hope it's a good one.'

Thanks to Mamsell we had a delicious feast and then, to our surprise, mother took a small bottle of her own home-made cherry liqueur from the cupboard. It tasted wonderful. Hans-Dieter was also allowed a tiny glass and pretended the drink had gone to his head, giving a good impression of a drunken boy. Mother laughed and joined in a game of charades. She reminisced about happier times in Düsseldorf with dear father, now far away. Then we remembered our little sister alone in the bedroom and I fetched her into the sitting room to join us. Mother lit the candles on the tree and together we listened to the wireless and heard how people in bomb-torn cities all over Germany were awaiting the coming of the New Year with hope of an end to the war and long-awaited peace at last.

We toasted little Ralf far away in Swinemünde and mother broke down for a moment. Hans-Dieter and I cried with her. We also thought of our grandmas and grandads and our lost friends, and prayed they were safe and the bombing we'd heard about would stop for them just for one night. And that made us homesick.

Then, as midnight came nearer, mother changed the mood. 'Come, children, let's be naughty and have one last drink to toast in the New Year. Let's open the window for a moment and listen to the small, lonely bell here in the village church.'

The clock finally struck twelve.

'A VERY HAPPY NEW YEAR!' mother cried out. 'May all our dearest wishes come true: that father will soon be with us again; also Ralfie, fit, strong and well; and for you Else and Hans-Dieter, little Marlene and myself, I wish a very happy and blessed 1943!'

Chapter 11

Boar Hunt

1 January 1943

I awoke very early next morning, and my first thought was, *Today's the first day of the New Year; it's also the day of the big hunt.*

As I lay in bed, I could hear voices and a lot of activity downstairs, not only in the house but also outside. It appeared many guests had already arrived. I looked at the time: it was only 5 a.m. Not much longer and Hans-Dieter would have to get up if he wanted to be ready in time to join the hunt.

The previous night, before I'd fallen asleep, so many thoughts had whirled round my head that, although it was late, I jotted them down in my diary:

Although it's a new year, I'm feeling quite sad tonight. So many worries.

I've been thinking of father in unknown lands, daily surrounded by danger, unable to do anything about it. How frightening that must be. How he must long to come home to us.

Then, little brother, Ralf, all on his own, away from the family – surely he'll cry for us? The notion's heartbreaking . . . How mother must worry, not knowing how long her little boy will be away.

Time's rushing past: to think that, in a few more days, school starts again and with it the ordeal of boarding in Stolp. How I dread it, but I've promised mother at least to give it a try.

Also, I've made up my mind NOT to go to the hunt. As yet mother doesn't know, but as soon as she gets up, I'll have to tell her. I know she'll try to persuade me to go, but I'm determined not to. No one can make me. I really don't want to and won't change my mind. I hate the thought of hunting animals, so I shouldn't be made to do something that revolts me.

I know Hans-Dieter will be disappointed, but he'll be well looked after by Johann and other adults. There will also be children from the village he'll know . . . no, Hans-Dieter won't be alone. Sylvia, on the other hand, will be furious. She'll say I'm letting her down, but perhaps she'll listen if I tell her why I can't go: I hope she'll understand. I want to spend today alone with mother. The last few days haven't been easy for her and she's had a lot to cope with. It will please her to have me around, and to talk together, just the two of us, will be special: mother and daughter, without constant interruptions; I desperately feel the need for that. The last few weeks have been so busy that this morning, to be alone with her (apart from baby Marlene) will be a wonderful treat for both of us.

71

Later that morning when I told her, I knew mother understood. She hugged me and planted a kiss on my cheek. She knew how I felt, but insisted I go to make my apologies.

Hans-Dieter was disappointed, but quickly forgot his sulk. He was far too excited and the fact I wasn't going completely went out of his head. With a hearty breakfast of porridge, bread and jam inside him, and dressed as if for the North Pole, he was out of the door like an eager foxhound.

I chose the quickest way backstairs to the kitchen, as I wanted to see what was going on outside. In the yard half a dozen sleighs were lined up in a row, ready to leave. They looked similar to Otti's sleigh, which we'd ridden in to select Christmas trees from the forest. Each sleigh was well kitted out: warm muffs for feet and hands, and fur blankets to sit on and to cover knees. The horses harnessed to the sleighs were getting impatient, stamping their feet and blowing steam through their nostrils. They had bells round their necks and whenever they moved a pleasant jingling sound could be heard.

Also in the yard stood three or four large haywagons with boards fixed to either side for people to sit on, and with snow-runners instead of the usual wheels. Those wagons were for the estate workers, who were needed as beaters, and their reward at the end of the day would be the result of the shoot: rabbits, hares, pheasants and partridges. There were few women attending the hunt, as they preferred to stay at home and enjoy a day of leisure. Some village lads, allowed to take part as additional beaters, laughed and fooled about as they got impatient to be on their way.

Sylvia came running towards me. 'Else, why aren't you coming with us? I was so looking forward to being with you. Now I'll be the only girl and that's not much fun.'

'Sylvia, I'm sorry I can't go – my mother needs me.'

I didn't want Sylvia to know how I felt about the shoot. She wouldn't have understood and I wanted to keep my thoughts to myself. But I said I'd try to go on the next hunt in February.

Uncle Kurt carried the hunting horn and put the mouthpiece in his pocket to keep warm. If he'd left it attached to the horn in that bitter weather, it would have taken the skin off his lips.

Frau Krause appeared from the kitchen, carrying a large tray with glasses of hot punch. Each person was offered a glass, and a big cheer went up: 'Good health to you, Frau Krause, and a happy New Year!' Then, as the sun started to rise over the horizon, I could see Uncle Kurt lifting his horn and fixing the mouthpiece. He blew the signal and the sleighs started moving.

It was a grand sight: a long line of sleighs slowly wending their way through the snow-covered country lane towards open fields and the forest.

I stood a few minutes longer, watching the last wagon slide out of sight; then, shivering with cold, I turned and ran down the kitchen steps.

Oh, such wonderful warmth greeted me! Frau Krause was now preparing breakfast for her staff and Baron and Baroness von Puttkamer. It smelled delicious and made my mouth water. But mother was waiting upstairs and that morning we'd have a leisurely breakfast together. I was looking forward to it – just the two of us. A very special treat!

Luckily baby Marlene was still asleep and mother and I would have breakfast undisturbed. I had a feeling she wanted to talk to me, and I wasn't wrong.

After her first cup of coffee, she relaxed and, looking across the table at me, said, 'Else, next Monday, 4 January, you and I need to travel to Stolp to meet the family with whom you'll board. I'll arrange with Frau Schröter, the lady of the house, that she can expect you to come to her after school on Monday the eleventh. There's a daughter called Anneliese, but I think she's a little younger than you, so she'll be in a lower class. I hope you get on: it would be good to have a friend. Please Else, give it a try. I know how you feel, but I'm certain this is best for you and I promise again that, as soon as the days lengthen and the cold weather disappears, you won't board any longer.'

'Mother, where's Herr Schröter?' I asked. 'You've not mentioned him. Is he a soldier like father?'

'I don't know, child, but I'm sure once you're with the family, you'll find out.' Mother went over to look at a calendar on the wall. 'I also want to tell you, Else, that I intend to visit little Ralf on 23 January and return four days later. Fraulein Dorothea has offered to look after baby on the days you're at school, and Frau Ruch, my friend in the village, whom you haven't yet met, will look after Hans-Dieter. I must go and see how our little boy's progressing. The worry about his well-being gives me no peace at all.'

After breakfast, mother saw to baby Marlene. I offered to help, and while mother prepared a bottle of warm milk, I tested Baby's bath water so she could have a little splash. How that tiny girl enjoyed the water! I sprinkled it on her tummy and she shrieked with laugher and waited for more. But not too much – it wouldn't do to get her cold. 'Out you come, my little darling. I'll wrap you up quickly in a warm, soft towel, dry you and dress you in nice clean clothes. Then you'll be the prettiest baby in the world.'

Meanwhile mother had prepared baby's bottle.

'Should I feed her this morning, mother?' I asked. 'I know you want to go to help Mamsell in the kitchen. I can finish up here, and when Marlenchen has finished her bottle, I'll bring her down to you in her basket.'

'Oh no,' was mother's answer, 'I can't have you feed her every mealtime. Little Baby will think *you* are her mother and I'm only Auntie. That wouldn't be right, would it? Thank you for your help, but it doesn't mean I can shirk my duties. You do understand, don't you?'

'Of course I do, mother. I certainly don't want to take your job away.'

As soon as our room was tidy and baby fed and made comfortable, mother placed her in her basket and together we carried her downstairs to the kitchen. There she was welcomed with oohs and ahs, admired and cooed over. Mother could see the little one was tired and wanted to go to sleep, so when Frau Krause suggested we leave baby in her room, mother gladly accepted the offer. The kitchen was extremely busy that morning. Of course, it was always busy, but that day was exceptional. Everyone seemed to rush about, yet there was order amid the upheaval.

That day Frau Krause needed all the help she could get. In the evening, when the hunt was over, many guests would arrive for dinner. Frau Krause wanted to do the manor proud and no effort was spared. Dinner would be a grand affair, talked about for days afterwards. Other landowners would hear and their turn would come. Rivalry was a fact of life and each guest would want to outdo the other.

Mamsell and her staff were kept busy, and I soon joined in.

'Else, please clean the Brussels sprouts for me,' asked Mamsell. 'That's a great help. You'll find them in the sink with a basin and a sharp knife. Don't cut your finger; take your time.'

I found the sprouts and, as I cleaned one after another, thought what a lovely name we'd given them in Germany: *Rosenkohl*, 'rose cabbages'.

In the coldroom mother arranged a variety of meats and cheeses onto large silver platters. Such a wide selection: pork, liver sausage, salami, smoked and boiled ham and another type I hadn't seen before. Everything was home-made by Frau Krause. The cheese platters looked particularly inviting. I loved cheese and the sight of so many different kinds made my mouth water. However, the rule was 'Look but don't touch.'

Not only was there a cold buffet that evening, but hot food would also be served: roasted hares with stewed apples, fried potatoes, Brussels sprouts and a delicious gravy from the meat juices, flavoured with red wine. Then a sweet course with jellies, fruit cakes and pastries, and all through the evening a lot of wine, cognac and other spirits from the wine cellar would be consumed. The whole feast would last for hours, until early the next morning.

It was a blessing food was still plentiful in Pomerania, whereas in other cities throughout Germany, provisions were getting more and more difficult to obtain.

At midday Marlene started to cry. 'Mother, can I take her upstairs, prepare her feed, and give it to her. I've finished all the sprouts, so I can look after her.'

'Very well, Else. I'll stay a while longer, but I'll join you upstairs as soon as I can.

After I'd seen to baby Marlene and had settled her in her cradle, I wondered what to do next.

I know, I thought, *I'll write a letter to both our grandparents in Düsseldorf. I haven't written to them for such a long time, and while I wait for mother, I'll have the chance to make good my neglect.*

I'd finished the letter before mother came up. She looked tired. 'Come, sit down and tell me how it's going downstairs in the kitchen. Is the dining room ready?'

'You should see how beautifully Trudi has laid the table for the feast. It looks wonderful: white damask tablecloth, damask serviettes and gleaming crystal glasses. Down the centre are silver candelabras, each with three white candles. Each candle holder has a strand of ivy twisted round the stem: the green of the ivy and snow-white table linen makes the whole picture stunning. Frau Krause can be very proud of her staff: they've all given their best, including Dunja and Anna. Such a credit to her training.'

By 3 p.m. it was almost dark, and soon the weary hunters would return. Indeed through the windows we could see lanterns from the sleighs as they came up the long drive. Loud singing floated up from the wagons: a happy sound, telling of a successful hunt. We heard the wagons drive into the yard, and then the sleighs came to a halt outside the main entrance.

After a few minutes, someone ran up the stairs: Hans-Dieter burst into the room, full of energy and excitement and, even before he'd taken off his outdoor clothes, was chattering away about his wonderful day.

'Slow down, child!' mother tried to calm him. 'You'll have plenty of time to tell us how your day went. But first, your slippers; then a hot drink and something to eat; and afterwards, we'll all sit down and listen to your tale about your first hunt.'

Our little lad didn't know where to start. So much had happened to him throughout the day that to find a beginning was impossible for him. Mother had to help.

'Tell me, Hans-Dieter, did you ride in a sleigh today?'

'Oh no! I rode in a wagon with the men and boys from the village. It was great fun, much better than a sleigh. We sang and laughed and told silly jokes. Everyone was very jolly, and I was so happy.'

'It sounds as though you had a wonderful time. Did you come home on a wagon?'

'No, mother, I came back in Fraulein Dorothea's sleigh. She wanted me to help her with the horses, because we were beginning to feel the cold.'

'That was very kind of her, but now, Hans-Dieter, tell us about the shoot. Else and I can't imagine what you did all day.'

'All right, I'll tell you everything; and Else you must listen, because you missed it.'

By now mother and I could see that our boy was in no state to do much talking. He almost fell asleep trying to eat his meal: the long day and fresh air had totally exhausted him.

'I tell you what we'll do, Hans-Dieter. Tomorrow morning, when Johann brings the peat, we'll ask him to spare us some time. Then you both can give us all the details of the shoot. Now it's bedtime. I know it's still early, but you've had a busy day and will soon be asleep.'

All was quiet now in our room. Hans-Dieter fell asleep instantly, and looking at him lying there so peacefully made me realise how exhausting his busy day must have been. Marlene, though, was still wide awake, making babbling noises and playing with her tiny hands. She was so contented, but was it any wonder? Mother sat in her chair, gently rocking the cradle, and the motion had a soothing effect on our little girl.

While we were occupied and quietly talking, mother mending Hans-Dieter's socks and I with my knitting, we could hear the arrival of sleighs, and voices talking and laughing.

Guests were arriving – ladies, whose husbands took part in the hunt were coming to partake of the grand and sumptuous dinner. What with food and drink in plentiful supply together with heaps of goodwill and high spirits, we'd most likely hear the merrymakers into the early hours!

I'd worried about the hunt all day and mentioned it at bedtime: 'Mother, I've promised Sylvia I would take part in the next hunt, but really don't want to. I hate the thought of taking part, but don't know how to explain my strong feelings to her. Could you talk to her, mother? It would sound better coming from you.'

'Oh no, my child; you don't get me to do your unpleasant work. You and you alone know how you feel, and that's what you must convey to Sylvia. If she's a true friend, she'll respect you for being honest and admire you for standing by your beliefs.' Mother packed away her work and made us a last hot drink. 'Don't worry any more tonight. Trust me: it will sort itself out at the right moment. Things are never as bad as they seem.' She took the empty cups to the sink. 'Now it's time for bed. We've had a busy day and tomorrow will be no different. I won't be far behind you, so I'll say good night.' As usual, there was a gentle kiss on my forehead and a loving embrace. Mother then went to her room to prepare for bed.

2 January 1943

The next day started with a bright blue sky and brilliant sunshine. There had been a sharp frost during the night and the crisp snow sparkled in the dazzling morning sunlight. It promised to be a beautiful day and, quite early, men and women from the village arrived to prepare for the evening's get-together. After the day of a hunt, villagers always celebrated the capture of the boar. Repeated each year, the gathering, with its gaiety and laughter, was a tradition no one, old or young, would want to forgo.

When Johann called with the peat, mother asked him to join us for his coffee break. Always one to oblige, he promised to return at 11 a.m.

There was no doubt about it: Johann enjoyed drinking his coffee in a warm, comfortable room. Far better than a cold garden shed, and a generous slice of stollen was a welcome extra bonus! He made himself comfortable on the seat surrounding the tiled stove.

'Come, Hans-Dieter, sit by my side, and together we'll tell your mother and sister about the hunt. I'll start; then you go on. But if you get stuck, I'll continue.

'The hunt's divided into two parts. The first part, during the morning, takes place in a large field – yesterday it was the one nearest the forest. In the field, only small animals and birds are shot: rabbits, hares, pheasants and partridges. After a midday meal, the beaters go to the forest hoping that, with luck, a boar can be sighted and shot by a chosen shooter. During the hunt, only one boar can be killed: that's the rule and for that, one shooter's responsible. Lots are drawn: yesterday Fraulein Dorothea fired the lucky shot.'

'But going back to the morning, when we arrived at the field – Hans-Dieter, you go on.'

'We were divided into two groups,' Hans-Dieter continued. 'One group went with Uncle Kurt – I was in it – and the second group went with the forester, Herr Lehmann. We had to make a large circle, already staked out round the field. There were seven or eight beaters and one man with a gun, and so it went on, until both groups met at the top of the field. Every beater carried a thick stick: a branch, pole or walking stick, whatever they could find. When the circle was complete, Uncle Kurt blew his horn and we all started to walk towards the middle of the field. The men with guns walked backwards. They were not allowed to shoot into the circle. That's too dangerous. Am I right, Johann?' Hans-Dieter asked. 'You go on.'

'The shooting starts as soon as rabbits or hares run out of the circle,' Johann continued. 'It's the same when pheasants or partridges are disturbed and fly into the air.'

'Fraulein Ottilia gave me a walking stick,' Hans-Dieter interrupted. 'I waved it in the air and shouted with all the others, 'Ho, ho! Hare, hare! Imagine the noise, mother. If the windows were open, I'm sure you'd have heard us.

'The dogs fetched the dead animals for their masters. Rabbits and hares were put on one heap and birds on another. Uncle Kurt selected a few birds and hares; then, at the end of the shoot, the rest were distributed as a reward among the estate workers.'

'Hans-Dieter, tell us, what did you have for lunch?' mother asked.

'We had pea soup with ham from a big urn, didn't we Johann? It was the best pea soup I've ever tasted. Yours is lovely, mother,' he added, 'but that was even better.'

'After lunch we went into the forest,' Johann continued. 'Again we formed a large circle and, beating against trees and making as much noise as we could by shouting, we soon disturbed a large and very angry-looking boar. When wild boars are disturbed and frightened they become dangerous, and it's well advised to stay at a distance. This time, Fraulein Dorothea fired the well-aimed shot, which killed the animal outright.'

'It was a brilliant shot, mother, but I was very sad when that big animal keeled over, dead. I don't like to see animals killed and tonight, when it's roasted on a spit, I don't want to eat it.'

'It will be a happy get-together when the boar's roasted: the village people will be part of it,' answered Johann. 'I'm certain you, your mother and sister will enjoy it. To shoot and then roast a boar is a tradition that has gone on for many years. They're preparing it as we speak.'

'But now,' said Johann, rising, 'I must be on my way. There's work to be done and I've stayed longer than I intended. Frau Hopp, thank you for your kind hospitality; your cake's delicious! Perhaps you can teach my wife how to bake the cake; that would be wonderful.'

'We must thank *you*, Johann, for helping Hans-Dieter tell his story. The hunt has left a big impression on him. I don't know whether he'd wish to go again: only he can decide that.'

After Johann had gone to his duties in the garden, I resolved, even stronger, never to attend a hunt. I couldn't understand what seemed to me the pointless killing of innocent animals for fun. I also had to give my opinion. 'It's fine for Fraulein Dorothea, Ottilia and Sylvia. It's their tradition: they've been brought up with it. But it's not mine.' I must try to make Sylvia respect my point of view.'

We did go out and watch the preparations for the hog-roast, though. The paddock in the centre of the farmyard had been cleared of much of the snow, and strong young men were assembling the spit on which the carcass of the boar would be slowly roasted. The device had to be sturdy, for the animal was heavy, and help would be required to turn the spit at regular intervals. A fair-sized hole had been dug, deep enough to prevent the meat from burning before it was cooked and after the fire was lit, it was covered by an iron grating for added safety.

Ladies from the village arranged their plentiful contributions on trestle tables, all of which had been carefully prepared days before. Baron von Puttkamer contributed his usual barrel of beer for the adults and home-made apple juice for the children. In the centre of the paddock, boards were laid out to give young and old a chance to dance to music provided by a violin, two accordions and a mouth organ.

It promised to be a jolly evening and I was looking forward to it. I could see my young brother was also affected by the fun and the light-hearted spirit found in our small community. Rarely could such a joyful, friendly occasion take place in a city. There, neighbourly friendliness and warm hospitality are missing most of the time: people keep their distance, prefering a chosen circle of friends where outsiders are rarely included.

The paddock fire was lit quite early in the morning, and peat and large logs of wood created smouldering, slow-burning embers. To roast the bulky wild pig to perfection, plenty of time was needed, and the heat had to be intense to slow-roast such a huge animal. Constant supervision and basting were necessary, and it all required experience and a large amount of patience.

Many people were arriving from outlying villages. Also present were gentlemen who had participated in the hunt, and their ladies who had all spent the night in the manor.

There was my girlfriend Gisela and other children who travelled daily by train to school in Stolp. Very shortly I'd no longer be part of that friendly group, at least for a month or two. Oh no, I had to board with a family I didn't know and was determined *not* to like. As the sun disappeared over the horizon, the temperature dropped, and everyone knew once again it would be a frosty night. It was a wonderful evening, without a cloud in the sky; just a deep purple, like velvet, with millions of stars sprinkled on it as far as the eye could see. And the clear half-moon, with its milky collar, was a sure sign of more snow to come.

Soon there'd be dancing and singing and merry-making, and the air was full of the delicious aroma of roasting meat. The butcher's apprentice had received his instructions and had the honour of carving the first slice. The large carving knife was sharp as a razor and he looked proud to be given such an important task. Later his father would take over; but, for now, he basked in his father's admiration.

Sylvia and I had been busy all day, helping wherever we could. Then it was time to have a short while to ourselves. Gisela Krämer had also helped; her mother would come later. As I looked up, I saw mother approaching. Someone must have volunteered to look after our baby. Excellent! Now mother wouldn't have to rush back, and could spend some time with her friends. It would do her good, for she hardly ever had fun, and that night would be a tonic for her.

'Gisela, come and meet my mother,' I said. 'I've told her you'll be here tonight and she's looking forward to meeting you.'

The music and dancing, the laughter and happiness that surrounded us, gave me a feeling of true friendship and belonging. How fantastic it would be if that feeling could last for ever . . .

Suddenly there was a lot of shouting and hand clapping and people calling to each other, 'The boar's cooked! The boar's cooked! Come and be served; it's hot and delicious and there's plenty for everyone.'

The butcher's lad was ready with his carving knife and after his cutting of the first slice of succulent pork and a large piece of crisp and crunchy crackling, a big cheer went up. That made the poor boy's face turn scarlet with embarrassment, and yet everyone could see how proud he was to be the centre of attention.

I went up to my mother, who was sitting with the other ladies, and by the sound of their laughter I knew they were enjoying a good gossip. But I had to ask her something that had worried me all evening.

'Mother,' I whispered in her ear, 'will there also be pork for the Russian prisoners? I've seen them looking at us through the fence, and the lovely aroma from the roasting meat must have wafted across to them. We have so much food here, far more than we can eat. Surely we can spare some for the Russians.'

'Child, child! Why do you always worry so? Be careful what you're saying: not all people have warm-hearted feelings like you. These are village people. To them the Russians, prisoners or not, are considered enemies, and people here are frightened of them.'

'Why, mother? They can't do us any harm; they're behind barbed wire.'

'Leave it now, Else, please!' Mother was embarrassed and anxious. 'This is not the time or place to talk about it, but I'll have a word with Uncle Kurt to ask him what will happen to the rest of the meat should there be any left over. I'm certain there will be.'

I was too young to understand what was happening to the village people, who always appeared so kind. Sometimes, during a conversation, there was a look of utter hatred in their eyes and I asked myself why that should be. What were they frightened of?

It was getting late, my feet were icy cold, and I could see Hans-Dieter also stamping his feet. He had to be feeling the same. 'Come Hans-Dieter, let's call mother and ask if we can go home.'

But she'd already had the same thoughts.

'Let's go home, children: baby Marlene and a lovely warm room are waiting for us. I'm so glad we don't have to walk any distance; just think of the poor people who have to travel quite a few kilometres before they're home. Oh no, I don't envy them one little bit.'

Off we went, mother in the middle, Hans-Dieter holding her hand on her right and I, taking her left arm. After we'd shouted good night to all our friends who could hear us, amid the din of music and dancing, we started our short walk home with a joyous feeling of togetherness.

After little Marlene had been fed and made comfortable, and Hans-Dieter was washed and in his pyjamas ready for bed, I asked mother if we could both stay up a little longer, as I wanted to talk to her.

'Of course, Elslein. Is something worrying you? Come and sit with me; tell me what it is.'

'Mother, this evening I overheard two men talking about the war in Russia, how our soldiers are suffering in the bitter cold Russian winter and that the war's not going well for Germany. They said our soldiers don't have sufficient warm clothes to cope in such cold weather, and, because of that, many soldiers are freezing to death. Can that be true, mother?'

'Oh my child, the worrying thoughts you have in that small head of yours! You just wait; everything will come right in the end. We must have faith in our leader, who has promised us a wonderful future. I firmly believe the war will soon be over. Once spring's here, our soldiers will win back all the ground they're losing now and Russia will realise they're no match for our German army.'

I'd listened to mother's words, but they didn't put me at ease. I knew she was wise, and wanted to believe her. But were her words really what she also believed, or was she just trying to put *my* mind at rest? Was I too young to have a premonition? Or had the way the two men talked unsettled me? I was brought up to believe in our leader. He'd made a promise to his German people and had said a promise made by him would never be broken.

'Else, now that we've talked, tell me, do you feel more at ease?'

'Yes, mother, just silly thoughts that go round and round in my head. But they're gone now; I can go to bed with an easier mind. It was good to talk to you, and I'm certain Uncle Kurt will take some food to the prisoners. Don't you think so, mother? We had a lovely day, didn't we? But in February, when the next hunt's held, I'm still determined *not* to go.' I smiled at her and said good night.

'Good night, my child. Sleep well.'

Chapter 12

Doll's House

4 January 1943

The feeling that someone was standing by my bedside woke me from a deep sleep. I knew it was mother. As I opened my eyes just a fraction, I could see she was standing as still as a statue, just gazing at me.

I opened my eyes wide. 'Good morning, mother.'

'Ah, good morning, Else. I'm glad you're awake. It's almost time to get up – we have a busy day before us. I'm on my way to the bathroom. Will you wake Hans-Dieter? And as soon as I've finished, you two can go in. I'll see to little Marlene, bathe and feed her, and then, when all's done, we'll have plenty of time to breakfast together.'

'Yes, mother, don't worry. Hans-Dieter and I will be fine.'

I was still angry with my mother about the arrangements she'd made for me. Today we had to travel to Stolp. Why did it have to be? Life was good here with my family and to have to live away, and only come home at weekends – I didn't like it one bit. I didn't want to accept mother was acting in my best interests. I'd tried to prepare myself, but that didn't stop me from grumbling and being thoroughly miserable at the injustice of it all.

I went to the side of Hans-Dieter's bed. 'Come on, Hans-Dieter; wake up. We mustn't hang about this morning. Mother and I have to travel to Stolp and you'll stay with Frau Ruch.'

'Else, why can't I come with you? I like riding on a train and won't be any trouble in Stolp.'

'No, Hans-Dieter, that's not possible; but, if you must, when we sit down to breakfast, ask mother what she has to say about it.'

As soon as mother entered the room, Hans-Dieter blurted out, 'Mother, can I come to Stolp with you and Else? I promise to behave myself and I'd love the train ride. I really will be good, honest. Please can I come?'

Mother looked at me. 'Else, what do you think? Should Hans-Dieter come with us?'

Feeling as grumpy as I did, I could only answer, 'I don't care, mother. It's up to you. It doesn't bother me whether he comes or stays behind with Frau Ruch.'

'Goodness me, Else, at least try to cheer up! What's the matter with you?' As mother poured Hans-Dieter a glass of milk, she said, looking at me sternly, 'You're not normally so difficult. Your sulking's gone on long enough: now that's an end to it. You make *me* feel guilty and I only want what's best for you. To judge the Schröter family without having met them is unfair and unworthy of you. After all, it's only until Easter you're boarding with

81

them. Then the days will be longer and spring will have arrived. After the Easter holidays, you can again travel daily to school with your friends.'

'Yes, mother', I replied grudgingly, as I heaped a spoonful of jam onto my sandwich and viciously took a large bite.

'Every Friday after school you'll come home,' she continued, 'unless you have important lessons on Saturday mornings.'

'Yes, mother.'

Then, looking at Hans-Dieter, she added, 'It's best you stay at home today. It's not a good day for you to come with us. There will be another time soon, I promise, when you and I will do something nice; just the two of us. Now, let's all cheer up; you Else, in particular.'

'Yes, mother.'

'You and I, Else, will try to make the best of our day together and I hope we can enjoy ourselves. I thought we could have lunch in Café Reinhardt. Apparently, according to Fraulein Dorothea, it's an elegant establishment and the food's supposed to be excellent. I also have something to tell you, something that will surprise you: it's a little secret I can share with you.'

I cheered up instantly. 'Oh, what is it?'

Mother smiled. 'I have a letter for you. It came this morning but you were too bad-tempered for me to want to give it to you.'

'Mother, I'm so sorry – I surrender,' I said, using a word I'd often heard on the wireless. 'And you win!'

After we'd finished breakfast and cleared everything away, Marlenchen was put into her basket and together we carried her downstairs to Fraulein Dorothea, who was waiting to receive our little bundle. We knew baby was in good hands; there was no need to worry, and we could leave her with an easy mind.

'Come, Else, quickly now. We must be on our way. The three of us can go together. First, we'll leave Hans-Dieter with Frau Ruch; then you and I will hurry to the station.'

Outside it was bitterly cold with a fierce easterly wind sweeping across the Pomeranian plains. It hit us head on and mother, Hans-Dieter and I had to fight to stay upright. There'd been a sharp frost during the night and the trees and bushes again looked as if they'd been sprinkled with icing sugar: a lovely sight. Thankfully no further snow had fallen, which made walking much easier once we left the drive and reached the village street. We still had to walk with care, though, Hans-Dieter holding mother's hand and she and I linking arms, all the while watching our step – one false move and down we'd go, the three of us, onto the icy road.

Frau Ruch lived in the high street in one of the estate worker's cottages. Her husband had been a farmhand, responsible for livestock and stables. After war broke out he was conscripted into the army, and lost his life in the Russian campaign, which had begun in June 1941. She liked Hans-Dieter and agreed to have him, while mother and I went to Stolp.

We soon reached the cottage, which was tiny, but neat with freshly painted woodwork and snow-white net curtains at each window. Fronting the cottage was a small garden, now deep in snow. I wondered what the little garden would look like in spring and summer, and imagined a carpet of flowers, colourful and sweet-scented.

Mother knocked on the door, which was immediately opened by a handsome young boy. This proved to be Frau Ruch's son, Egon. He was home from school in Berlin and seemed to know not only who we were, but also about today's arrangements. He very politely asked us in and called to his mother to say that we'd arrived.

Frau Ruch came into the living room, wiping her hands on her apron, and greeted mother warmly. She'd already met Hans-Dieter, and said hello to him. Turning to me she said that mother had told her a lot about me, including my long journey to Pomerania. Flatteringly she said that she thought I'd been very brave, and asked Egon if he thought so too.

'Yes', he said. 'A very brave thing for a girl to do. Well done Else'.

I couldn't help feeling that he sounded rather sarcastic. He was rather aloof but very good looking; somehow I thought that he knew it.

Frau Ruch asked Hans- Dieter if he minded staying with them for the day, and he tried very hard to sound grown up when he explained that he would have liked to have gone with us, but that it had not been convenient. However, he pointed out, he was planning to help Johann, so he would do that first, returning to Frau Ruch later. She smiled and said that would be fine. On his return he could play with Egon's sister, Inge. At just seven or eight Inge was a pretty little girl with bright blue eyes, just like her brother.

I glanced at Egon again. My word, he was handsome! With his blue eyes and blond hair, it wasn't difficult to see he was of Aryan descent – pure German without Jewish blood. That of course was a most important requirement to be admitted to the exclusive Adolf Hitler School, where each boy was rigorously trained to be a high-ranking officer in one of the German forces.

I'll always remember that first meeting with Egon, who was on his Christmas holiday. One look at him and, despite my reservations, I was smitten. He was incredibly smart in his black uniform – to me he was amazing. Never before had I seen a better-looking boy and in his presence became tongue-tied and shy.

'When do you go back to Berlin, Egon?' I asked. 'Will it be soon?'

'Oh yes, very soon. Only a few more days and I'll return to school. Your holidays are also soon over, aren't they?'

'Yes, next week. My mother wants me to board with a family in Stolp. That's where we're going today. I'm not happy about it, but mother has promised it's only till spring. Then I can travel daily again with my friends.'

'I'll also be back for the Easter holiday. Perhaps, you and I can go out, then? A few walks in the countryside and just talk. Would you come, Else?'

'Oh yes!' I answered. Then realising I sounded too eager, I added, 'I'd like that. I'm sure I'll have some free time.'

'Right, that's a date. Now I'll look forward to Easter.'

Then mother interrupted. 'Else, we must make our way to the station. If not, we'll miss our train.'

'Ready, mother, when you are.'

'Katrin, thank you for having Hans-Dieter today; and you, Egon, take care when you're back in Berlin. I don't suppose it's quite as cold there as here. Surely you don't have as much snow?'

'No, Frau Hopp, we don't and what there is soon turns to slush. But when it's fresh and newly fallen, it looks just as beautiful as here. Once the snow lies deep, it stays for a long time – too long sometimes – but here, we're used to it.

'Come, Else,' mother urged, 'put on your coat and bonnet, and don't forget your gloves. Say farewell to Frau Ruch, Egon and Inge; also to Hans-Dieter. Then we must be on our way.'

Now we really had to hurry if we didn't want to miss our train. The icy road made walking difficult, but we made it to the station, and, when we got there, had a few minutes to spare before the train arrived.

The carriage was almost empty, so mother and I could both sit by a window. I quite looked forward to my day with her. How strange? All of a sudden, I didn't feel angry and miserable any more! I glanced at her sitting opposite me and suddenly felt full of remorse. How horrid I'd been that morning. How could I have been like that when I knew she only meant the best for me? I took a close look at mother, sitting in her corner reading a newspaper she'd bought at the station kiosk. What a pretty woman she was! Always so elegant, she wore her fur coat with hat to match, warm gloves and fur-lined boots. To me she seemed perfect!

She must have felt I was watching her, for she glanced up from her reading and gave me a tender smile. 'Are you feeling better now, Else, and a little less angry with yourself, with me and the world?'

'Yes, mother, I *do* feel better. I'm sorry I behaved the way I did. I shouldn't have done that; it wasn't fair to you. I'm truly sorry.'

'It's all right, child. We'll forget all about it. Now make yourself comfortable and read your letter, while I get on with my newspaper.'

Of course, the letter! I'd forgotten about it. I took it out of my handbag and scanned it closely. How much I missed my closest friend, Marlies – would she also be missing me?

I opened the envelope and began to read:

Dear Else,

It's a long time since I last wrote to you, but I had to put it off again and again. We have so many air-raids here in Düsseldorf, both night and day. We seem to live in the shelter, and when I do go to school, lessons are always interrupted. You don't know how lucky you are away from sirens howling all the time and bombs dropping, making you fear one of them will surely hit your house and bury you under tons of rubble.

Oh, Else, how I wish this terrible war would end. Then you could come home and we could be together again.

You'll be surprised to hear that we also have a lot of snow this winter. We try to have fun: snowball fights and build snowmen. I'd like to take my toboggan to Grafenberg where we always went. But my mother won't allow it. She wants me near her. My father's kept very busy: he seems to work night and day. Always so many people hurt, every doctor's needed, and Papa has to be constantly on call. He wanted mother and me to be evacuated to a safer part of Germany. But she's refused to go. She wants to be near father, and I'm not going on my own.

Please, Else, write again soon. Let me know how your little brother is getting on. Is he improving? We were sad to hear he's in a sanatorium; perhaps he'll soon be well again.

My parents send their love to you all, and so do I.

I think of you and will always be your best friend, no matter how long you have to be away from home. When you come home, who knows, there may be nothing left standing here in Düsseldorf. Not if the bombs keep on falling, as they do now.

With all my love,
Your best friend Marlies

After I'd read my letter, I folded it carefully and put it into my bag. What Marlies had written left me deep in thought.

'Tell me, Else,' mother asked, 'how are Marlies and her family? Are they coping in the city, surrounded by constant danger?'

'I think they take each day as it comes. I do wish Marlies could be here; at least she'd also be safe. She and her parents send their kind regards. Would you like to read it?'

'No, child, that's not necessary. You've told me all I wanted to know but when you write back, send my good wishes and kindest regards.'

As the train bowled along towards Stolp, I wanted to look out of the window, but couldn't – the glass was covered in a thick layer of ice. By order of the government, trains were not heated, as fuel was in short supply: the public had to put up with shivering. But I wanted to look out. Putting my face close to the windowpane and breathing on the glass, I managed to make a peephole and through it was able to watch the countryside rush by, covered in snow and not a human being or animal in sight. I imagined the world to be empty of people, apart from us on the train as we hurtled along, not knowing where our journey might take us. My imagination was running wild when suddenly I remembered mother had some news. 'What is it?' I asked her. 'Is it a secret?'

'Well yes, in a way, but I don't think it will remain a secret for long. Just for now, let it be between you and me.'

'I promise, whatever it is, I'll keep it to myself.'

'This morning when I took baby to Fraulein Dorothea,' mother revealed with a broad smile, she told me that at the beginning of summer she'll be married.'

'Married to whom, mother?'

'She's engaged to a gentleman also called Puttkamer. He's a high-ranking officer in the cavalry and, like your father, is fighting in Russia.'

'Do you know when the wedding will be, mother?'

'I think it may be a June wedding, but I'm certain that soon everyone will be talking about it and we'll have more details. I have a feeling it will most likely be a grand affair.'

'Will they be married in Glowitz or in Berlin?'

'Else, it's no good asking questions – I don't know much more than you do. Let's wait and see.' The train jolted and slowed down. 'Anyway, my child, we're approaching Stolp. What will we do first? Go to the Schröters, then have some lunch and afterwards take a stroll through Stolp? I've been told it's a delightfully elegant town. How do you feel?'

'Mother, whatever you suggest is fine with me. I'll be happy when our interview with Frau Schröter is over. I'm not looking forward to it.'

'I don't know what you're worried about. Think of it like this: you're the boarder, I'll pay for your board and the Schröters will look after your comfort. That's all there is to it.' The train came to a halt at Stolp station. I knew that station well now: the school interview with Fraulein Dorothea, half a term's journeying back and forth with my friends . . . But it seemed such a short while ago, that first time I'd arrived there from Berlin. Then it had been dark and I'd been tired from the long journey and was so hoping mother would be there to meet me. Now, of course, I knew why she'd been unable to come. But for me it had been a very traumatic day.

After the shelter of the railway compartment, the blast of the icy east wind pounded us with full force. The station was open at both ends and the platform offered no shelter to shivering travellers.

Mother hurried me out of the station. 'I wish we could get a hot drink, but there's nothing available,' she said. The station restaurant's closed; perhaps Frau Schröter will offer us something warming. I could do with it and I'm sure you could too.'

Mother had the address in her handbag, but neither she nor I knew how to find the house. It was on the Mühlentor, which was near the river Stolpe, a short walk from the Hexenturm, the Witches' Tower. Appropriate that!

'Come, Else, let's be on our way. It can't be so far but, all the same, we must walk carefully: it's very slippery and I'm surprised how deep and tightly packed the snow lies. It will take many weeks of warmer weather before it finally disappears.'

There were plenty of people from whom we could ask directions and soon we discovered the way.

The Mühlentor was a wide avenue, flanked on either side by large, majestic oaks. At that time of year the trees were bare: instead of green leaves, the branches were covered with thick layers of snow. It seemed a wealthy neighbourhood; the houses were grand – not houses really, but villas with ornate front gardens. What struck me most was that it was so quiet; not a sound to be heard, and even the birds didn't feel like singing. Could that be the witch's influence?

Stolp was not a large town. In school we'd been told there were about fifty thousand inhabitants. But where were they at that moment? It appeared as if the town was empty.

We soon found the house we were looking for. Mother rang a bell and immediately a young girl about my age opened the door. 'Good morning,' mother said, pleasantly. 'My name is Frau Hopp. My daughter and I have come to meet Frau Schröter. Is she at home?'

'Yes, she is,' answered the young girl, haughtily. 'My name is Anneliese and I'm the daughter of the house. Step inside. I'll call mother.' She turned regally and called out, 'Mami, can you come? Frau Hopp and her daughter have arrived. Should I usher them to the drawing room?'

'Yes, Liesel, do that. I'll only be a minute.'

Almost as soon as we stepped inside, the drawing-room door opened and, like a whirlwind, Frau Schröter entered. She spoke fast: 'How do you do, Frau Hopp? I'm pleased to meet you . . . and your daughter. Else, I hope you'll be very happy staying in our house. I'll now talk to your mother. Go with Liesel to her room; she'll show you where you'll sleep while you're here.'

I glanced at mother at that instant dismissal, but she winked; so, reluctantly, I left her and followed Anneliese. Should I also call her Liesel? Her mother did, but perhaps it was too early for me to be so informal. Anyway, if she didn't want to be called Anneliese, she could tell me– I'd wait and see.

Anneliese showed me her bedroom. I was speechless: it was more than beautiful . . . it was grand! Very large with a tall window leading onto a balcony, overlooking the garden, the bedroom was, as my teacher would say, a 'symphony' in pink and white . . . pink voile window curtains and the same material and colour draped over her bed. There was a thick white carpet – no wonder Anneliese had asked me to remove my shoes – and a white sofa with pink scatter cushions, large enough to seat three people in comfort. Looking around me at that lovely room, I felt a small twinge of envy, but was immediately ashamed – how could I be so petty minded? After all, it wasn't my fault I was an evacuee, and appearance wasn't everything. My home in Düsseldorf was just as nice; there was no reason why I should be envious of Anneliese's bedroom.

But the toys she had . . . I was astonished. Dolls of all descriptions, too many to count; a doll's house; shop with scales and a till and many drawers for flour, sugar, peas, beans and lentils. And there were teddy bears and soft toys galore . . . everywhere . . . on the bed, sofa, on chairs and on the floor . . . I didn't know what to say! Whatever could Anneliese ask for when Christmas or her birthday came round?' How could she possibly desire anything, when she had so much? I picked up a baby doll.

'Don't handle my doll!' Anneliese reacted. 'Put it down! These are my belongings: no one's allowed to touch them. And that includes you, Else. Remember that! You're just a refugee.'

Oh dear, what would I have to put up with? My life there would *not* be easy or pleasant. It was even worse than I'd thought. I wondered what mother would say when I told her.

Anneliese barking at me interrupted my thoughts. 'Come, Else, I want to show you where you'll sleep. Follow me.'

She took me along a corridor, opened a door at the end, and there it was . . . my bedroom . . . a small, dingy, narrow room with a tiny window looking over the backyard. I was disappointed, to say the least. I didn't know what I'd expected . . . but certainly not that. Not in such a huge house.

Anneliese must have noticed I was unhappy and smiled wickedly. 'You're only here during the week and then it's just in the evening. Mami will allow you to sit with us, so this room, after all, is simply for sleeping.'

'Anneliese, can we go downstairs now? You've shown me many things, but now I'd like to return to my mother.'

'Not yet, Else; you haven't seen everything in my toy cupboard. I want to show you my games and my books . . . and many other things . . .'

'There will be plenty of time later, Anneliese.' Too much! 'I don't have to see them today.'

I could see from her face that I'd angered Anneliese. Most probably she was used to getting her way. All of a sudden she pouted churlishly and replied irritably, 'Oh, Else, if you feel like that, have it your own way. But when you live here, don't think I'll be at your beck and call.'

With that she ran downstairs, opened the drawing-room door and, with the sweetest smile and impeccable manners, she approached my mother: 'Frau Hopp, we had such a wonderful time, Else and I. I showed her my toys and she was most impressed because there were so many. Have you finished talking to my mother? If so, perhaps you'd like to go now. Soon my father will be home; he doesn't like strangers in his house.'

'Anneliese, please don't be impertinent!' scolded Frau Schröter mildly. 'Frau Hopp was just saying that she and Else must be on their way, but you're too young to give your opinion.'

'I agree with Anneliese, Frau Schröter. I also think it's time we left you,' I added.

As we were about to go, Frau Schröter said to me, 'We're looking forward to having you next Monday after school; it will be most pleasant for you to be our daughter's companion. She's often on her own and that's not good for her. She needs company and I hope you'll be just the person to provide it.'

I disagreed inwardly, and hid a frown. I intended to avoid her as much as I could, the rude hussy! Frau Schröter and I shook hands, I made my customary curtsy and mother and I left the house, at last.

'Mother, I don't think I can possibly be happy with that family,' I said, as we held on to each other for support. 'I haven't even met Herr Schröter, and from what I've heard of him, I don't think he's a nice person.'

'Else, you can't form an opinion of a person before you've met them. I've told you that before, and say it again – wait and see: you may be pleasantly surprised.'

I paused and squeezed mother's hand to gain her attention. 'You're right, mother. I'll bear in mind what you say. But that Anneliese – you have no idea!'

But it was no good, for mother didn't want to hear any more. So I changed the subject. 'Can we have something to eat and drink now? I'm thirsty and so very hungry.'

'So am I, Else. Let's go to Café Reinhardt and see what they have to offer.'

'Anywhere's all right with me, mother, as long as I eat something – you don't want me to faint from hunger, do you?'

We went to the end of the Mühlentor where three people stood at the corner, talking. Mother asked the way to Café Reinhardt and was given directions.

We had to turn left at the entrance to a large park, which had to be truly beautiful during the summer months. Past the Witches' Tower – surely a good place to imprison that horrid girl, Anneliese! We crossed a small bridge spanning a shallow stream, and, after a short walk, saw the station road. But just as we reached the end of the park we noticed a small, cosy-looking restaurant.

'Else, what do you think of this?'

'Yes, mother, it looks fine. Let's try it. But what about Café Reinhardt? I was looking forward to going there.'

'I'll tell you what, Else; this afternoon, after we've walked around Stolp, we'll finish our day by visiting Café Reinhardt and I'll have a small pot of coffee and you may choose a piece of cake.'

'Thank you, mother. I wonder if Café Reinhardt really is as elegant as Fraulein Dorothea described it?'

By now we'd reached the small restaurant at the edge of the park. It seemed quiet, not many customers, but it was Monday and the middle of winter. People didn't eat out as often as they would in summer, and certainly not during the week. We entered and the proprietor gave us a friendly greeting, before guiding us to a table in a corner by a window. He handed mother a menu; and after studying it, her verdict was 'Good wholesome food. If it tastes as good as it sounds, I think we'll both be satisfied. Have a look, Else. Tell me what you'd like.'

I felt grown up, reading the menu. To start with, I chose a clear chicken broth with tiny dumplings. Then I had a small pork steak, with fried potatoes and green bean salad. I also wanted to select a dessert, but mother insisted I wait. 'When you've eaten all that's put before you and if you still have room for more, then we'll see what there is for pudding.'

As we waited for our meals, I looked around that charming little restaurant. In the corner of the room stood the tiled stove –a regular feature in most houses, restaurants and other public establishments – with the usual basket of peat standing to the side. I counted ten small tables arranged at random around the room, each covered with a blue-and-white chequered tablecloth and a small vase with a single sprig of evergreen. Very elegant!

Suddenly, out of the window, I noticed it was snowing again. 'Mother, look how large the snowflakes are.'

She was deep in thought and hadn't heard me. 'What did you say, child?'

'I only said it was snowing; but you were far away. Were you thinking of father or Ralf?'

'Yes, darling, I was thinking of your little brother. I do miss him.'

'But you'll see him soon, mother. When are you going to Swinemünde?'

'I think Tuesday the nineteenth would be a good day to travel. I'll ask Fraulein Dorothea if she'll look after baby Marlene. You know, Else, it's very difficult to know what's best to do. There's also Hans-Dieter. You, of course, will be with the Schröters in Stolp. Never mind, I'm sure I'll find a solution.'

'You know, mother, it needn't be a problem. I have the answer. You travel to see Ralfie, and instead of me being with the Schröters, I'll come home and be there for Hans-Dieter and Baby. Don't you think that's a brilliant idea?'

At that mother laughed. 'I thought you might suggest something like that, child; let's wait and see. Now, here comes our lunch. Tuck in and enjoy it – I know *I* will.'

After we finished our meal, we went out into the falling snow with the intention of having a good look at Stolp, but I had the feeling mother would prefer not be out of doors.

'You know, Else, this is a bad day for walking through town. It's cold and unpleasant and I think we should keep the outing for another, warmer, day. When you're with the Schröter family, I'm certain there'll be many opportunities for you and Anneliese to explore the town. It will be much more fun for the two of you than it is with me on a day like this.'

'But, mother, what about our treat in Café Reinhardt?'

'That I've promised you and that you'll have. I'd first just like to go to the department store. I must buy one or two things, not only for myself but also underwear for you. Your's urgently needs replacing.'

I'd only been in the department store once, and that was the day I'd come to Stolp with Fraulein Dorothea. The lift mesmerised me. It was old fashioned, with iron gates on every floor. They had to be opened before one could enter. *Most probably a safety measure*, I thought; but whatever, it was fun, and I rode up and down as often as I could. I loved it, but the lift attendant didn't find it as amusing as I did.

The large department store fascinated me. There were so many things one could buy and many floors on which to buy them. In the basement was the food department. In spite of it being wartime with constant reminders of food shortages, in that department store there was no sign of scarcity. On shelves and in cabinets mouth-watering delicacies were on display for sale to anyone who had the money and inclination to buy them. There was smoked salmon – where had that come from? Many varieties of fish – I could understand where they'd come from. Being so close to the sea, despite restrictions, it was still possible to fish in waters close to the shore. Then the cheeses: all home-produced by local dairy farmers. Various smoked sausages, always popular, were also on display. What an abundance of delicacies when, in many parts of Germany, food was far from plentiful and strictly rationed.

Ladies' fashions were on one floor; on another, garments for gentlemen and boys, with separate departments for baby articles and household linen. On the top floor was an elegant restaurant. But not for us today – mother and I were going to have our treat in Café Reinhardt, and as soon as she finished shopping, we'd go there.

In the entrance hall near the lift I waited, and waited . . . and waited. Where was mother? What *was* she doing? Surely she couldn't still be buying? She'd said she wouldn't be long, but here I was, still waiting. It felt as if I'd waited for hours: I was bored and very impatient. Should I look for her? But where could I go? The department store was large, and mother could be anywhere. Most probably she was gossiping with a sales assistant on one of the many floors. Down came the lift again. Would she be in it this time? Yes! With a sigh of relief, I stepped over to meet her as it came to a stop.

'Mother, where *have* you been? I've waited such a long time and nearly came to look for you.'

'Well, Else, I'm here now. I had to buy lots of things, and wanted to make my selections carefully. Anyway, let's be on our way to Café Reinhardt to treat ourselves to something special. You, my child, deserve it.'

I was happy now, certain all the waiting would at last be worth it.

Café Reinhardt was a truly stylish and elegant establishment. Small tables and chairs were carefully placed to appear at random, not too close to each other, allowing customers to converse without being overheard. Waitresses in little black dresses with tiny white lace aprons and small headbands to match were dashing soundlessly between tables. With eyes everywhere, they made sure every customer was served speedily and efficiently with courtesy and a friendly smile. There were so many delicious cakes and gateaux on display that it was most difficult to make a choice. They all looked wonderful. A large chocolate gateau had pride of place in the centre of the display; there were iced cherry cakes and mocha walnut cake and many more besides; also a selection of different tartlets and small pastries. Such a variety! In the end, I decided on a large slice of cherry and chocolate gateau and a cup of creamy hot chocolate. Meanwhile mother enjoyed her pot of coffee. It was always a special treat for her.

While I was eating, I observed the people around me. They all seemed so at ease, laughing and talking to each other in subdued voices, giving the impression they hadn't a care in the world. How I wished I could be like them: grown up and sophisticated. But before that could happen I knew a few more years had to pass. What would mother say if she could read my thoughts? She'd surely tell me to enjoy being young and not wish my precious childhood away. But at thirteen I felt I had so long to wait, with many boring teenage years before me.

While we talked about our day in Stolp, mother kept looking at her watch and I realised she was eager to get home. Perhaps she didn't want to spoil my enjoyment, but I knew what she was thinking. So I said, 'Come on, mother; I'm ready to go to the station now to catch our train. Thank you for taking me to Café Reinhardt, I've enjoyed it very much. My piece of cake and chocolate drink were delicious and, apart from going to the Schröters and meeting Anneliese, I had a lovely day. Hans-Dieter will be awaiting our return and wondering if we have a small surprise for him. I've also missed my little sister.'

Mother looked at me and smiled. 'How lucky I am to have a daughter like you, and, with the four of you, that includes little Ralf, even though he's not with us, how could I ever be lonely?'

Happy in each other's company, we linked arms and braved the extreme cold again. Mindful of the slippery road that could so easily make us lose our footing, I grabbed an iron railing. Immediately my glove stuck to it.

'Else, you mustn't touch frozen metal. It's dangerous! Thank goodness you were wearing gloves; otherwise it would have burnt your skin.'

I managed to peel my glove off the railing without tearing it, and carefully we continued on our way along the tree-lined road to the railway station.

We soon reached the station and there stood our train, ready to depart. That day it wasn't very crowded, so mother and I soon found a window seat where we could huddle in the corner to keep warm. The compartment was icy cold and the window as usual covered in a thick layer of ice; but at least we were sheltered from the cruel wind that howled across the platform. The temperature must have been way down in the minus figures. I felt cold to the core and thought mother couldn't possibly feel any different, even though she wore her fur coat.

'Mother, how are you?' I asked her. 'Are you very tired? It's been a long day.'

'Yes, child, I am. My feet are so cold that not even my boots are able to keep them warm. And what about you, Else? Just as cold as I am?'

'Yes.. My feet are like two lumps of ice at the end of my legs.'

'Come and sit beside me,' mother said. 'My coat's roomy and if I open it you can snuggle close and we'll both soon feel warmer.'

'Thank you; you're right – there's plenty of room for both of us.'

'Listen, Else, I have an idea,' mother giggled conspiratorially. 'When the train's moving and if we're still the only passengers in this compartment, we'll both stand up and perform a dance. We'll clap our hands, stamp our feet and pretend we're performing a Russian mazurka or Spanish tarantella.'

'Mother, we can't do that! What if someone hears us? They might think we're dismantling the train.' But dance we did – our health was more important than our dignity!

It must have made a very funny picture. Anyone observing us would have wondered what we were playing at. Even I thought we were ridiculous, but we laughed so much that tears ran down our cheeks. It was good fun and, best of all, we soon warmed up. Before we realised it, we were approaching Glowitz station.

It was quite late when we arrived. Snow had started to fall again and the light reflected off the snow. The road was slippery, the wind bitter and it was difficult to stay on our feet – we had to support each other.

We passed the dairy and were approaching the post office, when I saw my girlfriend Gisela by her front door, underneath a lantern, talking to a girl I didn't know.

'Mother, can I stop and talk to Gisela? Just say hello? I havn't seen her since the boar party.'

'If you talk to Gisela, I'll have to go on. I must fetch Hans-Dieter. It's late and they must be wondering where we are.'

'In that case, I'll come with you; you can't walk alone.' I waved at Gisela and called out, 'Come and see us tomorrow afternoon if you feel like it.'

'Is that all right?' I asked mother.

'Gisela's always welcome.' Mother smiled, and Gisela waved.

Mother and I continued, slipping and sliding down the icy road surface. Luckily it wasn't far to Frau Ruch's cottage and it was a relief to step inside, to escape the cold.

Hans-Dieter was pleased to see us, but he and Inge were engrossed in a card game.

'We won't be long, mother. Please let us finish.'

'It mustn't take too long. I need to ask Frau Ruch if you've behaved yourself!'

'I was really good, wasn't I, Frau Ruch? Inge and I helped with the washing-up after lunch, and I brushed the snow away from the back door.'

'Yes, Hans-Dieter, you did a wonderful job. A man couldn't have done it better.' Frau Ruch removed her apron and placed it over a chair.

I hoped to see Egon once more, but he was out and I didn't dare ask where he'd gone.

Soon Hans-Dieter's game was finished and mother was anxious to go at once. 'Come, children, quickly now. Don't forget, we have a baby waiting, and we still have to battle the weather. The wind through the park will be fierce and the snow may be deep.'

'Will you be all right?' Frau Ruch was concerned. 'If Egon were here, he could have escorted you.' Can I lend you anything to keep you warm?'

I didn't hear mother's reply, as I was wishing Egon could have escorted us!

It was wonderful to be home again. The struggle through the howling gale was exhausting, but the trees gave us a little protection and we focused on the black hunk that was the outline of the manor. No lights shone out to welcome us, because of the blackout curtains. But soon we were able to stamp our feet outside the back door and remove our snowy boots in the lobby.

Our room was wonderfully cosy and Johann had left the peat basket outside our door. Mother asked Hans-Dieter to bring the basket inside and to stoke the fire, as it had burned so low it could easily have gone out. Hans-Dieter knew what to do. I offered to help, but, with an indignant look on his face, he informed me he was quite capable of managing.

Meanwhile mother went down to fetch baby Marlene, and after Hans-Dieter had finished seeing to the stove, we both made a start on our evening meal.

Mother returned out of breath, carrying baby in her basket. 'What a little heavyweight she is,' mother commented, 'a proper little dumpling but oh . . . so very cuddly.'

Mother looked contented, hugging her little daughter. She was a proud mother, but at forty-two it seemed to me she was getting a little old to have such a young baby. I looked on in admiration.

Mother interrupted my thoughts by saying that there had been letters from father and my grandmother that day. She wanted to bathe baby and then read them. I was more impatient and said that Marlene was fine for the moment, and mother should read the letters straightaway. I was desperate to know how father was, and when he would be coming home.

Mother gave in and settled into her chair. With Hans-Dieter beside her and Marlene on her lap she opened father's letter first. And soon she was crying. I was terrified and pleaded to know what had had upset her.

Imagine my relief when mother said that she was crying tears of joy! Father was coming home soon and would be there for Marlene's christening.

'Where is he now mother? Does he say?'

Mother of course reminded me straightaway that father would not be allowed to say where he was. This was war time and it was forbidden to divulge the location of any military units.

Quickly, mother opened grandmother's letter. The good news was that grandma would also be coming to see us. Sadly though, grandfather would not be able to make it. He had some problems with his legs and the doctor had advised him not to travel. He sent his love and we were happy that he said he would make it when the better weather arrived.

Chapter 13

Back to School

5 January 1943

Only three more days until the end of our holidays. That meant we had to go back to school and I had to get ready to board.

Sylvia had already returned to her boarding school in Berlin and we had to wait until Easter before we could meet again.

I was happy to travel to school by train with Gisela and a few young people from Glowitz and other surrounding villages. We talked about gifts we'd received for Christmas and how we'd passed our holidays, and then we all had a moan about the beginning of a new term. We grumbled about getting up so early each morning and the long days we had to endure.

'It's all right for you, Else: from next Monday you don't have to travel any more. Lucky you! No more getting up early – you can have a lie in most mornings, and going to school will be no distance.'

'It all sounds good,' I answered, 'but give me the opportunity and I'd willingly change places with any one of you. I don't want to board – it's my mother's idea.'

Monday, 11 January 1943

The fateful day arrived all too quickly.

After school I waited for Anneliese to finish her lessons. On that first afternoon I wanted us to walk home together. Anneliese chatted away, but I didn't take much notice of what she was saying. My mind was far away at home with my family. I had a lump in my throat and felt like crying, yet knew that was something I could *never* do, especially in front of Anneliese.

Frau Schröter must have been watching for us. As we entered the garden she opened the door and greeted me kindly. She did try to make me welcome; perhaps she saw I felt strange and uncomfortable. 'Come in, Else. Welcome to our home. Let me take your coat. Anneliese will show you upstairs to your room. When you're ready, come to the kitchen for a warm drink.'

Her kind words did make me feel better, but the lump in my throat wouldn't go away. For the rest of the day I found it difficult to talk; tears were never far away, but after a while I settled down. I was longing for evening to come so I could to go to bed and be alone with my thoughts. Anneliese tried to cheer me with her constant chatter. If she'd only be quiet and let me be! I also knew that soon I had to meet Herr Schröter. Anneliese had talked about him many times; she adored her father and I imagined him to be kind, friendly and very approachable.

'When's your father coming home, Anneliese? I look forward to meeting him.'

'Else, that could be anytime. Sometimes he's home very late. We could be in bed by then. Don't worry – you'll meet Papa and will certainly like him. My father's a *very* nice person.'

I was glad when the day was over and I could crawl into bed. I felt miserable and homesick, abandoned and very alone. I wanted mother, yet was angry towards her. I felt sorry for myself and when I couldn't hold back the tears any longer, I cried and cried, until at last sleep overcame me.

Yet the days flew by. I was busy at school and afterwards homework took up most of my evenings. I didn't want to play with Anneliese: she was too young for me. She could keep her dolls and soft toys. I didn't want to play with *them*. I much preferred to take a book, sit in a corner and transport myself into another world. There was no time to be homesick; only at night in bed, in my poky little room, where I cried myself to sleep, longing to be with mother and my family.

In a large room that also served as a library I found an extensive selection of amazing books. When I mentioned to Frau Schröter how much I liked to read, she gave me permission to help myself.

The first week I spent living in Stolp went by quickly and, on the whole, uneventfully. Except . . . I had a big quarrel with Anneliese, which, at the same time gave me the opportunity to tell her just what I thought of her and her behaviour.

Anneliese was a silly girl, as I suspected, always wanting her own way – if she couldn't get it, she'd stamp her feet and have one of her famous tantrums. Her mother was powerless to calm her. Anneliese threatened to tell her father, which she always did.

We'd started the day on which we had our confrontation in a friendly and harmonious way. I was walking to fetch something from my room when, outside Anneliese's bedroom, I noticed a few items of clothing belonging to one of her dolls. I stooped to pick them up and knocked on her door. No answer. 'Anneliese, are you there?' Still no answer, so I opened the door to her room and stepped inside to lay the little garments I'd found on her bed.

At that moment Anneliese came running upstairs, saw her bedroom door open and discovered me in her room. 'Else, what are you doing? I've told you *never* to enter my room without my permission, and here you are, with my dolls' clothes in your hands. How dare you!'

I said nothing; just let her go on raging and fuming because I knew that no reaction would make her angrier than ever.

Eventually she *had* to stop. She was shaking with temper: I stood and waited.

'Anneliese,' I said, as she gasped for breath, 'just listen to yourself. You act like a spoilt child, yet you always pretend how grown-up you are . . . or, at least, you try to give that impression. I don't want anything to do with you and can do without a friend like you. You can explain to your mother what's happened. All I ask is that you're honest.' And with those words I left her.

After our evening meal, while I was in my room absorbed in a book, Anneliese knocked on my door. 'Else, may I come in for just a minute?' she mumbled, standing on the threshold. 'I . . . I apologise for my behaviour. I was horrid and unfair to you . . .' I didn't reply, so she continued, 'I promise it won't happen again. Please, Else, let me be your friend. You're welcome to enter my room any time . . .' Still she waited for my reaction. 'And you can call me "Liesel" . . . only people I like best call me that.'

I looked at Anneliese standing there and could see she actually felt ashamed. I was unsure if she was truly sorry to have behaved so childishly, but this was a start. 'Very well, Liesel, let's forget what's happened. Please now let me get on with reading my book. I'll see you at breakfast tomorrow morning. Good night!'

Chapter 14

Heil Hitler, Sir

14 January 1943

On the Thursday, during my first week in Stolp, I heard the telephone ringing downstairs in the hall. I heard Frau Schröter coming out of the drawing room to answer it and realised from the way she spoke that she was talking to my mother. I heard her say 'Good evening, Frau Hopp. I hope all is well with you and your family? Would you like to talk to Else? She's in her room doing homework. I'll call her; just give me a minute.' Frau Schröter walked to the bottom of the stairs and called up to me, 'Else, can you hear me? Please come downstairs. Your mother's on the telephone.'

Mother wants to talk to me on the telephone? I wonder why? I do hope nothing's wrong. I rushed downstairs, excited and anxious at the same time.

'Hello, mother. How are you and Hans-Dieter and baby? Is everything all right?'

'Yes, Else, we're all fine. In fact I have news for you. You'll be surprised to hear that grandma is coming, tomorrow.'

'How lovely, mother! What time will she be arriving?'

'Listen, Else. Please don't interrupt me. Grandma will arrive at Stolp railway station in the early afternoon. You should be able to meet her and travel with her at your usual time, to arrive here in Glowitz just after 4 p.m. I've asked for the sleigh to be made available to meet you both. Miss Dorothea sees no problem with that.'

'But, mother, what should I do if grandma isn't there?'

'Then, child, you must come home without her. Don't stay and wait for a later train; it's too dangerous on your own. Are you listening, Else? Come home at your usual time, even if grandma hasn't yet arrived.'

'Mother, don't worry. I'll do as you say. I hope grandma can make the connection and travel with me to Glowitz.'

'Yes, Else, so do I. Goodbye until tomorrow, darling. We're looking forward to having you home.'

'Night, mother. Kisses and love to the three of you. Oh, I nearly forgot: Hans-Dieter doesn't believe in kissing any more. Just give him a hug and tell him it's from me.'

While I was talking to mother, the front door opened and Herr Schröter walked in. At that moment my good manners deserted me. I stood and stared at a tall imposing figure, who gazed at me with eyes that bored into me. It felt as if he could see right through me, which left me tongue-tied and lost for words. Herr Schröter was tall and very handsome, with hair that was almost albino white. He was dressed in a black uniform and wore shiny black boots and a full-length black leather coat. It dawned on me the uniform was that of the Schutzstaffel (SS), Adolf Hitler's personal guard. When I looked at Herr Schröter, I was reminded of Egon. That's what he'll look like one day, I thought. He'll also be proud to wear that awesome uniform. I'd heard of the SS and had noticed that when people talked about them they spoke in a whisper. I couldn't work out why.

Herr Schröter stepped towards me. 'Ah, here you are, Else. At last we meet. *Heil* Hitler and welcome to my home. I hope you feel comfortable here.'

'*Heil* Hitler, Sir, and thank you,' I said, raising my right arm in salute. 'Yes, I'm happy to be living with your family.' I paused. What else could you say to a man like that? I then added, 'And Liesel and I are good friends.'

'Now where's my little princess? Isn't she coming to greet me this evening?'

'Here I am, Papi,' shouted Anneliese, running towards her father, jumping on tiptoe to give him a big hug. 'You met Else? It's…nice…to have her staying with us; she's company for me.'

I wondered whether Liesel really appreciated her father coming home most evenings. How lucky she was! I felt jealous and could feel a lump forming in my throat.

'Run along, children,' he said. I'll see your mother, Liesel, and then I must rest for a while. My day has been very busy and after dinner I still have more work to do.'

That night, as I lay in bed, I couldn't get Herr Schröter and his black uniform out of my mind. There was something sinister about being all in black and yet he appeared pleasant. Was that an act he was playing? Or could he still be a good man despite the uniform he was wearing?'

Next day I was very excited. It was Friday, I was going home and, best of all, grandma was coming to visit us – so much to look forward to. Wonderful!

When Liesel and I were ready for school, Herr and Frau Schröter remained at the breakfast table, both totally absorbed in their own adult world.

Suddenly, on our way to school, Anneliese gave a big sigh.

'Liesel, whatever is the matter? Are you not well?'

'I'm well, Else, but you're so lucky to be going home, while I have to stay here on my own. I think my parents are planning a dinner tomorrow evening for important people from father's department, and I won't be invited to join them at the table. I'll have to eat my meal in my room or in the kitchen with Helga, our maid. That's not exciting.'

'I'd like you to come home with me, Liesel, but it's not possible. You know today my grandmother's coming to visit us. It could cause an upheaval, as space will be limited. I'll return to school on Monday morning and, on the way home, you can tell me all about your parents' luxurious dinner.'

'All right, Else,' she said reluctantly, 'and you can describe your grandmother's weekend.'

I thought lessons that Friday would never end. But eventually they did and when the 2 p.m. bell rang, I knew the weekend had begun. I didn't loiter behind until it was time to go to the railway station. Instead, as soon as we were dismissed, I grabbed my small case, shouted goodbye to my friends and off I flew.

'Else, why are you in such a hurry?' Gisela called out. 'Wait, I'll come with you – we're in plenty of time.'

'Yes, Gisela, but for all I know, grandmother's already arrived and is waiting for me.'

But we needn't have hurried. When we arrived at the station, I searched up and down the platforms: Grandma was nowhere to be seen. 'Oh, Gisela, what should I do if she doesn't come before our train leaves? I must find out if the Stettin to Königsberg train has already gone. Give me a minute; I won't be long.'

What a relief! When I reached the information desk, I was told the train from Stettin was due any minute on platform one. I raced up the stairs to where Gisela was waiting and, in my excitement, danced about until she told me to calm down. 'You'll have a heart attack, Else, if you go on like that. What kind of greeting would that be for your grandma?'

'Look, Gisela, there comes the train! I must run to the other platform. Stay here, or, if you like, come with me.'

Together we ran to platform one and reached it just as the train, with much huffing and letting off steam, came to a halt. The doors opened and many people stepped down from their compartments. 'Help me look, Gisela. She's an elderly lady, about sixty years old, dressed in black for certain, but very elegant.'

Suddenly there she was. The train had numerous carriages but I could see her in the distance, a smart elderly lady wearing a black felt hat. 'Grandma, Grandma!' I shouted. 'Here I am!' As fast as I could, I ran towards her, almost knocking her over in my excitement.

'Steady, child. You'll fall and hurt yourself. Now calm down and introduce me to your charming girlfriend.'

'Come here, Gisela. Meet my beloved grandmother. She's travelled all the way from Düsseldorf to be with us. And this, Grandma, is my best friend, Gisela. I've mentioned her in my letters to you. But come on, talk on the train to Glowitz. We must go back to platform two.'

'Not so fast, Else. I'm not as young as you are: my racing days are over.'

'Sorry, grandma, but we really must hurry. Our little train doesn't stop very long. It shuttles back and forth between Stolp and Glowitz all day long, so those who want to travel further can change trains.' I ushered her along the platform to the steps. 'Grandma, do you only have that small case you're carrying?'

'No, Else, this is my hand luggage. The rest is being sent directly to Königsberg.'

We returned to platform two, where some of my travel companions had gathered. The boys, as usual, were laughing and fooling around, closely watched by the stationmaster, who wanted to make sure their tomfoolery didn't get out of hand. They kept glancing curiously at my grandmother. A lady from the city rarely travelled on the small local train to the outlying villages.

When we were seated and the train was moving towards Glowitz, Grandma commented on the amount of snow lying everywhere.

'Have you no snow in Düsseldorf, Grandma?'

'No, child, not any more. It's long gone.'

'Grandma, how long will you stay with us?'

'I'll stay until Monday, 25 January, and then, when you travel to school, I'll accompany you to Stolp to catch my train to Königsberg. Your mother wants to visit little Ralf in Swinemünde, and Hans-Dieter and baby Marlenchen will have me to look after them.'

'Grandma, why can't I stay at home with you or, at least, come home in the afternoon? I'd help you as much as I could and keep you company.'

'I don't think so, Elslein. You must understand, mother pays Frau Schröter to look after you, which she seems to do well. It would be unfair to disrupt her household with you coming and going as you wish. If you're as sensible as I think you are, you'll understand what I'm saying and agree I'm right.'

'Yes, grandma, of course you're right. Mother says the same.'

'Frau Hopp, do you often travel to Pomerania?' asked Gisela.

'No, Gisela, not Pomerania. My home's in East Prussia. When I was a child I lived in a small village near Königsberg. Three of my sisters are still there and I visit them as often as I can.'

'Do they also visit you in Düsseldorf?' asked Gisela.

'No, they look after a large farm and, now they're older, it keeps them fully occupied.'

I could see that Gisela could go on and on asking questions. I felt I had to intervene, as grandma was tired and it showed in her face. 'Goodness,' I called out, 'here we are already in Klenzin. Only five more minutes and we'll arrive in Glowitz.'

Johann was waiting outside the station with the sleigh to take us to the manor. That was nothing new to grandma; she remembered sleigh rides from her childhood. Old memories must have come rushing back to her – I was certain I saw unshed tears glistening in her eyes.

How pleased mother was at our arrival.

'Mother,' she called out, 'how lovely to have you here with us. How was the journey? Not too stressful, I hope.'

'The only place I felt slightly nervous was crossing Berlin. Soldiers were everywhere. It touched my heart to see those young boys go off to battlegrounds where possibly many would lose their lives. Tell me, Lene, how's little Ralf? Any sign of improvement?

'Slightly, mother. The news from Swinemünde is encouraging, but I must see for myself. We all miss that little lad and the worst thing is, next week's his birthday.'

'Yes, Lene, I hadn't forgotten: in my bag's a gift for him. Please take it and say it's from Grandma.'

'Thank you, mother. He'll be four years old and it's sad we're missing so much of his growth and development. That's why I want to go next week; not only to be there for his birthday but also to see for myself if his health's improving.'

Grandma had removed her heavy winter coat and fur-lined boots. Now she was sitting in mother's favourite chair and, with a strong cup of coffee in her hand, could at last relax and recover from the strain of her long, tiring journey.

Asking about her son, my father, Grandma said, 'Lene, how's Willy? Have you heard from him?'

'Yes, mother, as far as I know, he's well. I don't know where he is – everything's top secret – but I've a feeling, reading between the lines, that he may be somewhere near Moscow. I don't know what to think, and I live in constant fear. But then, I'm not the only one: thousands of wives, fathers and sweethearts are in the same position. Worry, worry and more worry – it's never ending.'

'Do you think he'll be home for our little one's christening?'

'I think so. At least Willy hopes he *can* get leave for a few days, but who knows?' Mother shrugged her shoulders. 'I'm not the only one, but that doesn't make it any easier. Every morning, when the postman calls, I think, *is he bringing a telegram*? And when he goes and there's none, I'm so relieved. Then I'm happy – if only for a while. I cuddle my children and once more I'm at peace with the world.'

Mother turned to me. 'Now where's my big, responsible daughter? Come here, darling; give your mother a hug. I'm so glad to have you home, even if only for a short weekend.'

There was much chattering and exchanging of news. Hans-Dieter also wanted Grandma's attention and, all in all, it was bedlam in our small set of rooms!

Later, when Hans-Dieter was asleep and I'd retired to mother's bedroom, I heard her and Grandma talking long into the night. Grandma had been offered a small room in a passage near ours. It must have been late when she and mother at last retired for the night. Mother had to wake me to go into my own bed, but I was so sleepy that I couldn't even remember next morning how I got into it.

The weekend went by all too quickly. Mother and grandma had a lot to talk about; they had to make up for lost time and mother was hungry for news from home.

The weather was lovely and, although there was frost at night, no new snow fell and the sun shone every day. I was able to visit Gisela and a few other friends; and all that, together with being at home with my lovely family, made me very contented.

19 January 1943

Mother left early that morning to visit Ralf and I couldn't concentrate in class for thinking of her. I knew Grandma would have liked to accompany her, but visitors, other than a parent, were not allowed. We often thought of our little brother, far away in Swinemünde. Was he homesick or had he got used to being away from us? As long as he was treated well, he'd be happy. Mother would tell us about her journey and visit as soon as she returned at the weekend, and then I'd also be home to share her news.

As soon as I saw mother the following Saturday, I knew she was pleased with little Ralf's progress.

'Mother, you can't believe how well that child's looked after,' she told my grandmother. 'Ralf's the youngest patient in the sanatorium; everyone loves and makes a fuss of him. Matron acts as if he's her own child, and I can't describe the wonderful birthday party they laid on for him. If it continues like that, instead of being happy, Ralf will cry when he has to return to us.'

'Lene, don't think like that. Ralf won't forget you're his mama.'

'That may be so, mother; I did tell Matron that under no circumstances should she encourage my little boy to call *her* Mama. When I see how happy Ralfie is with her, I feel resentful and jealous, yet I should be grateful he's so well looked after.'

The days of my grandmother's visit went by quickly. In no time it was my last weekend with her, and I watched her pack her bag to continue her journey to Königsberg.

'Grandma, it's such a short visit with us. I wish you could stay longer.'

'Don't be sad, Elslein. In exactly one month, I'll return. Then father will also be here and together we'll celebrate your little sister's christening.'

That weekend I frequently noticed something else: grandma and mother, sitting close together, talking in restrained, subdued voices. They both looked serious, which made me long to know what it was about. I assumed it had something to do with the war, but, as a child, I wasn't included in their conversation.

Once I heard grandma say to mother, 'It's hard to believe our propaganda minister, Dr Goebbels, tells us the whole truth. The reports in the daily newspapers sound more genuine than the nonsense he comes out with.'

'Hush, mother! You don't know what ears are listening!' Mother glanced not at me but at the window and door. 'But I agree: papers, at least, tell us a little about the savage fighting and how our soldiers are suffering in the bitter cold Russian winter. They mention thousands of lives being lost in the siege of Stalingrad. I fear dear Willy's among them. How much longer can our soldiers hold out? That's what I'd like to know.'

'Lene, there's nothing *we* can do. Sometimes I think it's better not to listen to the wireless or read newspapers. We don't know what to believe. Are we told the truth, or is it propaganda dished up by Dr Goebbels in order to appease the German nation?'

I could hear only snippets of conversation between mother and grandma. Much of it I couldn't understand. One thing puzzled me, however. Were they both beginning to doubt the words of our leaders? If so, mother must be careful; so must grandma. It was easy to overhear: I'd heard talk of outspoken people disappearing for good. But mother had always been a staunch supporter of Adolf Hitler. Was she now having doubts? Never! Not mother, yet . . .

On Monday, 25 January, Grandma started her return journey to East Prussia. I travelled with her as far as Stolp, where I saw her safely onto the train to Königsberg.

31 January 1943

That day we heard officially that the German army had surrendered at Stalingrad.

As only scant news filtered through, the horrors of the battle for that city were still unknown to the people of Germany. It would be many months before the city's devastation and the carnage of possibly thousands of men, women, children and soldiers of many nations would become known to us.

As the defeat and surrender was announced, German people around me seemed stunned. 'But on the radio Goebbels keeps emphasising we're winning,' they said. 'Could this be the beginning of the end?'

My mother buried her head in her hands as tears streamed down her cheeks. All she could say was, 'Dear God, have mercy on all those affected one way or the other.'

What's it all for? Can someone please tell me?

Chapter 15

Marble Shelves

February 1943

The boar hunt to have taken place on 6 February was cancelled. News of the fall of Stalingrad and the devastating defeat on many battlefronts in Russia had severely dampened the German people's spirit. It left no room for rejoicing or merrymaking.

But instead of no shoot at all, Baron von Puttkamer and other landowners from surrounding villages decided to postpone the boar hunt to Saturday, 20 February.

'Goodness me,' mother exclaimed, 'this is going to be a busy month. What with baby's christening, father's hopefully coming home, grandma's arrival and the many preparations for one thing and another, we'll be rushed off our feet.'

'Don't panic, mother. It's not that bad. You have my help and Hans-Dieter can lend a hand. Frau Krause is used to mayhem in her kitchen; she remains calm no matter how much chaos surrounds her. She knows how to stay level-headed in any situation and restores peace and order in no time.'

As for me, I was delighted! Mother had insisted I not miss one lesson at school but, instead of staying in Stolp, I was allowed home not only at weekends but also each evening during the week before our numerous events.

20 February

The long-awaited day of the postponed boar hunt had finally arrived. At breakfast Hans-Dieter constantly pestered mother to let him join the hunt with other children from the village. mother was getting annoyed. 'Hans-Dieter, stop it! Very well, go. But don't think that just because you know how to plead, you'll get your own way all the time. When you return this afternoon, there'll still be work for you and tiredness won't be an excuse.'

'What will I have to do, mother?'

'Never mind now, Hans-Dieter, but I'll think of something! Now get your warm clothes on and I'll check. It's bitter outside and you'll have to wait until everyone's ready to come home; no excuses about returning earlier. Be good and listen to your Uncle Kurt. Stay close to him: he'll see you don't get into danger. Now give me a hug, and off with you!'

I was glad Sylvia was at school and wouldn't attend the hunt. I didn't need to feel guilty about staying away.

I hurried downstairs to the kitchen. Mother would follow with Baby as soon as she'd completed her housework. Everyone was too busy to notice me. I wanted to explore and there was no one to prevent me. Many storerooms had doors wide open. However, one door, the one nearest the bottom of the stairs, was closed. I gingerly tried the handle, but, to my surprise, it was locked. I'd ask Johann what the room contained. Meanwhile, I investigated others.

The next tiny room had slatted shelves where fruit was stored. Apples and pears of various varieties, all harvested from the manor orchard, lay spaced out along the slats. The delicious fruity aroma was inviting; I picked up a crisp green apple feeling the rough skin with my fingers: somehow, I resisted the urge to bite into it.

'Not without asking, Else!' I told myself. 'But if you ask nicely, Mamsell is sure to say, run along and help yourself.'

Then followed the cold store where perishable goods were kept on marble shelves. Thick walls ensured an even temperature and a small, wire-netted window built high into the wall was never closed.

Next to the cold store was the larder, full of preserves and such like. I saw jams and jellies, many kinds of soft fruits in bottles and a great variety of vegetables, bottled, canned or pickled. That was a labour of love carried out by Frau Krause with the help of Lotti every year during the summer season. Everything was home produced from the huge manor gardens; there would be no shortages throughout that long, cold winter.

Steps at the end of the passage led to the backyard and from there to the gardens. Beside them was one room I hadn't noticed before. I tried the door – it opened, and I peered into the dim interior. Bar upon bar of peat was neatly stacked from floor to ceiling, and the room was filled with a wonderfully earthy fragrance. Johann's domain . . . no one would dare enter it without his permission.

I sat on one of the steps and gazed down that long passage. *Well, Else*, I thought, *you've inspected each room on the right. Now what's on your left?*

The first door I opened led into a dining room reserved for Johann, Frau Krause and her kitchen staff. I had to peep inside the staff-room. Only once before, on a morning soon after my arrival, when Hans-Dieter and I had had our breakfast there, had I been inside. Now it was orderly, with the table set ready for lunch. I tiptoed out, and pulled the door closed behind me.

There was one shut door left now. From sounds behind it, I gathered it would lead back into the kitchen. As I opened it and stood for a moment looking at all the bustling activity.

I entered the kitchen quietly and greeted Mamsell. She stood close to the cooking stove, wielding a large wooden spoon, stirring the contents in a pan, the size of which I'd never seen before. It was huge! Whatever was inside that big pot smelled delicious and made my mouth water – and it wasn't even ready yet!

'What are you cooking, Frau Krause?'

'Soup for this evening; and when it's ready, you'll have a taste.'

'Thank you, Frau Krause. Please tell me, is there something I can do to help?'

'Oh, I expect we can find you something. See your mother first; she might like you to look after Baby.'

'I'd much rather have some proper work, Mamsell. Can I help Anna cut up vegetables?'

Anna stood by the big sink under the window, peeling potatoes. On a wooden draining board at her side lay a huge pile of sorted vegetables: carrots, onions, celeriac, turnips and many more – all needed to be prepared for the evening's meal.

This time there was no grand dinner after the shoot. Instead Fraulein Dorothea and her grandmother, the Baroness, had asked Frau Krause to prepare a cold buffet accompanied by hot vegetable soup and a substantial venison ragout.

Lotti was in the scullery, her hands deep in hot water and soapsuds, trying to cope with ever-mounting piles of dirty dishes, pots and pans. 'Poor Lotti,' I thought, 'her hands must get so red and painful.'

When I'd finished helping Anna and Lotti, Mamsell asked me to take two silver condiment sets to the dining room.

Trudi and Maria were there preparing the beautiful, spacious room with wood-panelled walls. From the centre of the ceiling hung a magnificent crystal chandelier, which gave the decor a splendid, sophisticated elegance. The two girls had almost completed their work and I was enthralled. The table was laid to perfection: silver cutlery gleamed, and highly polished crystal glasses, large and small, sparkled as they reflected glittering rainbow colours from the chandelier. Sideboards and side tables waited to accommodate platters with various cold meats and cheeses. Later, everything would be displayed in readiness for guests to help themselves, with Trudi and Maria close by to give a helping hand. How I wished I could mingle with the guests. Trudi and Maria would wear black dresses and little white aprons. I'd have felt nervous but important; and afterwards, when all the guests had gone, I could eat and drink as much as I liked. There was sure to be food left over, but everyone would have to eat quickly before the Baroness came to hide it away!

Just as I returned from the dining room, the back door opened. It was the postman. 'Frau Hopp, I have a fieldpost letter for you. I'm sure it's from Herr Hopp. I hope all's well!'

Mother ran along the passage. She had been busy in the cold store arranging platters for the evening. As she ran, she wiped her hands on her apron, nodding anxiously at the postman as he handed her the precious letter from father.

'Mother, will you let me read father's letter?'

'Wait, Else, I'll let you know what father says. If it's not bad news – he may tell us when he's coming; I hope, in time for baby's christening. Now, please go; let me read my letter in peace.'

After mother had finished reading, I saw her put it back thoughtfully, fold the envelope and slide it into her apron pocket. I tried to read her expression. Was it good news or bad?

'Mother, does father mention when he's coming home?' I ventured, cautiously.

'Else, we'll just have to wait and hope. Don't be impatient; we may have to wait until the last minute.'

Mother must have known all the time what was going to happen, but she gave nothing away – everything is uncertain in war anyway. Was there a surprise Hans-Dieter and I were to be kept in the dark about? She certainly didn't look sad.

'By the way, Else, have you spoken to Dunja today?'

'No, mother. Where is she?'

'She was in the dairy separating the milk for butter and cream. But now she may be in the laundry room, sorting washing and finishing the ironing while she looks after Baby. Go and help her; she'll be pleased with your company.'

As I walked slowly towards the laundry, mother called me back.

'Else, when you've helped Dunja, take Marlenchen upstairs. Time's getting on. Not long now till Hans-Dieter comes home; he'll be cold and hungry. I'll follow you shortly, and then we'll all sit down and have our evening meal.'

Chapter 16

The Parcel

While we were sitting at the table having our evening meal, mother looked up and spoke to Hans-Dieter and me. 'Listen, you two, I want to talk to you. Next Monday you don't have to go to school. I've spoken to your teachers and they know I need you here at home.'

I was intrigued. With only a few days to go I didn't want to miss any more lessons, and was surprised that mother thought I should. Mother explained that she had something she wanted us to do. Something so important that it couldn't wait. Needless to say I pestered her for more details and she said that on Monday morning Hans-Dieter and I must go to the station to meet the eleven 'o clock train. There was a parcel to be collected from it.

A parcel! We were astonished. What could it be? In answer to our questions mother said only that it would be too heavy to carry, and that we should take the toboggan. We tried to find out more, but eventually mother said, 'No more. Just go and collect the parcel. You have asked enough'.

22 February 1943

The day dawned bitterly cold. It had snowed during the night and it was still falling.

'Mother, what time do you want us to leave for the station?'

'The train should arrive about 11 a.m. Give yourselves plenty of time; rather be too early than too late. The train will *not* wait for you. Go across the field – it's much quicker. But be careful, because it's very icy and you could easily fall and break a limb.'

At 10.30 Hans-Dieter and I started walking towards the station, pulling our toboggan behind us. We didn't have long to wait, for in the distance we heard the train puffing nearer and nearer.

'Here it comes, Else!' Hans-Dieter shouted, jumping up and down in his excitement. 'I can see the steam!'

Closer and closer the train came towards us, slowing down as it approached the station, and, with much hissing and screeching of brakes, it eventually came under the canopy. Such a noise!

'I wonder what's in the parcel mother wants us to pick up?' Hans-Dieter asked for the umpteenth time.

'I don't know, Hans-Dieter. Stop asking that question. How should I know what's in the parcel? Wait and see!'

We stood and waited. The train slowly clanked towards us and then, after another sighing hiss, jerked to a stop.

'Come on, Else, let's run to the front of the train where the goods wagon is. Then we can watch our parcel being unloaded.'

Only a few passengers were stepping down onto the platform, doors clanging behind them – people we didn't know. But as it was Monday and still early in the day, we didn't expect many passengers to alight.

Suddenly my eyes came to rest on a man, a man in a field-grey uniform – a soldier. He was standing on his own, waiting for something or someone.

'Dieter, look!' I shouted. 'I believe that's father! I'm *sure* it's him. Come on, let's run and see!' I ran towards him, straining my eyes to confirm my sighting. I couldn't see his features, as he was wearing his army cap, but the man's stature was similar to father's: not too tall, yet upright.

Eventually I was satisfied and shouted, 'Father! Father! We're here!'

But he'd already seen us, and we ran towards each other. What joy! We hugged, and it was so good to feel his arms around us. My love for him overwhelmed me and I couldn't speak. All I wanted was to touch his face and feel he was real.

'Oh, father, mother sent us to pick up a parcel, and here *you* are! What a surprise and how wonderful!'

Dieter and I were both dancing around our father. We were so excited that we didn't notice he was holding something in his other arm, warmly tucked away in his woollen scarf.

'Children, see what I brought for you, all the way from Russia.'

We looked, and what was peeping out of a corner of his scarf? Two little black eyes looked up at us, and Hans-Dieter and I knew it could mean only one thing – a little dog!

'Father, you've brought a puppy for us! Such a little thing . . . Is it for us to keep? Where did you get it?'

'Yes, children, this little girl dog's for all of us to keep. Poor little Puppy lost her mother on the battlefield. I found and nursed her, and carried her all the way from Russia. I've named her Senta and I'd like you both to look after her and give her a loving home.'

'What breed is she?' Hans-Dieter wanted to know.

'She's a German Shepherd dog. As yet she's very small but she'll soon grow. If you care for and love her, she'll give you love and loyalty in return. But come, my darlings, we can talk about this later. I can't wait to see your mother. I'm sure she's anxiously waiting for us. So let's get going. If we three march like soldiers, it won't be long before we're home. Let me put my kitbag on your toboggan.'

'But Else,' Hans-Dieter reminded me, 'Mother asked us to pick up a parcel. Have you forgotten?'

I laughed. 'Dieter, don't you realise? *Father* is the parcel! "A parcel" was mother's excuse to send us to the station, without giving her secret away and because she said it would be a big parcel, we had to take our toboggan.'

As we walked back across the field my mind was preoccupied, wondering how mother would react when she saw us with a puppy.

'Father,' I said, 'do you think mother will be angry when she sees the puppy? I hope we can keep her, but of course we must also ask the Puttkamer family; they may not allow us to have a dog.'

'Don't let that worry you, Elslein; I'll make sure that Puppy can stay – leave it to me.'

As we approached the farmyard, we could see mother standing by the back door. As soon as she saw us, she couldn't wait a moment longer. As fast as she could, she slithered across the icy yard to meet us and when father saw her coming, he passed the puppy to me and ran to catch her.

'Willy, Willy!' mother shouted. 'How good it is to have you home! I was so afraid that, even at the last minute, something would prevent you from coming. Oh, how wonderful! At last we're together again; we have so much to talk about and I have many things to show you; I don't know where to start.'

Mother couldn't stop hugging and kissing and touching father, either. I thought she'd smother him, but he just laughed, picked her up and swirled her round and round, until both were utterly out of breath.

Meanwhile, Hans-Dieter and I, puppy in my arms, stood there; just for a moment almost forgotten by our parents. Then, still in father's arms she looked round, and in total surprise called out, 'Else, what on earth's that you have in your arms?'

'It's a puppy, mother, a German Shepherd puppy. Father brought her for us all the way from Russia. Please, please can we keep her? Don't say no; look how small she is and so lovely. She's a little girl-dog and father has named her Senta. Please, mother, say she can stay with us?'

'Is that true, Willy? Did you really bring that little dog for the children from Russia?'

'Yes, Lene, I did; but let's go indoors now. Later we can talk and I'll tell you how I came to rescue that beautiful little dog and bring her home with me. Meanwhile, Else, take Puppy among the bushes where she can relieve herself. She's very clean and knows what to do. When she's ready, bring her indoors, she must be hungry and tired; after all, she's very young.'

'Willy,' said mother, letting go of his hand, 'I'll go on. Hans-Dieter can stow the toboggan away and I must see to little Marlene. Don't be long. You haven't seen your newest daughter. She's still so small. You'll love her.'

'Very well, Lenchen, you go ahead. I'll wait for Else and together we'll introduce Senta to the household.'

'Willy, show her to Frau Krause, our Mamsell. Puppy will welcome leftover titbits from the kitchen. Now, I'm going! Sort the toboggan, Hans-Dieter, and you two hurry up.' Having said that, mother left us.

Father had made a little collar for Senta and in his pocket carried a strong piece of cord, which served as a lead. We put her on the ground and walked a little way into the park.

'It's beautiful here, Else. Mother was lucky when she was allocated a home in Glowitz Manor. He breathed in fresh air and listened to the stillness broken only by a crowing cockerel and the lowing of a cow. *What a contrast to the battleground*, he must have thought. 'As soon as possible,' continued father, 'I must introduce myself to Puttkamer, and then mention our dog.'

After the little dog had squatted, staining the fresh snow yellow, father said, 'Come on, Else. Let's go. I can't wait to meet my new little daughter.'

Just a few minutes of walking in the snow had tired puppy and she was shivering. It was also sufficient for father and me. I could see he wanted to be with mother more than anything.

The news of father's arrival spread throughout the house within minutes. Frau Krause and Johann were first on the scene to welcome him, and the rest of the staff soon followed. But father didn't linger: he was tired and overcome with emotion. I had to get him upstairs as quickly as possible, before the family appeared to greet him and delay us even further.

Of course, puppy was the talk of the 'downstairs department' and was much admired. But even the little dog couldn't be bothered any more; all she wanted was to have something to eat, and then sleep and be left alone.

When at last we reached our apartment, mother hadn't been idle. The table was laid, a meal prepared and a delicious aroma of freshly brewed coffee wafted through the room. In the centre of that homely picture stood mother with Marlenchen in her arms.

'Come, Willy, now we're all together be one of us. Come and meet your little daughter.'

Father looked at his tiny girl in mother's arms, whom he'd not seen before, and tears welled up in his eyes.

'Hello, my darling,' he said to Marlenchen. 'I'm your Papi. Will you come to me?' As he stretched out his arms the little girl was ready to go to him, without hesitating. She smiled and her tiny hand touched his face. My father was overcome with tender love.

'Lenchen, she's beautiful, a delightful little girl! Thank you for giving her to me. What a wonderful family I have – only our small son, Ralf, is missing. May he soon be well and one of us again.'

'You're not the only one to wish that, Willy. Every day I pray his good health will be restored. May God grant us our request.'

'Lenchen, I'm so glad you and the children are safely tucked away here in Pomerania. May it remain like this until this dreadful war's over.'

In the corner, near the stove, mother had already prepared a comfortable bed for our puppy. From somewhere she'd obtained a basket and, together with one of her cardigans, had created a snug resting-place for little Senta.

Suddenly there was a hesitant knock on our door. Father went to open it and Trudi stood there, carrying a tray laden with delicious food from the kitchen. As he took it from her, Trudi curtsied. This is with compliments from Frau Krause. Please accept her good wishes for a happy homecoming.'

'Thank you, Trudi,' my father replied, 'and please thank Frau Krause for her much appreciated kindness.'

It was a happy little family enjoying their first meal together in Pomerania. I couldn't take my eyes off my father. I wanted to get close to him, talk to him and have him listen to my problems. I knew they were only trivial, but it was important to me to have father hear about them. But I couldn't talk now; later, when we were all sitting together, I'd talk. And if it weren't possible that day, then it would have to be the next.

While we were having our meal, and mother fed Marlenchen, I noticed how desperately tired father was. He must have been hungry, yet exhaustion prevented him from enjoying his food. A thought occurred to me.

'Mother,' I said, 'I have a really good idea. When you've finished feeding baby, put her in her cot and she'll soon be asleep. Then you and father can lie down in your room and have a good long rest. Hans-Dieter will take puppy into the park, won't you Hans-Dieter? And I'll wash up and tidy this room. What do you think of that, mother?'

'Else, you're too kind. It's such a lovely idea. Don't you agree, Willy?'

But father was nearly asleep. He just smiled, patted my cheek and with a great effort got to his feet. 'Come, Lenchen, show me where to go. Else's right and sensible; she'll know what to do. You come with me: I've been without you for too long.'

Later, as we sat together in our living room, I had a most intense feeling of true happiness. Father looked rested and relaxed, and mother couldn't do enough to help him feel at home.

Hans-Dieter had returned from walking the puppy and couldn't wait to tell us how much fun it had been to romp with her in the snow.

Only two more days and grandma would be with us again. What bliss! This time she was breaking her journey from Königsberg to be at Marlene's christening.

Mother mentioned that she and father had decided to travel to Swinemünde to see Ralf on Monday, 1 March, and to return two days later. They also thought it best that, while father was on leave, I didn't lodge with the Schröter family but returned home each evening. When I questioned what Frau Schröter might have to say about it, father assured me he'd talk to her and explain the situation to avoid any unpleasantness.

Hans-Dieter was lying on his stomach trying to play with the puppy, who much preferred to sleep.

'Dieter,' father called out, 'come and sit by my side. Tell me about the boar hunt. I know nothing about it.'

Hans-Dieter had hoped father would ask him and, once he started his tale, there was no stopping him.

'What happened to the boar?' father asked.

'When we had the hunt just after Christmas, the boar was roasted here on the farm. We had a party and everyone from the village was invited.'

'And what happened last week?' father asked.

'Mother told me there was to be no celebration because of the terrible fighting in a place called Russia. That's where you are, father, aren't you?'

'Yes, Hans-Dieter, I am. Now tell me more about the boar.'

'We didn't have a party here. The boar – that's a wild pig. Did you know that, father?'

'Yes, Hans-Dieter. Go on.'

'Well, it was sent to another village, but I don't know which.'

'My, Hans-Dieter, what an adventure! Now tell me how you're getting on at school.'

When father had finished listening to all Hans-Dieter's news, it was my turn.

I'd been sitting in the corner by the window, trying to darn a hole in one of my thick winter socks. Mother had shown me how it was done, but I didn't like the job.

'Come, Elslein,' father encouraged. 'Come and sit here and talk to me. There's so much I want to know. Let's start with your long journey from Oberwiesenthal to Glowitz? What an adventure! You were very brave.'

It was so good sitting there, next to father, talking to him. He had abandoned his uniform and instead wore trousers and a warm pullover. He was smoking his pipe, as he listened to me; he looked content and completely relaxed.

'Tell me, Else, are you happy staying with the Schröter family?'

'Not really, father. The family's so different from us and I'm nervous of Herr Schröter. He wears a black uniform and is in the SS. I don't know what he does, but it must be something important. Many days he comes home late and often stays away overnight. Anyway it's only until Easter, and then I can travel to school with my friends again.'

'Stick it out, Elslein. Mother meant well and at least while I'm home you're with us every evening. Now show me your homework. I'd like to know how you're progressing at school.'

The day passed quickly. It was hard to believe father had arrived only that morning. It was as though he'd never been away: family routine returned instantly. Now we were together again, something I'd dreamed about and sorely missed.

We were all tired and mother suggested an early night for everyone.

'Tomorrow we have a busy day,' she reminded us. 'School for Hans-Dieter and you, Else. Father will have to introduce himself formally to Baron and Baroness von Puttkamer. He also intends to broach the subject of Puppy; I hope he'll obtain permission for us to keep her.'

Mother had arranged to meet Fraulein Dorothea and Mamsell in the dining room to discuss arrangements for baby's baptism. It would be performed by the local parish pastor, in Glowitz Manor on 26 February.

Trudi and Maria would prepare the dining room for the occasion. On a raised platform a table altar would be decorated with candles and greenery, and a bowl in the centre would represent the font. In front of the dais a half-circle of chairs were to be arranged for the Puttkamer family, grandmother and my parents; also for Hans-Dieter, me and a few invited guests. Members of the household staff would also be welcome to join in the celebration. Open doors to the music room would allow Miss Elisabeth to play suitable hymns for the occasion. The room plan, when complete, looked festive and mother was delighted with the result.

When she rose to return to our apartment, Fraulein Elisabeth stopped her. 'Frau Hopp, please wait a moment. I have something for you.' Folded over her arm she carried a most exquisite christening gown, together with a delicately knitted bonnet and baby jacket.

'Frau Hopp,' she said, 'will you accept this for the baptism of your little daughter? The gown's very old and has been in the Puttkamer family for many years. The last baby to use it was Sylvia. Everyone in this family would be delighted for little Marlene to wear it. That is, of course, unless you have your own gown.'

'No, Fraulein Elisabeth, I haven't. This is wonderful; I'd love to accept it. Our little girl will look like an angel. I'll thank the Puttkamers myself later, but for now a heartfelt thank you to you.'

24 February 1943

It was the day of my grandmother's expected arrival. Once again I was to meet her at Stolp station, and it was a joyful moment when the train arrived and I saw Grandma stepping onto the platform.

Many questions later I was satisfied to know she'd had a good journey, had enjoyed being with her sisters and was now eager to meet her son, my father, whom she hadn't seen for many months.

Once again Johann met us at the station in Glowitz. This time he'd come in a tiny sleigh, just big enough for the three of us.

The meeting between my father and his mother was very emotional. 'My son, my son, how blessed I feel to see you again! Your father and I have prayed for this moment. It's such a shame that he's too ill to be here today. May God take care of you as He's done so far.'

Hans-Dieter and mother, who stood there with Baby in her arms, also greeted her warmly. Grandma marvelled to see how much our little girl had grown in such a short time.

Then she made a fuss of our puppy, which was dancing around, wanting to be petted and loved.

'What have we here?' she asked. Where does this beautiful little dog come from?' And Hans-Dieter was the one to pass on the tale of Senta, the little dog that had travelled from Russia to be with us.

It was a contended family that evening, sitting around the dinner table. The conversation flowed and there was a lot of laughter, enjoyment and happiness because we were all together again – something we'd taken for granted in the past, but now in wartime we realised what a special blessing we had.

Grandma asked a lot of questions about father's involvement in the war. Where was he stationed? Was there much fighting? Did he think we were still winning the war overall?

My father was gentle with his answers. How could he possibly alarm his elderly mother? What good would it do? He tried to respond to Grandma's questions as best he could, but even I noticed a hesitation in his voice as he hunted for the right words.

Chapter 17

When will I see you again?

'Come along, Hans-Dieter; it's time you were in bed.'

'Do I have to, mother? I'm not tired.'

'You must be; you've had a busy day. Put your toys away – it's school tomorrow and that means up early.' While mother talked, she picked up pieces of Meccano to encourage Hans-Dieter to get a move on and stop dawdling.

'Is Else coming to bed as well?'

'No, Hans-Dieter, not yet. She's older than you and is allowed to stay up a while longer.'

Reluctantly my young brother went on his way to the bathroom, grumbling to himself because his sister who, after all was only a girl, had permission to stay up later.

'Mother, where's father?' he asked as he returned from the bathroom in his pyjamas.

'Downstairs with the Baron. He invited your father to share a drink with him. Don't worry, child, as soon as father returns I'll send him in to you. Have you cleaned your teeth? Then say good night to grandma and puppy, and quickly into bed.'

'Mother, I just remembered: who'll take Senta out tonight?'

'Father will do that. Don't worry, Hans-Dieter. Your puppy will be well looked after for the night.'

At last Hans-Dieter settled and baby was prepared for the night. Peace and quiet reigned in our living room – heavenly! Perhaps I could now have half an hour to write my diary. I'd finished my homework and my schoolbooks were ready for the next day. There was nothing else I had to do.

Mother and Grandma were having a quiet conversation. I couldn't quite hear what they were saying, but had a feeling they were talking about me. Then I heard the word 'confirmation' and knew exactly what they were discussing!

I confessed I was trying to listen. How I wished they'd speak a little louder. I only pretended to write studiously when all the while I was trying desperately to catch their words.

Grandma was getting agitated and raised her voice: 'I'm surprised, Lene, that you always let Else have her own way. She is, after all, still only a child and important decisions like this should be made by you and Willy. She'll be fourteen years old in September and it's right she should be confirmed by then.'

'I know what you're saying, mother, but Else doesn't want to be confirmed; not yet.'

'Tell me, Lene, why not? She must have a reason?'

I'd listened to their conversation long enough. Now it was my turn to have a say.

'Grandma, of course I have a reason. I'm sad to be hurting your feelings, but it's *my* wish not to be confirmed. Adolf Hitler's birthday's on 20 April. I want to renew my oath of loyalty to him and our country. I'll promise to live only for the good and greater glory of our nation. The ceremony's called *Fahnenweihe* (flag blessing) and the renewal of our oath of loyalty and obedience will take place beneath the banners in every district of Pomerania.'

'"Oath of loyalty?" Banners? *What* ceremony are we talking about? Who's brainwashing her?'

'She's a member of the Hitler Youth, mother. As difficult as it may be to understand, we must respect Else's feelings.'

'Lene, I've never heard anything so absurd. Does Else believe Hitler represents God?'

'Grandma,' I said, 'I don't think you understand. Of course I know Hitler's not God, but we honour him and want to show him how much his leadership means to us. I wish you could be with us. It'll be a wonderful day; many of my friends will take part. The ceremony takes place in the town hall in Stolp and important people will be present, including high-ranking officials from the government. And many banners will be lined up in the large reception hall. It will be a grand sight and a most wonderful celebration of our leader's birthday. If you could be there, Grandma, you'd understand what an awe-inspiring occasion it will be.'

'Well, child, I won't be there, but if it makes you happy, who am I to say that what you're doing's not right? But do tell me, Else, does this mean you don't wish to be confirmed in a church at all?'

'I don't know, Grandma. Perhaps as I get older, I may feel different, but I'm certain that now's not the right time. Sorry to upset you, but please understand: I must do what feels right for me.'

26 February 1943

'The day of our baby Marlene's baptism,' my diary says. 'The day we've looked forward to for such a long time!'

The ceremony was scheduled for 11 a.m. Everything was ready for the service; and when I sneaked downstairs to peep into the dining room, I was awe-struck at how beautifully it had been arranged.

The Puttkamer family had done their utmost to make that day a memorable occasion for my parents and little sister. Sadly mother's sister, Katie, and brother, Richard, who lived in Düsseldorf, were unable to join us. Uncle Richard was a captain on a minesweeper and away at sea somewhere in the Atlantic. Aunt Katie was to have been one of the godmothers and Fraulein Ottilia had agreed to stand in for her. I was very fond of my Aunt Katie, whom I hadn't seen for some time, and was most disappointed she couldn't be with us on such a special day. But such was wartime – families were scattered far apart.

'The Grandparents are safe in Düsseldorf, aren't they?' I had to ask.

'I hope so, child, but who can tell? At present, no one's really safe – least of all in a big city like Düsseldorf.'

My parents had invited Herr and Frau Schröter and Anneliese to be our guests, and they were 'delighted to accept the invitation'. Gisela's parents, Herr and Frau Krämer, also had an invitation to join us, but unfortunately couldn't spare the time, as Friday was always a hectic day for them in their shop and post office. Gisela, however, was allowed to come and it was lovely for us girls to enjoy each other's company. Frau Ruch and her small daughter, Inge, accepted my parent's invitation to join us. That pleased Hans-Dieter, as Inge would keep him company – even if she was 'only a girl', it was better than being on his own. Today he'd planned something special: he wanted to show her some baby lambs, which had been born just a few days before.

Grandma was looking forward to being second godmother, and father, as the only male in our family, had reluctantly agreed to be godfather. 'You do realise you're taking an enormous risk choosing me, Lenchen?' father reminded her. 'You're taking a gamble; let's hope it comes off.'

'I know, Willy, but you're a gamble I'm more than willing to take. We'll all survive; you wait and see. And our daughter will have us to guide her on her path of life, throughout the years ahead.'

When mother put the exquisite Puttkamer family christening gown on baby Marlene, I thought she looked like a little angel – and she behaved like one throughout the ceremony. As grandma carried the fair-haired baby in the procession to the dais, followed by the other godparents, the child's bright blue eyes twinkled, reflecting the lights of the crystal chandeliers. She laughed and gurgled at everyone around her.

The transformed dining table, moved into the centre of the dais, made a simple but effective altar. A snow-white tablecloth displayed two silver double candlesticks – each one carrying white candles. Two crystal basins with winter-greenery were a perfect addition, and just to the side was a large silver bowl that, when filled with warm water, was ready to serve as the christening font. The scene looked magnificent.

Our village pastor blessed the water and conducted the service. He spoke of the life that, with God's guidance, lay before our little girl. He reminded the godparents that Christian duties and responsibilities rested on their shoulders and asked them always to carry out their obligation to the best of their abilities. He told his small but attentive congregation that for little Marlene the future was in God's hands but, like a new book, still an undiscovered secret.

Finally he drew attention to the uncertain future that lay before us. There was a murmur of agreement. He asked for God's helping hand, not only for our baby but for all of us, during these turbulent and violent times. At the beginning of the service we sang the German version of 'The Lord is my shepherd' and, to conclude the ceremony, gave a rousing rendition of that beautiful and well-known German hymn 'Now thank we all our God'.

After the service, Frau Krause and her kitchen staff organised an impressive, tempting cold buffet. She knew how to whet the appetite of every guest present and we were invited to tuck in.

Hans-Dieter and Inge, who'd both behaved well during the ceremony, escaped immediately afterwards. They soon came back from the stables where they'd been to inspect the newborn lambs. 'Else, you should have seen them! They're lovely, so soft and cuddly. I wish I could keep one, but Uncle Kurt said, "Better not; Puppy might be jealous!"'

After we'd eaten, Gisela, Anneliese, Inge and I went with Hans-Dieter to look at those little lambs, gambolling around or feeding from their mothers. About half a dozen of the tiny creatures, only a few days old, were frolicking in the straw. They were delightful! We were tempted to pick them up but were told not to, because if we touched them their mother might reject them. I wanted to tell mother, but she was too occupied with her guests to listen.

Father was standing by the window talking to Herr Schröter, who today was out of uniform. Civilian clothes made him appear more approachable.

Grandma was deep in conversation with Frau Ruch. Those two had become instant friends. They appeared to have much in common and to be completely at ease in each other's company.

Mother waved to me from the corner of the room. 'Else,' she said, 'would you take baby upstairs and giver her a feed? She's so quiet, yet she must be hungry.'

So I took my little sister upstairs, gave a sigh of relief and was delighted to be away from the hustle in the dining room.

It has always been a tradition in my family that every time a new baby's christened, a small white satin purse is attached to the christening robe. Godparents and guests, who wish to, put a gift of money into the little bag and later a bank account's opened. The christening money makes a sizeable start and gifts are always added to it.

When I'd taken baby upstairs and had removed her christening clothes and moneybag, I could feel it was stuffed full and quite heavy.

'My, you're a lucky little girl,' I said. 'So many people gave you money. You'll be rich – richer than I'll ever be.'

Baby smiled at me with her angelic smile and her little hand touched my nose.

'Now, my friend, my little girl, you must be fed. You have a delicious dinner – mashed potatoes and carrots with a blob of butter – followed by a scrumptious drink of warm milk. Then, after an extra big cuddle, it will be time for you to have a nice long sleep because you're very tired. You, my little one, have had a busy day.

Just after 4 p.m. mother and Hans-Dieter came upstairs. I asked her whether all the guests had gone and she replied that everyone had left by 3 p.m. Mother and Frau Ruch had stayed to help Trudi and Maria clear and tidy the dining room.

'Now I'm here, Else, I can see how well you've managed to look after your little sister. Thank you, my child.'

'It wasn't difficult, mother. You know I always enjoy it.'

'Did you remember to say goodbye to your friends?' mother asked.

'No, I didn't. I picked up Marlenchen and came up. It didn't occur to me.'

'Else, how could you? What must the girls think of you? Where were they?'

'As I left, Gisela and Anneliese were sitting on the bow window seat, whispering together, watching everyone around them. Anneliese appeared most impressed with the grandeur of the room and the splendid building. Gisela has been here before but it was quite new for Anneliese.'

'It wasn't courteous to leave without saying goodbye. But it's done now, Else: you just have to apologise when you see them next.'

Suddenly I remembered I'd also left without speaking to Frau Ruch and Inge. She too must have thought I lacked good manners. I would have to make another apology there as well; I couldn't have mother apologising for me.

'Where's grandma, mother? Is she still downstairs, or has she gone to her room?'

'She and your father will come upstairs together. I don't know where they are, but father will look after her. The last I saw, he was talking to the Baron. It's a blessing that Herr Schröter didn't wear his uniform. That wouldn't have gone down well – I know how the Baron feels about the SS. He's a man of the old tradition and can't come to terms with the way things are changing in our country.'

When at last my father came upstairs, he was solemn and unsmiling. Not until later, with Hans-Dieter in bed, did I find out why.

Father was angry. He was pacing the floor, trying to keep his temper under control. Then he exploded! 'That man Schröter is an impossible bigot! And to think, Else, you live in his house. His mind's corrupt and he talks poison: his political beliefs are totally warped! There he stood with me by the window, going on and on about our glorious leader and how great our empire will be when we emerge victorious from this war.' Father threw up his hands. 'Of course, first of all – so he says – we must rid ourselves of the vermin that lurk and hide in corners. He was talking about the Jews. "There are still far too many of them. But never fear," says Schröter, we'll get them, every one of them, and wipe them out once and for all."'

'Hush, Willy, not so loud!' mother put her hand in front of his mouth. 'You know what they say – walls have ears. We're warned everywhere we go.'

'Yes, I know, Lene, but to think our daughter has to live with people like that sickens me. I can't bear the thought of two young people being brainwashed. And I include Anneliese in this assumption.'

'But, father, I hardly ever talk to Herr Schröter. Most of the time he's not at home.'

'That's just as well, child. I'll travel to Stolp before I return to the front. I'll see Schröter and inform him that from the end of March you'll be able to live at home again.'

Saturday, 25 February 1943

Next morning, at the breakfast table, Father addressed Hans-Dieter and me.

'Listen, children, your mother and I have decided to visit your little brother in Swinemünde next Wednesday, which is the first day of March. I know that's also the day Grandma wishes to return to Düsseldorf. If Frau Ruch will care for you, Hans-Dieter, and Fraulein Dorothea agrees to look after our baby, we can leave together Monday morning.'

'What about me, father?'

'You, Else, will go to school and on to Schröter's. Grandma, mother and I will travel together to Stettin, where Grandma changes trains to Berlin and on to Düsseldorf. We'll carry on to Swinemünde.' Turning to Grandma, he said, 'Of course, mother, if you like you can stay here till we come back. That's up to you.'

'When will you return, Willy?'

'Lene and I will return on the third of March and, sadly, on the fifth my short leave will be at an end. I must get back to the front and my battalion.'

'Willy, in that case I might as well stay until you and Lene return. I can look after Baby, and Hans-Dieter doesn't have to stay with Frau Ruch. At least, when you come back, I'll have one more day with you. Who knows when we'll meet again?'

'Father, I'll also have just one day left with you. When will I see you again? Will you be able to get any more leave?' Father shrugged. 'Please, Vati, take care. Don't let them hurt you. We all need you and I can't bear the thought that something might happen to you.' I left my chair, fighting to hold back the tears that threatened to spill out of my eyes. All I could do was put my arms around his neck and whisper in his ear, 'Vati, we love you. Please come back to us.'

Chapter 18

Clever Dr Goebbels

Friday, 5 March 1943

That morning my beloved father had to return to the front in Russia.

In the evening I'd write in my diary everything that had recently happened, because I thought I was leaving childhood behind. I was sitting in bed, alone with my thoughts, and Hans-Dieter was already sound asleep. That boy always had such busy days; father's not being there any more would be reality for him only when he awoke the next morning. Mother retired early that evening – I knew she was very unhappy. How I wished I were older, and then perhaps she'd confide in me. But to her I was still a child and she felt she had to keep her sadness to herself.

The previous night my parents had had a long talk. I'd wanted to go to bed to leave them undisturbed, but father would have none of it. 'Else, come and sit with us. You're almost an adult and your experience of life has made you grow way beyond your years. Mother wants to ask me some questions, which I'll try to answer as best I can. Just remember, child, what we talk about in this room's for our ears only. Do you understand that, Else?'

'Yes, father, you can trust me. I won't let you down.'

Mother wanted to know where father was stationed. He told her that when he'd left, his battalion had been in bitter combat with the Russian army near the town of Kharkov, Russia's fourth largest city, a great industrial area about 400 kilometres east of Kiev.

'Every day the battlefront changes,' father added. 'Sometimes we gain perhaps half a kilometre and then, during the next battle, the Russians take it back again. But what's really against us is the ferocious Russian winter. Temperatures of minus forty and more are endured daily and, to top it all, we lack manpower and equipment, of which Russia has an endless supply.'

'But, Willy, surely the government must realise our soldiers can't function unless they're adequately equipped?'

'Yes, Lene, you'll find this difficult to understand. The government promises to send reinforcements, and we wait and wait, but nothing happens. Empty promises, just to keep up morale. Slowly we begin to realise we're being hoodwinked, but the German soldier's such that he shrugs his shoulders and carries on with what he's got – sad but true.' Father blew his nose. 'Not only do we put up with incredible cold, but freezing snow and icy winds cause terrible frostbite. I can only predict that, under these conditions, we cannot possibly win. If we can recapture Kharkov it will be a real victory. I only hope that re-enforcements arrive soon. Perhaps they have by now, but if not, I don't know what will happen.'

'But what comes after Kharkov, Willy? Will you be moved again to other battles?'

'I don't know, Lene. First I must return to my infantry battalion, and what happens after is very much an open question.'

I really should have tried harder to sleep, as it was well past midnight. But so many thoughts were going around in my head and keeping me awake. Was my beloved country really letting her soldiers down? That was the first time I'd heard anyone question the situation. Normally I wouldn't have believed them, but coming from father?'

That day Grandma also returned to Düsseldorf. Dear Grandma and Grandad. Were they safe? Daily on the wireless we heard of heavy bombing raids. How could people do such things to each other? The large cities in the west of Germany were frequent targets, particularly in the industrial area of the Ruhr. But the daily newspapers scarcely mentioned what was really going on in the air, at sea or on the battlefields of Europe and other parts of the world.

Mother and I listened together to the news on the wireless. She seemed to have her doubts too. 'Our propaganda minister, Dr Goebbels, is very clever, Else. He talks only of German victories, but is he telling the truth or does he only want to boost morale in the German nation? There are rumours everywhere and wherever people meet there's whispering: "Have you heard . . .? Can it be true . . .? How will it end?"'

I also thought of my little brother in Swinemünde. My parents were pleased with his progress and, if he continued to improve, Matron would bring Ralfie to visit us. But first the weather had to be warmer, without snow. Mother couldn't wait to have her little boy home, if only for a short time. She feared he'd grow away from us and perhaps wouldn't know us any more. But I didn't think that would happen: he couldn't get our love from anyone or anywhere else.

Sunday, 7 March 1943

What should I do that Sunday? I'd decided to visit Gisela later, and together we'd make up our minds how to spend the day.

But after breakfast I first had to take Senta for her walk. She'd been so good throughout the night, but once I said the magic word 'walkies', she'd be up, out of her basket and dancing around me, knocking me over in her exuberance. If I took her that morning, Hans-Dieter could go out with her in the afternoon.

I wondered where Father was now. He had such a long way to travel; it surely had to take many hours – days even – before he reached Russia and his batallion. I missed him very much and couldn't understand why there was a war to separate us. There had to be other ways.

It snowed again during the night and I heard the wind battering the windows. It made me shudder, but I was warm in bed – what a heavenly feeling.

I tiptoed to the window and watched the sun rising over the frozen lake and the ice sparkling like diamonds. The sun's rays cut through the clouds and opened up a clear blue sky. In the distance one small bird tried to greet the morning with a tentative song. Another perfect day!

March was a strange month. Winter didn't want to back off and struggled with spring for supremacy, but gradually lost the contest. Days were lengthening, as yet only by a few minutes, but there was a little warmth in the weak sunshine. People looked more cheerful and greeted us with a smile. Everyone was tired of winter, and farmers especially waited impatiently for the snow to disappear. Fields needed to be tended for the summer crops, and the animals were eager to emerge from their winter quarters. They too wanted to be free again.

Spring began officially on 21 March, and from then on, slowly at first, but faster and faster, winter had to give way to spring. Would our war do likewise, and give way to peace? And if so, which side would surrender?

I promised myself I'd be patient and stay with the Schröters until the Easter holiday. But Easter dragged its heels in 1943, falling at the end of April. I could only resign myself and make the best of a bad situation.

It must have been very late when, at last, I went to sleep. I dreamt I was standing on a stage surrounded by my many friends. We were rehearsing a play but couldn't agree who should be the main character. There was a lot of shouting and arguing, and the noise in my dream woke me up. The image was so vivid that it unnerved me and it took me a while to wake up to reality. What could it mean?

Chapter 19

Café Reinhardt

15 March 1943

We heard on the wireless that, after fierce and bloody fighting, Kharkov was back in German hands. A few days later mother received a field postcard from my father telling her that his regiment would very likely be moved to another location.

One Friday afternoon towards the end of March 1943, as I was waiting on the Stolp station platform for my train to take me home, I met Fraulein Ottilia. I hadn't seen her since the day of the christening, but knew her horses and estate affairs always kept her fully occupied.

'Good afternoon, Else,' she greeted me. 'It's a pleasure to meet you. Now we can travel together and keep each other company. Tell me, are you still interested in learning to ride? It's quite a while since we last talked about it, but I've not forgotten – have you, Else?'

'No, Fraulein Ottilia, I'm looking forward to it; a lovely idea, although at present I have mixed feelings about it,' I admitted. I wasn't at all enthusiastic at the prospect of learning to ride. Never having sat on a horse, the animal frightened me. They were big and powerful, and it would take a lot of courage for me to get up on one of them.

Fraulein Otti (she'd told me to call her that, to make our relationship less formal) laughed at my fear. 'Come on, Else, you're made of sterner stuff. You wait and see – there's nothing difficult in getting on a horse. Once you're up there and get the feel of it, I'm certain you'll love it. Come to the stable tomorrow morning. Together we'll look at the horses and, when you see how gentle they are, you'll soon lose your anxiety.'

'I hope so,' I answered. 'I'd hate to disappoint you.'

'I have a horse I think you'll like, Else,' Fraulein Otti continued. 'Her name's Bella. She's not too large and she's not frisky. No, when I think about it, she'll be just right for you.'

All decisions seemed to have been taken away from me. Was I ungrateful? Should I look forward to riding with pleasure? Mother seemed to think riding would be good for me. Would it? I didn't know – I'd just have to wait and see. 'But, Fraulien Ottilia, I have no suitable clothes to wear and, most importantly, I have no riding hat.'

'That can soon be remedied, Else. Look in the downstairs cloakroom; there you'll find all the clothes you need. Most of them belong to Sylvia and she must be more or less the same size as you. She won't mind you using her gear. Go on; see if you can find something to suit you tomorrow morning.'

127

'Thank you, Fraulien Otti. You've been very helpful. I'll meet you at the stables in the morning.'

And the next day, when she met me in the stables and introduced me to Bella, all my fears were gone, and I fell in love with the horse. Who would have thought that could ever have happened to me? But it was true – I was actually looking *forward* to learning how to ride.

It wasn't difficult. Fraulein Otti said I was a natural and I did feel comfortable sitting on a horse. But riding wasn't the only thing: there was far more to learn, such as cleaning out the stable once a week and grooming Bella whenever I had time. Uncle Kurt Lemke, our kind estate manager, often helped me. 'That's a little secret between us, Else. I know how busy you are. Say no more about it; just come whenever you have time.'

As March ended, in a final act of defiance, winter again asserted itself, for during the night a lot of snow fell.

Spring, after all her waiting, burst forth with beautiful colours, blue skies, warm sunshine and longer days. Brightness was everywhere, and the drabness of winter was fading fast. Who would have believed there was a war on?

April arrived at last, a month that promised a variety of important events – a pleasant change from the long and dreary days of winter.

For me there were many exciting dates to think of. Easter, although significant in the religious calendar, wasn't until the last weekend of the month. Before that, on 20 April, was Adolf Hitler's birthday, and as always every German town and village commemorated it with rallies, parades and many celebrations. Everywhere flags flew from houses and public buildings. All over Germany the Swastika fluttered in the wind in honour of our beloved Führer who would lead his country, in the face of all adversaries, to a triumphant final victory.

There was to be a grand celebration in the Stolp town hall. The *Fahnenweihe* ceremony was scheduled for Sunday, 18 April, and many high-ranking officers and government officials were to attend. The words of our oath of loyalty and obedience, which the Hitler Youth and Girls had to chant in unison, had to be relearned – there was no room for mistakes.

We also had to remember the words of the Horst Wessel song of the storm troopers, always sung at the end of the German anthem. And we had to know every part of Adolf Hitler's life story, from his childhood in Austria to his fighting in France during the First World War, and his gradual rise to power in the late twenties and early thirties.

Mother had promised me a new uniform, and we went to Stolp to order it. As soon as it was ready, I was to collect it to wear for the following Sunday's rally.

18 April 1943

The *Fahnenweihe* was a splendid event. Hitler Youth carried banners from all districts of Pomerania into the grand hall and lined up on either side along the walls, an impressive sight, and I felt proud and privileged to be part of such a great occasion.

All the time I was waiting for my name to be called I had a huge lump in my throat. I was a happy girl that day, but most of all felt incredibly honoured to be a *German* girl.

Father would have loved that occasion and would have been proud of me. I missed him terribly. *Tonight*, I thought, *when all this is over, I'll write and tell him about our wonderful day.*

But mother was there with Hans-Dieter by her side. I could see her talking to Gisela's mother and wondered what they were discussing: most probably how well everything had been organised.

We Hitler Boys and Girls had to stand to attention, waiting for our names to be called. When it was my turn, I stepped forward, raised my right arm in a salute and, before receiving my certificate, renewed loud and clear our oath of allegiance.

Herr and Frau Schröter and Anneliese were also present. Herr Schröter, a high-ranking SS officer, looked splendid and immaculate in his impressive black dress uniform. Not long ago it had scared me to see him in it, but now I was used to it and I admitted to myself that it really was incredibly smart. Anneliese had to wait another year before she could take part in the *Fahnenweihe*. She was already talking about it and the big party her parents were planning in her honour.

Earlier I'd felt rather let down that we weren't going to have a party. But mother explained, 'Please, Else, try to understand our position. Our friends and relations are in Düsseldorf. We, here in Pomerania, are only visitors.'

'Yes, mother,' I answered. 'It really doesn't matter.' I pretended I didn't care, but I was disappointed.

'Don't be sad, Else. Frau Krämer and I have talked about this. We've decided to treat you and Gisela to an afternoon in Café Reinhardt.'

'Oh how lovely, mother! Yes, that will be wonderful, don't you agree, Gisela?'

'What about me?' piped up Hans-Dieter. 'Can I come too?'

'Of course you can, Hans-Dieter. After all, you're one of us.'

As usual, Café Reinhardt was crowded with elegant people dressed in their Sunday finery, enjoying their usual Sunday afternoon treat of coffee and mouth-watering cake. A delicious variety of cakes of every description were on display in a glass cabinet. Such a wide selection made it extremely difficult for Gisela and me to make our choices.

The hum of subdued conversation blended in with the elegance of the café, and Gisela and I loved it! Although we weren't allowed coffee, we three young people each enjoyed a steaming mug of delicious chocolate.

My diary entry for that night reads -

> Today has been an extraordinary day. I feel honoured to have been part of it and knew that it's an occasion that will stay in my mind for the rest of my life.
>
> I'm wrapped in a feeling of happiness on this special day. To me, Adolf Hitler's an icon, to be admired, loved and revered . . .

When I wrote those words I didn't realise that within a few short months my illusions would be shattered – my happy, trusting, innocent world would be lost for ever.

Chapter 20

A Carved Heart

April smiled on us in 1943. We'd been deprived of warm sunshine for many months and now waited impatiently for longer days. As the spring sun thawed the earth, the last remnants of snow vanished. Bushes and trees dripped with melting ice and, here and there, where the snow had melted, the first snowdrops gingerly showed their heads.

21 April 1943

The beginning of our school holidays! That was the day I said my final farewell to the Schröter family. Thinking over the time I'd spent with them, I admitted it hadn't been so dreadful after all. Once we'd got used to each other Anneliese and I had managed to live side by side in harmony and even friendship.

'I'll miss you, Else,' she said the evening before I left. 'The house will be empty without you: I'll be on my own every day, feeling lonely.'

I tried to cheer her. 'Don't be sad, Liesel. We'll meet at school. We can still remain friends and I'll ask mother if you can visit us. It's an easy journey: I can meet you at the station in Glowitz. I expect your parents will allow you to come.'

'Else, that will be wonderful. Please don't forget to ask.'

On the last morning, my bag stood packed and ready in my room and, as soon as the school bell rang, I rushed to say goodbye to Liesel's mother. Her father wasn't at home but I left a message to thank him for his hospitality. Then, having done my duty, I collected my case and made my way to the station.

As my train neared Glowitz, excited anticipation welled up within me, for I knew I'd soon see Egon again. Since he'd returned to Berlin after Christmas, I'd received only one letter from him, a friendly note reminding me not to forget our date at Easter. As if I would! His mother, Frau Ruch, had of course heard from him more frequently. Each time I met her she told me Egon had written and sent me his regards.

'He always asks after you, Else, and says how he looks forward to seeing you again.'

Now he was due home, could he be there already? That would be fantastic! Would he have changed while he was away? I hoped not. Taller, perhaps. More handsome? He was a kind person and I wanted him to stay that way. I knew how strict the training was in Berlin. There were only three Adolf Hitler schools in Germany, and young men fortunate enough to be accepted and trained there had to endure harsh discipline in order to succeed. Life for Egon was certainly not easy.

When I arrived home and walked through the yard towards the back entrance, I was greeted by a delicious aroma of baking from the kitchen. Frau Krause and her staff were busy preparing for Easter. They were making cakes and biscuits, soft white rolls and spicy loaves. Almost every pan in the kitchen was in use on the stove.

Frau Krause had hard boiled lots of eggs, and Dunja stood near the window colouring them: red, blue, green, orange and purple. When all the eggs were done, she arranged them in a large round basket on a bed of hay. To complete the nest, Dunja took a fluffy toy chicken and placed it on top of the eggs.

It was easy to obtain Easter egg colouring in the village hardware store. It came as many-shaded powder in small packets. Mother also bought some for us, and Hans-Dieter and I loved to paint the eggs with our own patterns.

'Do you realise,' mother declared, 'how lucky we are to have lovely fresh eggs from the farm? We all appreciate them, don't you agree?'

Dieter and I nodded, and then mother sent me down to the kitchen to collect the eggs she'd ordered from Mamsell. They were in a basket waiting for me.

'There are two dozen here, Else,' Frau Krause told me. 'Now *do* be careful: *walk* upstairs in case you trip. The eggs would make a dreadful mess and you'd celebrate Easter without any, as all I have are in that basket!'

'I'll be careful, Frau Krause.' I put the basket over my arm. 'Mother's waiting to cook them so Hans-Dieter and I can decorate them tomorrow. We do that every year; it's great fun. If only Ralf could be with us, he'd love painting eggs, and himself as well!'

'By the way, Else, have you heard of our Easter morning custom for girls like you?'

'No, Frau Krause. What is it?'

'Well, Else, talk to your friend Gisela. She can explain it to you.'

I thought Frau Krause was making fun of me, as the kitchen staff were smiling. But, sure enough, when I asked Gisela, she had the answer.

'There's an ancient custom in Pomerania that on Easter Sunday morning, young unmarried girls must take a pitcher and before sunrise, walk in silence to the forest. There, they hope to find a spring of water coming from the east to fill their pitcher and wash their face in the clear cold water just as the sun's rising. The girls then bow to the sun and make a secret wish, after which they take the jugful of water, and pour it over their heads.'

I laughed! 'Gisela, that sounds silly. What for?'

'They want to be beautiful,' Gisela answered. 'The clear spring water will make them so. But it can only be on Easter Sunday morning before sunrise; any other time and it doesn't work. Will you join me, Else?'

'Of course, Gisela, I'd love to be beautiful. You tell me what time and where to meet and I'll be there.'

We had to wait until Easter Sunday, but that would soon be here; meanwhile there were plenty of things to do.

Thursday before Good Friday, 22 April 1943

There was a knock on our living room door.

'Go and see who it is, Else.' Mother was baking, her hands covered in flour. 'It may be Johann with a message from Mamsell.'

I ran to the door and who should be there but Egon! I must have blushed crimson, for I could feel the heat burning my cheeks. For a moment I didn't know what to say.

'Else, where are your manners?' mother called out. 'Come in, Egon. It's so nice to see you again. You've been away a long time. Are you well? I must say you're taller every time I see you. Your mother and Ingrid must be pleased to have you home, and I know Else has been looking forward to your homecoming.'

We talked awhile and then Egon suggested perhaps I'd like to take a short walk with him. 'Do you mind, Frau Hopp? I won't keep Else long – unless you need her to help you?'

'Go on, you two; I can manage. Just don't stay too long, Else – I may need your help later.'

Why was I so shy with Egon? It wasn't like me! Normally I could talk and be easy with anyone. But with Egon I was lost for words. Thank goodness he had plenty to say – his school, life in Berlin . . . Gradually on that walk I felt my shyness disappearing: it was brilliant! We arranged to meet again and take longer walks through the country lanes. I couldn't wait.

One thing, however, I found strange. Egon didn't want to talk about his Berlin course. I had the impression it was another world there, yet I didn't like to ask. Perhaps he'd open up later. Would he tell me if something was troubling him? I loved his company and, I might have been wrong, but I thought he liked mine too!

Easter Day, 25 April 1943

Gisela and I went to the forest to wash our faces in the spring coming from the east.

The previous evening I'd made the necessary preparations before bed, and mother woke me in silence when it was still dark. She handed me a jug and off I went. Dawn was just breaking as I met Gisela and, together, without speaking, we went into the forest. She knew the way to the spring and we waited there in silence for the sun to rise. As the first rays appeared over the horizon, we filled our pitchers and waited again. Then, as the sun came up, I washed my face in the fresh cold water, bowed to the east and made my special request. I couldn't say what it was – to be beautiful, or to find a rich and handsome husband . . . like Egon. Whatever I wished for, I wasn't sure it would come true, but then again it didn't matter: I'd have other wonderful things happen to me instead.

After my wish, I took the jugful of cold water and poured all of it over my head. Gisela laughed at me and I laughed at her. Now we were able to talk and, dripping wet, made our way home.

Easter Monday, 26 April 1943

Perhaps my wish had come true?

In the afternoon Egon called for me, and together we walked through country lanes into the silent forest. It was still very cold but we were well wrapped up. Already the sun gave out a pleasant warmth as it tried to melt away the last remnants of snow. It was a joy to be out of doors. In the forest the snow still lay deep with a crisp top crust where the sun couldn't reach it, but in places where rays peeped through the trees the snow had melted. It left dark moist patches where soon the first spring flowers would create a colourful world of their own. It was, as yet, too early in springtime to find many flowers, but we found a sprinkling of snowdrops and winter aconites. Just another week or two and tiny lilac crocuses would peep out of the dark, moist soil.

All around us the forest was in stillness, as if the world were asleep. No bird sang and no wild animal disturbed the peace; all we could hear was the occasional rustle of a tiny creature scurrying on nimble feet through the undergrowth.

I felt transported into an enchanted world, and perhaps Egon felt the same. There was no need to talk – we were as one, totally captivated with the serenity of our surroundings.

Then Egon broke the spell.

'Else, can you wait a moment? I'd like to do something that will remind us of our day together in the wood.'

'What, Egon?'

'Wait and see. I won't take long.'

I saw him take a penknife out of his pocket, go to a large tree and start carving the trunk. I was curious, but Egon made me wait.

'I'll be finished soon, Else; then you can see.'

I sat on a thick branch of a fallen tree, swung my legs and waited.

'Egon, what are you doing? I'm getting cold. Please hurry!'

'Come here, Else. I'm finished now. See what I've done.'

I went over to the tree and looked. With nimble fingers, Egon had carved a heart into the treetrunk with his and my initials ER and EH in the centre.

'What do you think of it, Else? It will always be here and when I'm away again, come into the forest, look at it and think of me. Yes?'

'Of course I will, Egon; it's perfect! But I may wait till you return and we'll come together.'

Slowly we made our way home.

'Come in, Egon. Mother will have a hot drink to warm you before you go home.'

We'd had an enjoyable walk together and I hoped it was only the first of many. It was the beginning of a wonderful friendship and I wanted it to last for ever. But what would the future hold?

The next day the postman resumed delivery of the mail. Mother had seen him coming on his bicycle and was eager to find out if perhaps he had a letter for her. We hadn't heard from my grandparents for some time and I knew mother was concerned about their well-being.

'Postman, do you have a letter for me?' she called down, standing on the top landing.

'Yes, Frau Hopp, I do. I'll leave it here in the hall on the small table.

I was in our living room, giving my little sister breakfast, and at the same time keeping an eye on Hans-Dieter. I heard mother racing upstairs. Completely breathless, she burst into the room waving a letter at me.

'Else, you won't believe this. I have a letter from your father posted in Germany. Let me see . . . posted in Stettin. Unbelievable! I must see what it's all about!'

'Mother, calm down. You'll be ill if you go on like that.'

'You're right, child; please carry on seeing to Baby and I'll read this letter in my room. Later I'll tell you and Hans-Dieter what father has to say.'

Mother stayed a long while in her room. I was getting anxious yet knew she'd come out and talk to us when she was ready. We waited, and Hans-Dieter bombarded me with questions, which I didn't know how to answer. All I could say was, 'Wait, Hans-Dieter, till mother comes out. Then you can ask her all you want to know.'

After quite some time mother joined us in the living room. She was calmer now and more her usual self. Father's letter was open in her hand and I knew she'd talk to me later. But first she had to appease Hans-Dieter. He wanted the answer to many questions, but mother knew just how much she could tell him to satisfy his curiosity.

'Come and sit by my side, Hans-Dieter, and I'll tell you what father says in his letter. Then you can go out to play. I'll talk to Else, later.' She winked at me. That meant she'd share father's real news when Hans-Dieter was out of the way. I smiled: a secret adult language between us.

'Mother, does father mention me?' inquired my young brother.

'Yes, of course he does, Hans-Dieter. He speaks of every one of us and sends his special love to you. He wants you to work hard at school and help me as much as you can, and to remember you're the man in the house while he's away.'

'Mother, do you think father will get leave again soon?'

'Child, I don't know. He talks about fighting in many big battles, and while that's going on no one will be granted leave to come home.'

'Are the German soldiers winning?'

'Well, sometimes the German army wins; at other times, a battle's lost. The fighting goes on and on, and many soldiers on both sides are wounded or killed.'

'Mother, where's father? Can you tell me that?'

'No, son, I can't tell you where he is at present. I don't know myself.'

'What else does he say, mother?'

'He mentions that the snow's slowly melting, leaving behind dreadful muddy conditions. Lorries and wagons get stuck and sink deeper and deeper. Many poor horses pulling the wagons lie down and die.They're too exhausted and weak to carry on.'

'That's very cruel, mother. Those poor, poor animals!'

'But your father's well, Hans-Dieter. I think you'd make him very happy if you wrote him a nice loving letter. Will you do that?'

'Of course I will,' Hans-Dieter replied with a grin. 'But, mother – can I go out and play now?'

'Yes you can, Hans-Dieter. Don't forget, though,the puppy needs to go out. Take her and give her a run in the park. Then bring her back and you'll be free to go and play with your friends.'

After Hans-Dieter had left us, mother gave a sigh of relief. 'At last,Else. I thought that boy would never stop asking questions; he can be so exhausting. But then, of course, he's at an age when he wants to know everything. You and I can now have a few peaceful minutes, which will give me a chance to tell you a little more from father's letter.' As I sat beside her, she continued: 'He says he's in Smolensk, a town situated in central Russia that's still in German hands, but no one knows how much longer the German army can hold out. The battles fought there are ferocious and daily there are more and more casualties. But, as I said earlier, your father's well. Please God, let it remain so.'

What else does he say, mother?'

'Well, child, there really isn't much I can tell you, but reading between the lines, conditions must be bad; food and ammunition in desperately short supply and morale among the soldiers low. They sit in the trenches, waiting for a new battle to begin. I now ask myself, how can we possibly win a war when the conditions they put up with are so utterly abominable?'

'Oh, mother, those poor men! It sounds dreadful. I'll sit down this evening to write father a letter; then he'll get one from all of us.

'Else, you know father has never doubted the outcome of this war. He was convinced Germany would win, but now he has a strong feeling it's not going to happen.'

'Really? That's frightening, mother. My thoughts are always with father and I worry a lot.'

'So do I, child, but there's nothing either of us can do.' Mother got up and stretched. 'Now, dear girl, I must go down to the kitchen. Frau Krause has kindly invited me to take morning coffee with her. I can't keep her waiting: her time's precious and it's already 11 a.m. I'll not be long. Please look out for Marlenchen, and should she cry please see to her. I know I can rely on you. I can always rely on you – and that may be important some day.'

Chapter 21

Coalminer's Daughters

I was sitting by the window in our living room, darning a pair of Hans-Dieter's socks.

Silence surrounded me – mother was still downstairs in the kitchen talking to Mamsell, baby Marlene was peacefully sleeping in her cradle and Hans-Dieter was out playing with his friends. Johann had just brought a basket of turf and had disturbed Senta, curled up by the fire. He came a little later that day and didn't appear his usual cheerful self. When I asked him why he was so subdued, he smiled and assured me everything was fine. But he left almost immediately and again I was alone in the stillness of my room.

I wanted to be on my own with my thoughts. Father's letter had worried me.There were so many questions going around my head, but no one could answer them – not even mother, and she knew most things.

I couldn't ever remember father complaining. He was always so confident of our imminent victory, but now? He talked of food shortages and the lack of ammunition and equipment, of Hitler's promise of reinforcements, which, up to the time he'd written his letter, still hadn't materialised. He also mentioned low morale among the soldiers. For me that was difficult to believe. Could there ever have come a time when our soldiers would lay down their weapons and refuse to obey orders? No, I couldn't even entertain the possibility – our German soldiers were too honourable to contemplate such an action and would fight on, whatever the consequences.

What was happening to Germany? Everything had been going so well, but now suddenly the war was turning against us. That evening, when I wrote to father, I had to remind him of the great things Adolf Hitler had accomplished for his German nation since he'd come to power in 1933. I was a Hitler Girl and still believed he intended to keep the promises he'd made to the German people.

It had been his birthday just a few days before, and the newspapers couldn't praise him enough. Would they do so if they didn't believe in him? I doubted it!

Suddenly I heard mother's steps running upstairs. 'Hello, my child,' she greeted me. She looked into Baby's cradle and then came and hugged me tightly. She looked far more cheerful and when I asked her why, she said how pleasant it had been to talk to Mamsell and laugh and joke with the kitchen staff.

'You know, Else, it's surprising the difference a little laughter can make. You feel uplifted and can face the days to come with optimism. Mamsell's so confident,' mother continued. 'She believes in all things good, and in her presence it's impossible to feel despondent or doubtful.'

Mother could see how downcast I felt and, taking my hand, said, 'And you, my child, must stop brooding. No good has ever come of it. We must accept what's before us. We can't avert the course of destiny.'

I looked at mother but couldn't speak. I'd been so wrapped up in my thoughts and worries that I couldn't immediately find my way back to cheerfulness. I was glad to see her smiling again and wanted to do the same.

There was a sure way to make me forget the gloomy thoughts I'd harboured all morning. *I know what to do*, I thought. *I'll take Puppy for a walk in the park and down to the lake. She'll enjoy it and so will I.*

We ran through the park – still covered in crispy snow. We rolled in it and I laughed and Senta barked and, almost out of breath, we raced towards the lake where the ducks and geese scattered, startled by the noise we made.

I felt so much better. My puppy was the *best* gift I'd ever had. I adored her and believe she loved me too.

We stayed a while longer and then, with cold feet but rosy cheeks, I raced back home with my little dog close at my heels. We burst into our room where mother was preparing lunch. Although still in my damp clothes, I raced up to her to give her a big hug. 'Mother, I feel so much better now. The walk with Senta has really cheered me up'.

Saturday, 1 May 1943

Egon had to travel back to his school that day. But Berlin would be unpleasant, for air raids had started, and continued night and day with unfailing regularity – like so many cities throughout Germany it had become a dangerous place.

We went out together one last time, walking through the fields and into the forest. Then, when the sun shone, it was almost possible to see nature awakening, as spring was fully on its way.

We were so lucky to be living in the countryside, but much of the time took it for granted. But we appreciated our good fortune when, now and then over the wireless, or in letters from Marlies or grandma and grandad, we heard of the daily suffering in other parts of Germany. Here in Pomerania we didn't hear the fearful sound of sirens day after day; we didn't run to seek protection from falling bombs, or scramble out of blackened ruins. Grandma talked about the effects of a bomb alert: streets emptying in minutes as people fled in fear to the nearest shelter, not knowing if their homes would be standing when they ventured out again after the all-clear. How grateful I was we'd been spared all that, and prayed the war would be over before bombing reached us in Pomerania.

The last few days of our Easter holidays were at an end, and that day we returned to school. This time, however, during school term, I didn't have to remain in Stolp with the Schröter family. Instead I could travel home daily with my friends – brilliant!

During the night I became very ill. I awoke with alarming pains in my joints, which were hot and swollen, and felt utterly unable to move. Frightened and, in panic, I called mother.

She didn't know what was ailing me but, in her usual quiet way, tried to calm me and with cold compresses managed to alleviate the pain and swelling in my joints.

'We must wait until morning, darling, before I can call a doctor. I'll give you something to ease your pain and will stay by your side and not leave you. Lie very still: move only if it's absolutely necessary; then you'll feel more comfortable. As soon as the night's over, I'll ask Fraulein Ottilia to telephone the doctor. I'm certain help will soon arrive.'

'Mother, move your chair by the side of my bed and hold my hand? When you're near me, I don't hurt so much.'

Mother had given me some liquid to drink. It made me feel drowsy, eased the pain and helped me to drift back to sleep. I could just remember asking where Fraulien Dorothea was and mother telling me she was in Berlin, making preparations for her forthcoming June wedding.

15 May 1943

Fortunately we had a doctor living in the village, whom Fraulein Otti contacted very early with a request to call on us as soon as he could.

I awoke feeling extremely ill and boiling hot: sweat covered my body.

'Frau Hopp, your daughter's gravely ill,' stated the doctor, after examining me. 'I think it's a form of rheumatic illness but can't be sure. Little is known about that illness and it takes a specialist to make a correct diagnosis. Else must be admitted to Stolp hospital without delay.'

'But Dr Hoffmann,' mother asked, 'how can I get my child to Stolp?'

'I'll see to that, Frau Hopp. Leave it to me. I have a car at my disposal and have to be on duty in the hospital this morning. Else can come with me. You can also travel with us. Can you make arrangements for your son and baby daughter?'

'The children will be taken care of: there are many willing hands to help out in a crisis,' mother answered. 'I do hope someone in the hospital can tell me what really is wrong with my daughter.'

She'd taken a blanket and pillow to lay on the back seat to enable me to travel to Stolp in comfort. Before we left she gave me one more spoonful of medicine to ease my pain and make me drowsy. Mother sat in the corner of the back seat holding me, my head in her lap. Gently, as she always did when I was ill, she stroked my forehead – the pain eased and I drifted into a restless sleep. The road to Stolp was far from smooth, as potholes and deep ruts had to be negotiated. Each time the car went over a bump, I came to with a jolt and felt the awful pain in the joints all over my body.

I can't remember arriving at the hospital, being placed on a trolley and taken to a room, but vaguely knew I was lifted into bed and felt the joy of lying in comfort between crisp, cool sheets that eased my burning body. I was drifting in and out of consciousness.

Sometimes, as if from a distance, I heard subdued voices. I sensed someone leaning over and touching me. It wasn't mother's hand – perhaps a nurse or a doctor?

Later, when I was getting better, mother told me the consultant had been pleased to treat me. 'You're my little guinea pig,' he told me in his best bedside manner, and thus managed to put me at ease.

'Frau Hopp, I must point out one thing,' he warned mother. 'Very little treatment is known for this painful illness. Research is gradually making headway and one day, I hope in the near future, there'll perhaps be a breakthrough and a cure found.'

'That will be a godsend,' mother replied. Please let it be soon – the pain's so severe.'

I was unaware how many days had passed, but remember that day when, as mother sat beside my bed, the consultant entered my room and addressed her with some excitement: 'Frau Hopp, I need to talk to you about a new treatment for rheumatic illnesses, which has now been made available. It's a course of eight injections – widely tested and found to be of great benefit to patients. They're not cheap, but are you willing to let me try them on your daughter? I can only obtain them from Berlin. If you agree, I'll order them immediately.'

'Please, Doctor, try anything that will help her. I do want my child to get better. To see her in such severe pain saddens me more than I can say.'

My illness lasted a long time and the road to recovery was slow. The weeks I spent in hospital dragged on and on. Daily I waited in vain for the injections to arrive from Berlin, and all the time I was in agony and hardly able to move in my hospital bed.

Many doctors examined me. I was very young to have rheumatic fever, and my being a girl puzzled them even more. 'Usually boys and elderly people are troubled with this illness,' they told me. 'Rarely do we see a young girl like you so severely afflicted.'

As for treating me, I sensed no doctor really knew what treatment to give me. They even thought the illness was contagious and I was isolated in a room on my own. But I was cared for with great kindness; and when I felt in low spirits and homesick, I received encouragement from the nurses, who tried to boost my morale.

I was confined to bed and had to lie flat on my back with only a small pillow to support my head. Just for a few minutes, twice a day, I was lifted onto a chair while nurses straightened and refreshed my bed. I was also on a strict diet: plenty of milk and milky puddings – semolina, rice or tapioca, which I called frogspawn – and anything that could be cooked in milk. For lunch it was chicken, cooked one way or another, or fish; for breakfast, perhaps a boiled egg or the hated porridge. The nurses knew how much I disliked it. For a special treat they sprinkled a little sugar on top, a precious commodity that made me feel obliged to eat all of it.

Mother could visit me only once a week, as it was a long journey from Glowitz to Stolp and she had commitments at home. But when she did come, it was a joy to see her. I wanted to hear all the news from the manor and we'd laugh over snippets of juicy village gossip. I was amazed how cheerful she always seemed in front of me. How could a mother with two very ill children in long-term care in different hospitals, in quite different towns, manage to laugh?

Once, when she came to visit, she really *did* have important news for me. 'Fraulein Otti came to see me yesterday,' mother started her news enthusiastically. 'By the way, she sends her love, hopes you'll be well soon . . . and she wants me to tell you that Bella, your horse, is well and awaiting your return.'

'I also miss her, mother, and Senta and Hans-Dieter and little Marlenchen and –'

'And then, Else, Fraulein Otti told me something very interesting,' mother interrupted.

'What is it, mother? 'Do tell me.'

'Very soon another refugee family will be coming to the manor, a woman with *seven* girls! Her name's Frau Fronzeck, and they come from Wanne-Eikel, Westphalia, where the coalmines are. Her husband, like father, is fighting in Russia, and their home in Wanne-Eikel was completely destroyed in an air raid.'

'Mother, how amazing! I'm longing to see them. Seven girls. That's incredible! I hope they're fun.'

Mother and I chatted away. She talked about Hans-Dieter and how difficult it was to get him to write to father. 'Don't be angry with him, mother. After all, he's a boy and letter-writing's too much like hard work. And my little sister? Is she progressing? Please give her a big hug from me.'

The time mother was allowed with me flew by, and when she had to leave, I cried and clung to her. Oh, how I wished she could take me with her.

'Darling girl, be patient,' she soothed. 'Soon the injections will be here. Then you'll see: it won't be long before you're allowed home.'

One afternoon Fraulein Dorothea came to visit. What a surprise! I assumed she'd gone to Berlin in connection with her forthcoming wedding and had called in on her way back. I didn't let on, though, that I was aware of her wedding plans; if Fraulein Dorothea wanted me to know, she'd tell me herself. She'd brought a basket of apples and pears from the fruit store, which sadly I was unable to eat. Acid in fruit was harmful, so I was told, and would only intensify my joint pain.

When I'd almost given up hope, the consultant came into my room. 'Else, you'll be delighted to hear that the injections have arrived from Berlin, at last.'

'How wonderful, Doctor! Will you start treating me today?'

'Yes, Else, you'll have your first injection this evening and a second the day after tomorrow. There are eight injections altogether, and you'll be given one on alternate days.'

'If they make me better, Doctor, can I go home?'

'I can't tell you as yet, Else. We must see how you react. Meanwhile, you must remain in bed; lie still and try not to be impatient.'

When I awoke that morning, the day after the second injection, I knew something was working. I felt greatly refreshed, for I'd slept all night; it was the best undisturbed sleep since my illness had started. And, most incredible of all, the pain in my joints was much reduced. It was a miracle! I hoped the doctor would allow me to go home soon.

But he wasn't prepared to let me go just yet. 'Don't be impatient, Else. One or two more days will make little difference. You've only had two injections: I can't discharge you until you've had at least four. If I see you're truly on the way to recovery, I may consider it.'

28 June 1943

After another few days of improvement, the doctor came again.

'*Please*, Doctor, may I go home now?'

'First I must speak with your mother. You'll need intense aftercare; use of your legs will only be gradual and at the first sign of pain or swelling you must rest and put your feet up. This is not a short-term illness, young lady. Be patient and listen to your mother.'

'Thank you, Doctor. I'll take care to do all that's asked of me.'

'That's what I like to hear. I'll instruct your local doctor to give you your injections. He'll also receive detailed information on how to act should the need arise.'

When at last arrangements were made for me to leave hospital, mother came to fetch me. Dr Hoffmann, our local doctor, had once more offered to drive us in his emergency car. I was delighted to be going home and when I arrived, the welcome I received from everyone touched me deeply. I fought back tears of joy that welled up in my eyes, and the lump in my throat left me speechless.

Chapter 22

Four-Leaf Clover

July 1943

I was overjoyed to be out of hospital and at home again, surrounded by my loving family. Hans-Dieter was also pleased to see me and went out of his way to be kind and helpful. 'How long would that last?' I wondered. We loved each other dearly but our relationship sometimes erupted into arguments and shouting matches.

Yet being home helped me towards recovery. I was determined to return to good health as quickly as possible, for soon my little brother Ralf was to come for a visit and I wanted to be well by then.

Without my help mother was very busy: everything rested on her shoulders. However, Frau Krause had kindly released Dunja from her kitchen duties and each morning she was free to help mother with her chores. Mother appreciated an extra pair of hands and Dunja enjoyed the change of routine.

Mother found a place for me to sit in the park. A large copper beech gave welcome shade on hot July days. Blue skies, warm sunshine and tranquil silence surrounded me, interrupted only by occasional sounds from the farm and the joyful song of a blackbird high in the tree. Peace to read my books without interruption; Baby in her pram beside me; Puppy Senta at my feet, resting her head on her paws. Little black eyes, ever watchful, guarded her territory and growled for intruders to keep their distance.

'My tree' stood close by the manor entrance. Everyone who called stopped to talk to me, to admire my little sister and handsome puppy, who also wanted to be fussed.

Dr Hoffmann continued to give me injections, which helped tremendously. After each one I felt better and ever more my usual self.

Gisela, my girlfriend, came to see me whenever she could be spared. After her day at school, she helped her parents in their shop and post office and cared for her elderly grandparents, both frail and in poor health.

Hans-Dieter remained a great help and tackled duties he'd normally shirk. He fed and walked our dog, ran errands for mother or me and even shopped in the village store, a chore he usually hated.

Communication from the sanatorium indicated that soon they'd consider a home visit for Ralf to see how he'd cope, as his health was also beginning to improve, though he was nowhere near coming home for good. My fitness also improved daily and, like mother, Hans-Dieter and I also became excited at the prospect of seeing my little brother again.

The most important thing was to walk again, and I wanted to take Ralf through the park and down to the lake to feed the ducks. Also, with their visit, I had to be well enough to help with mother's extra workload.

It was marvellous to think my little brother would be with us. Hans-Dieter and I hadn't seen him for some time. How much had he grown? Would he still remember us?

While I was recuperating, mother asked for homework for me, in case with such a long absence I'd fall behind and find it too difficult to catch up. Gisela happily acted as the go-between, bringing it and then returning the completed work.

Every day I practised walking and every day saw an improvement. Then, one day, when I found I could walk downstairs unaided, I was thrilled. 'Mother, Mother, come and watch! I don't even need my stick!'

Mother came running. Mamsell, wiping her hands on her apron, rushed out of the kitchen, with Dunja and Anna trailing behind. I was shouting in my excitement, and from all over the house everyone came to see what was going on. I was ecstatic, so proud of my achievement. 'Now Ralfie can come, mother, and I can walk with him to feed the ducks on the lake. Isn't it marvellous?'

Mother was delighted and hugged me. 'Darling, your determination's paid off. Now we'll look forward with confidence. Dr Hoffmann must be told the injections have worked miracles.'

In July, Fraulein Dorothea's wedding would take place in Berlin. Mamsell told mother that the elderly Baron von Puttkamer had agreed to give her away, and he and his wife would journey together to support their granddaughter on her special day. Fraulein Elisabeth would travel with them.

I had a vision of a grand aristocratic wedding: bridesmaids and many guests in splendid attire. I imagined how *I* would dress to attend that wedding. But then mother told me it was to be a small wartime ceremony. I felt rather sorry for the bride and groom.

'While the family's away', Mamsell announced to her staff, 'we can have a few easy days. Not many, because the house must be thoroughly cleaned. Maria, you and Lotti will spring-clean the bedrooms and bathrooms. Trudi, you're in charge of all the living rooms, including the dining and music rooms. Frau Ruch has agreed to help. If we work hard, we should complete the work in a couple of days. Then you can have time off and, if possible, visit your families.' She faced each member of staff in turn: 'Are you all in agreement?'

'Yes, Frau Krause.' The staff would do anything to get time off to go home.

Frau Krause had told mother the newly married couple could visit Glowitz Manor only for a long weekend, as time was limited. The young groom, a high-ranking officer in the German cavalry, had to return to his battalion on the Russian front.

'Mother,' I asked, 'how do I address Fraulein Dorothea now?'

'Else, you must call her *Baroness*. Her title is *Baroness Dorothea von Puttkamer* and she'll want to be addressed like that when appropriate.'

'That's strange, mother. She was Voeltheim, but now she'll be a Puttkamer like her grandparents. Is it so important that names carry through generations, or is he a distant cousin?'

Somehow I thought the young Baroness would be different, now she was married. But no, she was her usual smiling, efficient self, a wonderful help to her elderly grandparents. I never got to know her husband. I was so in awe of him that I tried to avoid him whenever I could.

24 July 1943

As mother, Hans-Dieter and I were eating our evening meal, there was a knock on our door.

'Should I see who it is, mother?' asked Hans-Dieter.

'Eat your meal, child,' mother answered. 'I'll answer the door.'

When mother opened it, we could see a lady with four little girls.

She introduced herself. 'Frau Hopp? I'm Frau Fronzeck. Sorry to disturb you during your mealtime. We arrived a short while ago and I was eager to make your acquaintance.'

'Pleased to meet you, Frau Fronzeck; no need to apologize. We've looked forward to your arrival. It must be as strange to you as it was for me, but Glowitz Manor is a happy refuge and I'm certain you and your children will soon feel at home. If you have any questions, I may be able to answer them. Don't hesitate to ask.'

'Thank you, Frau Hopp. The Baroness has told me your daughter's the same age as my Sieglinde. Perhaps they may become friends.'

I left the table, approached Frau Fronzeck and said, 'I've been very ill, but am getting better. I look forward to meeting your daughters – do you have many?'

'Else!' mother admonished me. 'That's impolite and you should know better!'

But Frau Fronzeck laughed. She was a big woman and when she laughed, her whole body shook. She laughed often and loud: sometimes it could be embarrassing. 'It's fine, Frau Hopp. Not many women have seven daughters: quite a novelty. We're used to being stared at. I have my Mother Cross in gold to wear with pride.'

I knew about the Mother Cross: Mother had been presented with a bronze one after baby Marlene was born. Adolf Hitler, wanting to encourage mothers to bring many babies into the world, enticed them with a generous child allowance, special wartime rations and the Mother Cross for those with more than three children: bronze, silver and gold, depending on the number of children born.

As we got to know the family, we learned what it meant to live in a mining area and with the dangers underground workers faced. Coalmining was so hazardous that, although miners were exempt from enlistment, Herr Fronzeck had enlisted in the army.

'I do miss my husband,' Frau Fronzeck told mother, 'but then I'm glad to be free from the fear of more babies. I like being without a husband and constant tiny babies. One day, I hope, he'll come back; but then we'll start all over again.' She saw the funny side of it and laughed until she was weary. Hans-Dieter quickly offered her a chair.

Early August 1943

Gisela, Sieglinde and I became firm friends. 1943 was the last summer we young people could be light-hearted and free. We enjoyed every new day without worries or trouble – it was a good life and we didn't notice the dark clouds gathering. The three of us were inseparable, and just had to wait for Sylvia to arrive from Berlin to complete our 'four-leaf clover' as we liked to call ourselves.

Sylvia came, but she was not happy about our friendship with Sieglinde.

'Else,' Sylvia said to me soon after her arrival, 'she's a miner's daughter! She comes from the *coalpit* . . . how could she possibly be one of us?'

I was aghast. 'Sylvia,' I answered, 'you surprise and disappoint me. You're privileged, but that gives you no right to deride people less fortunate than you. Sieglinde's father's a miner – a hazardous occupation. Now he's fighting on the Russian front – just like my father and your brother-in-law and thousands of men from all over Germany. Perhaps, as we speak, he may even be dead! And you think yourself too grand to associate with Sieglinde, his daughter?'

'But, Else –'

'No, Sylvia, you've no excuse. Accept Sieglinde as one of us, or we want nothing to do with you. Go and think about it: I hope you come to the right decision.'

And with these words, Gisela and I walked away.

Only a few minutes passed and Sylvia came running after us: 'Please wait for me,' she called. 'I want to talk to both of you.'

'What is it, Sylvia? Have you thought about what we said?'

'Yes, Else. Of course I want to be one of you. You and Gisela are right: I'm so very wrong. My grandparents would be furious with me for being conceited, and I'm ashamed. Please forgive me.'

We shook hands and embraced. Then I announced, 'Now our lucky four-leaf clover will be complete. Let's go and call Sieglinde.'

Whenever possible, Gisela, Sieglinde, Sylvia and I were together throughout the summer, and my three friends were a definite part of my successful recovery. At the end of the summer holidays, when I was better and Sylvia had returned to boarding school, the three of us continued to travel by train to Stolp; we went to the same school and shared the same classroom, and then, after lessons, we came home together.

Of course, my best friend was still Marlies in Düsseldorf. But she was far away and I hadn't heard from her for some time; the letters I wrote remained unanswered and there was no way of discovering why.

Frau Fronzeck's daughters, with their blonde hair and blue eyes, were very pretty: they'd have stood out in any crowd. Hanna, whose full name was Hannelore, was ten years old, and although she wanted to be with us, we didn't let her and told her to find her own friends.

I could never quite remember the names of the other girls, right down to the baby, who was only eleven months old. Our days, however, were full of happiness and laughter and I have memories of a golden summer, for we were blissfully unaware of the darkness about to enshroud us.

Chapter 23

Field Postcard

2 August 1943

At last, after she'd waited a long time, a letter addressed to mother arrived from Swinemünde. 'This is about little Ralf!' mother called out. 'Come, Else, be with me when I read it.'

It informed her that Matron, Fraulein Stein, would bring Ralf personally to visit us mid-August. She asked mother to make all the necessary arrangements for her and the child to be met at the station with some form of transport. Her letter sounded like a demand, and mother was none too pleased. 'That woman has grand delusions,' she exploded, anger showing on her face. 'How can I possibly be civil to her?'

'Mother, just treat her with your usual distant politeness. Don't let her see how irate you are. You're Ralf's mother and have priority where your child's concerned.'

Mother booked a room for Fraulein Stein at the inn in Glowitz: small, but homely and clean, for the landlord tried to make his guests welcome.

'Mother, will Ralf stay here or with Matron at the inn?'

'Else, how can you ask such a question? Of course our little boy will stay with us. Matron may protest, but Ralfie will remain with us. No argument! It's only a few days and Dr Hoffmann has promised to be available if needed.'

'Well done, mother. I knew you'd say that.'

14 August 1943

The day arrived, a beautifully warm summer's day. Everything was ready to welcome our little brother and excitement built up inside mother. She couldn't sit still for a minute. Fraulein Ottilia had offered to send Johann in the small landau to the station, but mother had decided not to go. She'd wait to greet her little lad at home. She peered out of the window every few moments – she couldn't stop herself. She didn't want to miss the arrival of the small coach as it entered the park and drove up to the main door.

At last came her joyful call: 'Here they come!' And without waiting, she rushed down, through the kitchens, out of the back door and around the house until she reached the front entrance, where she almost collided with the horses just as Johann was bringing them to a standstill. Mother was laughing and crying at the same time; she could hardly contain herself for the horses to steady. All she wanted was to get at her blond little four-year-old boy, whom she hadn't seen for months. He was small and looked frail, and mother longed to hug, kiss and cuddle him.

But Ralfie didn't want to go to mother! He turned away with a cry and buried his face in Fraulein Stein's coat. Mother was stunned – this was not what she'd expected.

Becoming angry, she directed that anger at Matron. Six months in a little boy's life is a long time: mother didn't want to believe that during those months when Ralfie had been away from his family he'd slowly grown apart from us. The few days when mother had visited him were too short to bond again. When she'd left, he'd remained in his secure, familiar surroundings. It was no good blaming Matron. She'd been kind and caring and over time had become his substitute Mama.

But mother didn't like it. I tried to calm her, to make her see reason, to point out she was being unjust to Fraulein Stein. The woman had, after all, done her best at all times during Ralf's severe illness to compensate for his Mama's disappearance. I believed mother had a vision of her little son running joyfully towards her with outstretched arms. But that hadn't happened and I could see the hurt in her face.

'Let's go upstairs, mother,' I tried to persuade her. 'Have patience: Ralf will come to you.'

Mother put her arms around me and laid her cheek against mine. 'You know, Else, you may still be young but you're wise beyond your years.'

'Thank you, mother. That's a lovely thing to say, but my wisdom comes from your guidance, and without it I'd be nothing.'

I was right, though: before two days had passed, it seemed Ralfie had never been away. Mother and Fraulein Stein became more tolerant of each other, owing to Matron's patience. Mother wanted replies to numerous questions about Ralf's treatment in the sanatorium.

'Matron,' mother asked, 'how much longer will we have to wait for Ralf to be discharged?'

'I'm sorry, Frau Hopp, but I can't answer that. When we return to Swinemünde, Ralf will have a thorough check-up and much will depend on the outcome, but, guessing, I'd say, you're likely have your little boy back before autumn's over. I'll telephone you as soon as I hear and you'll receive a detailed letter from the consultant.'

For a few short days we were a proper family once more, without Matron's presence, for she was happy to rest in the village inn. The weather was kind to us and we spent much of the time out of doors. Hans-Dieter, Ralf and I, and often mother as well, walked through the park, Senta running ahead, nose to the ground. We fed the ducks and then visited the horses in the stables. Bella gently accepted a carrot from Ralf's little hand. He showed no fear and shrieked with excitement, when I lifted him onto her back: 'Let me ride, Else. Please let me ride!'

'Not today, Ralf. Bella's tired and we must let her rest. But when you come out of hospital, you and I will ride her together – promise.'

Our rooms were quiet after Ralf and Fraulein Stein returned to Swinemünde, but we hoped that in a few weeks, our little brother would come back for good.

23 August 1943

Kharkov had remained in German hands until that day. But by then the Russian army was fast advancing across Russia and the German army was retreating. The majority of German soldiers knew by then that they were fighting a lost cause. There was insufficient equipment and ammunition, and all promises of re-enforcements and secret weapons were empty words, as father had predicted – only meaningless promises to keep up morale.

But for us, hardly aware of that setback, the summer holiday passed speedily and was great fun. I was well again and looking forward to returning to school after my long absence. But the young Baroness had one more treat in store for us towards the end of the holidays. One morning she called on my mother, just as we were finishing breakfast.

'Frau Hopp, please forgive the intrusion. Will you give your permission for Else and Hans-Dieter to come to Stolpmünde with me today? Two naval ships are anchored in the port and, for one day only, the public's invited to see what our mighty navy has to display. It's a rare opportunity, and perhaps it may interest your young people?'

'What kind of ships are they?' mother asked.

'One's a destroyer; the other's a minesweeper.'

'Oh, a minesweeper. That's a ship my brother serves on. Who knows, Else, perhaps you'll meet Uncle Richard,' mother said smiling, as she winked at the Baroness.

Of course, Hans-Dieter immediately became very excited. 'Mother, that's wonderful. Please say we may go. I'd love to – you'd like to go, wouldn't you, Else?'

That wasn't what I wanted at all. Travel to Stolpmünde? Yes, that could be exciting, but what was there to do, apart from looking at boring old warships? The beach was out of bounds and people were permitted to walk only on a certain path that had been made safe from landmines. Yet if I refused to go, I'd be considered ungrateful, and perhaps Hans-Dieter would miss out. I didn't think Baroness would just take him. So what could I do other than say, 'Yes please, Baroness, I'd love to; thank you for asking us. Hans-Dieter and I love surprise outings.'

And, as it happened, our day out was excellent. Baroness was fun to be with and, as we entered the ship, smart young naval boys surrounded her and tried to outdo each other to be of service to her – and thus also to us.

And then, when we came home in the evening, I had one more *big* surprise.

Frau Ruch had left a message with mother that Egon had come home for just a few days' holiday, and that he'd very much like to see me as soon as I could manage it. How wonderful! I'd given up hope, thinking that other plans had prevented him from leaving Berlin.

When we met the following day, it was as if he'd never been away. He hadn't changed: as always he was well mannered, pleasant; but there was something different, which I couldn't place.

'Tell me, Egon, are you well? Are you perturbed?'

'Else, I'm fine; I have no worries. We've worked hard during the last few weeks. We're training to be soldiers and it seems we're being prepared for battle. Rumours – one doesn't know what to believe. No one tells you anything. You ask questions and you're fobbed off, told to wait for answers: "all in good time". Soon we may be moving out of Berlin to a different location.'

'Do you know where, Egon?'

'No, Else, I don't. And even if I did, I couldn't tell you. Everything concerning the army's hush-hush. Let's enjoy our few days together and forget about war and fighting, bombs and destruction. We can't stop what tomorrow has in store; let's just live for today.'

This time, when we said goodbye, Egon kissed my cheek. I could feel myself blushing, yet was flattered and didn't know what to do. I felt shy. I'd never kissed a boy before but wanted to kiss Egon. I had to stand on tiptoe to reach his cheek. He was much taller than me, but I did it! And then, to cover my embarrassment, I said, 'Now, Egon, you've had my kiss. Please don't forget me: I'll always think of you.'

It saddened me when I had to say goodbye to him, as it would be Christmas before he'd be home again – at least that was what I hoped.

September 1943

On the first day back to school the headmistress visited our classroom. 'Good morning, girls,' she addressed us. 'Have you had a good summer holiday?'

'Yes, thank you, Fraulein Mertel,' we answered with one voice.

'Good, because I have news for you. It may be a shock.' There was a murmur of expectation, which died down immediately Fraulein Mertel raised her hand. 'Listen, girls,' she announced, 'I must tell you that you're requested to take part in harvesting the new potato crop. Your form mistress has the details, plus a note for your parents, which you need to return with their signature.

There was much excitement among the girls. Time away from school! Potato picking! Great fun, so they thought. But the reality was very different: how disappointed they'd be when confronted with the actual task. The weather was foul, the earth wet and muddy, and, to make matters worse, each potato had to be back-achingly picked up by hand and transferred into baskets handed out by the farmer.

I should have been delighted when I was told it was out of the question for me to take part, but I wasn't. I was the odd one out and therefore unhappy. But Dr Hoffmann and mother were adamant. After my lengthy, serious illness, I couldn't possibly crawl on my knees: I'd be asking for trouble.

'But mother!' I cried. 'How embarrassing. The girls in my class will look down on me. They'll think I'm shirking.'

'Nonsense, Else; they know how ill you've been. Believe me, they'll understand.'

The day before my fourteenth birthday we heard news that the German army had occupied Rome.

As far as we knew, father was still fighting in Smolensk, but letters from him were irregular and each time a field postcard arrived it told us little. Then, towards the end of September, we heard on the radio that the Russians had retaken Smolensk. War victories were like a see-saw, rocking between one side and the other. Would our father survive all that?

A few days later, mother picked up an official letter off the silver tray at the bottom of the stairs. Was that the news she'd been dreading? After a short hesitation, she tore it open. I watched for her reaction over the landing banisters. For quite some time mother stood there, at the bottom of the stairs, staring at the words, the paper shaking in her hand. She seemed stunned.

My heart skipped a beat. Father . . . was he DEAD?

We'd never mentioned the word, but were all aware it might be a possibility one day. My head swam. Was this the day? I stared around wanting familiarity, wanting other adults to help us make sense of it. And the Puttkamer family portraits on the panelled walls all seemed to focus their eyes on me: elders, barons, matriarchs, generals . . . 'This is life,' their eyes said. 'We know. If it's true, you'll have to deal with it and help mother accept it.'

'Mother!' I ran down the wide staircase to her side. 'Mother, talk to me. What does it say?'

She stared at me, but it took a while for her to answer. 'Injured,' she croaked. 'Hospital.'

'What does the letter say about father's injuries? Are they severe? They must surely be, for him to be hospitalised? May I see the letter?'

She handed it over and I scanned the words. It informed her that father had been wounded, that he'd been rescued and admitted to a military hospital in Kiev, Russia. It said his injuries were not life-threatening.' I sighed with relief: father was alive!

'It tells us nothing.' Mother came back to life and walked wearily up the stairs. 'I'd like to be on my own for a while. Look after Marlenchen and Hans-Dieter; I'll be with you soon.' And with those words she went to her room and closed the door firmly behind her.

I was worried and, following her, curiosity made me listen at her door. I could hear sobbing and knew my mother was crying. No doubt she'd thought the same as I had. What mixed relief: not dead, but wounded. Where? Was he in pain? Neither of us could be there for him, nurse him, love him. I left her alone; I was no help to her but knew that in a short while she'd come back to us and feel better for having wept.

Mother entered the living room, smiling. 'Children,' she said to Hans-Dieter and me, 'your father's alive, thank God. Perhaps some good may come of his injury.'

'What do you mean, mother?'

'We never know, Else. It's possible that when your father's well again, the army will send him home for a while to regain his strength.'

But that wasn't to be. Weeks passed and a second official letter arrived. Father's injuries had much improved and he was to be sent to Guernsey in the Channel Islands to convalesce.

The year was slowly nearing its end. Although October days were still warm and sunny, they were shortening and already the evenings felt decidedly chilly. Leaves were falling, brown and yellow, red and gold, and the park grounds were soon covered in a thick, colourful carpet.

'Not long now and it will snow,' mother said. 'The wind's coming from the east and that heralds cold weather. I pray the coming winter will be less severe than last year, or our soldiers will be unable to survive.

Chapter 24

You're not my Mummy!

A wonderful thing happened in October. Mother received a letter from the sanatorium in Swinemünde telling her that our little Ralf was now well enough to return to us. We'd waited throughout September for news, to no avail. Now Fraulein Stein would bring him home on the last day of the month. She was coming herself to instruct mother on what to do in case of an emergency. She also wanted to consult Dr Hoffmann.

After a deep and dreamless sleep, I awoke just as dawn was breaking. My window was slightly ajar and through the opening I could hear the dawn chorus in the park in full throat. I lay and listened to the multitude of small birds competing with each other to be heard.

Before long I was wide awake and my immediate reaction was to get out of bed and enjoy the start of that brand new, beautiful day. I pushed back the bedclothes and put my bare feet on the floor. Chilly that morning! I looked at Hans-Dieter, still fast asleep with a little smile on his face. Was he having an incredible dream of his adventures the day before? Or perhaps he was dreaming of his little brother who was to come home that day.

I tiptoed to the window behind me and pulled the curtain to, so the light wouldn't disturb Dieter.

It was going to be a glorious day. The sun was rising fast over the stables, and soon the shining red ball hung in the sky, seeming to rest on the edge of the barn roof. Bright rays of sunlight were turning autumn leaves into pure gold. The day was fresh and lovely and I felt like running in bare feet through the dewy grass in the park; but no, impossible at that time of year, much too cold, and anyway too much to do on that important morning.

Not very long now and Fraulein Stein will arrive to bring my little brother home to us, I thought to myself.

Our room was pleasantly warm but the stove needed more turf and the basket held plenty for me to stoke up the fire.

I know what I can do! Make a cup of coffee for mother and take it in to her. She'll like that and it will help her make a start to her busy day.

This time mother wanted to go to meet her son. Johann, always so kind, had prepared the small, four-wheeled carriage and had promised to take mother to the station. As yet there was plenty of time, but I could hear her moving about in her bedroom. I rushed to her door wanting her to stay in bed, but she was up, nursing my little sister, and I knew that once again she'd beaten me to it.

'Mother, I have a cup of coffee for you. Do you have time to drink it?'

'Child, how wonderful! You're a treasure!' Her eyes lit up when she saw the small tray with her own coffeepot and smelt the delicious aroma coming from it. I knew then that her day was made.

'Good morning, mother,' I greeted her, planting a kiss on her forehead. 'Did you sleep well?'

'No, I didn't, my child: too many things to think about. And you, Elslein, did you have a good night?'

'Yes, mother, but I awoke very early. The birds singing loudly in the park prevented me from sleeping. Although it's cold outside, it looks like it will be a lovely day.'

'Please, Else, take little Marlene and dress her. I must bathe and get ready; then, while you and Hans-Dieter wash and dress, I'll prepare breakfast.'

I could see how happy my mother was. It was agony for her to wait until it was time to go to the station – the longing to hold her little boy was almost too much for her to cope with.

One minute she was nagging Hans-Dieter (something she rarely did); then she'd joke with us and in the same breath panic, thinking Johann might forget to come in time.

How we got through the morning I never knew. Breakfast was over and cleared away; beds made and rooms tidied, and now all we could do was sit tight and await Johann. We should have stayed in bed longer instead of getting up so early. We sat around with time on our hands and mother couldn't stop looking at her watch.

I'd decided to stay behind with Marlene and Hans-Dieter, who wanted to go out to play with his friends.

'Can I, mother? Please can I go out? I promise to be back for lunch and not to get into mischief or make myself dirty.'

'Go on, son; just go,' mother answered with resignation. 'But don't forget Fraulein Stein will also be here for lunch. You mustn't be late.'

'I'll remember. Anyway, I want to see my brother.' Hans-Dieter was glad to escape. He couldn't get out fast enough.

At last there was a knock on the door. 'Frau Hopp, are you ready?'

'Yes, I am!' mother answered. 'I've waited for this moment since early morning. Thank you, Johann. You're very kind.'

When they reached the station, there was still time for the train to arrive. Johann told me later that my mother was so excited she couldn't stand still. She walked up and down the platform, telling everyone who would listen that her little son was due home from Swinemünde, where he'd been a TB patient in a sanatorium.

And then at last a puff of smoke appeared in the distance, followed by the unmistakable sound of a steam engine approaching. Mother knew that in a few minutes she'd be able to hug her little boy.

But when they all later returned to the manor, Ralf was crying bitter tears and mother was very upset. I had to ask Johann why they all looked so downhearted.

'Else,' he told me, quietly, 'Fraulein Stein was the first to alight from the train, followed by Ralf, very smart in a new outfit, given to him as a farewell present from Matron.'

Mother was convinced Ralf, unlike last time, would come running to greet her. She approached him, arms wide open to enfold him, but he turned away – he didn't want to know her. As mother bent down to pick him up, he burst into tears and sobbed, 'No, no, I want Aunt Ellie! Go away! I want my Aunt Ellie!'

Mother was at a loss. She didn't know what to do or say. She stood there helplessly, looking for guidance from Fraulein Stein.

'Frau Hopp, please don't worry. Your little son will soon come to you. Give him time and he'll realise *you* are his mummy and a very special person. Don't be impatient; listen to my words.' And mother, although reluctantly, had to acquiesce.

Johann had bustled everyone into the warm carriage. The morning, which had started so promisingly, had become chilly as the clouds gathered, and a cool wind blew from the east, making the day most unpleasant.

Off the carriage went at a trot through the village, up the drive, through the large gates into the park and came to a halt outside the back entrance.

Once more mother tried to pick her boy up, but he wanted nothing to do with her. To make matters worse, he told her, 'You're not my mummy. Aunt Ellie's my mummy. I don't like you.'

I'd come downstairs with baby in my arms just as the carriage arrived and could hear what was going on. I could see how upset my mother was. 'Mother,' I said, 'take Marlenchen so I can see if Ralfie will come to me.' I approached Ralf and knelt in front of him. 'Hello, little brother. Have you come home to us? I'm your big sister, Else: I love you and want you to stay with us for ever and ever and never go away again. Will you come to me, now? I'd like to give you a big hug and a kiss. Will you let me?'

He came to me straight away, that little brother of mine. It was strange; I'd feared he wouldn't remember me, as it had been over two months since he'd last seen me. Come, Ralfie,' I said, 'let's go upstairs. Now you're four years old, can you climb stairs by yourself?'

'Of course I can! I'm a big boy now.' And with those words he took my hand to show me what he could do.

When we reached our sitting room, I sat him on my lap and started to talk to him. I told him about mother, Hans-Dieter and myself and tried to make it clear to him how happy we all were to have him home again. 'Soon Hans-Dieter will come home. He's your big brother and he'll play with you sometimes, and teach you many boy tricks. He'll be your friend.'

As we were talking, he looked at me and gave a most angelic smile. 'Else,' he said loudly and clearly. Then he snuggled up to me and, with that, the ice was broken.

Mother had prepared a light lunch for us. There was bouillon – a clear broth with a variety of root vegetables. That was followed by slices of cold meat, salad and mashed potatoes. 'Mother, what kind of meat's this?' I asked. 'It's so dark.'

'Oh, it's beef, Else. Uncle Kurt gave me a large joint. It was more than he needed and I was glad to receive it.'

After lunch Fraulein Stein went over to Ralf. 'Now, my little boy, should we do what you always did while you were in Swinemünde?'

'What was that, Aunt Ellie? Oh, you mean I must go to sleep.'

'That's right. Now you're well, and we want you to stay well. Come, follow me; first into the bathroom and then, hop, hop into your little bed.'

And then he surprised us by calling, 'Mama, will you come and tuck me in?' And mother beaming all over her face, followed him meekly. She was 'Mama' once more.

After Ralf was settled, Fraulein Stein asked me to walk with her to the inn, where she'd spend the night. Next morning mother was to visit her and they'd go together to meet Dr Hoffmann, who'd promised to be available for Ralfie should the need arise.

In the evening, when Hans-Dieter and Ralf were both asleep, I asked mother once more what meat we'd eaten for lunch. She looked at me long and hard: 'Else, it was horseflesh. One of the horses was injured and had to be put down. Uncle Kurt decided to distribute the meat among the farm workers. Frau Krause also had a generous piece, which she shared with Frau Fronzeck and me. I know you don't like the idea of eating horseflesh, Else, but there's a war on and meat's hard to come by. We must be grateful for what we can get. There may come a day when we wish we can have a little meat, no matter which animal it comes from. Now don't fuss. You enjoyed it at the table, so let's now forget all about it.'

'Yes, mother,' I answered, 'I understand, but I hope I never have to eat horseflesh again. I'd rather go without.'

Later on the Monday, before Matron was to leave, she wanted to come and say goodbye to her little charge, but mother asked her not to. It would only upset Ralf once again. Mother wanted the farewell to be quick and matter of fact, and her judgement proved to be a sensible decision.

Mother was trying really hard to get close to her son and, with a great deal of patience, was succeeding. The following morning I could hear Ralfie's joyful laughter in the bedroom with mother joining in. Quietly I opened the door a crack and peeped in. Ralf was playing with her on her bed and together they were having great fun. I knew then that without a doubt everything would be all right.

Chapter 25

Rumours

10 November 1943

It was 4 a.m. when, too restless to sleep, I reached for my diary beside the bed and fumbled for my precious fountain pen:

> Today's my little sister, Marlene's, first birthday.
>
> It's also our dear father's birthday! Wherever you are, 'Happy Birthday, father!'
>
> Tomorrow, the eleventh, one year ago, I arrived in Pomerania. Often I think back to that long, long journey through Germany on my own, and on my arrival the surprise of being presented with a new little sister. Such a tiny baby . . . yet look at her now, sturdy and bonny, crawling around and pulling herself up to stand independently, but not always with success!
>
> It's still early and very dark. Hans-Dieter is sleeping soundly, curled up like a dormouse, and from mother's bedroom not a sound. She'll soon wake up: five o'clock is usually her time. When she comes to give me a call, she'll be surprised to see me wide awake and writing my diary.

The torch in my hand was throwing a beam onto the page, but my writing was wobbly, as I was not in the most comfortable position:

> But then I must hurry up. My train leaves Glowitz station just after six o'clock. This morning I'll walk across the fields. It's far quicker than walking through the village, but it will still be dark: only the moon to guide me along the footpath.
>
> Last night we had the first flurries of snow. I hope it won't have snowed all night. Winter comes soon enough . . . how well I remember last year's snows. Once it starts to snow in Pomerania it goes on and on until well into spring.
>
> When I think back, it has been an eventful year:
>
> My long illness – how thankful I am that's over. I feel much stronger. I was very lucky to be one of the pioneer guinea pigs for the injections: they'd told me there was no cure. I could have been crippled for life.
>
> And then Ralf, so small, yet so very ill. Thank God he's recovered! We're really glad we have him back home . . .
>
> Father wounded fighting in Smolensk, Russia, and being handed over to a military hospital. He so nearly could have been killed. Then, when he was

able to travel, being sent to Guernsey, in the Channel Islands. At least we felt he was safe there, but no: when we last heard from him, he was waiting to return to his unit in Kiev. How could they put him through that again? Though it can't be Kiev. On 6 November it was announced on the wireless that Kiev had fallen back into Russian hands . . . So was his regiment there at the time? If so, I wonder how many of his friends were killed in that? Perhaps he was safer being in the Channel Islands . . . So father, where's he now? What are his wounds? Are they healed and where were they? Have they changed his looks? Dear Papa . . .

Mother told me that Frau Krause somehow appears to be very well informed, though won't say where from. Rumours are rife, but her information has certainly been reliable so far. According to her there are battles being fought all over Russia and bitter fighting on all Russian fronts, and our German soldiers are not advancing as they were only a few months ago. Instead the rumour is they seem to be retreating, ever closer to Odessa on the Black Sea. Now if father's once more in the middle of ferocious fighting, who knows when next we'll hear from him again? Apparently the Russians are almost in Poland.

The official news is that, to date, our German troops are holding back the advancing enemy – if that's true – but winter starts early in that part of the world and when it really begins, it comes with a vengeance. What will happen then? And who knows if Dr Goebbels is still feeding our German nation propaganda? Many people question his words. But only in whispers!

Suddenly I heard mother moving about. It must have been almost 5 a.m. Just a few minutes more, and then I'd also have to get up. I wrote a little faster:

It has been a glorious summer this year with an abundant harvest in fields and gardens. In October we had a very moving harvest festival thanksgiving service here at Glowitz Manor. It was held in the farmyard and most of the village were assembled. The local pastor conducted the service. It was so natural and very moving with our farm animals close by and bundles of corn, fruit and vegetables in a circle round an altar erected in the centre of the paddock.

Frau Krause was in her element with the bountiful harvest. How she loved preserving and bottling fruit and vegetables from the home garden. The shelves in her storerooms were filling rapidly and she was justly proud of her handiwork. Dunja and Anna had been a great help, and Frau Krause was generous with her praise, assuring them, much to their delight, that she couldn't have managed without them.

I closed my diary and jumped out of bed just as mother entered the room.

'My, Else, you're up and about early this morning! Have you not slept?'

'Yes, mother, but when I awoke, I wanted to write a few thoughts into my diary, which I've neglected recently.'

I looked out of the window. It was very dark but the light covering of snow broke the blackness and would help me find my way across the fields to the station.

Mother sat with me as I ate breakfast. She drank her cup of corn-based coffee while I had a glass of milk and a thick slice of bread and jam. I smiled to myself knowing that, as soon as I left, she'd treat herself to a cup of *real* coffee. Rations were getting shorter even in Pomerania, and the abundance of food we'd had not so long ago was no more. We were still lucky living in the countryside, but Stolp and the other towns nearby were beginning to feel a scarcity of provisions. Mother had somehow got the real coffee via the black market.

'Child, dress extra warmly this morning. Let's hope the train's heated.'

Before putting my outdoor clothes on, I ran to the bathroom and found I was bleeding. I was terrified. I burst into tears. *I'm ill!* I thought. *Surely not again after feeling so well?*

I rushed into the living room.

'Mother,' I sobbed, 'I'm bleeding! Whatever's the matter with me? I'm frightened.'

Mother looked at me and smiled.

'Else, you're a young woman now. You're fourteen years old. What you're experiencing's completely normal. I've expected this and am prepared. Perhaps you were awakened early by a tummy ache?'

'Yes, I was. But mother, why? I can't go to school like this, can I?'

'Of course you can, child. You're not ill. You now have what we call your 'periods': they'll occur once a month. Tonight, when you come home, we'll sit down together and I'll explain to you exactly what's happening to your body. The most important thing is, don't worry. What you're experiencing is a natural process of becoming a woman.'

I must admit, what was happening to me played on my mind all day. I knew my mother would explain it all to me, but I didn't want to talk about it, not even to Gisela, my best friend. It was my secret, and I wanted to keep it that way.

December 1943

Slowly the year came to an end, and with December came Advent. It should have been a time to start Christmas preparations, but somehow the festive feelings were absent that year.

Many German people were beginning to wonder what life would be like a year hence. I was surprised to realise the war appeared to have spread throughout Europe. Little information about other countries had been given to us on the news. Now it was worse, for announcements of victories were almost non-existent. We very rarely received a letter from my grandparents. The last one told us that Grandma could no longer travel to East Prussia. The place where she grew up, Gumbingen, not far from Königsberg, was near the Polish border and once Russia started its advance towards Poland it would take no time for them to reach German soil.

But the last time we'd heard, Grandma and Grandad's little house near Düsseldorf was still standing. She implied the inner city had been badly hit; yet suburbs and outer areas remained relatively untouched. In my diary, the night after we heard the news of my beloved city, I wrote:

> I'm very worried about my dear friend Marlies. I've received no news from her for a long time. I've written – many times – but had no reply. Is her house still standing? Perhaps both our streets have been hit? I pray she and her parents are alive and well . . . perhaps, by now, they've also fled to safety somewhere.

> For quite some time now, we've had no news from father. It's so worrying; we don't know what to think . . . we can only pray that he remains safe. We heard he was in Odessa, and that town, as far as we understand, is still held by the German army.

And the next night I continued:

> One snippet of wonderful news has been given to mother today. It's the first Sunday in Advent. The senior Baroness von Puttkamer announced that her granddaughter and the cavalry captain are expecting their first child in March 1944. How exciting for them! And what a boost to the morale of the young baron fighting on the front somewhere on Russian soil. I do hope they can get a message to him.

> The young Baroness, Fraulein Dorothea, and her sister Ottilia, are at present in Berlin. Shortly before Christmas they'll return to Glowitz, together with Sylvia and their mother, Frau von Voeltheim, to spend the festive season with their elderly grandparents and Fraulein Elisabeth. The family nanny, Ida Affeld, is also to travel with them. I've never met her, but Sylvia has often mentioned her with affection.

> The manor will be full this Christmas. Frau Krause will love the challenge of stretching the sparse rations and I'm certain she'll manage the celebrations somehow.

That year, once again, mother was invited to celebrate Advent with the Puttkamer family in their drawing room. Hans-Dieter and I, with the little ones, were of course also included, as was Frau Fronzeck with her seven delightful daughters.

'Mother, do you think we'll have a goose again?'

'Of course we will, Elslein. Mamsell has already said so and we can all look forward to it. Luckily here in Pomerania geese are plentiful, as are potatoes and vegetables. That's something we'll not be short of and it makes me realise how fortunate we are, living in the countryside.'

As always our dear mother made Christmas a memorable occasion. Gifts might not have been as plentiful as in previous years, but what we received was all home-made and very useful: scarves and gloves, pullovers for the little ones and warm socks for Hans-Dieter and me. For mother I was able to get an attractive pen and pencil set in Stolp. Hans-Dieter gave me a few pennies from his pocket money to put towards mother's gift, so I could say it was from all of us, and I knew she'd be delighted to find it under the Christmas tree.

On Christmas Eve our small tree looked charming and decorative. The candles, left over from the previous year, gave it a special sparkle that reflected in the silver ornaments.

Our little sister, now one year old, shrieked with delight when she saw the tree with candles alight. And Ralfie, quite the big boy now, took notice of everything going on around him. Forgotten was Swinemünde, his illness and 'Aunt Ellie'. He was home and happy, and mother, once again, was the most important person in his young life.

So the year 1943 came to an end, with 1944 still a mystery. At the dinner table, before mother started carving the goose, she said, 'We'll pray now for happy days, for the end of the war, and to be reunited with our dear ones scattered to the far corners of Germany and other parts of the world. We'll say a special prayer for our dear father, Grandma and Grandad in Düsseldorf, not forgetting Uncle Richard on a boat somewhere.'

'And for Marlies,' I added.

'And for *everyone everywhere!*' said Hans-Dieter finally, with his eyes on the steaming dinner.

Chapter 26

Do your Best for the Fatherland

January 1944

A lot of snow and extremely cold weather ushered in 1944. The temperature dropped to thirty degrees below freezing and everything was frozen hard as steel. The lake in the park had a thick lid of ice, as smooth as glass.

Baron von Puttkamer had opened the gates of the park and offered the village children a frolic on the ice. Hans-Dieter and I joined them. There, with much shrieking and laughter, we could slide and skate or use our toboggans to race down the bank on one side, directly on to the ice, the momentum carrying us right across the lake. It was terrific fun for us young people.

Just a few more days and then back to school, so we had to make the most of that useful winter weather.

We didn't know if trains were running on the Stolp–Glowitz line, because snowploughs fixed to the engines would be needed to clear the track, but, with the normal German efficiency, things would soon be in order.

One morning in January, after school assembly, soon after Ralf's fifth birthday, the headmistress, Fraulein Mertel, asked us girls to remain seated, as she wanted to make an announcement.

'Girls,' she began, 'the government has ordered our establishment to be converted into a military hospital. Many soldiers, some of them badly wounded, are being sent from the Russian battlegrounds back into Germany and we don't have adequate facilities to accommodate them all. Therefore our school and the boy's grammar school will combine and lessons be structured accordingly. Your hours of tuition will rotate weekly. One week, the girls will have their lessons from 8.30 in the morning until 12.30 p.m., and the boys from 1 p.m. until 5 p.m. The following week the timetable will reverse: boys will attend in the mornings and girls in the afternoon. Except for those girls and boys who live outside Stolp and need to come in by train. They'll only have morning lessons, either with the boys or girls, whichever the case may be. Now, do you have any questions you'd like me to address?'

I raised my hand.

'Fraulein Mertel, please can you tell us when this new system will start?'

'Very soon, I think, Else. The teaching staff from both schools will meet tomorrow afternoon to finalise the new structure.'

'Fraulein Mertel, will we keep our own teachers and the boys theirs?'

'Listen, girls,' Fraulein Mertel emphasised. 'Apart from the different hours you'll spend at school everything else will remain the same. Now, go to your classes. Your form mistresses should be able to answer any other questions you have.'

Of course there was a lot of chatter on the way to our classrooms. To us girls it was very exciting to share the school with the Grammar boys. We'd be certain to meet occasionally, for that could never be completely avoided.

What concerned Gisela, Sieglinde and me was the envy we'd cause, because we were the only girls from our class who'd share lessons with the boys every other week. But what could *we* do about it? The teachers had made that decision and we had to abide by their rules.

Yet the system worked.

Our school became a military hospital. After only a few days of ceaseless, non-stop preparations, the hospital was ready to receive its first consignment of casualties.

February 1944

One afternoon the three of us had left the school building and were on our way to the station. Having been delayed during lessons, we now had to hurry. Our train left Stolp at 4 p.m. and if we weren't there, it would leave without us.

Deep snow lay everywhere and the world was white. A strong icy winter wind blew cruelly from the east.

We were surprised to notice how much traffic was on the street leading to the station. How strange – a lot of military vehicles: Red Cross vans and lorries, ambulances and emergency cars from the hospitals. Whatever could have happened?

But soon it became clear what they were waiting for. A transport train full of wounded soldiers had arrived from the Russian front and were waiting to be transported to the new military hospital here in Stolp.

Those poor, poor boys and men! A look of hopelessness, horror and suffering haunted their eyes.

They were all severely injured. Red bloodstains on their bandages covering their heads and limbs contrasted starkly with the white snow. Some soldiers walked with crutches, while others were carried on stretchers, too ill or wounded to move unaided.

'Gisela,' I said, 'look at these poor boys, some hardly older than we are. How could they have been fighting in Russia?'

'Surely they're not old enough to be on the battlefront,' whispered Gisela. 'Seventeen? Eighteen? Too young to be so severely wounded.' We were both moved dreadfully by the sight.

The older men made me think of my father. Would *he* come home one day looking like that? *Dear God, I hope not!* But I scanned the lines of men, just in case . . .

The thought tugged at my heart and tears rolled down my cheeks.

Red Cross nurses were in attendance, ever ready to give a helping hand or offer a warm drink. Some soldiers needed help holding a cup with bandaged hands or struggling with crutches, while others needed support to walk. Nurses and voluntary helpers willingly gave assistance with kindness and smiles of encouragement.

It was all too awful! I couldn't comprehend what was happening in that dreadful war. I thought that if our soldiers were sent home so seriously wounded, surely soldiers from other nations would be in the same situation. It was all dreadfully sad.

'Oh, Gisela, if only we could help! It must be wonderful to feel you could cheer those poor soldiers up in some small way. Don't *you* think so?'

'I know, Else, and I feel the same as you. But for now we must rush to catch the train, or it will leave without us. If we miss it, we'll be stuck here and I'm cold and hungry.'

I nodded. 'At least we have warm homes to go to and hot meals waiting for us. They must be longing for a home-cooked meal, though I'm sure the hospitals will do their best for them, now they're safe.'

'Else, let's go! I'll race you to our platform.'

Spring 1944

After February came a lull in our lives. News from the front sometimes filtered through but no one told us what was actually going on. It appeared to be an advantage for the German nation to be kept in ignorance of the true state of affairs. But when we heard that the Russian army had entered Poland and was advancing nearer and nearer towards the German border, fear began to chill our minds.

What made matters worse was that weeks went by without news from my father. mother was dreadfully worried, as there was no one to turn to for information.

End of July 1944

Our summer holidays in Pomerania ran from the end of July to the beginning of September, and one day towards the end of term, during lessons, the headmistress entered our classroom.

'Girls,' Fraulein Mertel announced, 'I have in my hand a letter – an official communication, giving details of instructions, which I'll shortly explain to you. First, please be seated. Our school has been chosen to make available a group of girls and boys between the ages of thirteen and fifteen to spend three weeks near the East Prussian border to help dig tank defences.

'Should the enemy attempt to set foot on Prussian soil, we have to try with all our determination and dedication to prevent them from getting further into Pomerania. And you, German girls and boys, also have to play your part. The ditches we'll help dig will be reinforced with concrete. Blocks of concrete, called dragon teeth will be placed on both sides of the trenches for many kilometres along the East Prussian border.'

Arms were raised by those wanting to ask questions.

'Just a moment. You can ask me later; just let me finish what I have to tell you.' She raised her hand to quell the excitement. 'Our transport's scheduled to leave on the last Saturday of this month. Once you get to your destination, you'll be issued with work clothes and boots. You'll be shown your accommodation and issued with a straw mattress and blankets. All you have to bring are personal utensils, underwear and some clothes for leisure time.' Again she waited for the murmurs to die down. She was aware that that was probably the most unusual news she'd ever given out to her school. 'Now your questions, girls; but please, one at a time.'

My question was, 'Where will we go and how long will the tank defences be when they're finished?'

'To prevent the Russian army penetrating further into the Reich, Adolf Hitler wants to turn East Prussia into a fortress,' answered Fraulein Mertel. 'The east wall defence, when it's finished, will be almost 200 kilometres long.'

Gisela asked, ' Will our duties only be digging?'

'Mostly, Gisela. We must dig as deep and as hard as we can. Of course, you won't be alone: you'll be joined by hundreds of men, women, boys and girls – all striving to do their best for the fatherland and our leader. He's relying on us to excel. The East Prussian fortification must be so strong that it's invincible. Every shovelful of soil that we'll dig out of the trenches is a shovel towards victory and for our beloved leader. Never forget that, girls!'

Fraulein Mertel paused for her words to sink in, and then continued: 'I'll now hand each one of you a letter. Please take it home and give it to your parents for their signature. Then bring it back to me tomorrow.'

When I got home, I gave mother the letter straightaway. She looked at it silently for some time. From the expression on her face I could see she was very angry. Of course, I was full of what we called 'our adventure' and wasn't prepared for mother's reaction. She was furious!

'Whatever is our government thinking of, sending young girls so far away from home to dig trenches for tank defences? That's no job for girls! They're not meant to lift spades of heavy soil. They could damage their bodies severely. And what then? Would that also be in the name of the "Fatherland"?'

'But, mother, I'll have to go. We all have to; there's no way out.'

'I know, child, but it makes me sad to think my authority over my own daughter can be undermined by so-called "powers from above".'

'Please, mother,' I tried to pacify her, 'it's only three weeks: they'll soon go by. I'd rather stay with you . . . (I knew those words would please her) but it might be fun to be together with other young people from all over Pomerania. I promise to take care of myself, but please sign the letter.'

Mother did, although reluctantly. I felt I'd won a battle I could easily have lost.

But before we left, I had to have the answer to one important question: Was Egon expected home during the holidays? I had to ask Frau Ruch. However, she couldn't give me a definite answer. 'You know, Else, that Egon's in the middle of military training and because of this he may be unable to get away. But I'll tell him where you are and if he does come home, you'll be able to meet when you return.'

Saturday, 26 August 1944

The day arrived quickly and at a pre-arranged time we assembled on the school playground. Names were called, after which we marched in pairs to the station where a train awaited us. We were all excited, full of chatter and laughter, looking forward to our *great* adventure.

None of us knew exactly where we were going. The countryside through which we sped was mostly flat, interspersed with small marshland lakes and mixed woodland. We passed small towns and sleepy villages, here and there a lonely farmhouse with domestic animals roaming in yards and meadows. Because of the war all signposts had been removed. Even the names of stations we passed through had been taken away, in order to confuse the enemy should he set foot on German soil.

Now and then the train stopped in one of these unknown places to admit more children, women and elderly men – anyone who wasn't already fighting – into empty carriages reserved for them.

After three hours of travelling, we arrived at our destination. A small town, nothing spectacular, greeted us. I was amazed at how many teenagers and grown-ups alighted from the train – hundreds of us.

We were silent, hungry and tired after the journey and all the excitement, and when our teacher gave the order to line up and follow her, we were eager to.

Gisela and I stayed together. Sieglinde wasn't with us, as she was required to help with her large family. We were assigned to a school with accommodation arranged in the sports hall. It was a large hall and all the sports equipment had been removed. Instead straw mattresses lined the walls on either side: at least fifty in all – twenty-five either side. On top of each mattress were two grey army blankets, a pillow – also stuffed with straw – and an enamel mug and plate; two spoons, large and small, plus fork and knife in a small linen bag. At the side of the mattress stood a metal locker just large enough to take our sparse belongings. Money and valuables were handed to our teacher for safe keeping, but we were allowed to keep a watch, if we had one.

'Girls, settle in as quickly as you can,' our teacher called out. 'Then come to the dining room for a meal. After you've eaten, I'll take you to get your work clothes and boots and inform you of your schedule, starting tomorrow.'

We sat at a long table with benches on either side. The meal was unremarkable, except for the yeast dumplings and custard, which stuck in my throat! I couldn't swallow them, despite being hungry.

I was suddenly very homesick and didn't want to be there.

Somehow though it didn't take us long to settle in, and soon a routine was established. Daily we had to work two periods of four hours each, one in the morning and the second in the afternoon. The morning shift started at 6 a.m.; but we had to be ready by 5.45 p.m., when a lorry was waiting outside the school to take us to our workplace. Digging was hard work, but the men had already loosened the soil. With our spades, we threw the soil into wheelbarrows, which were picked up by boys or men and taken away to be disposed of. We were glad when it was 10 a.m. and the lorry was waiting to take us back to our dormitory, where we could rest until 2 p.m., when the second shift started. That lasted until 6 p.m., when we finished for the day. We had a short break in between, but needed that. The weather was hot all the time, and it was thirsty work, but luckily fresh water was always at hand. Sundays were not rest days, but we worked only one shift – for us it was a morning period from 10 a.m. to 2 p.m., which at least gave us longer in bed.

Oh how we ached in the early days, despite our school physical education training. Of course we grumbled and protested, throwing our spades down on the soil heaps. For some of the younger and weaker children, the work was genuinely too heavy. Yet we had to go on, as there was no way out. The army staff were kind, but made sure everyone did what was required of them.

Behind the school, where we had our living quarters, was an orchard. It was a large orchard with many fruit trees, mostly apples.

One day, while we were digging, two boys came over to Gisela and me. They asked if we were interested in doing some apple scrumping.

I'd never heard that word but could well imagine what it meant.

'You mean stealing apples?' I asked. 'I don't like that idea. What if we're caught? We'd be in deep trouble!'

'Else, we don't mean pick them off the trees. There are lots of apples lying on the grass and if they stay there, they'll only rot.'

'How do you think we could go about getting some without being seen?' I asked.

'We've got it all worked out,' exclaimed one of the lads. 'Listen! This evening, when it's dark, we'll meet at the back of the toilets in the yard. We'll climb over the fence into the orchard and pick up as many apples as we can carry. Our overalls have elastic in the legs, which will make it easy to carry them.'

'But that's stealing,' Gisela whispered with a worried look on her face. 'What if the farmer hears us and comes to investigate?'

'If we're quiet,' I answered, 'no one will hear us. There are so many apples on the grass, it will take only a few minutes to get all we want. The moon will give us enough light to pick up the best. Come on, Gisela, say yes; it would be fun.' I did have some misgivings but hated the thought of being a spoilsport. I didn't think that what was proposed was actually stealing. After all, the apples were windfalls and I persuaded myself it would be all right to gather those.

As the evening approached, I put on my overalls and, at the appointed time, Gisela and I slipped out of the school building. Silently, we dashed across the schoolyard where, behind the toilets, the boys were already waiting.

'Quickly,' one of them whispered, 'let's get over the fence; there's no one about.'

And in no time we stood in the orchard. I didn't want to go too far, just in case, but there was no need. Apples were everywhere. I bent down and quickly picked up as many as I could with Gisela always close by.

The best apples were in the centre of the orchard. One tree in particular stood out from the rest. It was laden with big rosy apples, which looked so tempting that I imagined them to be sweeter and juicier – quite delicious! I stuffed them into my trouser legs, which made my legs almost too heavy to lift.

Gisela was still near me.

'That's enough,' I whispered. 'I don't even know how to get over the fence. I may have to leave some behind.'

Suddenly I heard someone approaching.

'Hush,' I whispered, 'It could be the farmer – and a dog? Gisela, I'm scared. Let's try to run for it.'

'No, let's wait, Else, hide behind a tree: he may not see us.'

But he did – we were soon discovered!

'Well, young ladies, what do you think you're up to? Don't you realise trespassing is a punishable offence? I'd better hand you over to someone in charge. I can't leave this unreported.'

Gisela and I were really worried now. The boys had disappeared – the cowards. Typical!

'Please, Sir,' I pleaded with the farmer, 'don't report us. We'll not take a single apple and promise never to enter your orchard again. We're both very sorry to be on your property.'

Then the farmer surprised us by saying, 'Now you two, take a couple of apples each and disappear. I don't want to see either of you again. Another time and I won't be so lenient.'

'Thank you, Sir,' was all we could say, tumbling all but two apples each onto the ground, and away we sped, over the fence and out of sight.

Back in our dormitory Gisela and I sat on our mattress each enjoying an apple. But I had a consolation: on my pillow lay a letter. I knew the writing was my mother's, and stroked the envelope and hugged it to me. I waited until I was in bed before I read it, twice over, while trying to stem the tears that rolled down my cheeks – I felt so homesick.

4 September 1944

I decided to sit in my corner and write in my diary:

> It's evening and very quiet in our dormitory. Most of the girls have occupied themselves: some are reading and some writing, and at the far end of the hall a group of girls are playing cards.

> Today I had a letter from mother. All's well at home. Marlenchen's a proper toddler now with little fingers into everything.

> Ralf's a healthy child again. He often asks where his big sister is and mother keeps telling him that she'll soon return home. Hans-Dieter, my big brother, is 'the man of the house'. He's such a kind lad and has been a big help to mother.

> The best news, however, is to hear that the Baroness, Dorothea, intends to visit Glowitz with her new baby boy sometime during September. They call him Gerhard, after his grandfather. The name is a well-established Puttkamer tradition.

> Very soon it will be my birthday. At last I'll be fifteen years old. No little girl any more, but grown-up, and almost an adult. I may not be home by then, but later I can make up for what I'm now missing. Mother will see to it we can celebrate my birthday, even if it's late.

> I'm longing to be home again. Although the days go by fast, the evenings are worse. There's little to do. We're not allowed into town but have to make our own entertainment. We sing and dance to wireless music, tell stories from where we live and sometimes, just occasionally, we touch on politics and the war. We all have our own opinions but must be careful expressing them so as not to hurt others' feelings.

> I'll be glad when three weeks are over and we can go home. Back to normal. It's all right here in a way: we get on well together. But, it's not like home … nothing can equal that.

15 September 1944

The day arrived when our designated stretch of tank defences was complete. For us school children the three weeks were up at last and it was time to go home. The adults, men and women, were to remain and extend the trenches further along the border. A new group of workers would join them, including pupils from other schools in Pomerania and East Prussia.

But our time was up. We were ready, our belongings packed and waiting for us to walk to the station. We were all in high spirits, laughing and singing as we marched along.

Oh it was good to be going back to Glowitz and my family, especially on mother's birthday! But my time away hadn't all been bad. It had taught us a lot – how to get on with people in large groups and in close proximity, to realise we're all different and, most of all, to be tolerant of other people's failings.

I'd been away for just three weeks, but it seemed far longer. Yet as soon as I was home it felt as if I'd never left. Ralf came running, arms open wide. I bent down to his level, gave him a big hug and whispered in his ear how much I loved him.

Little Marlene was delighted to be picked up. She seemed to have grown – could it have been my imagination? But she could run on her little legs and her tiny fingers grabbed everything in reach.

As for Hans-Dieter – he just looked at me. 'Welcome home, Else. Glad to have you back.'

But my mother! After she'd given me one of her famous bear hugs and a big kiss, her first words were, 'Else, you need a bath!'

'A bath, mother? I'm not dirty! I've washed every day except this morning; there wasn't time.'

'No matter, child; do as I say. Then, when you're ready, we can all sit down for a meal.'

'Lovely, mother. Home-cooked food! My mouth's watering just to think of it.'

It was wonderful to be back, and, it being Friday, I had almost three days before I had to return to school.

I asked mother what news I'd missed while I was away. She said she'd received another letter from Grandma and Grandad to say they were both in good health and that they intended to remain in their house. Their love and thoughts were always with us. From Marlies still no news. Where could she be? I hoped she was safe but there was no way I could get in touch with her.

I was sad when mother told me she still hadn't heard from father. I saw how worried she was and wished for a sign from him that he was well and surviving the war.

My birthday on 11 September had come and gone. That year it had been a day like any other, with hard work as usual. But I'd accepted that, and anyway mother had promised a belated birthday treat for me when I returned. I didn't want anything special; it was enough for me to be with my family and to have my normal life back.

Sure enough, as we ate, mother said, 'I also want to talk about your birthday, Else. You're fifteen years old now, an important milestone. We can't let it go without doing *something* special. Have you anything in mind?'

'Yes, mother, I have. Can Gisela and I travel to Stolp to see a film at the cinema and afterwards go to Café Reinhardt to have some cake and a cup of *real* coffee, if it's obtainable? Now I'm fifteen, I'm allowed to drink it, aren't I?'

Mother laughed. 'Of course you are, daughter. Quite grown-up now aren't you?' Then, after a pause, she added, 'But please Else, take Sieglinde with you. That young girl works so hard for her family and doesn't get out often. She'll be excited when you offer and, don't worry, it will be my treat to all of you.'

Saturday, 16 September 1944

It was a lovely birthday celebration after all. At the cinema the film we saw was a comedy. There was a lot of laughter and gaiety, and for a while we could all forget the serious world outside the cinema. We entered Café Reinhardt acting like ladies and felt grown-up.

When we arrived home, mother was delighted to hear of our successful afternoon and how much we'd enjoyed our outing to Stolp. She reminded us that, now we stood at the threshold of adult life, we had to be prepared to leave childhood behind.

I often wondered if the digging we'd just done was really necessary. The beautiful countryside where we'd worked seemed so peaceful, utterly disconnected from a war of bloodstained soldiers. Was it a waste of time digging tank defences? Yes, they were strong and looked formidable, but would they be able to halt an advance from the enormously powerful Russian army? Was all that hard work for nothing? And as for advancing enemy troops – that was too difficult even to contemplate . . .

'Mother,' I asked, when we were alone later that night, 'suppose, just suppose, the Russians do reach Pomerania, what do you think it would be like for us?'

Mother looked at me in grave silence for a moment or two, and I could see from her frown she was weighing up her answer.

At last she replied. 'Else, my dear, as I say you're now old enough to understand so much more. I don't know how the Russians would treat us if they came. But one thing I do know – they *won't* treat us kindly. Because our soldiers haven't always been kind to their civilians, there's a lot of hatred against us Germans. All I'd ask of you, my daughter, is to try to be constantly on your guard. Stay in the background and make yourself inconspicuous. It's well known Russian soldiers drink a lot, and who knows what they're capable of when they're drunk on vodka. I'll guard you as much as I can, but remember, I also have two little ones and Hans-Dieter: they'll all need my care.'

'I know, mother. I'll look after myself. Who knows? They may not be as cruel and malicious as they're made out to be.'

Little me and my dog

Papi can I stay here?

On a bicycle made for two

Snow in Glowitz (Pomerania) - 1943

Baby Marlene in the snow - January 1943

Marlene with Mother

Hans-Dieter with our parents

Don't I look like a proper soldier?

Else & Hans-Dieter found Easter eggs

Hans-Dieter the musician

Mother & little Ralph - 1941

Ralph, now a young man

Opa Hopp, Vati & Hans-Dieter

The four of us. Marlene,
Hans-Dieter, Ralph & I - 1970

Oma & Opa Barbier

Looking smart for the camera.
Hans-Dieter, Ralph & I - 1941

Dearest Mother, 80 years old

The Manor House, Glowitz (Pomerania)

Permits of entitlement for milk (from Russian administration)

The street where we lived

Chapter 27

Six Wagons

November 1944

Summer and autumn had gone and November, the forerunner of winter, had arrived. Already there had been a first fall of snow and a thin layer of ice could be seen covering lakes, ponds and the edges of rivulets. Farm animals were brought in from fields and meadows, back to the shelter of their winter quarters. People, young and old, enjoyed the leisure hours winter gave them in their cosy cottages, a secure haven away from the biting winds that swept over the flatlands of Pomerania from the east.

One day in November, much to the amazement of the people in Glowitz, six wagons came to a halt in the high street. Either two or four horses pulled each wagon and some had cows or an ox tied behind. Each cart was packed with precious personal belongings and whole families were sitting among furniture and household equipment. Old and young, from the tiniest baby to the most senior member were wrapped in blankets and featherbeds to keep warm in a battle to survive the icy Pomeranian winter.

The village people were most curious. Where had the wagons come from and where were they going? Mother had sent me to the grocery store and I was just as inquisitive. I also wanted to find out what was going on and, instead of returning straight home, stayed, trying to hear what the adults were discussing.

One elderly man, a spokesman for the evacuees, asked to speak to the mayor. A young lad was sent to fetch him, and he returned with the message that the mayor, who had a wooden leg and couldn't walk fast, wasn't far behind.

When the mayor arrived, he asked a lot of questions. But the replies were not to his liking.

From the old spokesman's account it emerged the people were refugees from East Prussia. They were fleeing from the advancing Russian army, which had entered Poland and was now pushing towards the East Prussian border. Their home was Prussia, and although their dialect varied from ours, they too were Germans and we could understand them.

What the old man said was horrific. He talked of families having to flee for their lives or be wiped out by large-scale massacres, of Russian tanks driving over and crushing wagons and all inside. The Russian troops weren't far behind and the only thing left was to flee to whatever safe haven could be found.

But the local government had ruled *under threat of execution* that everyone, young or old, had to remain and defend home and property in any way thay could. No one was permitted to flee.

But secretly people prepared their wagons, loaded them with precious belongings and as much food as it was possible to stow away. Then, under cover of darkness, they fled to escape not only the Russian army but also secret informers from their own neighbourhood.

'We got away safely,' said the old man, 'but we're only the first. 'Many thousands will follow us. Who knows when or how they'll get away. It's cold now, but daily the freeze becomes more severe. There will be many deaths: old people and tiny babies in particular. They can't survive the hardship of trekking in open wagons day after day in mid winter.'

'But where do all these people intend to go?' asked our mayor.

'We're happy to be in Pomerania,' replied the old man. 'We feel safe here; perhaps we can find a place to stay. The German army will soon arrive and defend our part of Prussia. They'll drive back the Russians and we can then return home.'

'Wait here,' said our mayor. 'I'll ask the estate manager if you can be accommodated, at least for a few days. But then, I'm sorry but you must move on. If what you say is true that more and more refugees will come this way, we must organise ourselves to receive them and be prepared to offer help wherever we can.'

'But where can we go?' asked the desperate people with angry raised voices. 'You're safe and have your cosy homes; we've lost everything.'

'Be that as it may,' answered the mayor, 'I'll do my best to find out if there are places set aside for people like you to find shelter. For now I'll see where you can make camp. You must have had a terrible journey.'

The refugees remained in barns at Glowitz Manor for five days. Then, one morning very early before daylight, they repacked their wagons and left.

20 November 1944

A few days after the refugees had left, a Russian prisoner of war came to see Johann. He wanted to speak to the estate manager, Herr Lemke, but couldn't find him anywhere. He had knocked on his door but neither he nor his wife seemed to be at home.

'I'll go and speak to the Baroness,' suggested Johann. 'Perhaps she has the answer.'

But she was no wiser, and just suggested he wait. Herr Lemke would surely be back soon.

When, after a few days, he and his wife still hadn't returned, the Baroness and Johann went to the cottage and found, to their consternation, that the doors were unlocked and on entering saw that, apart from furniture, all personal belongings had disappeared. So also had Herr and Frau Lemke. No one knew where they'd gone, but from that day on nothing was heard of them: they'd vanished without a trace!

A difficult time lay ahead for the young Baroness. She wanted to return to Berlin with her baby, but how could she? The estate was too much for her elderly parents to look after, so all responsibilities rested on her shoulders. She could rely on some of the Russian prisoners. They had been imprisoned on the farm for some time and the baroness knew them well. Now they could see her dilemma and were willing to do whatever work she asked of them. But others were more rebellious: they thought that now Herr Lemke wasn't around, they could please themselves. Mother feared some of them might escape, but surely they realised that if they were caught they'd be executed instantly

There were only a few estate workers, as the majority had been enlisted into the army, and most of those left were elderly and frail. But Fraulein Dorothea was grateful for any help they offered. Fraulein Ottilia wasn't available. No one knew where she was and mystery surrounded her absence, but it wasn't for us to question – it was none of our business.

Frau Krause, the mamsell in the kitchen, had told mother that it was now dangerous to be in Berlin. Air raids continued night and day and the bombardment of the city was horrific. 'The Baroness would be safe in Pomerania,' Frau Krause exclaimed emphatically.

Mother agreed it would be far better if the Baroness stayed in Glowitz, and indeed so much safer for her baby. But of course that had to be her own decision – we couldn't tell her what to do.

25 November 1944

It was evening and mother had already put baby Marlene into her cot; I was seeing to Ralfie. He'd had his bath and was in his pyjamas and now, as usual, wanted a story and a cuddle; then he'd also be tucked in for the night. Hans-Dieter was playing with his Meccano set and mother was about to sit in her chair and start to knit. I still had homework to finish for school on the coming Monday, after which I decided I would write to father or perhaps just sit quietly with my book. Outside it was dark and cold, and the wind howled through the beech trees in the park. It made the room even cosier.

Suddenly we heard a tremendous commotion on the farm: engines revving and men shouting. It sounded like a convoy of vehicles approaching somewhere near the park entrance.

'Mother, what's going on?' I asked. 'Who would come so late in the evening?'

'Else, turn out the lights. All of them. Then look behind the curtains to see if you can make out what's going on.'

I did as mother asked, but it was too dark to see anything.

Then heavy doors slammed downstairs. I thought I heard the Baroness talking and deep male voices replying.

'Mother,' I said, 'can I go and see what's happening?'

'All right, child, but don't stay long. And wrap up warm. Cover your head and ears.'

I grabbed a coat and scarf and rushed past the kitchen and out through the back door. There I could see Dunja and Anna also trying to work out what was going on.

I was astonished. The drive was lined with army vehicles! Huge lorries, small pickup trucks, motorcycles with sidecars, and one or two saloon cars for the officers.

German soldiers – many of them – had had their orders and scurried all over the place, yet in an organised fashion. Where had they come from? A battleground? Some had set up a field kitchen. They'd need warm food on a cold night such as that.

One soldier ran in my direction.

'Stop a moment!' I shouted. 'What are you doing here? Where are you going?'

'Can't stop, lady. Too much to do. Wait till the morning; then we may have time to talk.' And with those words he disappeared into the darkness.

I ran back upstairs and told mother what I'd seen.

'I know, Else,' she answered. 'A moment ago Fraulein Dorothea came to see me. The major's adjutant had approached her to ask for accommodation for himself and his superiors. She gave him the keys to the Lemkes' cottage. Then she asked me if I'd cook an evening meal for the three officers. I'll go downstairs and find out what it's all about.'

'Mother, are you willing to do all this?' I asked.

'I am,' answered my mother, 'providing you, Else, stay here with the children.'

'Of course,' I replied. 'Find out what they want you to do. But mother, please come back and let me know.'

So she wrapped up warmly, hurried across to the cottage and cooked for the officers. Hans-Dieter went to bed reluctantly because he wanted to see what was happening on the farm, but I told him we both had to wait until morning. He sulked a bit, but I reminded him that the next day would be a Sunday, not a school day. So he went to bed pacified and soon fell asleep.

I decided to sleep in mother's room, just in case the little ones needed my attention. Once, during the night, I thought I heard our living-room door open, but dozed off again, thinking I'd imagined the sound.

But it had been mother. After she'd finished serving the officers, she decided to spend the night in her own bed – or rather in mine, as hers was already occupied – and to return early next morning to serve breakfast.

26 November 1944

There was freshly baked bread and rolls from the field kitchen and *real* coffee, which the officers shared with my delighted mother.

After breakfast she returned and reported to us that she'd received important news, which she wanted to share with us. 'The soldiers you see here on the farm are all that's left of an infantry battalion of more than a thousand men. They're retreating because they can't fight the Russians any more. They've hardly a weapon between them and have almost run out of ammunition. They aim to get to the Baltic port of Gotenhafen [now named Gdynia] from where they hope to board a ship to take them to safety.'

'Mother,' I asked, 'wouldn't they take us with them?'

'I asked, child, but was advised to remain here. When the convoy leaves, no one knows what the soldiers will encounter on the way. It will be a march into uncertainty: we're better off staying where we are. But one officer told me, should the Russians come, not to stay in the manor. There will be looting and destruction and we wouldn't be safe. We must find shelter in a cottage somewhere in the village: the manor would be too risky.'

'But what about Frau Fronzeck and her girls? I met Sieglinde and she told me her mother would ask the soldiers if they could go with them.'

'That's up to Frau Fronzeck,' mother answered. 'We'll stay here. Who knows, the Russians may never come as far as Glowitz.'

'When are the troops leaving, mother?'

'Tomorrow. I'll cook once more this evening and, tomorrow, before daybreak, they'll be gone. But, Else, there's one thing we must do.'

'What's that, mother?'

'You, Hans-Dieter and I will sit down this afternoon and write a letter to father. The officers will take it and post it with their own mail. That way father's more likely to receive it. Agreed?'

'Yes, mother, Hans-Dieter and I will do as you say.'

While Marlenchen had her afternoon nap and Ralfie played with his toy army, mother, Hans-Dieter and I sat down to write letters.

We all had our own thoughts, but I found it a difficult letter to write. I tried to tell father all that had happened. I wanted him to know of our difficult situation and the uncertainty of not knowing what might be before us. But, most importantly, I told him how much we all loved him and asked that, whatever happened, he'd never lose hope and always believe that one day, when the war was over, we'd be together again. I then wrote:

> Dearest father,
>
> I wonder if this letter will reach you. But if it does, please don't be sad. We don't know how we can survive a Russian onslaught, but, if it should happen, mother and I are strong. We'll look after Hans-Dieter, Ralf and Baby and perhaps it's true that the Russians are fond of children and will leave mother and the little ones alone. Don't worry about me, father. I'll look after myself.

And I ended my letter with the words 'Goodbye, father. God bless you.'

Monday, 27 November 1944

Next morning all the soldiers left, and with them Frau Fronzeck and her seven girls. I watched Sieglinde, blonde hair glinting in the early morning sun, walk down the drive towards a lorry that would take her away into an unknown future. She smiled as she turned and waved up to me at our window. Her mother was waiting for her.

If only they'd known what lay ahead.

3 December 1944

It was already the beginning of December and all too soon the Christmas festivities would again be upon us. As far back as I can remember, Christmas was always a special occasion in our home, the highlight of the year. Weeks before, we started to prepare for that most important event. There were secrets, and small surprises left on our pillows. 'Who could have put them there?' Hans-Dieter and I wondered, excitedly. When we asked mother if she knew what the Christ Child might bring us, she'd smile sweetly, tap her nose and say to us, 'Just wait and see when the day's here.' Such happy days when we were together. Father loved Christmas: he was like a child and couldn't wait until Christmas Eve.

And now? Where was he now? Fighting in Russia somewhere near Odessa, we assumed. The German army had to fight bitterly to hang on to that part of Russia. Until now it remained in German hands, but for how long?

No news had come from father for quite some time. Mother had sent a parcel to him with the gloves, socks and warm balaclava she'd knitted. Also included had been a small tin of special biscuits she'd baked herself, and Hans-Dieter and I had put in our own self-made Christmas greetings. We hoped the small parcel would reach him.

Christmas 1944

That Christmas was very different from those that had gone before. But Advent Sundays were still something special. As in previous years, we were invited to join the Puttkamer family in carol singing and partaking of a glass of wine and a slice of stollen, the delicious German Christmas bread, baked as usual by Frau Krause.

Frau Voeltheim arrived from Berlin to be with the young Baroness and her baby, but her husband, the cavalry captain, was absent: his leave, like that of all other soldiers, had been cancelled. Her mother, Sylvia, and Frau Ida Affeld, the old nanny, had also come. Only Fraulein Ottilia wasn't among us, and her name wasn't mentioned except to toast her good health and safety. Mother was pleased to see her friend Ida again. They were fond of each other, their friendship strong enough to survive long after the war should their paths cross again. And Fraulein Elisabeth was there too, quiet and inconspicuous.

But the atmosphere had changed. The true spirit of Christmas was missing, for a gloom hung over us as we awaited something ominous, but unknown. We had a premonition something dreadful would occur in the not-too-distant future.

As always our little family had a small tree; and once more it was kept secret until Christmas Eve, when at last we were allowed to admire it. We also had a goose. Johann had seen to that, which made it possible for us to have a traditional festive lunch once more.

Presents were small that year, as the shops in Stolp and surrounding towns were virtually empty; but no one went without. All mother's gifts were handmade, all useful and reclaimed from discarded garments. Fraulein Elisabeth had found some old knitted jumpers and cardigans for mother, which she unpicked and unravelled; and after the wool was washed and dried it felt like new. Clever mother! She was a lady of her time. Two wars had taught her how to be thrifty – she could have coined the word 'recycle', but in 1944 it wasn't yet in our vocabulary. Her present from us was a small bottle of eau de cologne, which Fraulein Elisabeth had given to me; but I thought it would make a suitable gift for our mother, her favourite perfume.

Christmas morning

Hans-Dieter and I went to church, but mother stayed behind with the little ones. The service was festive and very moving as the pastor spoke again of uncertain times ahead. No one knew what the coming year would bring. We'd heard it all many times before and wanted something uplifting, but there seemed to be nothing cheerful to talk about.

We met Gisela and her parents and wished villagers we knew a happy Christmas. The church was less crowded than usual, especially for Christmas morning, and we wondered why.

After the service we hurried home, where mother greeted us with good humour. She made the best of any situation and gave the appearance of having not a worry in the world.

The tears she wept over father fighting in Russia were shed in the silence and privacy of her room. She never let us children know how deeply she was hurting inside.

Frequently, in the winter evenings, when Hans-Dieter and the little ones were asleep, mother and I would talk. She now treated me as an adult, which made me feel proud. She knew she could depend on me in any situation, but also pointed out there might soon come a time when her trust in me would really be put to the test.

'Mother,' I wanted to know, 'soon it will be 1945. Do you think perhaps this time next year the war will be over?'

'I wish I knew, my daughter. Adolf Hitler has promised us a new secret weapon, which he'll use soon now. Perhaps, just perhaps, it will turn the tide of war and bring it to an end.'

Mother was my best friend and I loved her deeply. The teaching and guidance she gave me on my path through life was invaluable and made me the person I am.

Chapter 28

Shadowy Shapes

January 1945

The last day of 1944 passed very quietly, as the village lay empty and silent under a thick blanket of snow. In years gone by, when the clock approached midnight there would have been a lot of rejoicing and merrymaking. Bells would ring in the New Year and village people would congregate in a joyous mood, shaking hands with friends and strangers alike. It was always a wonderful and moving occasion.

But not that year. Sad news from the Russian front had filtered through and by now we knew the Russian army was pushing forward into Prussia towards Königsberg (now named Kaliningrad) and Pomerania, only about 240 kilometres away from the defences we'd dug just a few months before. So we knew it wouldn't be long before they perhaps reached us and shattered our peaceful world.

As January moved on, more and more wagons with refugees rumbled into Glowitz. They were only passing through, hopeful that somewhere further on, they'd find a safer destination. Those poor people were a pitiful sight. They'd left their homes and belongings behind in Prussia and were now carrying only a collection of essential household goods and bedding to help them in their struggle to survive.

Facilities were needed to help all the passing travellers. Mother and a few ladies worked out a rota, taking turns preparing and supplying hot soup and drinks in the village hall. Soon a popular venue, with hot sustenance handed out to cold, hungry refugees, Hans-Dieter and I called it 'The Glowitz Soup Kitchen'.

As yet their numbers were small, but they all had a wealth of information. Their tales were horrific. Mother and her ladies tried to protect us young people from the worst stories, but rumours spread among my schoolfriends. We dreaded the thought that our small community could soon be exposed to such incredible hatred and gruesomeness. When would it be our turn? That question was in everyone's mind, yet there seemed little preparation in the village for an escape.

'Mother, can't we leave now, before it becomes too dangerous to be here?'

'No, my child; it's too cold for us to travel. Ralfie and Marlenchen are not strong enough to brave this bitter weather. Rumour has it the Russians will divert away to the south of us on their march towards Berlin.'

For my friends and me January passed by uneventfully. Days were much the same as before, with bitter cold, snow and more snow and icy winds whipping across the flat landscape.

Some afternoons, when Hans-Dieter and I returned from school with no homework, we were allowed to accompany mother, while Frau Krause looked after Ralf and baby

Marlene. We enjoyed helping her with the distribution of warm drinks and soup, and fresh bread brought over from the bakery.

Twice mother found small boys who'd become parted from their mothers and were desperate to find them. But what could she do? All she could think of was to put the children on the first wagon coming through Glowitz and ask the occupants to help the little ones find their families, or to hand them over at the next Red Cross station. It was a tragic situation.

31 January 1945

When we tuned into the radio to listen to the war bulletins, we heard appalling news. It was announced that on the previous day, 30 January, exactly twelve years to the day Adolf Hitler had come to power, a Russian submarine had torpedoed and sunk the jewel of the German navy, the *Wilhelm Gustloff*. That proud ship had gone down in the Baltic Sea, taking with it the lives of thousands of wounded soldiers and refugees, mostly women and children. A Russian submarine had spotted the *Gustloff*, a sitting duck without escort or protection from the air, and with deadly accuracy had fired three torpedoes. For most of the ship's passengers there was no escape from death in the icy Baltic. Of 6,600 souls, at least 5,400 perished. Some vessels in the vicinity heard the desperate SOS messages and rushed to the scene, but could rescue only about 1,200 people, a terrible tragedy. Of course, the German propaganda machine went into motion fast, for Dr Goebbels, the propaganda minister, was in his element. I well remember him shouting and ranting, promising revenge against the Russian enemy.

We'd heard it all before and took hardly any notice of what he said. Mother quietly went to the radio and turned it off.

'Mother,' I asked, later that evening, 'do you think Frau Fronzeck and her girls were on the *Gustloff* when it sunk? I can't bear the thought they might be dead. And all those soldiers who stayed here on the farm just a short while ago – could they also have drowned? It's too awful.' I burst into tears.

'Else, my darling,' mother replied, 'how I wish I knew. There's no one who can give us that information. Perhaps one day, when this war's over, we may find out what happened to the Fronzeck family. Did they survive or did they perish like so many others? As for now, there's nothing we can do. Do you understand, my daughter?'

'Yes, mother,' I sobbed, 'I understand what you're saying. I grieve for them and the other victims. It's very very sad.'

Disaster followed disaster as the tide turned ever more against us. We also heard on the radio that the siege of Königsberg had begun and that the Russian army had encircled East Prussia. Königsberg was declared a fortress to be defended to the last man.

'Mother,' I asked, 'what does it mean to be under siege?'

'It's not easy to explain, but let me try.' She scratched her head. 'A city under siege is surrounded by the enemy, in this case the Russian army. All roads leading into it are blocked: nothing or no one can get in or out. The enemy outside tries to force the beleaguered population into surrender. Food becomes more and more scarce, water supplies become contaminated and the enemy outside sends in a continuous barrage of heavy gunfire to destroy the city. Is that clearer, Else?'

'Yes, mother, I think so. It must be a dreadful situation. Wasn't it like that in Stalingrad?'

'And Moscow, I believe,' mother added. 'But I'm not quite sure.'

The siege of that magnificent city Königsberg lasted until 9 April 1945. It was totally devastated and all its inhabitants surrendered; many thousands died.

Just eleven days after the sinking of the *Gustloff* the radio announced a second terrible disaster had struck in the Baltic Sea. The *General Steuben*, again crammed with many thousands of wounded soldiers and refugees, had also been an easy target for the same Russian submarine that had destroyed the *Gustloff*. Just after midnight two torpedoes had made a direct hit and the *Steuben* sank in only seven minutes. Most passengers, still asleep, had no chance of survival, and drowned in the freezing waters.

The loss of life was phenomenal and the German people were devastated. How many more disasters at sea were to follow? So many passengers had embarked in the hope of finding a haven. So many wounded, anxious to reach safety where they could receive attention and much-needed care. There was even a hint of resignation in the voice of the radio announcer.

One February morning, Gisela and I were waiting at Glowitz station to catch the train to Stolp – little did we realise what that day held in store for us. For the first time the horrors of the situation were about to unfold before our eyes with unbelievable, yet stark, reality.

That morning there was an icy storm, and the snow, driven by the wind, swept across the flat, empty countryside.It was so cold that Gisela and I huddled in a corner of the station building, longing for the train to arrive. Dawn was breaking, and as we looked across the country road towards the forest, we saw, silhouetted against the sky, shadowy shapes emerging into the early light.

'Look, Gisela. What's coming towards us? Can you make it out? Not the Russians, is it?'

'No, Else, of course not! Wait a moment and we may be able to see better.'

'I think I can see the outline of horses,' I said. 'Gisela, aren't they refugee wagons?'

'The wind's so strong and this blizzard makes it difficult to see anything clearly.'

'Gisela,' I said, looking her straight in the eyes, 'if those are refugees – and we don't know how many – I won't go to school today.'

'But, Else, you must go. You'll get into trouble: Fraulein Mertel will want to know why.'

'I don't care, Gisela; I'm *not* going. I'll ask mother to write a note explaining my absence. She'll be glad of my help.'

The wagons were already nearer and we could see there were many.

'It's a proper wagon train. They must be from a village just outside Königsberg.'

'Else, please come to school. You can help your mother this afternoon when we come home, but do come now.' Gisela was anxious.

'Gisela, don't keep on. I've told you, I'm staying here; go if you want. Look, there are lots of wagons, about twenty at least. They're coming towards our village and I'm certain they'll stop in the high street. They all need a hot meal: I want to be there to hand it out.'

'All right, do what you think's best. Listen, I can hear the train coming. I wish you were travelling with me.'

'Go, Gisela. I'll speak to you later this afternoon.'

In the states of Pomerania and Prussia almost every village had a vast country estate, where the lord and his lady ruled kindly and cared for the inhabitants: a cottage for each tenant family, garden front and rear, and some domestic animals – a comfortable way of life for each estate worker.

In times of trouble the villagers rallied around the lord and his lady for guidance and leadership. But here was a most unusual situation. The Russians were coming, taking by storm each village and town they came across. As other refugees had told us, everything was happening very quickly. To flee was forbidden, but not everyone paid heed to this law.

Secretly the lord would order wagons to be built: one or two for the manor and one for each tenant family. All the horses from the manor farm were to pull them. Polish prisoners of war were willing to help, their fear of falling into Russian hands as strong as ours. French prisoners on many estates were also eager to support the people who'd been their masters during years of imprisonment. They too wanted to escape before the Russians arrived, and were eager to be part of the preparations. There wasn't a moment to lose, for this was a race against time. As each wagon was completed, it was handed over to a family who would pack and prepare it under cover of night.

The lady of the manor with her children rode ahead of the wagon train in her own private coach. She was the spokeswoman for the people under her protection and they, in return, were grateful for her leadership. The lord stayed behind. He was the only one not to leave his estate to its difficult and tragic fate. He had to shoot or cull all remaining animals, including his beloved dogs – a heartbreaking mission.

When all tasks were completed to his satisfaction, only then would he mount his favourite horse and ride off to join his wife and people. But frequently his family had to wait in vain for their lord to join them. Too emotionally distraught, he would as a final act take the gun he'd used to slaughter his livestock, point it at his temple and squeeze the trigger.

I watched the last railway carriage disappearing into the swirling snow with Gisela on board, and then ran towards the first coach that had been held up with the rest of the wagons by the oncoming train. I knocked on the frozen window and the door was opened a crack. Inside I could see a family wrapped in rich furs.

'Good morning, my lady,' I blurted out, wiping snowflakes from my eyelids. 'I live here in Glowitz. My mother and the ladies of the village run a soup kitchen for refugees. Can I lead you to the hall?' I paused to wait for her answer and then, seeing the little ones inside shiver, added persuasively, 'Please follow me. I'll take you where you and your children can find warmth and hot food.'

I ran on ahead as fast as it was possible on the slippery, icy road. Bursting into the hall, I first had to explain to mother why I wasn't on the train to school. Then I told her and the other ladies that many wagons of refugees were on their way into the village and would soon be arriving outside the village hall.

I could see that mother was busy, but had to ask immediately, 'Mother, what about the horses pulling the carts and the cows tied behind some of them? Most of the horses have spiked irons under their hooves to prevent them from slipping. But the cows have no protection and I've seen traces of blood as they walk through the snow. What can we do, mother?'

'Else, run to the manor and find the forester, Herr Lehmann. Explain the situation and ask what can be done. I hope he can provide food and shelter for the animals and for those people who wish to stay overnight.'

I ran as fast as I could and found Herr Lehmann in one of the stables. When he'd listened to my request, he agreed to come and see for himself what had to be done.

After a while, as I was busy chopping vegetables, I noticed him enter the village hall and look for mother.

'Frau Hopp,' he said when he'd gained her attention. 'We've a grave situation, which I don't know how to deal with. Three tiny dead babies – frozen to death – the distraught mothers have asked me what they should do. They'd like them to be buried, but the ground's frozen solid: no graves can be dug to lay the little ones to rest. Have you any advice?'

'Herr Lehmann, please see the mothers; tell them we'll find a solution. Ask them to be patient. Meanwhile I'll speak to my daughter.' Mother looked around for me. 'Else, just stop what you're doing. Run to the pastor's house and ask him to come. Tell him it's urgent: I hope he's at home. Go quickly, child. You're also needed *here*.'

Fortunately the pastor was at home. I explained my visit and he immediately agreed to hurry over to the hall. There he conferred with Herr Lehmann, my mother and the three ladies who'd tragically lost their babies. The pastor proposed the little ones be wrapped in white linen sheets and blankets. The mothers would then place the babies on consecrated ground in the cemetery and cover them with a deep layer of snow. The pastor would perform a burial service. He promised the mothers that, as soon as the snow melted, the babies would each be placed into a tiny coffin and laid to rest in separate graves with a small cross stating their names, dates of birth and death. That, he explained, was the best he could do, and the grieving mothers agreed they couldn't have wished for a better solution.

20 February 1945

The ancient, historic city of Danzig, completely destroyed by the war, was now in

Russian hands. After a fierce, prolonged battle against the superior strength of the Russian army, the German soldiers had capitulated and laid down their arms as an indication of surrender. So much bloodshed, with thousands of soldiers killed or maimed, and thousands more taken prisoner, not knowing where they might end up.

It was a sad day when we heard the news on the radio, for then we knew, without a doubt, it could only be a matter of weeks before the Russian army entered our village. For, with only the very top region near the Baltic Sea still open, Pomerania was already encircled. Glowitz was near the centre of this entrapment, as was Leba, on the edge of a large beautiful lake, and many other small isolated villages. What would become of us all once the trap was shut?

Mother tried to be optimistic. 'Come, children, let's wrap up warmly and walk through our lovely snowy park. Let's dream of springtime and happy days. What tomorrow, next week or next month will bring is a mystery. But, miracles happen – perhaps one's just around the corner?'

Chapter 29

The Russians Are Coming!

By the end of February we realised it wouldn't be long before the Russians entered our fairly isolated part of Pomerania. Particulary after the night of the phantom thunderstorm!

Hans-Dieter and I sat bolt upright in our beds when a sudden sharp crack of what I presumed was thunder echoed overhead.

'Else!' Hans-Dieter called out. 'What's that?'

'Don't worry. There must be a bad storm outside. Go back to sleep. We're quite safe.'

I lay for some time listening to the rumble in the distance. Strange. It was unusual for a thunderstorm at that time of year. Eventually I got out of bed and tiptoed to mother's room.

'Mother, are you awake?' I whispered.

'Yes, dear.'

'All that noise – can you hear it? Is it really thunder?' I crept to her bedside.

'No, I don't think so. Mamsell hinted this morning that the fighting's getting nearer. I think it's heavy gunfire we can hear. But nevertheless, we should be safe for a while – sound carries at night.'

After that, a distant rumble was heard frequently. Every day the ominous sound was getting closer and closer. Relentlessly, day and night, heavy gunfire could be heard from three directions: north, east and south. We felt threatened and frightened.

14 March 1945

A message came that the mayor of Glowitz had called the villagers to a meeting on the forecourt of the local bank. He had an important announcement to make and requested that every adult attend. The appeal was carried from person to person by word of mouth and also announced by two lads on bicycles: better than any loudspeaker. Because of the urgency, no man or woman could ignore the demand to attend, and mother was preparing to go alone.

'Can I come with you, mother?' I asked.

'Not this time, Else. You must stay and mind the little ones. Neither you nor Hans-Dieter will go out this morning; at least not until I come back.'

'Mother, please tell me what's going on? Something's happening. I must know what it is.'

'Have patience, child. You won't be kept in the dark. We'll talk as soon as I return.'

And true to her word, as soon as she came back, she sank into a chair and beckoned to us.

She was flushed, almost in shock. 'When I arrived at the bank, a crowd was already huddled together. Everyone was speculating why our mayor had called us, but we had to wait until he arrived. Soon he appeared on the balcony overlooking the forecourt and Glowitz high street. To everyone's surprise the mayor was in full dress uniform. A strange sight, quite out of the ordinary.' Mother paused, sipping the coffee I'd given her. After a few moments, she told us what the mayor had said:

> Dear friends, this is the last time I'll have the opportunity to speak to you. Very soon now the Russians will arrive in our village. It could be today; it could be tomorrow. No one knows exactly when, but I've been informed it will be soon. Therefore I implore you, go home now; remain indoors. Never, at any time, show resistance, but hang white sheets out of your windows as a sign of surrender.

'He paused to make sure we understood. When he was satisfied, he continued with this strange statement: "My job's done! For many years it has been my pleasure to serve you. Now may God protect you: Adolf Hitler cannot!"'

Mother's eyes were still round with amazement. 'Having said those words, our mayor lifted a heavy box onto the balcony wall, opened it and scattered its contents among us all who were standing below on the forecourt. It was money! Lots and lots of money: the bank's coffers. "If you don't take it, the Russians will!" he called out. And down it fluttered: mostly notes, but bags of coins also tinkled to the ground – all of it Reichsmark; hundreds and thousands of Reichsmark!'

Mother shook her head at the memory, before she continued, 'There was a gasp; then such a scramble as everyone struggled to gather as much money as they could. The mayor, in full uniform, looked down from the balcony and laughed and laughed. He sounded like a madman.'

'Did you pick up any money, mother?'

'Yes, I did; plenty of it.' She shoved her hands into her coat pockets and placed piles of it on the table: bundles, single notes and coins of all values. Hans-Dieter and I gasped and fingered the crisp new notes. 'How much is there?' we asked.

But mother's interest was no longer with the money. 'Leave it; we'll find out later.' She got up and removed her coat. 'Come to my bedroom, Else, and help me dress Marlenchen and Ralf.' Mother definitely had more to tell.

'Can I come too, mother?'

'No, Hans-Dieter, you stay here in this room. You mustn't go out. Don't touch the money till you help me count it. Get your favourite toys out. Else and I will only be a few minutes.'

Once in mother's bedroom, I wanted to know the rest of her story.

'Right, where was I?'

'You said he stood on the balcony and laughed. What happened then?'

'For a while he remained there, watching the mêlée below. Then he simply turned and walked through the door into the room beyond. Almost at once we heard a single shot and knew our mayor, as his final act, had taken his life.'

'What a terrible thing to do! I wonder why he did that? I liked him, mother: he was a kind person. He must have had a reason for doing such a thing?'

'Well, yes – he knew his life wouldn't be worth living when they came, as they'd probably torture and kill him. There was no more he could do for his beloved village. Now, Else, come on. We must get going. I want to leave this house: I don't feel safe here any more.'

'Where are we going?'

'Frau Ruch has asked us to stay with her and Inge. It may only be for a few days, so I've packed a small case for each of us. This house is almost empty. Frau Krause went to her home near Stettin; Trudi, Maria and Lotti have also gone to be with their families, as has Johann. He was most concerned about us but I tried to reassure him.'

'Who's here now?' I asked.

'Only Fraulein Elisabeth and the Baron and Baroness. All three of them want to remain, though I fear for them. It's their ancestral home. But Else, come now; we must hurry.'

It was a strange feeling walking through that large, almost empty manor. Not a sound could be heard as we passed room after familiar room. It was as though the old building was dying. I shivered. What did it know? The portraits, with their sad faces, stared down on us.

In the kitchen quarters, only Dunja and Anna kept themselves busy, pottering about.

'Will you be all right here?' mother asked them.

'Yes, Frau Hopp, we're staying. Nothing will happen to us; we feel quite safe.'

We went into the back yard, and from there around the house towards the large entrance gates. Everywhere was deserted, not a soul around, just an eerie silence hung over the farm.

The gates to the prisoners' compound were open, but no Russians could be seen. They'd taken their first opportunity to escape, probably during the night.Herr Lehmann had also gone, but before leaving must have put all the animals out to grass.

'The cows, mother, what happens to them? They have to be milked. Oh, mother, who will look after them?'

'I don't know, my girl, but I really can't be troubled with thoughts like that at this moment. Come, Else, we must hurry. I want to get to Frau Ruch's cottage. I don't know how much time we have – we certainly don't want to meet the Russians on the way.'

The village too was deserted. It was strange to see so many white sheets hanging from windows lining the street. No house or cottage was without one: a true sign of surrender without resistance. Perhaps that would save us from attack? Would the enemy respect the signal?

14 March 1945

I saw it before me like a film, unrolling in front of my eyes, never to leave me . . .

We were in Frau Ruch's small cottage. She and her little daughter Inge were sitting on a bench at the table. Mother was on the sofa, Marlenchen on her lap, Ralf and Hans-Dieter on either side. My faithful German Shepherd, Senta, lay at mother's feet; now and then a deep growl came from the alert dog's throat. The atmosphere in the room was heavy with tension. I was restless, afraid.

The Russians were coming and would be there any minute.

Earlier, refugees had told us the first footsoldiers were always from a punishment regiment. The lowest of the low, they were prisoners who'd volunteered to serve in a battle zone. By doing so, they hoped to shorten their prison sentences.

The vanquishers had official permission to rape and kill: they considered it the spoils of war. In a drunken stupor they'd go on the rampage and woe betide any woman they found.

'The Russians are coming! The Russians are coming!' A young woman ran down the high street shouting the dreaded words for all to hear.

Frau Ruch rushed to her front door, opened it and called out, 'Where are they? Have you seen them?'

'Yes, they're coming down the country road. Get inside; they'll soon be in Glowitz!'

And with those words she ran on, almost hysterically, to who knows where.

With mother's help I'd tried to disguise myself, for at fifteen I was very vulnerable. I'd tied a scarf over my head, roughed and knotted my long hair and wrapped an old shawl over my shoulders. I wore an ugly black skirt that had once belonged to mother and a torn and tattered jumper Frau Ruch had found among a bundle of old clothes. I deliberately cut my finger and mixed the blood from it with ash from the stove, before spreading the disgusting mixture over my face. I wanted to look foul and ugly, and wondered if I'd succeeded.

Suddenly we knew for sure that they were coming. The first sound we heard was the clip-clop of hooves over cobblestones.

I wanted to peep through the curtains but mother wouldn't allow me near the window. 'Else, come away from there! Leave the curtains shut,' she whispered loudly.

'Mother, there's a small gap: I can just see what's happening in the street.'

The first men were passing – rough-looking soldiers with jet-black hair, riding small shaggy horses. They were sitting very straight, eating what looked like peanuts and biting into raw onions!

'Mother, I think they're Cossacks from the Russian steppes. I've seen pictures in my schoolbook: they're very distinctive.'

The horses passed quickly without stopping, and footsoldiers followed them.

The appearance of these filled me with dread: their uniforms filthy, almost in tatters, many of them appeared to be drunk. Slurping from bottles, which no doubt contained vodka, they were ill-disciplined and rowdy, shrieking as some men let off rifle fire at anything that caught their eye.

I tiptoed back to my seat in the corner, but couldn't stop shaking for fear.

There was utter silence in our room, the almost tangible silence of terror.

Senta growled, and I said, 'Quiet, girl; not a sound from you. Come to me. Sit by my side.' I crouched down and put my head on my knees, sick with fear.

Suddenly a tremendous kick on the door. It flew open and two soldiers entered.

Uris! they shouted, pointing at their wrists. *Uris, uris! Davai, davai!*

Mother handed over her watch and Frau Ruch did the same. A small clock that stood on a dresser also disappeared. But what did it matter? We were far too frightened to resist.

Then one of the soldiers walked over to where I was cowering in the corner. He put a dirty finger under my chin and lifted my head, saw my blood-streaked face and, horrified, stepped back.

But that was too much for Senta. With a growl and then a bark she jumped up, leapt on the soldier and bit the sleeve of his uniform. There was a stunned expression, a grimace, on his face. He stood still for a moment; then lifted his rifle, pointed it at Senta's head and fired.

My dog fell. She was bleeding badly and in my brain I was shouting, *My dog, my dog! Oh! What have you done?* I dropped to her side.

The soldier laughed a wicked, dirty laugh. Once more he pointed his gun and fired again; then viciously kicked my beautiful dog, but her life was over. I wanted to cry and shout but not a sound escaped my lips. I cradled Senta's head, my heart breaking.

Then both soldiers left, banging the door behind them.

'Come, Else,' mother said, 'you have Marlenchen, while Frau Ruch and I carry Senta into the small shed at the bottom of the garden. As soon as we can we'll bury her, but we must be quick; I don't like to leave you alone, not even for a short while.'

I was too stunned to react. I felt devoid of any emotion and at that moment was certain I'd never be happy again.

15 March 1945

All through the night the soldiers continued to abuse us. But most of them just wanted to plunder and so they pocketed anything that took their fancy.

Towards morning we heard horses trotting over the cobblestones, followed by what could only be the sound of marching soldiers. It appeared they were leaving and the raucous noise of their voices told us that most of them, after a night of hellraising, were still extremely drunk. Then suddenly they were gone and an eerie silence descended upon the village.

As the morning wore on, mother, who'd been deep in thought for some time, approached me. 'Else,' she said, 'will you go with me to the manor? Now that the soldiers have gone, we can check if they've damaged our belongings. Perhaps we can go back to live there – if not, I'd like to see if there are some items we can bring with us. Will you come?'

'Of course I will, mother. We don't have to stay long this time, do we?'

'No, Else, just a quick look round. Hans-Dieter, Ralf and Baby will remain here with Frau Ruch. For the moment they're safe, and we'll be back soon. A new batch of soldiers could be here shortly, so we have to be quick.'

Just as mother and I left the cottage to walk down the high street, I glanced to my right towards the post office and Gisela's home. To my horror, I saw what looked like five bundles lined up on the pavement, each wrapped in a blanket.

'Look, mother, those bundles. What are they? People? Are they dead? Could they be Gisela's neighbours? Please, mother, we must find out!'

'You stay here, Else. Don't follow me. I'll learn what I can.'

Just then an elderly woman came out of her cottage next to the post office and I saw mother approaching her. They started talking and I saw the woman pointing to the upstairs windows. She was gesticulating and crying, and mother put her arms around her and guided her back to her own home.

Dead? They must be . . . Why? What had happened? I refused to believe it might involve my own dear friend. Gisela. I wanted to check those sleeping bundles, but my legs wanted to run away as fast as they could. Instead I stood rooted to the spot where mother had left me.

When she returned, she was deeply troubled and I dared not immediately bombard her with questions. She'd talk when she was ready. I made myself stand in silence beside her, despite my quivering, rebellious legs.

As we turned away from the tragic sight, mother tried to tell me what the woman had seen, but she mumbled incoherently, almost as if she were talking to herself.

'Yes,' she muttered, 'it was Gisela . . . and her parents and grandparents. According to the old lady next door, the Russian soldiers molested and raped Frau Kraemer and Gisela throughout the night, while Herr Kraemer and the grandparents were forced to look on. It must have been horrendous. Gisela and her mother suffered dreadfully –' mother shook her head as if to rid the vision from her mind. 'And in the morning, in desperation, and to avoid a repetition of such treatment, the whole family committed suicide together. Else – they ended it all.'

I couldn't believe it. What a horrendous thing to happen! Poor Gisela, my dear dear friend – *rape*. To have to take her own life? Imagine it! I burst into tears, as I couldn't cope with such news. Mother tried to console me, but my tears flowed like a waterfall. I was devastated, terrified when I thought of what might happen if a new batch of soldiers arrived.

And as mother and I continued down the street, villagers stopped us and told us of many people who had killed themselves during the previous night's horrific, sickening experiences.

'Come, Else, let's be quick; I don't want us to linger a moment longer than necessary.'

We hurried along the drive, but not a soul was in sight and the snow had almost melted. As we neared the large iron gates and entered the park, we saw Dunja and Anna standing by the front door of the house, both in uniform! Dunja looked splendid, dressed as an officer of high rank, while Anna wore the uniform of a private, much too tight, accentuating the bulk of her large body. The small pink handbag Sylvia had given me for Christmas two years before hung round her neck. She looked ridiculous! Mother wanted to greet them, but both turned away, pretending not to know us.

The front doorway was open and we entered an abnormally silent house. Not a sound anywhere! Quickly we climbed the grand staircase and a glance into the drawing room and music room showed the wanton destruction of those once elegant and finely furnished chambers. No need to look further.

'Mother, where's Fraulein Elisabeth and the old Baron and Baroness? Should we look for them?'

'No, Else. I daren't stop. Perhaps they're hiding. Let's just go upstairs, have a quick search of our rooms and get out of here, as fast as we can. I feel most uncomfortable.'

Our rooms were no different from those we'd seen downstairs – not much could be salvaged as everything was smashed. The precious china and old irreplaceable crystal glasses that had always been locked away, only to be used for special occasions were, like everything else, destroyed. They'd also found father's photographic record of the various campaigns in which he'd been involved – all missing, including a small box with his Iron Crosses of achievement in battle. This mother had hidden in what she thought a safe place, but no, it had been found. 'Else, their loss is dreadful, dangerous – I fear the contents may be used incriminate us. They could put us in a serious situation.'

'But they were father's, mother, not ours; I can't see that it can concern us?' I replied naively.

Mother's bedroom was just as awful. Everything was wrecked, her lovely coats and dresses torn to shreds. I couldn't imagine what they'd done with mine. Some were in the bathroom, totally soiled with vomit and faeces: it sickened me to see it.

We were able to gather a few things, but there was little worth taking and no time to search thoroughly. Mother was nervous and eager to get away. 'Hurry, Else, we must go as quickly as possible, before more soldiers arrive.'

But it was too late.

Downstairs, by the front door, a small group of soldiers were already talking to Dunja and Anna.

'*Stoi!* Stop!' one of the soldiers shouted, when he saw us, 'What are you carrying?'

Mother showed him her bag and I showed him mine. He took them and tipped the contents onto the ground. Then all of them started to trample on our few precious belongings. We could do nothing but stand and look on.

Anna laughed. For her, it was a joke – quite hilarious. But Dunja, the officer, showed her authority. *Stoi!* she shouted, and in her language, which we couldn't understand, she ordered the soldiers to return our belongings to the bags and hand them back to us. Then she lashed out at Anna with full force across the face, leaving a bright red handprint.

'Go, Frau Hopp, quickly now, and don't come back!' Dunja ordered. 'I don't want to see you again. I'm not your friend any more. From now on, you're my enemy.'

Mother picked up our bags. She looked at Dunja with great sadness. 'God Bless you, child and keep you safe.' With that, she handed me my bag, took my hand and, walking fast, didn't look back once. We left the park and Glowitz manor . . . never to return.

When we arrived at the cottage, Frau Ruch was most agitated. 'Lena,' she hugged mother, 'how glad I am to see you. The new batch of soldiers will certainly arrive soon. I don't want to be in this cottage when they come.'

'But where can we go?' mother asked. 'Do you know of a safer place?'

'To the dairy. I've seen others there. We won't be on our own: it's safer in a crowd.'

'Very well,' mother replied, 'I agree. Then let's not waste time; we'll leave immediately.'

Walking quickly, we all soon reached the dairy, a processing plant for the local farms. A villa next to it was the first house one reached when entering the village near the railway crossing that led to the station. It had belonged to the dairy owner, but was now deserted. Here was our new shelter. We were not the only ones, for the house had filled rapidly, mostly with women, some of whom I'd never seen before. All of them were older than me, but each, in one form or another, had tried to disguise herself. We were a motley group, but terror lined all our faces. There was little to do but wait.

We waited and waited, every sound magnified and analysed. Numb with apprehension, we listened for the hollow tramp, tramp of boots and deep rumble of wheels that signalled an approaching army.

Then suddenly, at terrific speed, an open military vehicle roared into the village and with screeching brakes came to a halt outside the villa. Two officers jumped out, ran up the few steps and with the butt of a rifle hammered against the door, demanding entry. Immediately it was opened, the officers pushed in and stared around. Not a word was said as they walked around the sad group of women and children, inspecting and counting them. One officer focused on me; he noticed I was cradling my left hand, swollen from a festering index finger.

He crossed over to me and, in perfect German, asked to see the finger. I showed it to him cautiously, fearful he might chop it off. But no – he studied it and announced it was an abscess and that he'd operate on it. He needed to make a small incision to release the accumulation of pus. I was too frightened to utter a word, but while he worked on my wound he told me with a smile that he also had a daughter about my age. Eventually I plucked up courage to ask him where he'd learned to speak such good German. He said he'd studied medicine in Heidelberg in Germany. When my finger was clean, he poured clear alcohol over it from a hip flask to sterilise it. Then he sent his companion to fetch a bandage from the car; and when it had been strapped, he studied my face and said, 'Under all that muck, you must be a pretty girl. Leave it like that: I hope it will protect you.' Turning to our group as a whole, he continued, 'Many soldiers are following, not far behind us. They'll select young women and have their fun with them. That's their privilege, because theirs is the victorious army and to them you're all as nothing.'

Once more, he gazed at me. Did I see compassion in his eyes? I couldn't tell. But he'd been kind to me and I was sad to see him go.

Chapter 30

Father's Iron Crosses

15 and 16 March 1945

For a moment, after the officers had left, there was complete silence in the room – then, like a torrent let loose, everyone started talking at once.

'You see,' said one of the women, 'they're not all bad: look how kind they were to Else.'

'Yes,' mother answered, 'but remember, there were only two of them and they were educated officers. Who knows what rabble's following after? It's no good becoming complacent; we must be constantly on our guard.'

Just then Hans-Dieter and another small boy burst into the room full of excitement.

'Mother!' Hans-Dieter shouted. 'Upstairs is a room full of toys. Can we play with them? We'll be careful and not break any; they must belong to the children who lived here.'

'Yes, my boy,' mother answered. 'Stay with Ralf and don't attempt to go out. Promise?'

'Yes, I promise; and I'll make the others listen to me.' Off he went to his own pursuits.

'Now I must go to the kitchen and see what there is to eat,' mother announced. We all seem to have brought something, so if we pool together there should be adequate food for all of us.'

'What can I do, mother?' I asked. 'Would you like me to see to Marlenchen? That little girl has been so good – not a sound except her contented cooing. She's a darling!' Then, on impulse, I rushed over to mother and flung my arms around her. 'Mother, I'm so frightened. What's to become of us? We're without a home and all our belongings are destroyed or stolen. I keep thinking of the future – everything seems hopeless. What can we do?'

'Elslein, my darling daughter, you and I must be strong. Our little ones depend on us. I don't know what the coming weeks and months have in store for us – no more than you do. But I haven't lost hope, and with you by my side I'm sure we'll survive and have a happier future.'

Then it was evening and another day was over. We'd all had a small meal and no one was very hungry – fear and uncertainty had stolen our appetites.

The children had settled for the night, tired from their playing and the novelty of a strange house; and sharing beds was an added thrill.

No one felt like talking, for everyone was preoccupied with their own thoughts. I looked from one person to another and thought to myself that the silence in that room was unhappy and fearful.

Suddenly we stared at each other. 'Can you hear it?' someone whispered.

A rumble in the distance! The sound of heavy motor vehicles – here they come! Someone pulled the curtain open a crack.

I crept near mother. 'Should I go and wake Ralf and Hans-Dieter?'

She shook her head. 'Wait awhile, Else; let's give them a few moments longer.'

Then we heard the first lorries crossing the railway line, followed by wagons full of riotous Russian soldiers. On and on they came, lorry after lorry passing by, seemingly never ending, into the village and down the high street. Through the chink in the curtains we could make out heavily armoured vehicles and tanks following them, and it took a long time before the last vehicle in the convoy, showing a Russian flag fluttering in the evening breeze, had passed.

'Where do you think they'll make camp, mother? The village isn't big enough for so many soldiers and vehicles?'

'I expect they'll drive onto the estate. There's the park and all the land surrounding the farmyard. Yes, child, there's plenty of room for them all. They'll also commandeer the manor.'

'What will happen to Miss Elisabeth and the baron and baroness?'

Mother's eyes filled with tears. 'None of them wanted to leave the house. Now they'll be defenceless against a drunken and unruly horde of Russian soldiers. I've seen this coming, Else, but they wouldn't listen.'

Mother wiped her eyes and I planted a kiss on her cheek.

'Dry your tears, mother; I hate to see you cry.'

After the traffic had passed and disappeared down the high street, the village lay in total silence. It seemed as if every house was devoid of living beings. People hid behind closed doors, birds stopped singing, no dog barked nor cat mewed – the silence was creepy and unnatural. But such stillness couldn't last long. Plenty of alcohol had made the soldiers noisy and now they were strutting and swaying in drunken stupor through the village streets. Breaking down doors, they shouted for women, 'Woman, come! *Davai, davai!*', and if they resisted, they were made to move at gunpoint.

Davai was a word we learned quickly. Everything was *Davai!* 'Let's go!'

It was a matter of time before the soldiers reached the villa beside the dairy and demanded entry. In their impatience to get into the house they broke down the door and forced their way into the room where everyone was cowering in terror.

One soldier, almost too drunk to stand, pointed at me and, despite my revolting make-up, shouted for me to follow him. What could I do? He must have been too drunk to notice how horrible I looked. I glanced at my mother and she looked at me. Did I have to comply with his wishes? 'Go with him, child, for your own safety. God look after you and keep you from harm.'

Then I saw that a second soldier was approaching mother and shouting at her to follow him. But she had Marlenchen on her lap; and when he was on the point of losing patience, mother pinched Baby's bottom really hard and made the little girl cry out loud in protest.

Immediately the soldier stepped back and left mother alone. She knew Russian people loved children. From then on, whenever she was on the point of being molested, poor little Baby had her bottom pinched! But mother was spared because of that.

To take mother's place, the second soldier grabbed another woman and we were both pushed out into the street. My heart thumped madly. There were two of us: perhaps we could escape together. We exchanged glances of support; all we had time for. The two men were so drunk they could hardly stand, but still had the presence of mind to know what they wanted. And they didn't want us together. The other soldier pushed his prey in the opposite direction towards the country road. I didn't know where they were heading. The last I saw of her was the fear in her eyes as she glanced back at me.

I was marched along the railway track, rifle butt in my back, with shouts of *Davai, davai!*

I tripped and stumbled in the darkness and had no idea where he was taking me. I shouted at him to go slower but he didn't want to hear. Anyway he couldn't understand my language any more than I could understand his. A field of allotments was on my right, neat little gardens prepared for the oncoming summer, and small garden sheds freshly painted. Was this where he was taking me? Now and then from behind the clouds I saw the sickle moon, but it soon disappeared and again the dark surrounded us.

Then, on my left, I noticed a small brick-built hut where railway workers left their tools and brewed coffee during their breaks.

The Russian pulled me along – no chance of escape! He also saw the hut and made for it. Holding me tight with one arm, he tried the door. It was unlocked and he kicked it open. It was dark inside, with only a thin beam of moonlight finding its way through a tiny, very dirty, windowpane.

I saw a pile of sacks in a corner and silently prayed he wouldn't notice them. No such luck – with all his strength he forced me down onto the pile.

My fear had turned to anger. I shouted at him, although he couldn't understand. I screamed; I kicked and struggled and used all my strength to ward him off. Again and again I tried to get up, but he always pushed me back. In the process he ripped my clothes, but in my desperation I didn't even notice. Without much success, he was fumbling with his trousers – no easy task in his drunken stupor. I was terrified! What did he want of me? I'd heard of rape, but didn't really know what it involved. I had to get away – but how?

My mind was working frantically. And then an opportunity presented itself – the soldier got tangled in his trousers. He almost lost his balance and I seized the moment to kick him as hard as I could in his groin, where I knew it would hurt him most. He yelped, howling in agony, but I didn't care! I jumped up, threw open the door and *ran* – faster than I'd ever run before.

But the Russian wasn't stupid. I might have hurt him with my kick, but the pain had sobered him to an extent. Abandoning his trousers, he followed, lumbering after me like a bear. But I was clear-headed and he was not, so I quickly outran him. I heard a gunshot. Where it came from I had no idea. Was it my assailant trying to hit me? *Please, dear God, let me be safe!*

Almost at the end of my strength, lungs heaving for breath, I reached the station building. All the time I ran, I repeated over and over, 'Mother, I'm coming! I'm nearly there!' My words became a chant to which my feet somehow responded. Yet the hairs stuck up on the back of my neck for fear he, or perhaps another soldier, would leap out at me.

Just a few more steps and I'd reach the villa and mother . . .

At the door something made me hesitate for an instant. Silence – it was too quiet. Those obnoxious drunken soldiers! What had they done? Mother? The children? Suppose they were all . . . dead? How could I even say the word? My heart thumped, but I couldn't go in. I didn't dare look at what was on the other side of the door, and reluctantly turned away.

I made for the bottom of the garden where I'd seen a coal shed. That was where I had to hide: if my assailant caught up with me, he wouldn't find me in the villa. The shed wasn't large but was stacked with logs and coal. With my bare hands I dug a hole in the coal heap. That was where I'd stay all night, no matter if by morning I was as black as a sweep.

There I was among the logs and coal, cowering in a corner of the dark, dank shed. I'd calmed down and my shaking had stopped. Now I felt secure, certain no Russian would find me. If only I could let mother – if she was still alive – know I was safe; but I was too afraid to risk going near the house.

I must have dozed, for how long I didn't know, but noises coming from the house had woken me. There was a lot of shouting and screaming and crying: over and over again I heard a baby cry. Little Marlene? Among the pleading voices of women I could make out the sound of bawling men and *Davai, davai!* Also a crash of breaking glass or china and smashing furniture. And always the helpless pleading of abused women unable to escape. There must have been many soldiers in the house. I cowered where I lay, and nothing would persuade me to leave that hiding place. What if my angry soldier had returned and was wreaking revenge on my family? Terror gripped me. The noise went on and on. I yearned to find out what was going on, but was unable to move.

Once more I slumbered – probably because I couldn't even turn over; the agony of my frozen muscles, the hardness of the lumps of coal and wood sticking into my skin demanded my concentration and vied with the sickening thoughts in my head.

I awoke as dawn broke. All around me was silence. Not a sound to be heard from the house. What had happened? I had to find out but was still too frightened to move. Perhaps the soldiers were sleeping in the villa? Mother? The children? Had they survived the night after all? Little Marlene – was her mama still with her? Mother was a good person; she had to come through for all our sakes. *Please God, look after her!*

Cautiously I moved my body, so stiff from squatting in the tiny corner all night. My teeth chattered and I was frozen to the quick.

Suddenly a distant door opened. I scrambled over to a small window and wiped it with my sleeve. Mother? My dearest mother was looking down the garden! Wiping tears from her face, she was searching anxiously for me. Poor mother! Now I had to get out! Quickly I rushed to the coalshed door, but it was stuck! I slammed my full weight against it and it burst open. Full of joy and relief I shouted, 'Mother, here I am! Wait for me; I'm coming!'

'Child, oh my dearest girl, how glad I am to see you! Quickly, come inside. You're so cold. We must warm you.'

'Where are the soldiers, mother? I spent all night in the coal shed and heard that horrific din in the house. It sounded terrible. I imagined awful things and was very frightened.'

'We're all right. The soldiers have gone. The children are fine; they're still asleep. Most of the women have found a corner to lie down in and rest. It's been a terrible night for us all.'

'But what about you, mother? Did the soldiers hurt you?'

'No, Else, I kept your little sister with me all night. Sometimes she slept, but often she cried, and because of that they left me alone. But tell me what they did to you? I was so worried and distressed, knowing I couldn't help you. My poor girl, what you must have gone through!'

'Mother, I'm fine. I escaped. But please let me wash. I'm filthy and want to get rid of the stink of that man! I'll soon tell you everything.'

It was good to talk to my mother. I told her every detail of my ordeal; and when I'd finished, she gave me the biggest hug ever. Then she looked at me, tears in her eyes, and said, 'Else, my girl, I always knew you have strength and determination. I'm so proud of you.'

How good it was to be with my family and friends again. The previous night's ordeal had been terrifying and, although I knew I'd never forget it, I wanted to put it out of my mind. Mother was so relieved to have me back that she couldn't pass me without touching me. It seemed as if she had to make sure I was really there, and wasn't just a figment of her imagination. But I had one question to ask her: 'Mother, the woman who was taken by the other soldier – has she returned? I don't know where they went. Is she safe?'

'Yes, Else, she came back very early this morning. She wouldn't talk to anyone but went straight upstairs. I haven't seen her since.'

I was still scared the soldier from whom I'd run away would return to take me again. I peered out of the corner of a window whenever I heard a noise. Would he forget me when he was sober? Was he sober? I hoped he'd be lying in a drunken stupor somewhere, until he had to return to army duties.

Now the street was empty and quiet, not a Russian to be seen.

'Where are they?' I asked mother.

'Today's a holiday for them and I expect they're sleeping off their hangover after last night's revelry and debauchery. Be glad it's quiet, Else; I doubt it will last long.'

Looking out of the window, I saw it was raining. A grey, dismal world. Befitting, I thought.

Mulling over what mother had said, I felt fear and revulsion at the thought soldiers could come and take me again. What would I do? How could I continue to protect myself? The men were so strong and trigger happy. I remembered the pistol shot behind me: I was lucky to be alive!

Our house had been tidied again and put in order. Everything broken or destroyed had been cleared away. Memories of the past night were swept out of the room, together with any signs of wanton destruction.

Hans-Dieter, Ralfie and the other children were upstairs, absorbed in their own little world. They were so small and innocent, and I hoped that innocence wouldn't be taken away from them overnight. I knew mother would protect the young ones with her life, if need be, and if I could I'd do the same.

Mother was in the kitchen, trying to prepare a meal for us. Most women were resting but I sat with my little sister, trying to put my jumbled thoughts in order.

I needed to talk to mother again. After a while I joined her in the kitchen, hoping she was on her own. 'Mother,' I said, 'can you spare a moment?'

'Yes, Else?'

'You told me how babies are made between a man and a woman who love each other. That's not rape, is it?'

'No, it's making love. Rape's evil!'

'But if a Russian soldier were to rape me, could I also have a baby?'

'Like last night? Yes, Else, sadly, you could.' She continued dipping plates in soapy suds for a while. Then she stopped and added, 'But he didn't enter you?'

'No, mother, I didn't let him get that close to me.'

'Else, listen to me! This is only the beginning. It will happen again and again until the day when some sort of order can be established in our country. But until then we have to grit our teeth and put up with it. It's possible we might both be raped. We might be made pregnant. There's nothing we can do to stop it. All us women have to be strong, you included. Else, do you understand?'

'Yes, mother, I'm trying to.'

'You ask me what rape is? Rape's wicked. It's when a man forces himself on a woman against her wishes. I still pray you'll never have to experience such a situation. Remember, Else, the soldiers who've conquered our country feel victorious and full of arrogance. They're at liberty to treat us as they wish. It's their prerogative and obviously they'll make the most of it.' She turned back to her task.

'Thank you, mother, for explaining it to me,' I said quietly.

'Else, I'll always try to answer your questions, though I fear my honesty hasn't put your mind at rest!' She gave me a kiss on my cheek.

Mother had cooked a tasty lunch for us. Now we wanted her to rest. Hans-Dieter offered to help me tidy the kitchen. Upstairs in the playroom he'd found a jigsaw puzzle and as a reward for helping me wanted me to give him a hand with it.

The women, who'd rested all morning, came with their children to join us in the living room. Now they looked more relaxed, chattering among themselves. One lady entertained us by playing the piano that stood in the corner of the room. She played a few well-known songs and some of us sang along with her. It was a friendly atmosphere and the talk was of happier days now gone, but also of hope they'd return.

'Else,' mother said, 'please go to the kitchen and make us some coffee. It's only coffee substitute, but better than nothing.'

I'd just walked into the kitchen, filled the kettle with water and lit the gas stove, when I heard a loud and impatient knocking on the front door. Someone opened it but was pushed aside by two Russian soldiers of senior rank. Without uttering a word they walked into the living room. In the stunned silence, a look of horror was on everyone's face. I'd quickly turned off the gas and rushed to mother. The soldiers looked around and, without speaking, pointed at four of the younger women and me. Then they made us understand by sign language that we had to go with them.

'No!' mother shouted, 'Not again! Leave my daughter here; she's already been out all night with one of your soldiers!'

One of the intruders pointed his gun at mother and, glancing at me, shouted, 'You, woman, come! *Davai!*'

'Mother, I must go with him. If I don't, he'll hurt you. Perhaps I won't be long. I wish I knew where they're taking us.'

I tried to make one of the soldiers understand I wanted my coat. He followed us into the cloakroom, but we had to be quick: they were impatient and wanted to be gone.

My dear mother looked as if her heart was breaking. I could see her eyes brimming.

'Darling mother,' I implored her, 'please don't cry. See! I'm trying to be brave and so must you. Wherever they're taking me, never fear – I *will* return to you!'

With a hug, a kiss and a smile that wasn't quite real I took one more glance at little Marlene on her lap and my two young brothers by her side. Would I see them again? Then I turned my back on them and followed the soldiers out into the wind and rain and a thoroughly miserable afternoon.

They marched us through the village, not the high street, but along the upper road, which led to the cemetery and church. The village was deserted and we still didn't know where we were going.

No words were spoken as we stumbled along at gunpoint; only our footsteps could be heard clattering over the uneven, slippery cobblestones. Near the church, one soldier took a bunch of keys out of his pocket. *Are they locking us in the church?* I wondered. But no, the leader tramped towards the nearby village hall, unlocked the door and ushered us inside. Then left.

There was one room, completely bare except for a table in the centre surrounded by four rickety chairs. In the corner I saw an old blanket that I took for myself and, as on other occasions, I crouched down and decided to remain there until someone could tell me what was going on. Why did they want us here? What was the purpose? Preparations for the coming night? I asked the other women but no one knew, so had to resign myself to sit it out and wait.

Time passed. I was getting hungry and thirsty; so were the others. Hours passed. Since the soldiers had left without saying a word, locking the door behind them, no one had looked in. We had no facilities whatsoever, no food, nor drink; only a small toilet in the corner of the building. The water had been turned off at the beginning of winter and there was no light; when evening came, we had to remain in darkness.

But we were not quite forgotten. The two soldiers who'd brought us there returned at last. They handed each of us a blanket and left a jug of water and a loaf of bread to share among ourselves. Up to now there were only the five of us. Would they bring more women to join us?

Questions we asked remained unanswered. Either they didn't understand or just ignored us. There was nothing to do but sit tight and wait for what would follow. We shared the bread and had a drink; then each wrapped up in a blanket, found a sheltered place on the floor and tried to sleep. It wasn't easy, as the room was cold, the floor hard and the fear and misgiving in each of us kept us awake. Perhaps that place was slightly more congenial than the coal shed, but then I'd been free and now I was a prisoner.

I must have dozed but was suddenly aware of someone shaking me. It was a strange soldier. He ordered me to get up and follow.

Immediately I feared the worst. 'No!' I shouted, pulling away from him, 'I don't want to come; leave me alone!' Was this it? Rape, the real thing? Where were the other girls? I peered into the darkness. They were either asleep or pretending to be.

His answer was, as usual, *Davai!* He dragged me to my feet and slapped my face hard.

'Pigdog!' I yelled, pushing him off me. 'You want to make me cry? No, never! Now take me where you want and bring me back so I can sleep again.' By now I was really terrified but wasn't going to show him. Where was he taking me? If only I knew, I wouldn't be scared. Or would I?

Out of the village hall we went, down the hill, his grip on my arm like a vice, his gun in my back, until we reached the high street. There we turned left, past the village shops. Soon the soldier pushed me through a gate leading to the cobbler's shop. Lights were burning. Why here?

He lifted the latch of the door and pushed me through in front of him. It opened onto a steep flight of steps, which appeared to lead into a cellar.

A cellar? I could hear voices. What did they want with me? Were they going to shoot me? Kill me? Or *just* rape me? I was petrified and tried to push him away, to turn him round and get back the way we'd come. But the doorway was too narrow.

'No! No!' I screamed, terror distorting my features.

He shoved the pistol into my face and barked some strange word, its intention clear.

I backed away and half fell down the stairs. Down we went and at the bottom entered a narrow passage with a wooden bench placed against the wall. The soldier pushed me onto it.

In front of me was a door with a small pane of glass in the top with a light burning in the room beyond. Why was I kept outside with that man towering menacingly over me? What chance had I of escape with his gun poking into my body? None!

Why were we waiting? What were we waiting for?

On the other side of the wall I could hear a conversation in Russian, but one of the voices had some authority. This was different. This wasn't the raucous, drunken rape situation I'd heard in the house the night before.

We waited and waited, until, after a considerable length of time, the door opened and another soldier beckoned me inside.

The room was empty except for a table at which an officer sat. *Ha, I thought, perhaps this is an interrogation. But why me? I have nothing to hide.*

I didn't say a word. The delay had composed me. I walked to the table slowly with my head held high and waited for him to speak. The room was dank and musty and water dripped somewhere. An ominous sound: drip, drip, drip . . .

After a while the officer looked at me and said, 'Are you Else Gopp?'

He spoke good German; however Russians can't pronounce the letter 'h' – it's not in their alphabet. So they use the sound 'g' instead. He called me 'Gopp' instead of 'Hopp'.

'I'm Else *Hopp*,' I emphasised.

'Did you and your mother live in Glowitz Manor?'

'Yes, we did.'

'Where did you come from?'

'We were evacuated from Düsseldorf in the Rhineland.'

'Where's your father?'

'He's a soldier in the army.'

'He's a Nazi!' the officer shouted, rising to his feet where he could tower over me. His chair clattered away from him.

'No, he's not!' I heard myself shout back. 'He's an ordinary soldier in the German army.' Dear father, a Nazi? Never!

'We found his Iron Crosses. Look, they're here on the table. He must be a Nazi!'

Drip . . . drip . . . drip . . . I stared at my father's medals. Those precious medals: we were all so proud of them.

'We have his picture,' he continued gloating at my obvious unnerved state. He's in uniform. He's a Nazi!'

'No, he's not!' I croaked. Then controlling my voice, I emphasised slowly, 'He's only a soldier! An officer like you, but fighting in the German army.' *Father! What would you say if you could see me now? What would you do?*

'Is he fighting in Russia?'

'When last we heard from him, he was fighting for his country in Odessa on the Black Sea.' I was fighting tears: they wouldn't see me cry.

'Ha!' the officer laughed and sneered. 'Germany finished! Finished for ever, and you can thank your leader, Adolf Hitler, for that.' He stopped and paced the floor dramatically before leaning over me and softly spitting out the words 'He can't help you any more because soon your Hitler will be dead!'

'Never,' I answered. 'He can't die! We need him and he wouldn't abandon his country or his people.'

'That's what you think. You wait: you'll realise I'm right.'

I stared at him genuinely astonished. 'How do you know all these things about me?'

'We have sources,' he sneered. 'We know everything. He'll abandon you! You can forget him!'

Drip . . . drip . . . drip . . .

Without looking up he added, 'Tomorrow morning, you, with the other village women, will line up in the high street. You'll march to Stolp. From there, you'll go to a railway station: a long, long march! There will be a train waiting to take you to Russia.' He glared at me and then spat out, '*You'll* get the same treatment you gave to Russian girls. You took them for cheap labour into Germany; you'll work long hours in Russia. See how you like *that*!'

'But I'm only fifteen years old.'

'Yes, but you were a Hitler Girl. You wore a uniform and idolised that evil man. You loved him, believed in him. Now see where it got you. He's a traitor! Every German person has to pay for his sins! It will be good when he's dead!'

I really did have to fight to keep my tears at bay now. I wouldn't cry in front of him – no!

There was another silence. Drip . . . drip . . . drip . . .

'I don't know what you'd like me to tell you,' I said quietly. 'Any questions you wish to ask me, I'll answer truthfully.'

'Where's your mother? Is she also a Nazi?'

I felt the colour rise in my cheeks, but kept calm. 'My mother has my little sister and two young brothers in a house in the village. She's a mother, not a Nazi! She's done nothing wrong. She and the children are innocent; so am I – and so is my father. Please, let me go!'

He smiled a sadistic grin. 'You'll never see your father again, ever! You'll be taken to Russia and stay there until you die!'

Then the officer spoke in his own language to the soldier who'd brought me and watched the scene from a corner of the room. Now he stood to attention, clicking his heels. His superior pointed to something he'd written. He now seemed calmer. Perhaps he believed me.

'Can I go now?' I muttered. 'Take me back to the village hall?'

Suddenly tiredness overwhelmed me. I just wanted to get away from that claustrophobic hole. My legs buckled and I grabbed the table to steady myself. I wanted to crawl back into my corner, any corner, where I could cry and no one would see. Then, I hoped, I'd eventually fall asleep. I was afraid, afraid of what the morning would bring and the enormous uncertainty of what lay ahead. Where would I end up? Russia?

I longed for my mother and wanted to be with her, to have her hold me tight.

Chapter 31

Goodbye, Dearest Mama

17 March 1945

I awoke, feeling stiff and very cold. The village hall floor was hard and uncomfortable, but, although ugly dreams had often disturbed me, I'd slept most of the night. It still had to be early, because the room was in darkness and I could hardly distinguish the few pieces of furniture scattered about – some trestle tables, a stack of chairs.

My four companions were still sleeping. I'd let them be. They'd come back to reality soon enough. If only I had a watch, then at least I'd know what time it was. But the Russians had stolen every watch in the village; even the town hall clock.

I lay for a while huddled in my blanket wondering what that day would bring. It wouldn't be a good day, that I knew; and then again, I asked myself, would mother come to rescue me? She wouldn't have a chance – she couldn't risk her life when the children needed her. Perhaps she might say goodbye? Someone, village gossip, must have told her we'd march to Stolp that day. If so, she'd surely be there to wish me well on my journey. Oh, I hoped so! I badly wanted to see her. But even if she came, we'd have no chance to talk.

I lay still and worried: my disguise would do my skin no good if I left it on, and my long hair, which I'd messed up, was tangled: I'd always brushed it daily – whatever would I do? I wished I could cut it all off; how much easier life would be. I felt filthy both inside and out, but had no toothbrush, no means of washing.

My stomach was rumbling: I was ravenous. I wondered if there was a little bread left over from the night before. Just a little piece would help; surely the others wouldn't mind? I crawled out of my blanket. Yes, there on the table I saw a small crust of bread. I took it and crept back to my resting place. It was a poor breakfast but better than nothing. After I'd eaten, I snuggled down again as best I could and tried to sleep once more – even if only for a while.

Did I doze off? I didn't know, but suddenly heard soldier's footsteps in heavy boots outside. A key was inserted into the lock, the door crashed opened and two soldiers entered. As usual they shouted *Davai!* Let's go! And a heavy kick on a table leg soon made us jump out of our makeshift beds and stand to attention.

'Hurry!' one of them shouted. 'You march to Stolp, now! *Davai, davai!*'

He put a jug of fresh water on the table and another hunk of bread, but nothing else; that frugal meal had to be our breakfast. My four companions grumbled about it, as did I. We all made an attempt to eat but it was no good – the dry bread stuck in our throats.

And then we waited.

Suddenly we heard voices outside and rushed to the window. A group of people had assembled in the high street and many soldiers were milling about. They seemed to have rounded up all the young women from the village, around fifteen to twenty of them lined up on one side of the street. On the other side, family members, mostly mothers, congregated, anxious to find out what was to happen to their daughters. I noticed my mother standing alone, a little away from the others. But she was there!

The soldiers entered our building and shouted for us to follow them. We left the village hall and ran down a slope to the others. It was such a relief to be let out, and a tremendous feeling of freedom, tinged with fear of not knowing where I was going, overwhelmed me. I looked around and noted my surroundings with a clarity never experienced before, the vivid detail of one sensing that, but for the will of God, they might never return.

It was downhill to where the lower road met the high street and I was running. We passed the old farm with white railings surrounding it, and the ancient chestnut tree that stood at the entrance to the farmyard. As yet its candle flowers hadn't opened, but it wouldn't be long before the tree unfolded its breathtaking splendour.

Oh, to be out in the fresh morning air! Although the sky was grey and the sun hid behind clouds, I didn't care. Just for a while I felt like a bird that had escaped from a cage.

But where were the birds? No singing or twittering – where were they all? Perhaps they knew how much sadness lay below them: from their vantage point they could see what was going on.

Opposite was the shop of Aunt Friedel, mother's best friend – but she and her husband, Ernst, had left weeks before. I wondered where they were? The shop was empty and abandoned.

As we four neared the bottom of the hill, we halted by the other group of women.

I cried out, 'mother, over here! See, I'm here!'

But the Russian behind me turned me around. I thought he was going to hit me, but no, he shouted what surely must have meant, 'Be quiet!'

Mother *had* seen me. She rushed towards me and took me in her arms. 'Else, my darling child, how are you? Have you been treated badly? I wish I could have more time to talk but I fear the soldiers are impatient to leave. Listen, I've brought your knapsack and in it you'll find a toothbrush, your hairbrush and a change of underwear. I also put in a warm pullover: the nights can still be cold.'

'Thank you, mother.'

'Wait child, I've also included a small milk can with a lid – it may be useful for many things – and a spoon, fork and a small enamel bowl. Look after them, they'll be useful wherever you are.' She was gabbling in her haste to say as much as possible, even if it was fanciful under the circumstances. 'When you eat, Elslein, never forget your manners. Always remember what father and I have taught you.'

'No, mother, I won't forget.'

'I hope I've thought of things you'll need. I've made sandwiches for you and added a piece of ham and some extra slices of bread. I couldn't bring more; you know, dearest, how very short we are of food.'

'Thank you, mother; I'll treasure everything you've brought for me. Look,' I pointed out to her, 'over there in the corner's Fraulein Elisabeth. I didn't know she'd be with us.'

'I'll try to speak to her,' mother answered, 'but it's difficult. Anyway, my child, I must spend every second left to us with you.'

'Mother, what will happen to me? I don't want to leave you!'

'I know, my child. My heart breaks to see you standing here. I can't bear the thought of you marching away from me. How will I know where you are? Will I ever see you or hear from you again?' Tears ran down her cheeks and she fought not to break down completely.

We clung to each other. My heart was screaming, 'Mother, take me home. I don't want to go. Mother, I don't want to go!' But the lump in my throat was so huge, not a sound came out of my mouth. My arms, however, told her everything my voice couldn't.

'How can I go on living, my child?' she whispered. 'Yet I have the little ones to care for.'

The soldiers were getting impatient. They were shouting at us to line up and march. *Davai!*

My dear mother released me and gently pushed me towards them. Again my feet strode me into line, but looking over at mother, my eyes swollen with tears and my heart bursting, I couldn't leave her. Once more, I ran to my mother and put my arms around her. 'Mother, look at me,' I sobbed, holding her cheeks to face me. *'I'll come back to you; that's a promise.* Never will they get me as far as Russia – I'd rather die. *Please, mother, wait for me.* I'll come back to Glowitz, no matter how long it takes, but promise me you'll be here?'

'Yes, my precious girl, I'll wait for your return!'

A soldier approached and roughly pulled us apart 'We leave!'

'Goodbye, dearest Mama. Kiss Marlenchen for me and hug my little brothers. Always remember, mother, I love you very, very much.' Words are like kisses when loved-ones part.

We were still standing attached to our families, but the soldiers were impatient. They shouted for us to start marching. I turned to join the other women. One soldier shot his gun into the air, a sign that our long march was to begin instantly. I looked straight ahead. I didn't want to turn any more, because my mother would still be standing where I'd left her. Most likely she'd still be crying; I couldn't bear to remember her like that . . .

We marched in silence, each wrapped in our own thoughts. I was also crying, as were most of the women. I sobbed my heart out; it felt like it was breaking.

What was mother going to do without me? How would she manage? I'd promised my father I'd look after her; now I had to break that promise. I wanted to scream, but what good would that do? The soldiers wouldn't hesitate to pick on me and would most probably beat me. The fear of that alone gagged my voice. My sorrow was immense, and all kinds of emotions flooded to the surface from deep within. My greatest longing was for mother to hold me. A child again, I felt abandoned. Would I ever see her again, hear her voice and feel her soft touch on my face? Would I ever manage to return to her as I'd promised? I'd try; that was for sure. If it was true the Russians wanted to abduct and transport us to their homeland in retaliation for what was done to their young women, then I was already determined they'd never get me that far. Once over the Russian border, there'd be no return.

Three soldiers marched with us. Their light brown uniforms looked shabby and none too clean, their jackboots worn and badly in need of a polish. One tramped in front, one in the centre and one made up the rear. They treated us indifferently and I wondered what thoughts were going through their heads? Hatred towards us? Perhaps compassion? Their faces were inscrutable.

Thank goodness it wasn't raining. Although it was overcast, with the sun hidden behind a thick sheet of cloud, it wasn't cold.

We marched until midday. Everyone felt weary and longed for a break. Occasionally the column stopped and we were thankfully allowed to sink into the long, cool grass at the side of the road, a comfortable resting place. Oh, my poor feet – tired and hurting. But I was lucky. My shoes were sturdy lace-ups and I had no blisters. Some were unused to that rigorous exercise and were already in a bad way. Still, it was good to rest, if only for a while. I enjoyed one of my precious sandwiches mother had packed into my knapsack. Dear mother, what would she be doing now? Oh, to be with her – what a wonderful gift that would be . . . *Perhaps this is all a dream; perhaps I'll wake up at home with my loved ones at my side* . . .

As I looked round, I noticed Fraulein Elisabeth sitting alone, away from the crowd. I walked towards her. 'Fraulein Elisabeth, hello. Are you well?'

She stared at me with vacant eyes and no response to my words.

'Would you like me to sit with you? Would you like to share my sandwiches? Mother made them; they're very nice.'

She still sat and gazed at me in silence. Whatever could have happened to make her act like that? Was she out of her mind? She looked like a haggard old woman. Her beautiful hair, which she'd always kept meticulously plaited into a neat bun at the back of her head, looked like a matted bird's-nest. Perhaps later, if we remained together, she might open up and tell me.

But now we had to march on, for it was still a long way to Stolp. Kilometre after kilometre we dragged ourselves along, getting more and more weary and dispirited. The road was deserted, and no sign of life anywhere – not even animals in the fields.

At last, in the late afternoon, we approached Stolp. We were exhausted and footsore, and longed to sit and rest our tired legs.

When we reached the town of Stolp, we were met by a sorry sight. Such destruction, with hardly a well-known landmark left standing. The beautiful old church I'd often visited, now only a heap of rubble.

I wondered where the soldiers were taking us? Suddenly I realised with shocking clarity that we were on our way to the county prison, which I remembered standing on the outskirts of town. Why would the Russians want to put us there? We were no criminals! But that was where they were taking us. As we approached the huge iron gates, I could see they were open, ready to receive us. We hesitated and it dawned on me that once we went through them our freedom would be gone for ever. Many women were crying and refusing to enter that forbidding place. But the soldiers knew how to deal with the situation. A blow with the butt of a rifle soon stopped any crying and we all knew we had to obey. No good arguing – to them we were nothing.

We had to line up in the prison yard and as I looked up at the imposing dark, sinister building, I could see women's faces staring down at us through many small, dirty windows with iron bars. How many women had they hearded into here?

The soldiers conducted a lengthy and drawn-out roll call, as none of them found it easy to pronounce our names.

At last we were told to line up and follow them. They led us through a long passage with heavy iron doors on either side. Behind some of the doors we could hear voices, but the guards took no notice. With their usual shouts of *Davai!* they herded us towards the last two doors and into what looked like two tiny prison cells. Other women already occupied both cells. They complained loudly, as they considered us to be invading the little space they'd been able to call their own. There was quite a rebellion at that point. After the first few had entered, some women refused to be forced into that claustrophobic space. They screamed and fought, yet the guards kept on shoving more and more in. Women, in their terror, turned and tried to attack the guards, but the combined male strength was too much for them. I too was pushed through a small gap into the heaving bodies. But when, at last, it was impossible to squeeze even one more frame over the threshhold, the heavy iron door was forced against us, until it clanged shut. The noise of that lock brought a shocking finality to our fate.

Under normal circumstances these cells would only have been suitable to hold two or perhaps three prisoners. But now, we were more than twenty women squeezed into each cell, and to get any form of comfort was impossible. There was no room to sit; we could only stand. Some of us were fortunate to lean against the wall, while the others had to stand and prop each other up – it was a nightmare.

We shouted and shouted and made a terrible noise banging the door with our fists. But no amount of screaming would bring the soldiers back to free us. They'd turned a blind eye and a deaf ear to our suffering. We badly needed fresh air, but the small barred window high up in the wall couldn't be opened, and a small vent in the top of the door was totally inadequate. Something had to be done.

Someone shouted, 'There's a bucket in the corner here! What use is that to relieve us lot?'

'Well, there's a large jug of water over here,' another replied. 'Even if we only have a sip each, it won't quench our thirst for long, so we can always use that!'

But there was no food of any kind. I still had a sandwich left, but most of the others had nothing. Surely they wouldn't let us starve? We had to admit defeat and were overcome by a feeling of helpless rage.

To make things worse, being in such close proximity to one another, together with the lack of fresh air, was bound to cause friction. Some women were snivelling, while others became abusive. It could easily have resulted in physical violence. Luckily there was one big, strong woman with a booming voice, who demanded that the offenders stop quarrelling.

'I reckon, if we're all to survive in this hellhole, we'd better establish some form of order.' She suggested that if we wanted to get through the night, a rotary movement be introduced at regular intervals. She also promised that as soon as a guard approached our cell, she'd ask for the window to be opened. Much later we discovered she spoke a little Russian, which often proved to be a great help.

Her proposal was that half the women should sit leaning against the walls while the rest stood in the centre; then, after a while, everyone had to change places. She thought that by doing it that way, there would at least be a chance for every woman to relax at some time during the night. The women who'd been in the cell before us were moaning the loudest, but our spokeswoman soon put them in their place.

Since our arrival in the prison, I'd kept silent throughout everything that had been going on. I must have been the youngest among them all and had no right to speak. Up till then no one had taken notice of me and that suited me well.

In my head I had a conversation with my mother, and talked with Hans-Dieter and my small brother Ralfie. In my thoughts I hugged my little sister and could imagine her smiling at me. It was all so real. The thoughts of home brought tears to my eyes, but I vowed I wouldn't cry: nothing would come of it and it would only make me feel worse.

18 March 1945

Somehow the night passed, but occasionally someone in the centre would buckle as their tired legs gave way or they literally fell asleep on their feet. They came to, startled and disorientated, but for the most part there was silence. The jug was passed round just to wet our lips. Although the water was in reality warm and stale, to us it tasted as fresh and cool as if it had come from a hillside spring.

As dawn was breaking, we heard the guards approaching. The door was unlocked and a soldier handed in a basket of warm bread and a large urn full of weak but hot tea.

'Eat,' he said. 'Then you come. We go up!'

Up? I thought, where could that be? Upstairs, into another cell?

The fresh, warm bread tasted wonderful and the hot tea put new life into us.

I was glad I had the lid of my milkjug; it served me well as a cup. Someone poured a little extra tea into my jug. What luck! I'd drink it later.

'Eat,' he'd said. 'Eat and drink. Then you go up!' Immediately we all shouted in unison. 'Up? Where's up? Another floor? Another cell?'

'Eat!' was his only command before he shut the door on us again.

'You must let us out,' shouted our big spokeswoman. 'We all need to wash and find a proper toilet. But most of all we need fresh air!'

Most of us desperately needed a toilet. Fifteen hours had passed since we were incarcerated and I was doubled up with stomach ache, but I dared not use the facility in that cell. It was totally inadequate and most unpleasant. But I also needed to have a wash; mother had included a tablet of soap, a flannel and small towel in my knapsack. How wonderful that she'd remembered! But what use were these without water?

The guard came back a little later, unlocked our cell door and marched us to a washroom at the end of the long corridor. There were also toilet facilities – very basic, but adequate for our pressing needs. The water was cold, but so refreshing! I splashed my face over and over and reluctantly made room for the next person.

We had to wait in the corridor until everyone had finished their ablutions. At last the guard relented, unlocked a door and let us out into a glorious fresh morning. The sun hadn't yet reached the prison yard, but the light breeze on my face and the blue sky above felt like a gift from heaven. It dimmed the memory of the awful night we'd all had to endure, packed together like herrings in a barrel. Out there, in that wonderful fresh morning air, it was easier to block out those thoughts.

We formed into small friendly groups where we talked together, learned our names and found out where we'd come from. After all, we were all in the same boat – or prison – and that alone helped forge a certain unity. By now there were many women in the prison yard, young and old, all with one thing in common: we were separated from our loved ones and fearful of what the coming days had in store for us.

One young woman, a little older than me, had gradually moved closer. I felt she wanted to talk to me, but waited for her to approach first. To help make it easier for her, I left the group of women from Glowitz and walked a little apart. She followed.

'Hello,' she said. 'My name's Ruth. Who are you?'

'My name's Else Hopp and I come from Glowitz. Where are you from?'

'I'm from Stolp, not far from here.'

'So how come you were captured?' I asked. 'You have only your slippers on,' I said, looking at her feet, 'and your cardigan's so thin: it can't keep you warm?'

'I know,' she said. 'I'd only left the house to go to our neighbour to ask for a drop of milk for my baby nephew. But as soon as I stepped outside two Russian soldiers grabbed me, and now here I am in this awful place. I don't know why I'm here. I have nothing with me. No coat or warmer clothes, no shoes, no food and no toiletries whatsoever.'

And with those words she burst into heartbreaking sobs.

'Oh, Ruth, you poor dear. Listen to me! Don't cry! Whatever I have I'll share with you. I like you! Will you stay with me? We can be friends and go together wherever they're taking us. Would you like that?'

'Thank you, Else. I'd be very grateful for that. Now I don't feel quite so bad, or so alone.'

Soon our precious time in the yard came to an end. A guard blew his whistle and a door at the side of the building opened. A herd of Russian soldiers came running into the yard like animals, shouting their usual *Davai*'s and ordering us with kicks and the help of their rifle butts to line up and return to the prison building.

This time, however, we went up concrete stairs. Higher and higher, passing lengthy corridors with cells on either side until, at last, we reached the very top.

In front of us was a narrow wooden staircase, which led to an enormous loft, a large storage place in the roof. It covered the whole area from one end of the prison building to the other. That was where our captors wanted us to exist until they'd decided we should commence our march, destination unknown . . .

The floor area had been covered with straw. Along the wall stood buckets to serve as toilets and on another wall they'd placed large metal containers with drinking water. We were all responsible to replenish them from a tap on the landing below every time they were empty. As we entered the loft, a blanket was handed to each of us, and as Ruth and I stood, undecided where to go, we noticed the majority of women had already found a place to call their own.

'Come, Ruth,' I said to her, 'let's find a distant corner where we can be private and won't always be disturbed.' Our corner, almost at the end of the loft and to the right of the stairs, was relatively private, away from the greater crowd of women – almost two hundred of them. We were happy to have, at last, a little seclusion and both Ruth and I preferred it that way. Having found the place to our liking, we immediately built a comfortable bed with one blanket to lie on and the second to cover us.

The loft had many skylights built into the roof. However, they couldn't be opened; but at least they let in plenty of light.

It must have been almost midday when two guards came up and selected four strong-looking women. One was our earlier spokeswoman with her booming voice, and the other three also looked tough. They were ordered to follow the guards. No one knew where they were being taken, but we didn't have to wait long for an answer. They returned, carrying two enormous pots containing what we assumed to be either soup or stew, or at least something warm and substantial to fill our empty stomachs. We were *hungry*! Too hungry to fuss, and all accepted the food without being too concerned about what it might contain.

A Russian guard also brought a box full of pieces of bread, which were handed out by the women who served the soup. It was our first warm meal since we'd been taken to the village hall three days before.

'Else, what should I do?' Ruth asked me. 'I have no bowl or cup or anything to eat with?'

'Don't worry – we'll find a way. Let's ask them to fill my milk can. Then you can drink out of the lid and I'll still have my bowl.'

Sadly I had only one spoon but, after all, what were fingers for? They made a useful substitute. I blessed my dearest mother for having packed those things; now they came in handy and would serve me well in the days to come.

'You know, Ruth, I'm very tired. I think after we've eaten, I'll try to have a sleep. What do you think? After all, we've stood up nearly all night and there's nothing else to do.'

'Yes, let's do that! I'd love to go for a walk, but sadly that's something we can only dream of.'

We crawled under our blankets and were soon asleep. The emotions and upheavals of the previous three days had exhausted me, and all I wanted was to sleep and forget about our desperate situation. But before sleep overtook me, my thoughts went to my beloved family – what would they be doing now? Would mother be safe from molesting Russians? Dear God, I prayed, take care of her and please let me soon be with them again.

The evenings were worst. As soon as it was dark the Russian guards would come, walk among us and select women, whom they commanded to go with them. They'd come nearer and nearer but somehow stepped over us, as Ruth and I hid our faces under the blanket. I curled up into a tight ball and didn't want them to see I was young. They'd surely also have ordered me to follow them. Their usual 'Woman, come. *Davai, davai!*' could be heard all over the loft, mingled with the terrified pleading of the selected women. But Ruth and I, in our corner, both remained unmolested. I thanked God for that.

19 March 1945

In a dark corner, not far from where Ruth and I had our bedspace, I could see Fraulein Elisabeth. She was sitting on her own, dirty and unkempt and her eyes looked haunted and fearful. She looked much older than her sixty or so years. I could hear her mutter to herself full of anger and discontent, and watching her frightened me. Yet I had to speak to her. I walked over and greeted her with a smile. There was no response, but I felt she'd recognised me.

'Fraulein Elisabeth, does it bother you if I stay for a while and talk to you?'

She turned her head slowly and gazed at me. 'No, Else, it won't bother me at all,' was her reply. 'Come and sit down and tell me how you are and where you're going. Have you been to school today? This is not a good place to stay; I'd have thought they could have put us in a better and more comfortable hotel, don't you agree?'

I realised Fraulein Elisabeth had no idea where we were.

'Tell me,' I asked her, 'are you well?'

'Yes, Else, I'm fine. And you?'

'I miss my mother,' I answered. 'I wish I could be home and that everything could be the same again, the way it was. Please, Fraulein Elisabeth, may I ask you a question?'

'If it doesn't take too long. You see, I'm in a hurry, but ask away. What's it you want to know?'

'I'm so concerned about the old Baron and Baroness von Puttkamer. Will you please tell me how they are?'

She stared at me in amazement. I watched in silence as her face gradually contorted in horror at some invisible vision in her tortured mind. 'But, Else, don't you know?' she whispered. 'They're dead!'

'Dead? When did they die? And how?'

'They were killed, brutally murdered.'

Again she paused and I waited patiently, not believing my ears.

Then she looked at me with deep hollow eyes and croaked, 'And before they were even dead, they were dumped, one on top of the other, into the kitchen lift. You know, that small dumb waiter, the cupboard that takes food from one floor to the other? Well, they were squeezed inside it, with no room to move, and left to suffocate. Then the Russians locked the door and threw away the key, ignoring their pathetic thumps and cries for help.'

Again she faded into a distant world, her hands covering her ears, a futile gesture, for their wails would never leave her.

'Oh, how dreadful!' I groaned. 'How could they possibly treat the old couple like that? That was inhuman! And what about you? Were you also molested?'

I turned my attention to her, that poor wasted creature before me. For a long moment the poor lady just sat and looked at her hands.

Then she answered, 'Me? I was their plaything, an object of fun.' Her mouth dropped open and she gazed sorrowfully at an invisible scene. She was a child, badly rejected and beaten, who'd lost its will even to cry, but whose worst pain was the injustice of it all. 'I'd cooked a beautiful meal for my Russian guests and laid the table in the dining room. How elegant that dining table could look. Do you remember, Else, how exquisite the china was?' I nodded. 'And when the Russians entered our house, I invited them to sit down and enjoy the delicious food I'd prepared. But what did they do, Else? What do you think they did?' She appealed to me with pleading eyes. This time I shook my head, but kept my silence. 'They wrecked my meal. They smashed everything in sight: the china with the gold crest on it; the deep red upholstered chairs; the family portraits slashed; those beautiful young faces slashed to pieces in front of my eyes.' She was looking up at them, her eyes creased with anguish. 'Else, I stood there horrified: I couldn't stop them –' As a governess, the horror of seeing all that historical beauty demolished in her presence was painted in furrows on her drained face, made even greyer in the dim light.

Again I waited in sympathetic silence, sensing there was more to come.

Finally she looked up into my face with those childlike eyes. 'And then they grabbed me and raped me all through the night, one soldier after another, one after another, after another – I was completely helpless, at their mercy. I thought I'd die; oh, I wish I had.'

It devastated me to hear her talk like that. Three elderly people all alone – what harm could they possibly have done? I looked at Fraulein Elisabeth and saw tears streaking down her dirty cheeks. My heart went out to her. I put my arms around her to try to lighten her grief. She sobbed and I spoke to her as I'd have spoken to an injured child. 'There, there,' I tried to comfort her.

It helped as she clung to me, the hug she must have yearned for ever since her trauma had begun. After a while, she cried herself out and lay in my arms, still, hardly breathing, a frail bundle of aching bones. I let the minutes tick by – I had nothing else to do.

Eventually she let me lower her onto her blanket; her large eyes blinked up at me.

'May I come again?' I asked, tenderly covering her with her coat.

'Yes, do,' she answered drowsily, 'but not today: I have too much to do.'

I got to my feet, looking at her sorrowfully as she slipped back into that protective world of a long-gone past when life was filled with safe trivialities. Her eyes had glazed: she no longer saw me or the loft with its imprisoned women. I tiptoed back to my corner, as a thin smile of madness involuntarily distorted her face, locking her away from us.

Chapter 32

A Place Called Siberia

19–31 March 1945

We settled into a survival routine, thankful for the respite. But most of us knew it wouldn't last.

Twice a day, every day, we were allowed downstairs to the prison yard. Split into two groups, each group of women had about fifteen to twenty minutes outside in the fresh air. It was a period we all looked forward to and enjoyed. It enabled us to stretch our legs, have a chat or just walk about. When the weather was really fine, it was a tremendous pleasure to be out of doors away from that horrible, stinking atmosphere in the bucketed loft under the eaves.

Usually we went down in the morning and again sometime during the afternoon. And we kept the same routine on Sunday, 31 March, the start of our third week in prison. As before, the guards came and shouted for us to line up and go downstairs. We were used to that by now and could see no difference from any other time. But as we stepped into the prison yard, we immediately felt a change in atmosphere. There were about ten or twelve soldiers in the yard, and from their behaviour most of them seemed to be very drunk. They were laughing, shouting and fooling about and, most surprisingly, were tampering with a machine gun, which they'd heaved to the centre of the yard. It was a terrifying beast – whatever was going on? We might have hesitated, but certainly didn't have a chance to rebel because no sooner were we all outside, than the usual shout of *Davai, davai!* made us run into line and stand against the prison wall.

What were they going to do? Surely they weren't going to shoot us?

I was beginning to panic inside. Many women began shouting, while others cried, but in answer they received a painful blow from a rifle butt. Then there were some on their knees grovelling on the floor at the soldiers' feet. It did little good, for they were soon hauled into line. They were pleading for their lives. *No*, I thought, *that's something I will* not *do!* I refused to beg for my life – if they wanted to shoot me, so be it.

We stood there, lined up against the wall looking into the yard. So this was it.

But that wasn't good enough for the Russians. They were shouting back and forth to each other. There was a change of tactics. With pushing and bawling they gave us to understand that they wanted us to turn round and face the wall. And because so many women were crying and pleading and wouldn't stop doing so, the guards became even angrier and more and more rifle blows rained down on our heads and backs, a nightmarish shambles.

Thosands of thoughts ran through my head. Like a reel from a motion picture, images of my life rushed through my mind, mostly of my family. Did mother fear this when she said goodbye? I was utterly confused. I didn't know what to think. What had we done to justify this treatment? Ruth, beside me, was sobbing and clinging to my hand.

'Else,' she whimpered, 'I don't want to die! I've done nothing wrong. Why should they want to punish *me*?'

'Hush, Ruth,' I squeezed her hand and felt some comfort from another human being. I didn't look at her though. 'I feel the same. Perhaps it's revenge. They blame us for something evil, which their women suffered.' I was talking rapidly in a hoarse whisper. 'I don't know, Ruth, I'm just as desperate as you. Any minute now, that monster will go off with a ricochet of bullets. We must drop to the ground instantly. It may save us.'

For quite some time we stared at the wall. The Russian guards were having a game with us. Still we waited; still they shouted at each other and pummelled us. They found our terror highly amusing. If one of us dared to turn a head to see what was happening, the Russians were only too ready to deliver a blow with the butt of their rifle or revolver. The tension was getting unbearable; fear made my legs weak and I felt ready to collapse.

And I wasn't the only one. *Shoot, will you! If you mean it, then shoot us and get it over with!*

Suddenly, quite unexpectedly with a clang, the large prison gates opened and in drove a jeeplike vehicle of the Russian army. I peered cautiously around. In it sat three officers and a driver. The car stopped; they got out and looked around, taking note of what was going on. They were clearly amazed. One officer immediately walked towards the soldiers still trying drunkenly to assemble and position the machine gun. In his language he shouted what we assumed to be a demand for them to stand to attention, which they, because of their drunken state, were quite unable to do. In fact they looked surprised to see the officers. Their companions had stopped hitting us and were backing away into the shadows.

Then, acting in unison, all three officers took their own batons and started to thrash the guards as hard as they could in front of our eyes. The blows struck the drunken soldiers, who fell about, scattering their rifles as they attempted to sober up. The officers dished out terrible punishment in all directions with rage and disgust. The soldiers had to take it: to defend themselves would have meant instant death. And their shouts for mercy fell on deaf ears.

There was stunned silence among us women, all of whom had felt reassured enough to turn around and watch what was unfolding before us. Never before had we experienced such a display of brutal punishment of Russian against Russian. We were all utterly numb with shock from the whole ordeal.

It was surreal. Was I playing a part in a feature film? No! This was real.

An officer approached and addressed us as best as he could in halting German.

'Now, you go back to your sleeping quarters. You have no man to fear: you're safe. Rest as much as you can. Tomorrow you leave this prison and march a long, long way. You start very early, but today rest and sleep.'

As we were used to by now, we lined up and climbed the stairs into the loft and to our bedspace in the corner. There was complete silence – our ordeal had been beyond words.

Immediately I rolled myself into the blanket with Ruth. We were shaking and both felt icy cold. Downstairs, in the yard, I might have appeared strong and calm, but I wasn't – that was only a front, not the real me. We hugged each other in silence, to get the life back into our bodies, life that had almost been taken from us.

As I lay there in my corner, I felt an almost physical rage envelop my whole being. I vowed then and there I *would* get away from that nightmare. I'd bide my time, do nothing hasty, but wait until the moment was right, and perhaps – with God's help – once again be reunited with my family.

I kept that thought to myself as I hugged poor shivering Ruth beside me. I hoped she'd be with me, but now wasn't the time to talk about it. Planning was no good: my escape had to be a spur of the moment decision. The opportunity would come – I was certain of that – and, with exhaustion from the trauma and thoughts of my mother and the little ones in Glowitz, I somehow fell asleep.

I must have slept for many hours. The dreadful events of the previous afternoon, combined with the inner turmoil and terror, which we'd all experienced in the yard, had left me physically and mentally drained. But now I was wide awake. It had to be very early, perhaps no later than the middle of the night. I had no way of telling. The darkness was intense but a faint light emanated through dirty skylights. It made the outlines of the sleeping women shadowy and almost impossible to distinguish.

Most were restless and didn't seem able to find serenity even in sleep. I could hear sighs and now and then a whimper. Some were talking in their sleep and it appeared many had uneasy dreams. No one was completely relaxed and able to find untroubled repose.

I had no idea what the time could be, but sleep was gone and, rolled in my blanket warm and cosy, I let my mind wander to my family. I felt like praying. I wondered, would God hear me in these dismal surroundings? He was supposed to be everywhere; perhaps he'd also listen to my pleas.

I folded my hands, closed my eyes and concentrated on my talk to God and asked him to take care of my loved ones and also of me. I needed his care.

God, are you out there somewhere? Are you with me? With my family?

Mother and father, will they be asleep? Will mother be tossing and turning, worrying about us? Will father still be somewhere in Russia in the trenches, fighting a lost battle and wishing it were all over? Please God, don't let him be taken prisoner. I've heard it said that when the Russians take German prisoners, they send them to a place called Siberia: far, far into the wilds of Russia. (Most probably we'd never see our father again, a thought I don't want to dwell upon.)

The little ones, Ralf and baby Marlene, can they keep their innocence, God? Too small as yet to see evil and experience horror and fear as long as mother's there to shelter them from harm. But Hans-Dieter, my nine-year-old brother, so vulnerable and trusting, will he be spared the shame many women, and perhaps also his mother, will have to endure? I hope so!

Once more, God, look after me and all the women here in this prison, in the same predicament as me. Take care of us today and in these frightening, unknown days to come . . . Amen. Oh, and thank you, Lord, for saving us all – a real miracle, but it really was a bit close to the line! Amen.

Now that I'd said my prayer, I felt better. I crawled out of my blanket and groped my way to the nearest bucket to relieve myself. Stepping over sleeping bodies was no easy task, for they lay about haphazardly, abandoned in restless slumber.

After I'd rolled back into my blanket, I lay with eyes wide open watching the faint light of a new day creeping into our wretched abode. I lay there, wondering what that day would have in store for us. We'd been told we were leaving. Could it be true? Or was it again just a ruse to keep us all on edge? It was a matter of waiting – we'd learn our fate soon enough.

Alone with my thoughts, I realised that since I'd said my prayers I didn't feel quite so unhappy. The previous day I'd been angry and full of hate: wicked thoughts had gone through my head and, in my anger, I'd determined I'd escape as soon as an opportunity presented itself. I still felt the same determination, but was calmer and the anger had left me with a renewed resolve to find my way back to mother and my family. But I had to wait, bide my time, carefully work out a plan and stick to it. It was imperative that once I got away I avoided recapture, which would mean certain death.

I must have slept again, because when I awoke and opened my eyes, it was daylight. There was a lot of activity around me: most of the women were already up and about. Ruth was sitting by my side, tapping my shoulder and shaking me.

'Wake up, Else. It's breakfast soon. I heard someone say we may get something special this morning. Probably our usual weak tea and lump of bread scraped so thinly with ghastly margarine that it's hardly noticeable.'

I sat up, rubbed my eyes and tried to return to reality. I folded my blanket, took the can out of my knapsack and walked over to the water container to fill it.

'I won't be a minute, Ruth. I must swill my hands and face. I hope there's still water left.'

I badly needed a wash: I was dirty and must have looked it. But there was only a little water left in the container. I longed for a bath; I hated being dirty and felt self-revulsion, but no one knew when – or even if ever again – we'd have a bath or a thorough wash. No good asking the Russian guards, as they didn't understand us anyway.

With my comb I tried to untangle my hair. It wasn't easy. Dirty and sticky, and it itched continuously. Perhaps I had headlice. Quite possible, with the conditions we were living in; but there was nothing I could do about it.

At last the women came from the kitchen carrying our breakfast. That morning we had porridge. Not made with water, but with milk, and even though we had no sugar, to Ruth and me it tasted wonderful. We were also handed a piece of delicious, freshly baked bread, a luxury that rounded off a perfect breakfast.

My can could hold sufficient porridge to satisfy both of us and I was pleased to see how well we managed between us. Our breakfast tasted good and we enjoyed it. We'd learned by now that if you're really hungry, the humblest food can be a banquet. And who knew when we'd be fed again.

As soon as we'd eaten, the soldiers arrived to take us downstairs. Quickly we gathered our meagre belongings and followed them. I was still hoping that perhaps we'd be given the opportunity to visit a toilet and swill our hands and face.

It's amazing how easy it is to hurry when you have to. Just a short while and we were lined up in the yard ready to move off.

A motley bunch of women, we were dirty and unkempt, but strangely didn't even notice this.

The big prison gates opened, and outside was the world and an unknown destination. Yet at that moment we felt free. There was a wonderful feeling of euphoria and lightheartedness. Soon we'd come back to reality with a jolt, but for just a short while we all relished being out in the fresh morning air, away from confinement and grey walls.

1 April 1945

On that day some two hundred German women marched onto a country road, leaving Stolp and, except for a lucky few, our former lives behind us. No one knew where the road would lead, for all the signposts had long before been removed: our final destination, somewhere in Russia, had never been disclosed to us.

Guided by a soldier, a shaggy horse harnessed to a rickety cart led the way; it carried a metal container of water.

Soon we left the last houses behind – no longer dwellings, but ruins left over from ferocious battles that had been fought there not long before. But ahead of us, on either side, we could see tended fields, which later on would bear vegetables and corn in the hope that someone would still be there to gather in the harvest.

In the distance appeared what looked like dense woodland, which told us we were leaving all traces of civilisation behind. We were in conquered territory that was once Germany, but now belonged to Russia and would soon be under Polish administration.

We were walking now, quiet and not inclined to talk any more. The chatter and occasional laughter that had accompanied us at the beginning had petered out. Now we were simply trudging along in silence, each person deep in her own thoughts and carrying again the burden of utter misery – a long line of women dragging their feet along that endless dusty road.

Sometimes one of us tried to sit down for a moment, but that wasn't allowed. A guard was instantly on the spot, shouting 'Get up. *Davai!*' and blows would rain down if we didn't immediately comply.

Ruth and I walked side by side without speaking. For a while we'd talked but now there was no more to be said.

Without warning, we were brought to a sudden halt. It appeared some women had requested a stop to go into the forest to relieve themselves, which the guards cautiously allowed. We took the opportunity to go to the front and ask for water to quench our dreadful thirst.

The guards nervously stayed at the entrance to the wood, all the time keeping an eye on each individual as she disappeared among the trees.

Suddenly we were in the centre of a tremendous commotion. There was shouting from furious soldiers who'd run into the forest, giving chase to shrieking women. The hapless prisoners couldn't escape from those fast-sprinting Russians. We heard pitiful screaming and crying and pleading voices and soon the soldiers emerged, dragging behind them three wretched and desperate women.

I'd had a sneaking feeling they intended to run into the forest to escape. Now they'd been caught and dragged back to the road where everyone could witness their fate. They screamed and pleaded and cried, begging for mercy, but the pleas fell on deaf ears. The guards ordered the three women to kneel at the edge of the road, drew revolvers from their holsters and shot each woman in the back of the neck. *Three women, alive just few minutes before, now dead, lying in the dust of a country road.*

It was horrendous, unbelievable. How could such dastardy action be allowed to go on? I'd heard father talk of the Geneva Convention, rules made to protect prisoners of war. We were also prisoners, so would those rules not apply to us as well? But there was nothing we could do. After all, what were three German lives, but scum and trash to our captors, nothing to be concerned about. Three enemies less to drag to Russia, and no one would be any the wiser.

I saw the bodies hauled into the ditch at the side of the road, left there as we were ordered to march on. Some women remonstrated and demanded the corpses be buried, but the soldiers wouldn't hear of it. '*Niet, niet!* No, no!' they screamed, and, as they always did, using their rifle butts they made us toe the line and march on.

They insisted we look at the dead bodies as we passed them, a lesson to show what would be in store for us should anyone else dare to try to run away again.

Three dead bodies and a few patches of blood were all that was left behind as we were forced to continue on our way. Three sad nameless souls stained each of our memories for the rest of our lives: their only memorial . . .

The guards were now in a hurry; it was as if they wanted to get away and forget their terrible deed. They were agitated and didn't quite know how to handle the situation. We let them see how angry we all were, and in the end they became frightened and all they could do was lash out at random and we, in return, were forced to comply with their demands as usual and walk on. Could we have overpowered them? Two hundred women against ten or twelve armed men? Not without more bloodshed.

No food, no rest, just walking and walking non-stop. Our legs threatened to refuse to carry us further, but always, from somewhere, we managed to gather a little more strength to drive ourselves onwards. We were shattered. All we wanted was something to eat and drink and, no matter where, a tiny corner to sleep to obliterate the shocking incident that had made a dreadful day so very much worse.

Chapter 33

Hotel on the Horizon

1 April

Never before had I felt as weary and footsore as I did at that moment. My legs refused to carry me further, yet I had to go on to save my life. Ruth, *still walking in her slippers*, was stumbling along beside me; she felt the same. We supported each other, though neither felt like talking; only our eyes, glued to the road prevented us from missing our footing. I was desperate to sit down, if only for a little while; but that was wishful thinking – the guards wouldn't let us.

Ever since the incident earlier in the day at the edge of the forest, they'd been on edge and wanted us to keep moving as quickly as possible. Where were we going? Why didn't anyone tell us our destination? All around us were fields and meadows and large forests stretching into the distance as far as the eye could see – beautiful in other circumstances, but today just endless monotony.

Here and there we caught sight of small clusters of houses, ruined and uninhabitable. Now and then we passed tranquil lakes and village ponds, deceptively peaceful and undisturbed – inviting us to jump in and cool our weary legs, but they were luxuries beyond our reach.

Suddenly Ruth stumbled and fell over. I stopped to pick her up, but it was enough to break the rhythm of the poor women following us. It caused chaos, as they tumbled over us and each other, whimpering and muttering.

A guard was instantly upon us, and his baton came down. It hit Ruth's cheek, which split open. Blood spurted out and trickled down her neck. She looked like a victim in a horror film. I couldn't believe what he'd done and wanted to attack him; but as I turned to face him, his baton struck my shoulder. The pain was excruciating and my arm instantly went limp. I couldn't hit him now although I still wanted to. I wanted to shout at him, scream defiance, but as I looked into his eyes – that coarse man with his squashed nose and filthy unkempt uniform – I saw his hatred and loathing for us, his face contorted with disgust. The revelation of how powerful his feelings of contempt were for us hit me like a second more potent blow: to him we were scum, the basest of creatures, and he wouldn't think twice about wiping us out.

He spat out words at us and, although we didn't understand them, their meaning was clear.

'Get up! Walk on, you cretins; don't ask questions. We soldiers know what we're doing, where we're going. Why should you know, you imbeciles? All you need to do is follow.'

I was so angry and miserable I felt like screaming. Yet what good would it do? It was monstrous not to be told where the road was leading or how much longer we had to struggle on before we could rest. Surely the Russian authorities must have given orders where we'd spend the nights? But if the sodiers knew, they certainly kept us in the dark, and up to then I'd seen no building large enough to shelter so many weary women.

My eyes were fixed on the ground, my head too heavy for my body. I was thirsty but too exhausted to hurry to the front to fetch water.

The day was coming to an end and dusk was falling – soon it would be dark. The sky was clear and very likely there'd be a frost that night. I was fortunate to have my warm coat and sturdy boots, but poor Ruth had nothing. I'd offer her the spare pullover mother had put in my haversack. Her slippers had almost fallen apart. Luckily we'd found some twine on the road that, wound around them, had up till then helped keep them intact.

If the guards wanted to walk much further, they'd have had a riot on their hands and lost more prisoners in the dark. We outnumbered our captors about ten to one, but they had rifles, revolvers and superior strength. Any argument to challenge their decision would only have resulted in more bloodshed.

'Else,' Ruth nudged me, 'look ahead. Can you see what I see?'

'What is it? I can't see anything. My eyes are sore. What do you want me to see?'

'Look again, Else. There's a building looming ahead in the distance, a large building. Can't tell what it is, but it's there and we're walking towards it.'

'What do you think it is?'

'A school or factory, or even an army barracks. Whatever it is, it's large. Perhaps that's where we'll spend the night. I'm so relieved. At last we may be able to rest our weary bodies.'

'Slow down, Ruth. Don't get your hopes up. You know what the Russians are like. Let's wait and see. I don't think there's one woman among us who isn't ready to collapse. Let's just hope our agony will soon be at an end.'

I had to admire Ruth. In spite of her inadequate clothing and footwear, she'd remained cheerful most of the way. She put me to shame. I had to pull myself together, because there were moments when I doubted I'd be able to survive our soul-destroying ordeal. I was depressed and in very low spirits. Ruth seemed to understand; smiling, she looked at me and linked my arm with hers. She was such a good friend; nowhere could I find a better one.

'Yes,' I answered, looking at her, 'you're quite right. I can see a large building in the distance, coming nearer and nearer. I also believe that's where we'll spend the night.'

'And once we're there, Else, we'll find a corner to lie down in and rest – heavenly!'

We hobbled on, a bedraggled line of weary women, while the large building slowly came nearer. As we reached it we recognised it must once have been a school, perhaps a boarding school. Large gates opened to what must have been well-tended, but now sadly neglected, grounds.

There were three separate sections to the building. The guards ordered us to stand in line and divided us into three groups, each group to be watched over by four soldiers.

'Stay close to me, Ruth,' I whispered, 'otherwise we may be separated.'

We were hustled inside and the doors were immediately locked behind us. There was plenty of room for all of us, however, and we were not crowded together. The classroom – a safe guess because of a blackboard on the wall – Ruth and I chose had a table standing in the corner. I made a beeline for it, reserving it for us to sleep under. But there was an argument because another woman also wanted the table. Yet I was having none of it. We were there first and I wasn't going to let someone else push us out.

As soon as we'd settled under the table and arranged our meagre belongings, I asked Ruth to stay there while I located toilets, washrooms and drinking water. I assumed there was also a kitchen somewhere, because, from along the corridor I could smell cooking.

I found a door marked 'Toilets'.

Oh, what bliss! Each of us must have been in terrible agony to find a toilet, but we had to queue. Nearby was the washroom, which had many basins in double rows – heavenly to hope that, as long as there was water available and once the first rush was over, I might treat myself to the luxury of having a complete washdown. Never before had I been among so many women. It was an eye-opener. They came from all walks of life and some were incredibly noisy, their speech common and often vulgar. Others, however, got on with what they had to do and minded their own business.

Although I was hungry, food didn't seem so important. First I needed to tell Ruth what I'd discovered.

'Ruth,' I called, as soon as I entered the schoolroom, 'apart from toilets and a lot of washbasins, there are also showers, but I don't know if they work. Somewhere along the corridor must be kitchens: I could smell something cooking. Go and see for yourself. I'll stay here and guard our belongings.'

It took a while for her to return, but, with so many women clambering for the same things, I expected that.

When she came back and handed me my soap and towel, she was scrubbed clean, her cheeks glowing after the grime had been removed. Her facial wound, though swollen and no doubt developing into a black eye, was looking healthier.

Now it was my turn.

I found a vacant basin and the cold water on my dirty head and neck exhilarated and refreshed me. I bathed my crushed shoulder: as I could wiggle my fingers, I felt sure nothing was broken. It was sore but I was getting some movement back. Suddenly I felt uplifted, as a faint glimmer of hope and cheerfulness enfolded me. I knew it couldn't last, but I was convinced everything would come right. I also knew with certainty that the next day or two would decide Ruth's and my fate.

When a large container of some kind of stew and a basket of bread were brought into the corridor with ample for all to share, my sadness and low spirits vanished. I stood in line with my little can, waiting to be served. I was assertive enough to persuade them to fill it to the top and returned to Ruth under the table. We had only one spoon between us but that didn't bother us in the slightest, for we took turns to eat and in no time at all had consumed every scraping of stew and also a slice of bread, which helped to satify us.

Now all we wanted was to relax under our table and watch what was going on around us. The women were laughing and chattering, their bellies full, appearing not to have a care in the world. But what would happen later when the soldiers had also eaten and drunk their fill of vodka, of which there seemed to be an everlasting supply? Then there would be screams instead of laughter, not only in that classroom but echoing throughout the walls.

'Ruth,' I whispered, 'I have to go and find out if Fraulein Elisabeth's in this building. I haven't seen her all day and want to know how she's coping. I'll soon return, but don't go anywhere and leave our belongings unattended.'

'You go, Else. I'll stay and wait for you to come back. Take care and try not to catch the eyes of any soldiers: stay inconspicuous.'

I walked from classroom to classroom trying to find Elisabeth, but it appeared she wasn't in our building. I could search no further, as all the doors to the outside were locked and there was no way I could find her that evening; it would have to wait until the morning.

I returned to Ruth, whose turn it was to prepare for the night.

I looked at our makeshift bed. There wasn't much I could do: we had no bedding, no blanket to cover us and had to be prepared to feel cold during the night. I shared between us the clothes I had. My coat would give us at least a small amount of cover and my haversack would serve as my pillow.

'Ruth,' I said quietly, 'I'll try to go to the kitchen to see if I can find something we can use for a pillow for you. Don't worry – I'll be gone no more than a few minutes.'

'Please be careful, Else. If the guards catch you, you'll be punished. They'll accuse you of stealing.'

I did find the kitchen and a sack, empty and fairly clean, and, best of all, no one saw me! Ruth was delighted. Now she could fold the sack into a makeshift pillow, and we could both settle down to a good night's sleep.

3 April 1945

The march continued for a number of days without incident. No more shootings, though a few women were missing each morning when we lined up. What happened to them, we never knew. Was it abuse, illness or inability to walk any further – or had they escaped? Who could tell? There was no chance for us to escape, for the guards kept a close eye on us. Day blurred into day, and kilometre into kilometre, and the night stops were inadequate. Time felt like an everlasting day. But one night stuck out in my mind.

We'd stopped at a barracks; and although we had to sleep on bare boards, the Russians had supplied each of us with a blanket. I must have dozed off but suddenly awoke to find someone fumbling with the opening of my haversack. In seconds I was wide awake and, in the dim light coming through the window, could see a woman trying to steal my belongings. Without thinking, I grabbed her cardigan with one hand and with the other pummelled her unmercifully. I seemed to have aquired the strength of a giant. I was furious!

'You evil beast,' I whispered hoarsely pinning her to the floor. 'Here we are, all prisoners, none of us with much, and you, you rotten thief, try to steal even the little we *do* have. I'd report you, but the Russians are no better: they'd probably only laugh it off. But everyone here in this room will be told tomorrow morning what you tried to do and *you* will have to live with the shame of being ignored by us. Now get out of my sight! The Russians call us scum; you're no better. Go and crawl into your hole.'

Once more I lashed out with all the anger that overwhelmed me, and the sound of my full hand making contact with her face gave me great satisfaction.

Next morning, very early, while most women were still asleep, I made my way to the washroom. I thought I'd be the only one there, but the large woman who'd spoken for us in Stolp prison was already washing, alone, peacefully humming to herself.

'Good morning,' I said, 'I don't know your name? Mine's Else; I come from Glowitz.'

'Morning, little one. People call me Molly. You know, *mollig*, 'plump'. It's not my real name, but it suits me.'

'Can I call you Molly?' I asked.

'Of course you can, little one. You conducted yourself well last night and sent that thieving bitch away: a dog with her tail between her legs. Well done! She'll be cold-shouldered. I don't think she'll try to steal again in a hurry.'

'Molly,' I asked, 'I know you speak some Russian. Do you know where we're going?'

'Well, Else, I can't tell you much, but one soldier told me they're taking us either to Bütow or to Könitz. Bütow has only a small station and somehow I don't think transport to Russia will go from there. But Könitz is a lot bigger and has a main railway line. Of course, it's further to walk but that wouldn't bother our 'kind' guards. They've a timetable and as long as they get us there in time without shooting too many of us, they'll be happy.'

'And when should we arrive in Könitz, Molly? Do you know?'

'As far as I could gather from their conversation, no later than tomorrow evening.'

'How will you cope, being sent to Russia, Molly?'

Molly looked at me long and hard.

'Else,' she said, 'I think almost all of us have some plan in our head. Whether we can go through with it is another question. But I, for one, like many others, am only waiting for the right moment to disappear. How about you, little one?'

'I don't know, Molly. I'll just wait and see. Who knows?'

As soon as I returned to our classroom, I saw Ruth was awake. I handed her soap and towel, and off she rushed, hoping to find an unoccupied basin.

Once again, as on the previous morning, our breakfast, when it came, consisted of some type of gruel, but this time made with water and looking stodgy and quite disgusting. The bread, on the other hand, was fresh and crisp and we all enjoyed it.

There was no hanging about that morning. Our guards seemed in a hurry and rushed us out of the building at speed. One of them had obtained from somewhere a long horsewhip. It was like a toy to him and he enjoyed flicking it. Wherever it landed it caused agony and a line of bloody flesh, much to the delight and amusement of that childish lunatic.

Before us another long day, another long march. We were all tired, for none of us had slept well and there was no spring in our step. It was such an effort to walk again, but we had no choice – we *had* to make our legs move on.

Ruth's slippers were in shreds: despite the twine binding them on, they couldn't possibly last all day. She was walking almost barefoot in agony on the rough country road. I had a spare pair of socks in my haversack and gave them to her: at least they'd protect her feet for a while.

It was cold that day, much colder than the day before. The sky was grey, with the clouds hanging low, and it looked like rain. Although we were in April, it could still snow. Not unusual in Pomerania. The dull, dismal weather made me shiver and I felt chilled in spite of my winter coat. Poor Ruth. Although she had my thick jumper, she must have felt frozen to the marrow; but I had no more to give her. Yet she never complained.

I trudged down the road with everyone else, but was unaware of anything except one dull thought that churned around and around in my head: *I've got to get away and it has to be soon! We have one more night somewhere; then tomorrow we reach Könitz, and it could soon be too late. I have to act quickly, keep my eyes open for the slightest opportunity.*

Please God, give me a chance. It has to be soon . . . or never. And please, don't let me be caught – and end up dead in a ditch.

Tonight I'd talk to Ruth. She had to decide whether to come with me or stay behind.

Soon the first raindrops hit my face like pins piercing the skin. The many lime trees on either side of the road gave little shelter, for they were still bare, showing only the first sign of swelling leaf buds.

I remember mother telling me that the long straight country roads, flanked on either side by lime, birch or beech trees, were a famous landmark of Pomerania. The people were proud of their country roads and tended them with loving care. The trees, many hundreds of years old, stood dignified in their splendour, and the villagers took turns to keep the roads and trees in perfect order. At least there were no potholes.

We were alone, our convoy like a snake crawling along an almost deserted country road. Only the occasional Russian jeep passed us, throwing dust in our faces. Sometimes a lumbering lorry caused us to scramble onto the bank to get out of its way.

5 April 1945

There was urgency in the Russians' behaviour that day. They were in a hurry and wanted us to move fast: no rest and no food while we were marching. Just water from the barrel on the cart whenever we were thirsty. Yet we women wouldn't be chivvied along. We'd become hard and immune to shouting and beatings and *we* set the pace. All of us were weary and footsore – nothing could make us move any faster than we were prepared to go.

After many hours of trudging, the Russians suddenly called a halt at the side of the road, where we were able to sit for a short while and rest our exhausted legs. But we were offered no food.

I made my way to the front of the line to get a drink for Ruth and myself from the barrel. Molly was in deep conversation with a guard, a heated discussion, but I was too far away to tell what it was about. Perhaps she just wanted to know how much longer we had to walk before nightfall.

When she'd finished talking, I sidled up to speak to her.

'Molly,' I enquired, 'did the soldier tell you anything? We're so tired, it's impossible to go on much further.'

'Yes, Else, the guard said we'd arrive early this evening. They're planning a celebration.'

'Why?'

'They've received news their army's entered Berlin and is advancing towards the chancellery and Adolf Hitler's bunker! They want to surprise and catch Hitler and his entourage alive.'

'Yes, but what about us?'

'Huh! Their celebration will consist of vodka, and more vodka! Some of them will get so drunk they won't even know where they are. But all the same, Else, keep out of their way and don't let them notice you. Be on your guard!'

I returned to Ruth and told her what Molly'd said.

A thought came to me: *If the Russians are celebrating and drinking so much, perhaps they'll all have such a hangover they won't notice if Ruth and I stay behind when they move on in the morning.*

I'll tell her about my hopes later – but for now I'll keep them to myself.

To keep walking in some sort of rhythm I allowed myself to dream of escape. It was imperative we fled before we were herded onto the train at Könitz. After that there'd be little chance of getting off this side of the Russian border. There was no knowing how deep into Russia they'd take us before the train stopped, making escape even more difficult.

That gave Ruth and me just twenty-four hours to get away.

The three women who'd tried to escape en route were shot. That ruled out virtually any chance of flight from the convoy – unless there was an incident – but I couldn't rely on that.

So we had only the small gap between arriving and leaving wherever they boarded us for the night. But where would that be? Another school? A hospital? At least there might be a maze of corridors, hidden cupboards or a cellar full of central-heating pipes. I hoped it wouldn't be another prison. We wouldn't have a chance of escaping from that.

'Look girls, our hotel's on the horizon!' someone shouted ahead of us, which broke into my reverie – a large building in the distance had caught the attention of the leading women. I pointed it out to Ruth, and we both hoped we'd spend the night there. I looked around. As far as my eyes could see, nothing but open countryside interspersed with large areas of woodland.

As we neared the building, it was obviously not a school but a vast complex of army barracks, stables and outhouses.

On arrival we were immediately marched into the main building, where we were divided into small goups and unceremoniously pushed into one of many empty rooms. Soon it was rumoured that this time we'd be given a blanket for the night, and food, which some of our women were preparing in the barrack kitchens.

The soldiers, in high spirits, were well on the way to being drunk, and each time they came near us, they'd shout, while laughing hysterically, 'Germany finished; Hitler finished; Russians in Berlin!'

They were taunting us and we tried to ignore them, but they wouldn't let us.

It was their evening of triumph and the long night would be for non-stop drinking until morning dawned. Who knew where they got their vodka, an everlasting supply.

Many times we heard their shout of 'Woman, come!' And each time, Ruth and I huddled deeper into our blankets hoping and praying that once more we'd be overlooked and spared the humiliating ordeal of being raped.

I still hadn't been able to find Fraulein Elisabeth. I'd have liked to speak to her once more, but that evening I didn't feel safe to go and look for her. I had no idea where she could be, but among so many women it was difficult to find anyone. I'd asked around here and there, but no one seemed to know her.

As usual Ruth and I had found a corner where we could settle for the night, wrapped this time in our blankets.

But first I had to find a washroom. I took my towel and soap and walked cautiously along a corridor, following the sound of many voices. Yes, there were washing facilities. I was able to swill my face and hands and quickly return to Ruth to let her go and do the same. 'Be really careful!' I whispered.

Our meal, when at last it arrived from the kitchens, was a kind of undefinable stew, together with a chunk of dry bread. It was better not to analyse what was floating in the stew. We were hungry, and it was either eat it or go without.

The soldiers continued to make pandemonium, singing and drinking and dancing their exuberant Russian dances: one of the guards played a mouth organ and the rest of them clapped their hands in rhythm.

We could hear the racket they were making, and to sleep was nearly impossible, in spite of our exhaustion. We were ready to settle down, but the urgency to escape kept me awake. I had to speak to Ruth immediately.

'Ruth,' I whispered, 'are you still sure that you want to follow me when I say "Come"?'

'Yes, Else, I've told you I will. When the time's right, just say the word: I won't fail you.'

'I was hoping you'd say that. Let's try to sleep now, even with that racket. We'll need all the strength we can muster.'

Next morning, on waking, I saw through the window a brilliant blue sky. Where'd the night gone? I'd slept soundly and now felt refreshed and determined to face that day, whatever it might have in store for me. Was the blue sky and bright sunshine a good omen? I hoped so, because that day was, I thought, a day of decision and so much depended on the outcome.

As usual our breakfast consisted of watery porridge and a drink of weak tea. Not appetizing but it filled and warmed us, and to eat and drink was necessary for what lay ahead. Food and drink could be scarce from now on.

The door was open. Ruth and I stepped outside while the others were still getting ready. I looked around and my eyes fastened on the outhouses, where once perhaps horses had been stabled. And as I was looking and taking note of all that surrounded me, a daring idea entered my head. It had to succeed, or else our fate was sealed.

There was one Russian guard standing near us. He swayed slightly, his eyes red and baggy, still somewhat under the influence of the previous night's celebration.

'Ruth,' I said loud enough for him to hear, 'before we move, I must find a toilet. The others are all occupied. Will you come with me?'

'Sure I will, Else, I have to go as well. Let's see what we can find.'

I approached the guard and tried to make him understand where we wanted to go.

Da, da (yes, yes), he answered. And, not at all concerned, waved us away.

'Come on, Ruth. We'll go now!' I whispered.

'Else, what about your haversack?'

'Leave it: it's not important. If we take it, the guard might become suspicious.'

Off we went towards the stables. 'Walk slowly, Ruth, just normally. Don't turn round.'

We entered a stable, empty, but for rows of lockers standing against two walls. There must have been four or five rows each with about ten to fifteen lockers, one behind the other.

'Quick, we must hide inside a locker,' I whispered conspiratorially. 'Look for one standing close to the wall at the back. You take one and I'll take another not too close to yours. Hold the door together from the inside; squat down. It will be tight and we'll get cramp but we have to bear it. And please, please, Ruth, don't make a sound. They'll come and look for us – be sure of that – and the slightest sound will give us away. We must both offer a prayer, hoping God will listen and send us more than one angel to guard us today.'

In the last row we found two lockers, unlocked. They had to be the ones to hide in.

We were only just in time. No sooner had I squatted down and held the door closed from the inside than I heard voices – Russian voices and footsteps across the yard. They were already searching the outhouses and shouting to each other. That guard was obviously not as comatose from liquor as I'd thought. Perhaps he'd remembered the three women at the roadside and had summoned help. Soon heavy boots were clumping on the concrete floor of the stable. Someone was looking for us. Was it just one soldier or more? My heart was beating so violently that I was sure it could be heard outside. Someone was trying the locker doors: I could hear it all so clearly. Wrench and slam. Wrench and slam. If he was consistent, he'd find us.

Then silence. Had he gone?

Ruth, please don't get out. Don't call to me, I pleaded silently. *I sense he's still here.*

And I was right. The boots started again – creeping this time – just a creak now and then, just a small rasp of a locker door being prised open with a stick or something.

Oh, please God, don't let him find us! I was trembling with the sheer terror of it all and feared I'd give myself away.

Should I give myself up? I thought. Perhaps he won't hurt us if I do that.

No, he'd shoot us dead on the spot. We've come too far – there's no going back!

And then I thought the footsteps were receding. Certainly there was silence again. Not a sound in the stable. Was he hiding? Ruth and I had to stay where we were for some time yet. I strained my ears – only distant voices of women, probably lining up to begin their march towards Könitz and journey into the unknown.

I must have slept a while. All around me was silence. I was too frightened to open the door, even a tiny bit. What if a guard had stayed behind, waiting for one of us to show our face?

I wondered how Ruth was faring, cooped up like me in her tiny locker? I hadn't heard a sound from her – perhaps she was asleep?

I was thirsty and badly needed a toilet. In agony with cramp, I couldn't move, not yet; I had to wait longer. This, for the first time in my existence, was literally a matter of life or death.

There was still no noise outside. I stayed still, slumbered again, awoke, was stiff all over, ached from head to foot, was paralysed. No wonder, having been sqeezed into that tiny space for such a long long time – would I ever move again? Not if I was dead.

Once more I must have slept, but then I was awake, wide awake – and not a minute longer could I stay confined in that narrow box. I had to get out, come what may.

Slowly, bit by bit, I opened the door and was surprised to see it dark outside. Only the light of a full moon outlined every shape in the stable. I appeared to be alone – no Russian silhouette. I crawled out of my locker, my legs too stiff to allow me to stand. Slowly I knelt and quietly called out Ruth's name, but received no answer. Would she have gone? Had she been taken?

Gradually I straightened up, numb, no legs, and nearly collapsed. Steadying myself, I looked down and could see feet – so presumably I still had legs. Now for the pins and needles, which would be agony! I rubbed my legs cautiously, keeping my silhouette to the minimum, not taking my eyes off my surroundings. And then the circulation started to return – oh, so painful. I wanted to shout and stamp my feet, but dared not. I knew that once I moved, it would get better. I crept to the door and peered outside – the world was empty. Just silence and an owl in the distant forest.

I had no idea of time. Was it evening, or perhaps the middle of the night? We'd lost a day.

But what did it matter? A wave of euphoria engulfed me. Freedom!

Never before had I felt so elated. We'd done it – we'd got out of the clutches of our Russian captors! I felt like laughing and crying at the same time.

'Come on out, Ruth', I said. Look, we're free! Now we can go home. Oh won't it be wonderful!'

'Ruth . . . Ruth?' No answer. I returned and tried to find her locker. Had she suffocated? Was she dead? 'Ruth?' Wherever was she?

Eventually I squeezed into a tight gap by the wall and prised open a small cupboard on its own. No wonder the guard hadn't been able find her. I could just make out a human shape slumped in the corner. 'Ruth? Are you alive?' I shook her gently, my heart thumping. Suppose she was . . . dead? I stared at her, feeling suddenly very alone.

After what seemed for ever, there was a grunt. 'Are we home?' she asked in a soft croak.

'Not yet, but we're on our way!' I replied.

Ruth emerged slowly, just as stiff and dazed as I was.

In our joy we hugged each other, laughing and crying at the same time – happy moments, but just for a short while.

I'd stepped into the yard to look around. 'Let's make for the fence and fields. I can't see anyone here,' I said in a normal voice.

'Hush, Else! I can see you clearly in the moonlight! How do we know the barracks are unoccupied? This could easily be an outpost supply camp of soldiers en route, or even living here, organising provisions between Russia and Germany. We've seen the jeeps and lorries.'

Instantly after Ruth's rebuke I felt stupid. Had I blown the whole escape? I suddenly saw enemy shadows everywhere.

We crept back into the gloom of the stable wall.

Then came the realisation that from now on we had to be extra vigilant. We *had to* avoid being detected. Capture would mean certain death. Therefore, before we could leave the shelter of the stable area, we had to decide on the best action.

Above everything else, we had to be silent, looking carefully around before making any move. Indeed it didn't look far to the edge of the forest, but to reach it, we had to cross a field and distance at night was deceptive. It wouldn't be easy in bright moonlight: most successful escapes I'd read about were carried out on a moonless night. Our silhouettes would be visible to the naked eye for some distance. We could only hope that no guard was on boundary duty, waiting for us to show ourselves.

We had to get out of the stabling without being seen and cross that field; there was no other way. It would be a matter of using the stalking skills I'd learned in the Union of German Girls as a Hitler Girl: I'd had no idea then how important they'd become. Now they'd prove their worth.

'Copy what I do, Ruth. Are you ready? Yes? Then let's go for it.'

We slid round the shadowy walls of the stable block, keeping alert for *anything* that moved. It wasn't easy. We were both jumpy. We saw things move that we knew couldn't – an old cart; a broken-down army truck; an oil can . . . We ran in small spurts from one shadow to another. Ruth stifled a shriek as a rat ran over her toes. I signalled for her to keep silent whatever happened.

Suddenly something grabbed the back of my coat. My heart stood still and I slapped my hand over my mouth. I turned my head around slowly . . . but it was only a coil of barbed wire! Ruth freed me with trembling hands. We were both shaking.

Getting out of the barracks was easier than expected: no high wall or barbed-wire fence; only a pile of rough concrete. No guard, but could there be dogs?

Now the field faced us: open, vast and brightly illuminated by a full moon.

We could see every hump and bump. There was no way we could go round the edge. One side was by the road; the other out of sight. We'd have to make it through the middle, aiming for any slight dip, tussock of grass, thistle – anything that would hide our outline.

The thought suddenly occurred to me that there could be a lookout tower manned by Russian guards, which would have a powerful searchlight. We must first camouflage any exposed skin with mud so it didn't show up. But they might see our eyes in a strong light.

'Don't look round, Ruth; keep your eyes on a certain point ahead. I'll do the same. And pray that no sudden voice yells into the night *Stoi, stoi!* If we hear that, for sure it will be the end of us.'

Dropping flat to the ground and twisting our legs as if we were swimming, we dragged ourselves forward, inch by inch. The field was vast and we appeared to get nowhere.

Inch by inch, clump by clump – make for the trees – every movement's a few inches nearer home. They say prisoners escaping over moorland in the dark often go around in a circle and return to captivity . . . Must not do that. Don't end up where you started.

Chapter 34

Thank you, Madam

6 April 1945

Ruth and I had made it! We'd reached the edge of the forest and then, for just a few moments, could relax. We were both utterly exhausted. Looking back, we could see how large the field was: to cross it crawling all the way was quite an achievement. Brightly illuminated by the light of that full moon, it was truly a miracle no one had seen us. The night was frosty and the stars twinkled in the velvet-black sky. If only we knew what time it was – perhaps nearly morning? But I doubted it: the night was too dark.

'Ruth,' I whispered, 'I'm so thirsty, I could drink a river dry and my tongue's sticking to the roof of my mouth.'

'Me, too, Else. Perhaps we can find a small stream – or a puddle. Even if the water's dirty, I'll still drink it.'

We stared at the coal-black woodland ahead of us. Safe as long as we were not too noisy, but creepy nevertheless.

Holding hands, we started to tackle dense shrubby trees. Twigs hit our faces, and brambles tore at our arms, legs and clothes. It was painful, but we had to get through it somehow – surely we'd reach a path leading to . . . somewhere?

'Ouch!' cried Ruth.

'You all right?' I whispered.

'Thorn through my foot! But I've removed it – it's not too bad.'

Suddenly, in the distance, I saw a light and pointed it out to Ruth.

She'd also seen it. 'Is it a person?'

'No, it's not moving. Perhaps it's a cottage or farm. Should we chance walking towards it?'

'They may give us a drink, Else. Surely we won't walk into danger, will we? But we don't know the time. People wouldn't take kindly to being woken from their sleep.'

We struggled on and slowly the light came nearer, drawing our spirits and thirst towards it.

Then we stepped into a clearing, where the bright moonlight pointed the way to a farm track. Now it was easier underfoot, and carefully we approached a farm with many outbuildings spread over a large yard. The light shone from a downstairs window – why no blackout? Was someone still awake?

Ruth hesitated. 'Do you really think we ought to knock, Else?'

'Of course; we must. They can only slam the door in our faces but I doubt they'll do that.

Anyway, I'm so thirsty, I must take that chance.'

We approached a large farm door. I knocked . . . no answer. Again I knocked, and after a few minutes we heard footsteps walking along a passageway. Someone was coming. A key turned and the door opened a crack.

I could see a man standing there, holding a lantern, a large dog by his side. It growled deeply.

'What do you want?' a gruff voice asked in German.

'Please, Sir, sorry to disturb you. We're two young girls. Please may we have a drink? We're extremely thirsty.'

'Who are you,' he asked, cautiously. 'Whatever are you doing out here in the dark? Where do you come from?'

'We're trying to find our way home, but we've lost our way,' I said, 'I live in Glowitz and my friend has to get to Stolp. We have no idea where we are.'

'You're German? You're wanting to come in?' asked the man, staring into the dark behind us. 'Is this a trick? Who else is out there with you? You're too young to be on your own.'

'No one. Really, Sir, our family are way ahead; we got parted. I'm sure we'll catch up with them eventually. Just a drink's all we need; then we'll be on our way.'

'You're hungry? Like something to eat?' The door was open a little wider and a welcome glow shone out of a passage door.

We looked at each other, but the temptation was too great. 'Yes please, Sir. We're very hungry, have had nothing to eat all day. A small piece of bread will be fine.'

'Well, wait here then if you're not coming in. I'll be a minute or two.' He stomped back down to the light. The dog lay across the doorway, staring at us with yellow eyes.

'Why didn't you go into the house, Else? At least we'd have been warm there.' Ruth looked longingly after the farmer.

'Use your head, Ruth. Out here we're safer. Too many questions. We don't know the man – even now he may be telephoning the authorities. If danger looms, we can make a run for it.'

But all seemed well. The man returned with two glasses of milk, nectar to our parched throats, a bottle of water and, for each of us, a small packet containing a piece of bread and some ham sausage. We thanked him gratefully, finished our glass of milk and told him we wished to be on our way.

'Follow this farm track,' he advised us. 'It leads you past two more farms before you come to a road. There you turn left and you'll be going in the right direction. Then ask again. Stolp and Glowitz you say?' He shook his head, stroking a stubbled chin. 'They lie in opposite directions, but both of you have some days to go! Not sure I'd like to walk all that way.'

And with those kind words and a reminder to be vigilant, he sent us on our way.

Once again we thanked him for his generosity and then, just before we left, I remembered to ask what time it was and we were surprised to hear it was only 11pm. We'd thought it was much later.

'Ruth,' I said, 'before I take another step, I must have something to eat. I'm ravenous.'

'You're not the only one, Else. Come let's find a place to sit and eat what the farmer has wrapped up for us. Look, there's a tree-trunk; that will do fine.'

We unwrapped our parcels and bit into hunks of bread and sausage. Never had food tasted so good as that simple snack, eaten in the deep forest in freedom with the moon to lighten the darkness of our night!

Finally, with renewed energy, we carried on. We must have at least two or three days' walking ahead. Neither of us was physically tired, as we'd dozed on and off all day in our tiny lockers. Yet we felt a weariness that told us we needed to find a place to rest until daybreak.

That shelter appeared in the form of a small wooden hut belonging to woodcutters or a forester. We tried the door – unlocked – and entered cautiously; it was dark inside and empty except for a few random items. It would keep us protected throughout the night and certainly be more comfortable than the barrack lockers.

'We'll stay until daylight; it'll be a lot quicker then than blundering around in the dark.'

Outside, in a cattle manger, we found hay to feed deer during the hours of darkness. We'd borrow some until the morning, when we'd return it.

The hut made a snug resting place and, with the silence of the forest around us, it didn't take long for us both to fall sound asleep.

Sunday 7 April

I awoke to the most wonderful dawn chorus. Birdsong filled the forest, to greet the new day. For a moment I wondered if my turbulent mind was teasing me – if the sound would fade and be replaced by the harsh reality from which I'd escaped. But I focused on a faint light slowly growing stronger through a tiny dirty window, and gradually became aware of my surroundings, of the small hut that had sheltered us throughout the night. A huge surge of feeling free flooded over me. I wanted to leap up, to run outside of my own free will. Suddenly life was wonderful again! It must have been very early, for the sun hadn't yet risen over the trees. The day would begin soon enough; then Ruth and I had to be ready to continue on our way towards home and our families.

I felt warm and snug in my haybed, the traumatic hours of the previous day pushed to the back of my mind. That was the first day of our hard-won freedom, and the wonderful feeling I experienced as I lay there had to spur me on for the rest of our long and dangerous journey.

Hungry and thirsty, I knew Ruth would feel the same. We shouldn't have eaten all the bread and sausage the night before. That was foolish. But we'd both been so ravenous, it never occurred to us to leave a little for the morning's breakfast.

Never mind, I thought, ever the optimist, *somewhere a kind person will surely open their door to us, give us a small bite to eat and a drink to refresh us.*

I made plans for the coming days.

Twilight was good: grey shadows and protection. We had to keep away from roads, walk along the edges of fields and forest . . . Now and then I heard the sound of military traffic in the far distance. We couldn't allow ourselves to be spotted. It would spell the greatest danger – imprisonment, torture . . . perhaps worse. The thought filled me with dread and roused me into action.

'Ruth, wake up! It's morning: we've slept enough. Time to get on our way. Someone might come and we don't want to be caught.'

'I know, I know . . .' Ruth's drowsy voice drifted from the straw. 'But I'm comfortable. I don't want to get up!'

'Neither did I, but before we leave, we've things to do. This hut must be tidied up, the hay put back where it belongs. No one must notice anyone has spent the night here. Come! As soon as we're done, we can get on our way – perhaps find more bread and water. Better than nothing.'

Reluctantly we left the woodman's hut. It had given us good shelter throughout the night, and I, for one, felt refreshed and ready to move off. But not Ruth. She was listless and not at all her usual self. No matter how hard I tried, I couldn't motivate her.

'What is it, Ruth? Aren't you well?'

'Oh, I'm not ill, Else, but I can't go on long. We've walked for days. I'm too tired and my feet are in a state: sore and ice-cold. I wish I didn't have to walk today.'

'But we must, Ruth. There's no other way,' I said, anxiously glancing around. 'Look, how would you feel if we were still in the convoy? Then you'd long to be free; and now we are, you sound as if you don't want to be! We must get food and drink as soon as possible. That's most important; then I'm certain we'll both feel better.'

'Sorry, Else; you try so hard to keep our spirits up and most of the time you succeed. You look after me when I should be looking after you; but today I feel very low indeed.'

'I know what will cheer you up, Ruth. If we can find someone to feed us, I'll ask if they have an old pair of shoes, boots or even slippers for you. If your feet are comfortable, you'll feel so much better. How's that?'

'Thank you, m'lady. You're so kind!' Ruth answered, a grin on her face and curtsying. Your wonderful idea has cheered me. Let's go on now – I promise to leave my depression behind.'

On the edge of the forest we saw before us a long, straight road that stretched in an unbroken line to the distant horizon. How much easier it would have been to walk along it, but that was impossible – far too dangerous. We had to continue our journey, keeping to the fringe of the forest, its shadows giving us protection. Quite often army vehicles roared up the road and time after time we had to duck behind a bank or hide behind bushes. Luckily we could see traffic approaching before we could even hear it, but it wasn't safe: so easy to have been spotted and *that* we had to avoid at all costs.

We'd now been walking for some hours by the sun's path, but had no idea of the actual time. Ruth's bare feet were painful and bleeding, but her determination inspired me.

Although we occasionally heard dogs barking in the distance, we were terrified of approaching a homestead in case we were handed over to the Russians. But as time wore on, and we passed the occasional dwelling, I knew we'd have to give in to our need for food and drink.

Echoing my own feelings, Ruth gasped, 'Else, I can't go on. We must stop at the next house; we'll have to take a chance.'

'I know; you're right. We can't go on like this, but we must be extremely careful. We're almost home and it would be heartbreaking if all our efforts were in vain.' We'd almost given up finding an occupied place of habitation, when, in the distance over the treetops, I noticed smoke coming out of a chimney.

'Look, Ruth. There must be a dwelling at the end of that farmtrack.' A rough path led down a slope. 'See the smoke? Where there's smoke, there must be people!'

'What do you suggest we do, Else?'

'Go and investigate. We might be lucky. Just be careful: make sure no Russians are lurking about.'

At the end of the track we had to cross a large farmyard. We hid for a while, but saw no military vehicles. So we walked to the house. I had a distinct feeling unseen eyes were watching us as we approached. But nothing could deter us now. We walked to the nearest door and knocked.

Immediately a woman opened it. I presumed she was a farmer's wife. I was wary, but she looked friendly enough.

'Good morning, Madam,' I appealed to her with extreme politeness. 'Please can you help us? We don't wish to take up your time, but could I ask you for a drink? We're both very thirsty. And perhaps, if you can spare it, we'd be grateful for a small slice of bread. We've had nothing to eat today.'

'You poor girls! Come in; come in both of you. Who are you and where do you come from? Wherever are you going in this remote area?'

I felt awkward. We were both filthy, faces grubby, hair matted. Our clothes were ripped in many places and covered in mud from crawling over sodden fields and navigating dusty woodland paths. I was ashamed of the state we were in: not a good impression.

The lady looked at Ruth.

'You poor girl – you're barefoot! What happened to your shoes?'

'They wore out long ago. I had socks on my feet, but I had to throw them away. They were in shreads.'

'Wait here, my girl; I'll see if I can find something to fit you. You can't walk with bare feet . . . no!'

'Thank you, Madam,' Ruth croaked. 'You're so kind.'

She returned with various pairs of shoes and boots and, much to Ruth's delight, one pair fitted perfectly. She was thrilled. 'Thank you, Madam. The shoes are wonderful. They feel comfortable and will keep my feet warm and dry until I reach home. Thank you!'

'I'm glad they fit, child. I can see you're pleased and I'm happy I could help.' She rubbed her hands on her apron. 'Now tell me your names and where you're going?'

'I'm Ruth, and I live in Stolp.'

'And I'm Else. I'm trying to get home to my mother in Glowitz.'

'Oh my dear girls! You have a long, long way before you. My goodness! It will take you days. Stolp's not quite so far, but Glowitz – that's two or three days' march. Can't you tell me where you've come from?'

'If you don't mind, we'd rather not. We've had many nasty experiences and now we'd rather forget them.'

'Please tell us, Madam, are there Russians on this farm?' My eyes scanned the yard.

'No, no, child. Don't you worry about that. Our farm's situated in a hollow. We haven't seen a Russian soldier for some time. I'm certain you're safe here, at least for a while. They pass by and don't even notice the farm. Yes, they've been here before, when they first arrived. That was a bad and dangerous time . . .' the woman mused, her eyes growing distant.

'Now come in!' she said, as she ushered us into her warm, cosy kitchen. 'Give me your coat, Else, and I'll dry it and give it a good brush. You'll look less conspicuous. What about you, Ruth? Where's your coat?'

'I don't have one, Madam. This thick jumper Else gave me has kept me quite warm.'

'Not adequate. I'll see what I can find; there are plenty of jackets and coats lying about. One's bound to fit you.'

'Thank you, Madam; that would be wonderful!' I answered. 'Do you live on your own?'

'No, I'm not on my own; but let's concentrate on feeding you with some of my tasty soup. I'll bring it to the table. Please, sit down. First I'll fetch a glass of milk for you: your soup will follow directly, together with a chunk of my own baked bread.'

And with those words she went over to her range from where an inviting aroma wafted towards us. Something smelt good: it made my mouth water with anticipation.

While we were waiting for our meal to arrive, I glanced at Ruth. She was pale and looked ill with dark shadows under her eyes. *Dear God*, I thought, *what can I do? Soon our ways will part and then she'll be on her own. How will she manage? Will she be able to reach Stolp without me to help her?* I was deeply concerned.

She gazed at me and I could see sadness in her eyes.

'Else,' she said, 'I can't eat just yet. I'm so tired.'

'Just a spoonful or two, Ruth. Go on. It will give you renewed strength. And please drink your milk; you'll feel a lot better afterwards.'

'All right, I'll have my drink, but the soup must wait until later.' She put her head on her arms on the table and closed her eyes. 'Don't worry about me; soon I'll feel better. All I need is a little rest . . .'

It was good to relax at last.

I was hungry and had been looking forward to my meal. I started to eat. The soup was delicious and I realised it was the first substantial meal we'd had in three days. Then I glanced out of the window and saw, coming down the slope towards the farm, a motorcycle with two Russian soldiers on it.

What should I do? Where could I hide?

'Keep calm, child. They won't hurt you,' said my host. 'Not in my house: here the Russians are friendly. Don't take any notice of them if they come into this kitchen. Just go on eating your soup. They'll soon go again.'

The soldiers parked their vehicle outside the kitchen door and, without knocking, entered.

'Woman,' they called to the farmer's wife, 'water, quickly!'

While they waited for their water, they stepped closer to the table.

I tried to ignore them. *Concentrate on eating; don't look up.* My hand shook so badly it was almost impossible to hold the spoon. All the while Ruth slept, oblivious to what was going on around her.

One soldier grabbed a handful of her hair, lifted her head and looked at her; then, with disgust on his face, dropped it back onto the table. Mouth open, comatose, she didn't wake up.

For a short while both soldiers just stared at me. I could feel their eyes boring into my back. Then one of them pointed at me: *You, woman, come!*

I looked up. 'Me come with you?' I answered with false bravery. 'Can't you see I'm eating?'

With an evil grin he picked up my bowl and flung it, violently, against the kitchen wall, soup and all.

'Now, you come!' He took hold of my arm and tried to lift me off my seat.

I struggled and kicked and screamed. Why didn't the woman come and rescue me?

'No, no! I won't come! I must stay with my friend. She's not well.'

But the soldiers were stronger than me. My screaming and feeble kicking had no effect. And the farmer's wife? She'd disappeared. Perhaps they'd abused her before . . .

My thoughts were frantic. What should I do? There was nowhere to run without putting myself in more danger. They both had guns.

Both soldiers wrenched me off my seat and, holding me tightly between them, marched me out of the kitchen, across the yard towards a large barn. I still kicked and screamed but my struggles didn't help; all the time I was getting weaker: I was no match for their strength.

I was terrified, to the point of panic. What was going to happen to me? What would they do? Rape me? Without a doubt. But would they also kill me after they'd satisfied their animal cravings?

There was nothing I could do. Between them they pulled me after them across the farmyard, and when my legs buckled under me, they slapped my face and ordered me to get up and walk.

One soldier kicked open the large barn door and I was pushed inside onto a bale of straw. I knew what they wanted, yet instinct made me fight it. But I was getting weaker and suddenly realised I could never win physically against two such strong opponents.

They grinned and enjoyed my distress, gabbling in their own tongue, incomprehensible to me. Although, they saw my terror, they ignored it. Perhaps it aroused them.

I pleaded, 'Please, please don't touch me! Please let me go!'

They found my pleading hilarious.

I struggled and nearly got up. One soldier, a huge man, pushed me down again, while the other knelt behind my head, grabbed my arms and held them tight, pinning me like a vice.

The first soldier ripped at my clothes and removed my underwear. I kicked and kicked with all the strength I possessed. I was terrified and in utter panic when I saw him pulling down his trousers. He swore as I caught his groin. Then, in the most brutal way, he fell on me with all his weight and raped me. I lay there, stunned into stillness.

But that was not the end of my ordeal. First one and then the other took his turn. One of them had more stamina: he came back again and again, until I thought I'd die. I didn't – I lost consciousness.

I awoke slightly. They were still there. I was befouled. Would I ever be clean again?

Please, dear God, let them stop. Let them go away. Or let me die. I don't want to live now I'm the object of their dirty work. If I had a gun, I'd kill them without the slightest pang of conscience. But I have no gun and they'll go on living. All I can do is lie on this bale of straw, feign unconsciousness and hope they'll disappear.

When they'd had enough and finally exhausted their energy, they left the barn. Minutes later I heard an engine start and, soon after, a motorcycle roared up the slope. The sound echoed far into the distance, gradually getting fainter and fainter, until at last it disappeared.

I lay quite still in my semi-conscious state, not wanting reality. I tried to pretend that my ordeal was just a nightmare – an ugly, terrifying dream, although I knew from the pain, the agony, my generally numbed physical state, what was the stark and grim reality.

I had to remain where I was. I certainly didn't want to move and get up, to go into the house and face Ruth and the woman. I thought shame was written all over me and that I'd carry the signs of my disgrace for the entire world to see for ever.

As from far away, I heard a door open and someone step into the barn. Panic rose inside me. Surely, not again – would I be subjected to abuse again?

But it was the woman from the farmhouse. She came to where I lay and without uttering a word, lifted me and cradled my head in her arms.

She helped me sit up, and gently stroked my face.

'Poor little girl,' she murmured. 'It's all over now. You must wipe it from your mind, not dwell on it.'

She saw my tears and wiped them away with a corner of her apron. Meticulously she picked each piece of straw from my clothing.

'Oh . . . Oh, Madam!' I uttered a voice that didn't belong to me.

She gazed into my eyes with great compassion. 'Hush . . . Be strong, Else. Learn to live through this: the horror will pass, I promise.'

'But I'll live it over and over again. I'm so disgraced.'

'Listen, Else: we'll go into the house. I'll prepare a small bathtub with hot water for you. You can sit in it and have a thorough wash. Believe me, afterwards you'll feel better. And by the way, please don't call me "Madam": my name's Frau Lutzig, Maria Lutzig. A 'madam' I've never been. Come with me now. Gently! Can you walk? Ruth's waiting; she's a lot better.'

'Thank you . . . I don't know what to do. How can I face my mother when I see her? She'll want to know what's happened to me. How can I tell her? And what if I should have a baby? How can I live with that? I'd rather be dead.'

'Now, now, Else! Let's not think of that now. Come with me. I'll look after you, and later you must have something to eat. Then we'll talk. You and Ruth should spend the night in my house. I've a small bedroom in the attic. No one goes there: it's hidden away. You'll be safe and undisturbed. And tomorrow morning, after a good night's rest, you'll be well enough to continue on your journey.'

'Thank you. Can I ask Ruth? I must hear how she feels about staying the night.'

'Good! Are you ready to come now, Else? I think it's time we leave this barn.'

'Yes, Frau Lutzig, but I don't want Ruth to see me. What am I going to tell her?'

'You needn't tell her anything. She's been asleep all the time you were out of the kitchen. No, Else, Ruth hasn't missed you. We'll tell her we spent time together in the living room, where you told me a little about your life in Pomerania before the Russians came.' Slowly she helped me out of that dreadful barn and across the yard. 'That's it – we'll enter the house through the back door. Are you calm enough now to face your friend?'

I looked at Frau Lutzig, and everything I'd endured at the hands of those filthy soldiers came back to me. I promptly burst into tears again, my heart breaking. The thoughts, playing over and over in my head, were too gruesome for me to shut out. I was full of hatred and wished, oh how I wished, I'd had it in my power to kill the brutes. I'd even lost my faith in God. I didn't want to believe any more. If he could turn his eyes away from so much evil on this earth, was he really there? Or just a figment of my imagination?

The joy on Ruth's face, when she saw me enter the kitchen later, touched me deeply. 'Else,' she called out, 'where have you been? I've slept a long time, and when I awoke you weren't here.'

'I was in Frau Lutzig's living room behind the scullery. We didn't want to disturb you.'

'And all the time you were out of the kitchen, I was asleep. You should have woken me.'

'Why? You obviously needed the rest. You look much better.' I tried not to look my friend in the eye. 'By the way, Ruth, Frau Lutzig has offered to let us spend the night in her house. She has a small, secluded attic room. We shan't be disturbed, and after a restful night we can start a new day, refreshed for another long journey. What do you think?'

'Yes, Else, I'd like that. Although I seem to have slept for some time, I'm still tired and a night in a proper bed sounds heavenly.

'Now, girls, follow me into the scullery where you can both have a wash. There's plenty of warm water. I've laid out a nightdress for each of you. They're a little old-fashioned but they'll keep you warm. Leave your clothes: I'll see to them. When you're finished, come into the kitchen and have supper.'

'You know, Else, that woman's very kind, don't you agree? After all, we *are* strangers. Why should she go out of her way to help us?'

'Perhaps she has her reasons. Don't question her motives; just accept with good grace.'

I looked at the supper Frau Lutzig had prepared for us, but to think of food made me feel ill. All I wanted was to shut myself away, alone with my thoughts.

Ruth touched my shoulder. 'What's the matter, Else? A few times now I've spoken to you, but you seem far away and don't listen.'

'I'm weary now and want to rest. I don't feel like eating – I just want to go to bed and close my eyes. Perhaps Frau Lutzig will let me go ahead; then, when you're ready, you'll follow.'

But when I entered the little bedroom in the attic with a comfortable bed in front of me, I couldn't lie down.

I'd never minded the dark, but that night the thought frightened me. Ugly images played havoc with my mind and I feared my dreams would turn into nightmares. I was afraid to sleep. As soon as I did, the violation of my body, the relentless and vicious attack I'd endured, which had gone on and on, would pass in front of my eyes like a reel from a film.

However, I crept into bed, buried my head in my pillow and cried bitter tears.

That day something deep inside my soul – I couldn't put into words exactly what, some precious thing that should have remained with me until a special time in the future – had been torn away from me.

8 and 9 April

Although I thought I'd never sleep that night, I must have, because the next thing I knew, Ruth lay asleep beside me and through the small skylight I could see it was morning.

I felt rested. Despite the events of the day before, it was the first sound sleep in a bed since I'd left the manor all that time ago. And somehow I managed to lock into the back of my mind the ugly images from the previous day.

A new day was before us, a day that would see the parting of our ways. Ruth would have to go on alone, but so would I, and my journey was further. I glanced at her: she was stirring.

'Morning, Else. Are you better?' She stretched and yawned. 'Did you sleep well?'

'Yes, I did. Wasn't it heaven to have a real bed! Should we get up? I can hear sounds downstairs; someone must be about.'

As we got out of bed, we noticed our clothes, including our underwear, clean, patched and neatly folded on a chair. Frau Lutzig must have placed them there while we were still asleep. What a kind lady she was: Ruth and I were grateful for her thoughtfulness. To be able to dress in clean clothing was a wonderful feeling.

I got dressed quickly and said, 'You know, Ruth, I wanted to talk about this yesterday, but didn't hear you come up. I think there's something very strange about this farm.'

'What do you mean, Else?'

' Since we've been here, we haven't seen another person except Frau Lutzig. There are no human voices, no animal sounds. In fact, there *are* no animals, as far as I can see. It's a creepy place. I don't want to stay here a moment longer than we have to. The sooner we get away, the happier I'll be. Come, let's go downstairs.'

'I know what you mean. It's as though something awful happened here. But we're safe enough. It's hidden away.' Ruth followed me carefully down the narrow attic staircase. 'But there's one thing I do dread. Not long after we leave here, we have to go our separate ways: we must both carry on without the other. I don't like that at all – it scares me not to have you by my side.'

In the kitchen, ready on the table, Frau Lutzig had prepared our breakfast.

'Good morning, girls,' she greeted us. 'Come and sit down, you two, and start your breakfast. Did you sleep well?'

'Oh yes, *I* did,' Ruth announced. 'I was soon asleep and didn't wake once. Thank you for seeing to our laundry.'

'Don't mention it. At least you'll feel more comfortable.'

'And you, Else?' Ruth encouraged. Then whispered, 'You've hardly spoken a word to the Frau. Are you not well or something?'

'I'm . . . fine!' I said aloud. But once Frau Lutzig was out of the kitchen I whispered, 'I can't wait to get away from here. It's spooky and frightening. Something's not right, yet I dare not ask – and neither must you, Ruth.'

'I've prepared a small bag for each of you,' the woman returned with her arms full of goodies: sandwiches and a small bottle of water each. 'That saves you knocking on people's doors; you mustn't put yourself in danger. You never know –' she glanced pointedly at me.

'Thank you, Frau Lutzig; you've been . . . most kind,' was all I could say. I found it difficult to speak at all. I threatened to burst into tears. Yesterday's episode was still vividly engraved on my mind and however hard I tried I couldn't wipe away the jumbled thoughts that haunted me.

'When you've finished your breakfast, girls, I'll explain the best route for you. It's not difficult: you won't lose your way.'

When we'd eaten, Frau Lutzig joined us. 'Now, let me see. Walk up the slope almost to the end. On your left's a field path. Take that: it will lead to the Bütow road. Don't walk on the road: keep to the edge of the field. Is that clear?'

'Yes, Frau Lutzig,' we answered together.

'When you reach the road, turn left. After about 6 or 7 kilometres, you'll see Bütow on your right.'

'Must we walk through the town, Frau Lutzig?'

'No, Else, ignore it. The town's not large; you'll bypass it. On the outskirts you come to a junction with roads branching in two directions. To the left's the Stolp road. Ruth, you must take that.'

'Yes, Frau Lutzig.'

'I have a feeling it may be the road you came on, but of course I can't be sure. But it's the road *you must* take: it will lead you to your city. If you stride along and not stop too often you may reach Stolp by evening. On the other hand, you may not; then you must find shelter somewhere. Understand?'

'Yes, Frau Lutzig.'

'As for you, Else, take the right fork, leading to Lauenburg. Just before you reach the town take a small road to the left: it will eventually bring you to Glowitz. You have to walk through dense woodland most of the way: you won't do it in one day, perhaps not two days, depending on how you feel. But once you leave Lauenburg and enter the forest, you should be safe.'

'Will there be somewhere I can spend the night?'

'I don't know, Else. You may encounter a woodman's hut here and there, where you can shelter. Most of them have reserves of straw or hay – winter fodder for deer and other animals. I wouldn't think they're locked; you'll be safe there.'

'Thank you, Frau Lutzig; we should be all right now,' Ruth declared. 'We ought to be on our way, Else. Are you ready?'

'Yes, I am.'

In my mind I mulled things over – nothing to take, except the most dreadful memories of my life. If only I could leave those behind. Again and again, awful reminders of the day before passed in front of my eyes. I couldn't shake them out of my thoughts. All I wanted was to leave that farm behind and never see it again.

Chapter 35

Parting

10 April 1945

After thanking Frau Lutzig for her great kindness, we finally climbed the slope, the slope where not many hours before an approaching motorcycle had blighted my life for ever. Ruth, however, with shoes on her feet and a jacket to keep her warm, was in high spirits. It had been a good stop for her.

What would she say if I told her about my ordeal? Not that I would. She'd blame herself for falling asleep. But if she'd woken, they'd have taken her too. At least she'd been spared that.

I wondered if she was looking forward to reaching home and seeing her family again. They'd be as shocked as my mother would be when I suddenly appeared in front of her. I couldn't wait to feel her arms around me. I'd talk to her and she'd understand how unhappy and dispirited I was.

As we walked along, Ruth became quieter and quieter. Suddenly she burst out, 'Else, what am I going to do? How can I carry on without you at my side? I know I won't manage.'

'Ruth, pull yourself together! I also feel sad and nervous about losing your companionship, but you can't come to Glowitz, and then go to Stolp, nor can I go with you to Stolp and from there return to Glowitz. Surely you understand that, don't you?'

'Of course I'm aware of it but I also know it's unlikely we'll meet again. I can't imagine how that could ever be possible and it makes me very sad.'

'But think, Ruth. Soon you'll be with your family again. That's what matters. I hope everyone's well and still in your house. Just think how joyful the reunion will be.'

'Yes, I know all that but . . .'

'Perhaps one day when things are better, back to normal, when I go back to school in Stolp, we may meet again. Now there's a lot of uncertainty. I can't even give you my address – I have nothing to write with and don't even know where I'll be. But you can tell me yours and I promise I'll write to you.'

'Please do, Else, and be assured I'll never forget you.'

'And I won't forget you, dear Ruth. What we've experienced will remain with me for the rest of my life. But now let's concentrate on the present. My priority's to return to my family; everything else is unimportant.'

Yet Ruth started to cry as if her heart would break.

'Don't cry, Ruth. Please don't cry.' I stopped to cuddle her. 'We've been thrown together and have faced a lot of hardship and suffering, but we must put all that behind us. Our friendship has been exceptional and if, God willing, we're to meet again, it will be a wonderful day for me.'

'Oh, Else!'

We held hands until the junction loomed up in front of us – the parting of our ways.

'Take care, Ruth. Please take care!' Again I hugged her. 'As soon as you see Russians approaching, either on foot or in vehicles, hide away, even if you throw yourself in a ditch.'

Suddenly Ruth held me at shoulder length and stared into my eyes. 'Else, tell me this – what should I do when I reach the place where the three women were shot. I can't bear the thought of passing them.'

'As you approach the spot, say a little prayer for them – and think how lucky you are to be alive. Don't stop; carry on and look straight ahead; try to push the hellish experience to the back of your mind.'

She nodded. 'I'll try, Else.'

'Now it's time to part, my dearest friend. My love goes with you – God bless you and see you safely home.'

'And you, Else: I'll never forget you.'

Once more we squeezed each other tightly; then we both turned and walked away without looking back.

Now I was on my own and already missed Ruth, my companion and friend. I was alone and there was no relief, no peace: I realised that throughout the weeks of capture, I'd constantly had other people about me, mainly dear Ruth – certainly her companionship had made it bearable. And now she was gone, I felt deeply lonely, a dreadful loneliness that enveloped me, magnified my predicament. I'd told Ruth to be strong, and I'd be strong, but it was extremely hard.

I'd been tramping for hours – well, a wide sweep of the sun, anyway. Progress was not always fast; it would be if I walked on the road, but I wasn't chancing it. I was skulking along on the bank near the vegetation, a small vulnerable bird picking her way between the edge of the forest and the long, straight road. I could see into the distance, but so could others, and I didn't want my silhouette noticed and investigated. I appeared to be the only human being around as far as the eye could see. But who knew? Nothing was sure after what had happened to me.

And what had happened was very real. Visions loomed in my head, far worse than I'd experienced in the night. I was alert, looking for danger everywhere. But what I saw were those two strong, stinking bodies creeping up on me, behind me, beside me out of the corner of my eye, waiting in front for me; they sneaked about in dark shadows, behind a tree, in the branches of a bush – everywhere. And always the faces – I had no way to escape them, no one to take my mind off them, off each horrifying, tiny moment of that ordeal. Hideous faces superimposed on a gnarled trunk stared down at me. I'd never forget those faces, harsh voices, leer of ridicule, the terrifying anger they thrust on me, into me. I'd cope with the physical pain, but the faces and my anger?

I'd found myself talking my thoughts aloud, gabbling away to myself. Perhaps for companionship, a proof of reality, the comfort of hearing a voice – unless I was going insane, which wouldn't be surprising when I thought of what had turned Fraulein Elisabeth's mind. Poor, dear woman; now I understood her, her trauma. I wondered what had happened to her? Was she in Russia by now? Or would they shoot her when they realised she was insane? Yet she was just a crazy, harmless creature. Would I lose my mind like her? No! I was too strong-willed. But if I ever had to go through that again . . . I could understand why those dear, dear friends in Glowitz had taken their own lives.

Ruth – would she stay safe? I now realised what risks women took with soldiers around. I was deeply concerned about her entering Stolp. She lived there and would feel safe; but being a garrison town, it would be full of Russian soldiers. She had to take the greatest care; I only hoped she'd do so.

Just before reaching the town of Lauenburg, I noticed on my left a wide dirt track leading into the forest. That must be the path Frau Lutzig had advised me I should take. It looked well maintained and frequently used and would be an easy and comfortable walkway to see me through the wood.

A little way along the path I stopped for some sips of water. I also had sandwiches left and ate one. The break did me good, renewed my spirit. Beams of sunlight danced through the upper canopy. It reminded me of the woodland where Egon and I had walked . . . Egon would have kept me safe. But where was he now? Perhaps he was with me in a way. I could feel his strength. Suddenly I knew my two taunting, haunting ghosts wouldn't follow me here.

The silence was interrupted now and then by a gentle rustle in the undergrowth – small woodland creatures: a bird or perhaps a rabbit or tiny mouse. I laughed quietly. At last I'd found that lost feeling of peace I so desired. There was nothing to hurt me here and I felt no fear.

As I wandered on, I noticed the day was drawing to a close. I was weary and my legs ached. After all, I'd walked almost non-stop since morning, except for the short rest Ruth and I had had before we approached the town of Bütow. I'd soon need a place to spend the night: a barn or woodman's hut, with straw or hay to keep me warm overnight.

Suddenly I noticed a building almost hidden by fir trees to my right. *That's it*, I thought, *just what I'm looking for*. Going closer, a sturdy wooden barn loomed up; and when I tried the door, it was stiff but unlocked. The barn was dry and warm with plenty of hay, quite sufficient to cover me and keep me hidden from spying eyes should anyone come into this remote place, which I doubted. There had to be a farm somewhere, but I hadn't seen one.

That was where I'd spend the night: no one would disturb me. I'd bury myself in soft, sweet-smelling hay and be able to find the rest I so desperately needed. First I'd eat another sandwich from Frau Lutzig's packet and drink more water from the bottle. How valuable that had been. What was left over, I'd keep till the morning.

I prepared my bed as far away from the door as possible. My nest was soon complete and I was pleased with my handiwork. For once I felt really safe, safer than in the farmhouse. I crawled onto a pile of soft meadow hay, pulled more on top and balanced some sheaves of corn over that. A real little home. I felt warm, cosy and secure. For a while I listened to the sounds of the forest – the hoot of an owl, and now and then the gentle churr of a nightjar close by. They made me drowsy and soon lulled me to sleep.

I awoke before dawn – something had disturbed my sleep. But when I tried to listen, there was only silence.

I closed my eyes and slept again, and had a dream.

I was dreaming of plums, bottled plums, jars of them standing on shelves in our cellar in Düsseldorf. They looked so inviting that I opened a jar and pulled out a large, juicy, blue plum. But that was forbidden – I shouldn't do it. Mother wouldn't be pleased if she knew. Much better to take a jar upstairs; if only it wasn't so heavy. No matter how hard I tried, I couldn't lift it from the shelf. I was struggling, but then heard voices.

I roused and in a semi-conscious state could still hear them.

Then I was wide awake and could hear deep male voices. Where had they come from? They were not German voices; they had to be Russian. I couldn't tell how many there were: perhaps a group of them standing outside the barn? I wanted to get up and investigate, but knew I had to keep extremely still, as I had in the locker. But now there was no metal locker to conceal me; just thin straw.

The barn door creaked open. Did anything show? A foot? The bag of sandwiches: what had I done with that? If they saw it, they'd catch me. What did they want? Suppose they'd decided to sleep here too? How awful! They'd find and rape me for sure. Then I'd go out of my mind. Or did they want to hold a secret meeting? They'd stopped talking. Were they looking for someone? Perhaps me? No, that couldn't be possible. They didn't know I was there. I was terrified, shaking, and had to clench my teeth to stop them chattering.

Now I heard what sounded like sticks, or guns? No they were bayonets, stabbing the straw. They intended to kill! Me?

Perhaps they were looking for German soldiers, prisoners of war who'd escaped (as we had) before they could reach Könitz. There, at the station, a train could also have been waiting to take them to Russia and prison camps far away from their homeland.

I lay completely still, not daring to move, holding my breath, urging my heart to stop pounding so loudly.

Boots rustled in the straw, scraped on the concrete floor. One almost trod on me, and I froze, gasped, shut my eyes. When I opened them a slit, I could see a muddy black toe close to where I was hiding. It was treading on my little finger – oh, how it hurt, but I'd not whimper.

He thrust into the hay, his bayonet narrowly missing my body; again he stabbed – *just beside my face*. But he missed and I had to summon all my willpower not to scream and surrender.

How I hated these people!

For a moment there was silence. I knew they were waiting for a giveaway sound. Then they must have realised their search was hopeless; they seemed to decide to leave the barn. I heard the door creak again and the latch click.

I lay, too petrified even to remove a straw tickling my nose. Had they left one man inside, just waiting for someone to crawl out of the straw? Time passed, but nothing else happened. Nothing. Not even a sound of voices outside.

After a while, life returned to my body. I appeared to be alone again, for I couldn't hear anything. Perhaps they'd disappeared by then.

All I could feel was a tremendous relief that they'd not found me and I was fervently hoping they'd not come back. For now, thank God, I might be safe.

I'd have loved to get out of that barn, but hadn't the courage to venture outside. I had to stay where I was. It was a dark night and in the dark the wood could be a dangerous place. In its vastness, I could so easily lose my way. Yes, it would be better if I stayed there until morning.

I was ice cold and shaking all over. It must have been the fear; but as soon as the danger was past, the cold would leave and I'd be warm again.

The soldiers who were there obviously hadn't found what they were looking for. By then they should have abandoned their search and, I hoped, left the forest. Or would they come back again later when it was light?

I was getting hungry, but there was only one sandwich left, which I wanted to keep until morning – but then again, I could eat it now: at least it would stop my tummy rumbling. I needed the last drop of water to quench my thirst. Perhaps on my walk I'd find a source to replenish my bottle – a stream or a homestead where even a slice of bread might be forthcoming

How far was it to Glowitz? Twenty kilometres or thereabouts? Perhaps a few more, or even a few less. I had no idea.

I'd try to sleep again and hope the rest of my night remained undisturbed. My bed of straw had saved me and might keep me safe again – and I felt warmer at last.

I folded my hands in prayer. This was a miracle – and I'd thought God had deserted me!

Dear God, I still can't believe how lucky I am. I give thanks to you with all my heart for taking good care of me. Please look after my family and also continue to protect me. I wonder if Ruth has reached her home? Please keep her safe – I think of her often . . .

Please let me find my way to Glowitz, and soon now. I can't go on much longer. I'm tired, weary of running and long to be with my mother: only then will I feel human again. Amen.

As soon as I'd finished my prayer I drifted into a sound sleep. The next thing I knew it was bright daylight and I crawled cautiously out of my nest in the straw; but the barn was unoccupied, apart from me. Perhaps I was safe. My body was stiff and I was covered in straw and felt dirty and badly in need of a wash. I also had an empty and rumbling stomach.

I hoped I might find a small brook in the depth of the forest to swill my hands and face and replenish my water bottle. I thought of the spring and well where I'd washed as a maiden on that Easter Sunday, so long ago now. I could bathe in one of those. Otherwise the rest of my body would have to wait until I reached home.

There was silence around me – I couldn't hear the dawn chorus. Was it so late in the morning that the singing had stopped and only an occasional chirp of tiny birds could be heard? Through a skylight I saw the sun was high in the sky: that could only mean it was already around midday.

Morning, 11 April 1945

I had to leave that barn, yet I was frightened of what might be outside. Had the soldiers who were searching for someone gone? Or were they still out there, lurking, waiting for their unsuspecting prey to appear?

Yet I couldn't stop there – I had to be on my way. All I could do was to be extra vigilant, and let my eyes be everywhere.

A final stretch and a last brush down with my hands to remove some of the straw from my clothes had to suffice. I ran my fingers – for want of a comb – through my tangled hair. Then, when I was satisfied I'd tidied myself and removed any signs of life in the barn as best I could, I opened the door and cautiously stepped outside into clear, fresh woodland air.

I was very frightened. Behind the trees I thought I saw Russian uniforms (real ones this time, not my haunting ghosts of the previous day) and imagined a forest full of soldiers trying to corner me. In each bush I passed I visualized Russian eyes watching every move I made. Yet there was no one – it was just my mind playing tricks on me again.

I was dwarfed beneath those ancient, trees and could have been the only person in the world, so complete was the silence that encompassed me as I strode along, knowing every step brought me nearer to Glowitz and home.

Occasionally a twig snapped, disturbing the silence and stabbing my heart with new dread. I'd stand still, stricken with fear – so near yet so far . . . but when nothing else happened, I presumed it was only a woodland creature, which I had no need to fear. And so the hours passed by.

Suddenly, as with weary steps I shuffled along, deep in thought and hardly aware of my surroundings, I encountered, hidden among the trees and hardly visible, a tiny cottage. It reminded me of the fairy tale 'Hansel and Gretel' that mother had told us many times when we were small. I stared at it. Was this the house of a witch? Would she be kind or was she evil, as in the story? Whatever, I'd soon find out. It meant knocking on her door to ask for some water to fill my bottle.

Gathering courage, I walked up an overgrown garden path and timidly knocked on a doorway. It was badly in need of a coat of paint and repair to the woodwork. No one seemed to have heard me, so I knocked again. I was about to give up, when, very cautiously, a wizened old lady opened the door a tiny crack. She glared, none too pleased to see me standing on her doorstep. Definitely a witch!

'Who are you?' she asked. 'What do you want?'

'I'm a German girl on my way to Glowitz. I'm thirsty but have run out of water. Could you please fill my bottle?'

She hesitated, and then grabbed it. 'Give it here. I'll fill it. Do you want a piece of bread?'

'Yes, please, I'd love some. You're very kind.'

'Where do you come from?' The door opened a little wider when she returned.

I thought quickly. 'I come from Bütow, where I wanted to visit my aunt, but she wasn't at home, so I decided to return to Glowitz. But last night, in the forest, I lost my way.'

'Where did you spend the night?' asked the old lady, eying me critically. 'Your clothes are covered with straw?'

'I found a barn full of straw for a bed and spent the night there.' I paused, but as that had satisfied her, I continued, 'Is it far to Glowitz, do you know?'

'Yes, I think it's quite a distance. Perhaps 15 kilometres, or more. You might not manage it in one day but of course you're young and can stride out.' As I smiled, she stepped outside to wave her thin finger back up the path. 'Go straight on; the path you came on leads to the end of the forest. Then, in the distance, you'll see the top of Glowitz church tower.'

14 April

As I stumbled along, far away, deep in my own world, I was suddenly convinced I could hear voices. I jumped into the shadows and listened . . . nothing. Phantom voices again. But there it was again – definitely not soldiers. I crept out. No one visible. The sounds seemed to travel on the breeze. I continued cautiously, straining my ears. Children laughing? Women calling? The sounds were still some distance away but I was absolutely certain that from somewhere in the near vicinity I could hear people. I walked along, a new spring in my step, listening carefully, but as yet couldn't make out where the voices were coming from.

And then I saw it, a clearing in the wood. Just a little way into the wood to my right was a large clearing devoid of trees and the ground free of bushes and undergrowth, and in the centre a huge fire burning brightly. It was a wonderful sight. I just stood at the edge of the woodland and looked, too overcome to take another step. I was still too far away to make out who these people could be. Refugees? Gypsies? No, impossible. There were no wagons. I could make out only small handcarts and wheelbarrows, but as yet they were too indistinct for me to identify who these people were. I was puzzled. Where did they come from and what was their reason for living in the forest? Were they homeless?

As the children played and shouted to each other, I worked out a few words and realized the party before me were German. My people, whom I didn't have to fear. Perhaps they knew Glowitz and would tell me if it were safe to go on. I certainly didn't want to walk straight back into a Russian trap and be caged again.

Suddenly a small boy moved away from his circle of playmates and pointing shouted, 'Mama, look! Someone's coming. It's a girl and she's walking towards us.'

Everyone stopped what they were doing and in complete silence watched me approach.

By now I felt sure I had nothing to fear from these people. They were as German as I was and, for some reason I didn't yet know, were living in the forest. But they were strangers and I was wary of them. My long walk and gruesome experiences had taught me always to be on my guard.

Then one elderly man turned towards me and shouted, 'I know who that is. It's Else Hopp from the manor – Frau Hopp's daughter! Look closely: you'll recognize her.' He beckoned the others. 'Don't you remember?' he continued, 'Frau Hopp refused to come. The Russians tried to force her, but she was adamant she had to stay in the village and wait for her daughter's return. They thought her mad, but she knew the girl would come – and now here she is!'

'It can't be? It can't be Else!' someone shouted. 'She'll be in Russia by now. How can it be her?'

'But I know Else,' the old man called out. 'I'd know her anywhere. She always stopped and talked to me – how could I fail to recognize her?' He dropped the axe in his hand and hurried towards me. Others followed, and in no time I was surrounded by people who knew me. As they approached, I too started to recognise a few of them.

They bombarded me with questions, too many to answer. It was overwhelming. Where had I come from? Why wasn't I on the way to Russia? Where were the others? All the women and girls from the village, would they be following later?

Sadly I had to tell them that, as far as I knew, I was the only one. I promised to answer their queries, but not yet. I also needed answers. It puzzled me to see them in the forest with their belongings. Would they return to Glowitz, and if so, when? I was anxious to reach my mother. Could it be that far? I had to walk on.

'Absolutely not!' was their answer. I'd never get as far as the village without being picked up by a Russian guard. No, I had to wait until morning. Then they'd all be allowed to return to their homes and, hidden from spying eyes, I'd be able to go with them.

There was a lot of excitement, hugs all round. So much talk: I wasn't used to it and stood rooted to the spot, stunned and overcome with emotion. I was silent, lost for words, and tears threatened to flood my eyes. Overwhelmed, my heart was ready to burst with happiness.

To these people I was a heroine. I'd escaped the clutches of the Russian army and now they'd do their best to keep me safe, hidden from prying eyes. They'd find a way to take me home without me being found, but for now I had nothing to fear.

I was ushered into their encampment. Each family tried to show me an act of kindness. Warm food and drink was offered and I suddenly realized how hungry I was.

First I was shown a small makeshift tent where I could wash in private. That was when I realised how awful I must have looked: still covered in dust and straw from the barn, my face partially blackened for camouflage and my body scratched and bruised from scrambling in the undergrowth whenever an army vehicle came by. They brought warm water, soap and towels and I experienced the most blissful feeling when, at last, I could remove all that dust and grime that had accumulated on my body over the days. I felt a new person and gloried in that delicious feeling of cleanliness.

Walking back into the circle of villagers, I noticed a mother and daughter approaching me. It was mother's friend, Frau Ruch, with her young daughter Inge! She put her arms around me and hugged me emotionally.

'Else, I still can't believe it's really you. Your mother will have the greatest shock. She was convinced of your return home and was determined to remain in Glowitz. How right she was!'

'But what can I do not to frighten her too much? My unexpected appearance so suddenly will distress her.'

'Don't worry, Else. I'll go ahead and prepare her. We don't want her to faint when she sees you standing before her.'

I was so incredibly lucky to have stumbled into this circle of friends from Glowitz, who were only too willing to give me shelter and soon take me safely home to my mother. To sit in their midst and listen to their story was more important than to talk about my exploits. Why had they left Glowitz and camped in this forest?

The old man who had been the first to greet me came to sit beside me. 'The Russian soldiers wanted our belongings, because in their homeland they're poor, having only the most basic commodities for their existence. In their eyes we're rich. We own things they could only dream of having and, as they've won the war, they think they're now entitled to take whatever they want. It's all there: they only need to grab it. Some of our devices they've never seen; they don't even know what they are – alarm clocks, watches, sewing machines and all electrical things. They don't realize that nothing will work without electricity, but are fascinated nevertheless. They want it all, and the only way to get it is by stealing it – the spoils of war.'

'But why did you have to leave your homes? Why didn't they just take what they wanted?'

'They didn't want resistance: the task of removing our belongings was easier without us.'

'So, if everyone had to leave, why's my mother not with you?'

'She refused to come. She was determined to stay behind. She's been fanatical about waiting for you. I don't know what would have happened to her if you'd never come back.' He looked sad: poor, dear mother. What she'd suffered! Then he roused himself and with a grin, added, 'She was right, of course. Here you are and tomorrow you'll return with us!'

That night I found shelter in another makeshift tent between Frau Ruch and Inge. It had been a memorable day, so long and full of drama and excitement. I was very tired but lay awake a little longer before sleep overcame me. I thought of our journey back to Glowitz next morning. My concern was also for dear mother, the boys and little Marlene. How they'd suffered. Should I have promised her I'd return? Suppose I hadn't – it would have broken her. Yet it had obviously kept her going. What would they say when I suddenly stood before them?

My last thought was for Ruth. She should be in Stolp by now. I hoped with all my heart the final part of her journey had gone well and she was safely reunited with her family. Would I ever know?

There in that small makeshift tent I felt secure and full of gratitude to the people of Glowitz, who'd received me with admiration and open arms. I'd have to say a heartfelt thank you to everyone and would never forget the way they'd welcomed me – it was incredible!

Before I finally closed my eyes, I gave a short prayer of thanks for my happiness.

Sunday, 15 April 1945

That night I had a wonderful sleep. All my anxieties had disappeared, and I was left with a tremendous anticipation that in a few hours I'd be back with mother again.

When I awoke, it was still early morning, but already the camp was a hive of activity. Everyone was up and about, preparing to leave the forest and return to their homes in Glowitz.

I wanted to be part of that busy crowd, but whenever I tried to be helpful, I was told to sit under a tree or assist with breakfast. I asked when we'd leave, but they told me not to be impatient, to wait for the moment I'd be summoned to my hiding place in a handcart. It took all the patience I could muster – I was eager to be on my way and was tempted to go on ahead.

However it was clear I'd be in danger if I did so. They were allowed to return to Glowitz by 9 a.m. Very likely Russian soldiers would meet and escort them into the village. On my own, I'd walk straight into that 'welcoming party'.

Breakfast was a simple meal: a slice of bread and dripping, or jam. But no one complained.

The old man came under the tree to keep me company. I asked him how long it would take to reach Glowitz.

An hour or so if we were lucky, he replied.

'I've prepared my handcart for you, Else,' he continued. 'I've made it as comfortable as possible. You must remain hidden all the way, for if soldiers should discover you, there's no knowing what would happen to you – and all the people here. After all this, what's an hour?'

'Thank you,' I said, smiling at him. 'I'll not give myself away. I don't want to put anyone in danger. It's brave of you all to help me like this.'

As soon as breakfast was over, the camp was dismantled. Rubbish was burnt and the fire doused with moist soil, so hardly a trace of human habitation was left.

Just after 7 a.m. everyone was ready to start the walk home, me with them. I was told to lie on the base of the old man's handcart, which was longer than the others. It was padded with a layer of blankets and, to cover me, he'd brought his featherbed, big enough to tuck me in securely on all sides. I thought that if they put any more on top of me, I'd surely suffocate. But more was to come. Clothes, pillows and, on top of that, two little girls who would ride in comfort. They didn't know I was beneath.

The position I found myself in was most uncomfortable. How could I possibly last like that for more than an hour? I couldn't stretch and lay cramped, my knees under my chin. But worse things had happened to me and this was different. At the end of this journey would come my reward – reunion with mother!

Now it was time to leave the forest. Each family, adults, children and the few belongings they now possessed, were lined up ready. Poor people! What would they find when they returned? Everyone knew their homes were ransacked. What was left was either too heavy to be transported, or of no interest to these uneducated, peasant Russian soldiers.

As I was lying on the base of the handcart, each bump in the road jerked my body and I was soon in agony. That, the featherbed, pillows and children on top, made it feel impossible to breathe. Claustrophobic, I started to panic. With my hand I tried desperately to move the bedding slightly away from the side of the cart and created a tiny peephole. At least now I breathed easier. The two girls had started to whine and it was a relief when their mother lifted them off and let them run about.

Once, Frau Ruch – Aunt Katrin – came close and whispered, 'Hold on, Else. It won't be long now – we're making good time. Remember, at the end of this journey you'll be with your family again.'

Who's pulling me? I wondered. I knew it wasn't the old man whose cart it was; he was too frail to pull me along.

Oh, how I wished I didn't have to lie there, cramp in my legs, aching back; yet, in spite of it all, I found my predicament very funny. *Wait till I tell you about it, mother*, I thought. *You'll laugh too! But at this moment my plight's deadly serious and, if I'm found by a Russian sentry, the consequences were unthinkable. I'd never forgive myself if I threw it all away for that.*

In the distance I could hear a church clock striking nine and then I heard a woman say Glowitz could be seen not too far away. I recalled the old woman in the cottage telling me about looking for Glowitz church tower at the end of the forest.

Once more Aunt Katrin came close to the side of my cart.

'Else,' she whispered, 'not much further. Be patient. When we arrive in Glowitz, I'll walk ahead to see your mother to prepare her for the surprise that awaits her. I know the cottage where she and the children were staying: I hope she's safe and still there. We'll make sure no Russians are about; then you can jump out of the cart and be reunited with her.'

I must have dozed for a while, because I awoke with a start when I heard someone shout, 'Russian soldiers – standing in the road!'

The old man, one of only three men in the group, went down the convoy and, calmly and quietly, urged, 'Walk past them, smiling and unconcerned. Behave as though the situation's normal. Perhaps they'll let us pass without stopping us. After all, we've *nothing* to hide, have we?'

Through the tiny opening I'd made I saw the soldiers, standing in the road, laughing and joking. A moment of terror gripped me. I wanted to scream and stuffed a fist in my mouth. I imagined a bayonet piercing the covering. Then, breathing deeply and slowly, I calmed down and forced the thought of discovery out of my mind.

Soon, without being stopped or molested, we were again on our way – the last stretch into Glowitz village. Now my excitement reached its highest point. Lying there at the bottom of the cart was more than I could bear. 'Hold on, Else,' I told myself. 'You've lasted so long, a few more minutes won't make any difference.'

All the time, Frau Ruch and Inge walked beside me, talking in a quiet voice, trying to keep my spirits up. I caught my breath when Inge said, 'Look, Mama. I can see the station. We'll soon be at the railway crossing.'

'Else, can you feel it as we walk across?'

'Yes, I can, but it's not as bumpy as I expected,' I answered, 'I suppose the tracks have gone.' Through the small peephole I'd made, I could see the village entrance. To my right, the dairy, closed down and empty. That building, with its coalshed, I'd rather forget.

'Else, we're coming to the old post office, Gisela's home, also empty – remember?'

'Yes, indeed . . .' And my heart bled for my dear dead friend.

The village was appearently deserted. Not a sound, other than the women, children and elderly men in our party; even they were quiet. The younger men were still away fighting, imprisoned or conscripted by Russians to rip up railway tracks. German trains were a different gauge to those in Russia, so the lines needed to be extended from the German border, to take prisoners deep into Russia, perhaps as far as Siberia. As a result, our valuable railway line to Stolp and beyond had been dismantled.

'Please, Aunt Katrin, can I come out now?'

'Not yet, Else. We must check no Russians are about.'

We turned down the low road, past a small cottage, where a latch clicked and footsteps sounded on the cobbles. Could it be mother? I heard Frau Ruch say, 'Morning, Helena! Are you and the children all right? Can I come in for a moment? I've news for you.'

'Certainly, Katrin. I'm so glad to see you all back safely.' It was definitely her voice!

'When we disappear inside the cottage, Else,' Aunt Katrin told me, 'get out of the cart.

Then wait a minute for me to prepare your mother.'

I was very stiff, hardly able to move, but bursting with impatience – after so long waiting for that moment, how could I hold back? I was shaking, my mind in turmoil. I *couldn't* wait longer. I ran to the door and opened it. I shouted the words I had dreamed about. 'Mother, it's me, Else! I'm home! Look, I've come back to you, just as I promised!'

Chapter 36

Promised to Poland

For a moment mother and I faced each other, too stunned to move. Then I flung myself into her arms and we embraced in silence.

'Else, my girl, my dearest child.' Mother's muffled voice, buried in my shoulder, croaked with emotion.

'It's all right, mother, I'm here. I promised you – it's really me!' I looked up into her eyes. Tears were streaming down the cheeks of my mother's beautiful face, the face I'd seen so often in my dreams. But she looked stressed and her hair had turned silver. Was it because of me?

Mother started babbling, 'Elslein, is it really you? Where did you come from? Are you well? How did you manage to escape? How did you get home?'

'Mother, wait. In good time. There's so much to tell you – later. Where are Hans-Dieter and the little ones?'

I looked over her shoulder and saw Hans-Dieter, Ralfie and little Marlene on a wooden bench in the corner, staring at me with a puzzled expression on their faces. They must have been wondering where their big sister had suddenly come from.

Letting go of my mother, I went over to them.

Hans-Dieter immediately jumped up, ran towards me and put his arms around me. 'Else!' he cried, 'I'm so glad you're home again. I . . . I've missed you.'

'And so have I, Hans-Dieter; in fact I've missed you all terribly.'

I wanted to hug him in return but he shouted, 'No Else, don't do that – you'll hurt me! You mustn't hug me: it's too painful.'

'But why, Hans-Dieter? What's happened to you? You're injured; I can see that. You have scars all over your body and I can see a large wound on your neck. What's happened to you, child? Have you fallen and injured yourself? Quick, say something; I want to know.'

'No, I didn't fall. Mother, can I tell Else what the Russian soldiers did to us at school?'

'Yes, child, go ahead and tell Else. Your sister will want to know everything about the gruesome story.'

'Well,' Dieter started his tale, 'I was at school and we were all in the playground kicking a ball. Suddenly three Russian soldiers appeared. They stopped and looked over the gate, watching us. I'm sure they were drunk; they could hardly stand and were shouting for us to let them into the playground. My teacher had heard the commotion. She approached the soldiers and asked them to go away. But they just laughed and shouted and kicked the gate. All the children were terribly scared.'

266

Hans-Dieter stopped, overcome with emotion.

'Go on, little brother,' I tried to encourage him; but then, when he looked at me, I saw tears in his eyes and he was shaking all over.

'Leave it for now, Hans-Dieter; you can tell me more when you've calmed down. I can wait until you're ready.'

'I'm ready now,' he replied. 'I want to go on talking.'

'Then I saw one of the soldiers remove something from his belt. I didn't know what it was, but I thought it might be a stick. He lifted his arm and with all his might threw it among us. Now I know it was a hand grenade. It hit the ground where Hansi my friend and I were standing and with an almighty bang the thing exploded. I didn't know what had happened but knew I was hurt. I fell to the ground and that's all I can remember.'

I gently put my arm around him. 'You poor boy; what a horrible experience.'

'Mother,' I asked, 'tell me when you heard about this.'

'A woman from the village came running to the cottage, shouting that something terrible was going on in the schoolyard. 'Come quickly, Frau Hopp; your Hans-Dieter's badly hurt. A hand grenade exploded among the children and many of them are injured, your son most of all. The doctor's been called. Thankfully he was at home and came immediately to give first aid to Hans-Dieter and his friend Hansi and other less severely injured children.'

As fast as possible, mother had rushed to the school, where she found Hans-Dieter badly hurt and bleeding profusely. 'Oh, if only my boy could be admitted to hospital,' wailed mother, 'but the nearest is in Stolp and it's impossible to get there.'

Frau Ruch had also come running. Her daughter Inge was unhurt but mother's friend was there to give support

'Lene, between us we must get Hans-Dieter home. The doctor will also help to carry him and your boy isn't heavy. Doctor told me he hasn't a drop of petrol and the Russians have confiscated his horse and cart. But he will do what he can to ease your boy's pain.'

The children were crying and wanted their mothers, who'd soon arrived to care for their little ones.

Between mother, Doctor and Frau Ruch they carried Hans-Dieter home. Doctor washed and bandaged his wounds and some ointment was available to ease his pain.

'Mother, are there still metal pieces in Hans-Dieter's body? Can they be removed or do they have to stay for ever?'

'I don't know, Else. Later, when times are more normal, I'll be able to find out from a specialist what can be done. Perhaps eventually the shrapnel in his body can be removed. I don't know. Meanwhile let's just be thankful Hans-Dieter's alive.'

Then I hugged Ralfie, my baby brother, with special love. 'Just look at you, how you've grown! You're almost as tall as your big brother. Are you a good lad and do you give mother a helping hand when she needs it?'

Timidly he nodded, still overcome and confused.

Then my little sister – so pretty with her fair, curly hair, and not a baby any more, but a real person – stretched out her arms, asking to come to me.

'Marlenchen, you're a beautiful little girl and I love you very much.' I picked her up, surprised at how heavy she was. 'I'm home and can help Mother look after you again.'

As I looked at my four dear family members, a feeling of belonging overwhelmed me. Carefully I put Marlenchen down, ran into mother's arms and, hugging her tightly, burst into tears.

'Come, Else,' mother said, gently, 'dry your tears. It's time we looked after *you*. I'll prepare you a bath. It will have to be in front of the kitchen range. There's no bathroom in this tiny cottage but, nevertheless, a good washdown will make you feel wonderful, followed by clean clothes: I've had them waiting for you. Then we'll have something to eat and afterwards you and I will talk.'

'Yes, mother, lovely. I have a lot to tell you.'

After we'd eaten a simple lunchtime meal and everything was cleared away, Marlenchen had her afternoon nap. Ralf also rested and Hans-Dieter occupied himself with his few toys, while mother and I sat together by the living-room fire and I tried to tell her what had happened to me.

There was so much to say – how could I talk about it all in one short session? It had to wait; later perhaps. Then it would be easier to talk about the horrors I'd lived through. But not yet; it was too soon. My mind was still in turmoil. So much had happened to me; I didn't know how to tell mother. Sometime soon I'd have to talk to her about the horrific episode in Frau Lutzig's barn. Could I speak about it, even to my mother? I had no idea; as yet, my courage failed me.

Once I started, the words tumbled from my lips. So much, so much . . . mother let me talk. She didn't comment or interrupt the flow until I felt I'd said enough for one session.

'But tell me, Else, how did you come to meet up with the Glowitz people?'

'Oh, mother, that was very strange; such a coincidence.' I went on to tell her of my parting with Ruth, my lonely days walking in the forest not knowing whether or not I was on the right path – knocking on doors, hungry and thirsty.

Mother was getting agitated; she was fighting not to show her distress and was wringing her hands in her lap. With deep emotion and trying to restrain her tears she whispered, 'Child, that you survived at all is truly a miracle. But let's not talk any more today; there'll be other days – all the time in the world to go on with your story.'

'Yes, mother.' Instantly I dried up.

'Now I want to discuss something completely different,' she declared. 'As you can see, Else, this cottage is small – too small for the five of us. I prepared for the day you'd come home, and for some time now I've looked for a larger place.'

'And did you find anything?'

'Yes I did.'

'Mother, there's one thing I must ask you. Where's the old lady who lived in this cottage?'

'She died, soon after the Russians took you away. All too much for her. The children and I were still living in the dairy. But it became more and more impossible for us women: we were molested continually by drunken soldiers – mostly at night.'

'Did they also abuse you, mother?'

'Hush, child; we'll talk about those things another time. Let me go on with my tale.'

Did she also have something to hide? I couldn't tell.

'I wanted to get out of the dairy, and as soon as this cottage was empty, I approached the old lady's son, who gave me permission to move in.'

'That was luck, mother.'

'Yes, Else, I was grateful to be offered this little home. But it's too small now we're five: we can't stay. I must also think of your safety. I've found an empty farm opposite the church and Aunt Friedel's shop.'

'I know the farm you mean, mother; it has white railings and the house stands on the corner.'

'That's right. I've looked around and it seems suitable for our needs. The house is furnished: it appears the farmer and his family fled in a hurry, leaving everything behind. We'll be comfortable. There are barns and in one of them I noticed a pigeon loft, very suitable for you to hide in, Else, should you have to.'

'When do you think we ought to go there, mother?'

'The sooner the better. If Aunt Katrin will lend us her handcart, we can go as soon as everything's packed. We don't have much left.'

'Hurray!' Hans-Dieter shouted. 'Ralf and I can pretend to be farmers. We can play in the barn, can't we, mother?'

'Yes, Hans-Dieter, but today you must help with the packing, because when we leave here, it has to be very early in the morning.'

'Mother,' Hans-Dieter asked, 'are there animals on the farm? Cows and pigs and chickens?'

'No, my boy. All the animals are gone – I don't know where they went. We'll be on our own and must all look after Else. No one must know she's with us. It's a BIG secret! Do you understand, Hans-Dieter?'

He nodded, seriously. He wouldn't tell.

Mother could see I was very tired. 'I think, child, it must be an early night for you. I'll make a comfortable bed on the settee, where you'll be undisturbed.'

'What about soldiers, mother? Will they come during the night and harass us?'

'I don't think so, Elslein. They don't know you're here and still believe I'm alone with the children – I'm sure they won't trouble us.'

We had our meal quite early that evening, after which the little ones, Ralf and Marlenchen, had their wash and were soon ready for bed. A prayer, a kiss and a hug, and four sleepy eyes were waiting to close.

Hans-Dieter, older now, was allowed to stay up longer. There was no school and, according to mother, no one knew if it would open again. In the meantime Hans-Dieter had daily lessons with her. Every day she gave him an assignment and no play was allowed until he'd completed his homework.

Mother and I sat a little longer in the tiny living room, illuminated by the soft light from the open fire. Happy in our companionship in that cosy room, mother on one side of the fireplace and I on the other, neither felt like talking. I watched the firelight playing on her careworn face and could almost feel the agony she must have endured, worrying every day I was away. But now she was smiling, relaxed and happy. We were together again and I vowed I'd do my utmost to help keep our little family together.

To be at home with my dear ones was truly a gift from God, who had indeed listened when I'd needed him and had answered my prayers.

18 April

It was still dark when I awoke and felt mother's hand on my shoulder.

'Elslein, wake up. It's very early but I want you to listen to what I'm now going to tell you. Are you awake?'

'Yes, mother, what is it?'

'I think the Russian soldiers moved out during the night. All of them. It appears there are none left and most of the Glowitz people are already in the street deliberating why. They're rejoicing that the occupation has left us.'

'But surely others will follow, don't you think?'

'I don't know for certain, child, but I think Polish soldiers will replace the Russians.'

'I remember, mother. At the summit meeting in Yalta in February this year between Stalin, Churchill and Roosevelt, Pomerania was promised to Poland.

'Yes, Else, that's right,' answered my mother. 'I think, any day now, the Poles will enter and occupy Glowitz. Anyway, as there are no soldiers to hinder us, we may as well make our move to the farm, as early today as we possibly can.'

Once my mother had made up her mind to do something, there was no holding her back. Today she wanted to get on with the move to Low Road Farm, which we'd occupy for as long as necessary. She asked us to help her and found a job for each of us.

'Else,' she said, 'wash and dress your little sister, ready for breakfast.'

'Yes, mother, I'll start straight away.'

'Hans-Dieter, as soon as you're ready, lay the table. Ralf must see to himself; then he can help you. I'll start preparing breakfast, so we can all sit down and eat together.'

'Mother,' I asked, 'what will we have?'

'Not much, Else,' mother answered. 'We've a jug of milk and a loaf of bread a kind lady brought us yesterday, before you came home. I'll warm the milk and you children can break a slice of bread into it. That will have to do.'

'That's fine,' I told her and, glaring at the boys said, 'We love bread and milk, *don't we?*'

They both answered, 'Yes, Else!'

We had breakfast; then got straight on with our jobs.

Hans-Dieter and I washed up, while Ralfie cleared the table. Then he went upstairs to help mother. She had to remove and fold the bedlinen, and then started on the living room. All our belongings – there were so few– fitted into a basket, which we'd take to the farm in Aunt Katrin's handcart. Amazing: all we owned on such a small wagon! To me it emphasised the sadness of our situation.

While mother and her three helpers were busy, little Marlene sat in her pram, supervising the activity around her.

Time flew by and by midday we were ready to leave the cottage. Neighbours knew we were moving and, with unselfish kindness, brought small gifts of provisions they could hardly spare. A lady from a neighbouring farm brought home-made bread, butter and cheese; another offered potatoes and cabbage; and one handed mother a small dish containing a few new-laid eggs. Their generosity was overwhelming. It was difficult for mother to hide the tears that threatened to run down her cheeks – she'd never realised she had so many friends.

Everything was loaded into Marlene's pram, and what didn't fit was stowed in the handcart. Then we were off down the road to our new home, a farm that didn't belong to us but that, we hoped, would give us shelter until the rightful owners returned to reclaim their property. It was a lovely morning as we walked down a deserted street to the farm: most people had been out early and had now returned home.

We had to make a few journeys back and forth, but by early evening were at last settled once more in a new home.

With the departure of the Russian soldiers there was an air of expectancy about the arrival of the Polish army. People were curious to know what the next few days would hold.

We reached the farm but, before I followed mother into the yard, I stopped by the railings and gazed across to the church and small village hall. I relived the hours I'd spent there, the walk across the high street in the middle of the night, where I was interrogated in a cellar: questions I couldn't possibly answer. The line-up outside Aunt Friedel's shop and my heartbreaking goodbye to mother, the agony of not knowing if I'd ever see her again.

Thank God I'm home! I thought to myself. *I must be so careful I'm not caught again.*

Mother had hurried ahead into the farmyard and I was now ready to follow her. I caught up with them outside the house. The door was open – someone had broken in. We entered cautiously, and were horrified at the wanton destruction that met our eyes. Soldiers must have lived in the place, for signs were evident in every room: floor and tables littered with empty vodka bottles and dirty, broken crockery.

'Well, children,' mother remarked, 'we have our work cut out. I need you all today, and by this evening, or no later than tomorrow, I want this place fit for us to live in.'

'Can I help?' piped up little Ralf.

'Oh yes, my boy,' answered mother, 'we couldn't do without you. Stay with your brother; he'll tell you what to do. Hans-Dieter, take all the empty bottles into the barn and leave them in a corner. Don't break any and cut yourselves. Be careful!'

'Right, mother! Come, Ralf. Follow me!'

In a small outhouse, at the back of the kitchen, we found brushes and buckets, and with a combined effort a cleaner and more wholesome house emerged.

Mother lit the kitchen range and laid the living-room fire; soon the warmth emanating throughout the rooms made the house more comfortable. Mother and I worked hard, but so did Hans-Dieter and Ralfie: the two lads ran back and forth between house and barn until the job was done.

'Now, upstairs,' mother took a breath. 'What will confront us there? From the glimpse I took earlier, I have an inkling of the immensity of the task. The bedrooms are filthy, but we can't clean everything today. We'll finish the rest tomorrow. Agreed?'

'Agreed,' said Hans-Dieter and I.

'Agreed,' little Ralf piped in.

'What a wonderful family!' mother said emotionally. When father comes home, I'll tell him how you've all contributed to our survival.'

'Mother,' I pointed out, 'at the end of this landing's a door. Do you know where it leads?'

'No, Else,' she answered. 'We'll see later. First let's finish here – there's still a lot to do. At least this one room must be ready to sleep in even if we must rough it just this once. I want you to have a decent bed tonight, Else. You couldn't have been very comfortable on the settee last night. And for nights before that, you slept without a proper bed. So tonight I'll see what I can do for *you.*'

'Mother, I don't want any special treatment. I'm happy just to be here with you. It's a very special gift: I'd put up with any amount of discomfort for that.'

'My child, you don't know what it means to have you back. Our Lord truly looked after you. Sometimes he performs miracles. Your return home must surely be one of them.'

We finished what we needed; then, as mother had promised, she took me to explore behind the 'secret' door. A narrow staircase led to a second door, which was unlocked. We found ourselves in a large attic: boxes, crates, baskets and old furniture were stacked at random all over the place. In a corner was a small concrete construction, a smokehouse, often found in the attics of old farmhouses, constructed to smoke hams, bacon, sausages and other joints of slaughtered animals that were hung from hooks in the wooden beams, for use during the long winter months.

The smokehouse door was open and mother peered inside. 'You see, Else, smoke from the living-room fire goes up the chimney and enters the smokehouse through slits in the wall.' She inspected it more fully. 'This will do fine, Else, should you need to hide quickly. It's clean and airy. You can even lock it from the inside; surely no one would look for you here. It will save you running across the farmyard, especially when it's dark.'

Downstairs I thought about my retreat options. 'Mother, before it's dark, I'd like to look at the pigeon loft. If it's dirty, I'll clean it in case I need to sleep there – I couldn't do that upstairs. Especially if I have to hide for a few days.' I turned to Hans-Dieter: 'Have you looked at it?'

'No, Else. Ralf and I have been too busy stacking empty bottles, *so* many of them. We did a good job, mother; we didn't break one. They're lined up, like soldiers on parade.'

'Thank you, boys,' exclaimed mother, 'a marvellous help; we couldn't have managed without you.'

It was late afternoon by the time we'd finished upstairs. We were hungry and it was time to think about supper. We had plenty of food supplied by kind neighbours, but mother decided to have something quick and easy just for one night. The next day she'd provide a proper meal.

'Mother, while you're getting our evening meal, I'll look at the pigeon loft.'

'Our meal's nearly ready, Else; the barn will be there tomorrow morning and Hans-Dieter can help you with the rubbish. You could hurt yourself now it's almost dark. Stay here – I cherish every minute with you.'

'Very well, mother. I'll stay.' I hesitated. 'Mother, this evening, when the children are in bed, including Hans-Dieter, I need to tell you something . . . private.'

'My child, that sounds ominous! You're worrying me.' Mother sat down and studied me. 'Of course, tell me anything that's disturbing you. I don't want you having nightmares!'

As soon as the evening meal was cleared, Ralf and Marlenchen ready for bed, mother and I faced a peaceful evening, just the two of us. Hans-Dieter, who'd found a pile of boys' books in a cupboard, had permission from mother to choose one to read. Among them were many of his favorites – such as books by Karl May about Winnetoe, the Indian brave and head of the Apaches, and of Old Shatterhand, a German prospector, who saved Winnetoe's life and became his 'bloodbrother'. Hans-Dieter loved books and sat in the kitchen, nose buried in one, oblivious to the world around him.

The house was silent as mother and I sat alone in the living room. It was bathed in a gentle glow from a log on the open fireplace, which crackled and hissed as flames took hold and began to lick at it from all sides.

Mother looked at me for a few moments. 'My child, can you now tell me what you've had to keep so secret? I'm your mother: nothing's so appalling and horrific that you need shoulder such a burden by yourself. You can always confide in me.'

I went down on my knees and slowly crawled towards her. Kneeling at her feet and burying my face in her lap, I started to talk. After the first few hesitant phrases, it felt as if a sluicegate had opened: words poured out of me. Soldiers . . . the barn . . . the pain . . . shame . . . the kind woman on the farm . . . Once I started I couldn't stop. Mother sat in silence, her hand gently smoothing my hair.

'My child,' she whispered, 'my poor darling daughter. That you survived such an ordeal is truly a miracle.'

'The worst of it all, mother, is I feel so dirty. All I'm telling you is stuck in my head – for the rest of my life.' Suddenly I looked up into her eyes. 'What if I have a baby, mother? A Russian baby – could I? I don't know, because I don't feel anything. All the time I was away I never once had a period. That's unnatural, isn't it, mother?'

'The reason for that, my child, could be the stress you were under. Somehow I don't think you're expecting a baby. But darling, there's nothing we can do but wait a little longer before we know for certain.'

'Please, mother, you must promise me that what I've told you this evening will for ever be a secret between you and me. You must never talk about it to another person, including father when he returns. I couldn't stand the shame, the embarrassment. Please, mother, please promise me?'

'Yes, my child, I give you my word. And that will never be broken for as long as I live. You can rest assured.'

We sat together for many hours that evening and I told my mother much more, of being in prison in Stolp, where, if the officers hadn't arrived in the nick of time, we would have been executed. I told of my escape, of Ruth, and how she'd followed me and become my dear friend and companion. I spoke of being hungry, of dreaming of plums, which mother had bottled and stored in the cellar. That made her smile. When she heard how close I'd come to death by a Russian bayonet she sat motionless listening to me, tears running down her cheeks.

We sat in silence, deep in thought for long moments. Suddenly she said, 'Enough now, my child. Lock it all away into the deepest recess of your mind. I have a plan, but will tell you about it when I've worked out the details. Now it's time for bed. Thank you, my dear girl, for confiding in me. Now I'm certain the heavy cloud you were under will lift and disappear. Come, let me give you a big hug. Good night, my child. God bless you.'

'Good night, mother. I love you. Sleep well.'

And with those words, we both made our way upstairs.

Chapter 37

The Permit

20 April. Adolf Hitler's birthday I remembered how we always used to celebrate that special occasion. Schools closed for the day, and boys and girls would wear their Hitler Youth uniform and march through the city, carrying their district banners, while singing with gusto the many familiar songs we always sang at our group meetings.

But in 1945 it was all very different. The German people were no longer interested in celebrating the birthday of a man who'd daily lead his people closer to the brink of disaster. They had more important things to think about, and uppermost in everyone's mind was how to survive the final downfall of the German nation.

In Yalta, at the meeting of their representatives, America, Russia and Britain had allocated Pomerania to Poland. In Glowitz the inhabitants had one thought: when would the Polish army arrive? Despite the departure of the Russian guards, no one was yet at ease. A few days' remission, but it wouldn't last. Russian military vehicles were regularly seen on the roads but fortunately none stopped for long. And rumours of the Polish army's approach were rife – as a few months previously, when we'd heard the Russians were on their way.

When would the Poles finally occupy Pomerania, and our village in particular? Worse still, would they throw out the local population – people whose families had lived there for generations – and replace it with their own nationals? If so, was it imminent, or would it be a gradual process over some years? No one knew for certain and there was much speculation. Every time mother went into the village she returned more concerned. No one appeared to know what was happening; it was all conjecture, but gossip was rampant.

Mother kept Hans-Dieter and me occupied tidying the farm and completing the work we'd started when we'd arrived. That day my job was to climb the barn ladder into the pigeon loft and clean it, in case I needed to live in it. The thought excited me, a novelty I looked forward to – occupying my own residence!

I don't think the pigeon house had ever been treated to so thorough a clear out as we gave it. Mother had found some bedding and soon I'd prepared a comfortable small hideaway.

As I climbed down (cleaning material in bucket, scrubbing brush in hand), I made out the sound of people shouting, a general commotion coming from the village. I hurried across the yard and hid by the house. Did mother or Hans-Dieter know what was happening? Excited voices were replaced by military vehicles: more Russians? Or the long-expected Polish army? Deep tones soon filled the air: marching and singing, as heavy boots reverberated on the cobbled high street. Across the yard I could see village people looking on in silence.

I rushed into the house and met mother coming out of the kitchen. 'Else, I'm glad you're here. I was just coming to fetch you.'

'Mother, it's the Poles! They're marching in to occupy the village, aren't they?'

'Yes, Else, and you must stay indoors. Please don't go out again – it's not safe. Do you understand? Else, are you listening?'

'Yes, mother. Don't worry: I'll do as you say.'

'What about me?' Hans-Dieter piped up. 'I can see what's going on, can't I? Please, mother.'

'If your friends are there, you can join them. But don't wander off; come straight home.'

'Yes, mother, I promise,' Hans-Dieter said, already halfway out of the door. And in a flash he was gone.

Wednesday, 9 May 1945

April was over and there we were already in the month of May. The days were longer and it was a lot warmer. May was a lovely month in Pomerania – the time finally to say goodbye to the bitter winter and to welcome in the summer.

Rumours about the surrender of Germany had been rife from the end of April. News filtered in that Mussolini was dead and Italy had surrendered. It was followed by all sorts of unfounded reports of other surrendering armies, but no one could tell which were true.

On that day, 9 May, Frau Ruch came running to the farm to give mother the news that the war in Europe was over. 'Apparently they signed a full surrender yesterday, west of the river Oder,' she said, unsure whether to be shocked or relieved. 'Fighting's to cease immediately.'

'Wait and see, my dear, how the Russians and Poles will celebrate. They won't let us forget we're the losers. But, most importantly, there'll be no more bloodshed. Our soldiers will come home and our prisoners be released – and soon everything will return to normal.'

'We may not need a permit any more; perhaps soon now we can travel freely again, mother.'

'You may well be right, Else, but let's bide our time.'

Mother and I were sitting with the two little ones in the living room, doing nothing, just waiting. But waiting for what? Mother was on edge.

Why was she troubled? Perhaps she was sad about the defeat. Yet surely the victorious Poles, who now officially occupied Pomerania, would treat its people kindly and with respect? Mother shrugged her shoulders when I suggested it. She was an astute woman and perhaps suspected problems rather than peace. She was certainly depressed and I wanted to cheer her, but didn't know how.

'You think there's more trouble ahead, don't you, mother?' I ventured, quietly.

'I know no more than you, Else. I do know, though, this is no life; not for you, my daughter, nor for Hans-Dieter and the little ones. Neither is it for me. What's here for us now? We originally evacuated to Pomerania for safety, but it's now more dangerous than anywhere else. We have nothing and even live in a house belonging to someone else. Any day now some Polish official could appear unannounced and order us out, saying he wants the premises for himself.'

'Yes, it's a cheerless existence. But what can we do?'

'And furthermore, Else, I'm dreadfully worried about your father. I don't know where he is, whether he's dead or alive – or a prisoner in a Russian camp. Everything's uncertain, so how can you expect me to be cheerful? Sorry, darling, I shouldn't need to burden you with my worries.' Then she got up and bustled about purposefully. 'Else, on Sunday, if you stay with Ralf and Marlenchen, Hans-Dieter and I will go to the morning service. Would you mind?'

'Of course not; go with an easy mind. Perhaps church will make you feel better. Prayers work wonders. I now know from experience – they got me home to you, didn't they?'

Mother nodded. 'That's decided, Else. Come to the kitchen and we'll get lunch.'

As I was helping mother to prepare our meal, I remarked, 'Mother, wouldn't it be best if I stayed in the barn tonight? Just in case – I don't want to be caught again.'

'Oh, my child! I'd rather you were in the house with us. You're afraid of Polish soldiers molesting you? I hope not, but if some should turn up during the night, you can disappear into the attic and hide in the smokehouse.'

'If you think I'm safe there, mother. I prefer to be near you, not on my own in a pigeon loft.'

At that moment Hans-Dieter burst into the house, full of energy and excitement, eager to relate the village news. 'I saw soldiers, mother, many of them, marching into Puttkamer's estate. They're camping there. They were friendly, smiled at us. One soldier gave Hans, my friend, and me some chocolate!'

'That's kind, Hans-Dieter. Now wash your hands and have lunch.' Mother seemed unconcerned.

'Can I go out again when I've finished my meal? Please say yes?'

'Where, Hans-Dieter? I don't want you going too far. Remember, my boy, if *anything* should upset you, no matter what, run home immediately. If soldiers ask if you have a sister, say she's only a baby. Do you understand, Hans-Dieter? You must *not* mention Else to anyone.'

'Yes, mother, I'll remember.'

A few days went by, but nothing untoward happened. Gradually mother relaxed and we began to assume the new occupational force would leave us in peace.

Saturday, 12 May 1945

Everything was quiet and normal. Mother decided to take Marlene in the pram and walk with Ralfie to the next village to ask a farmer for fresh vegetables and other provisions. She advised me not to leave the house. The risk of being seen by passing soldiers was too great.

As it was for my own good, I had to obey.

Mother's trip went well and they returned for lunch. During the afternoon, when we were all in the living room, Hans-Dieter noticed two Polish soldiers entering the farmyard. They knocked on the door. In a flash I ran upstairs, through the door at the end of the corridor until, quite out of breath, I reached the attic, where I hid initially behind old boxes stored in the smokehouse corner.

Meanwhile, as Hans-Dieter described to me later, the soldiers were shouting impatiently for someone to 'open up or else!'

Mother lifted Baby out of her pram and, holding her in her arms, answered the door. She politely asked them to enter and enquired if she could help.

In broken German, they wanted to know how many people were living on the premises.

'Only me and my children. You can see them,' mother answered, 'two boys and a baby girl.'

'Just the four of you?' One made a note.

Mother nodded, 'Just the four of us.'

The soldiers stared casually around, not particularly interested; then, without another word, they turned and left.

Mother let out a sigh of relief. 'Go to the attic, Hans-Dieter. Tell Else to come down; the danger's passed. Let's hope this incident is all we'll experience today.'

Sunday, 13 May 1945

Mother had decided to go to church with Hans-Dieter. She asked me to stay behind and look after our little ones. I'd like to have gone, but mother was adamant: 'Not this Sunday. We need to wait a week or so to see how things develop under the Polish takeover.'

Half hidden behind a curtain, I watched them cross the road.

No bells rang to call the villagers into God's house; neither was there much chatter – no harmless gossip, no subdued laughter, no usual banter between the elderly ladies of Glowitz and our neighbouring village. In fact few people entered the church that Sunday morning; they must have preferred to stay behind their own doors. The Russian experience was too vivid in everyone's mind, and villagers were suspicious of the new occupation. Only time would tell.

When, after the service, mother and Hans-Dieter returned home, I could see they were most distressed and very dishevelled. They'd been running and were out of breath.

'What's happened? Why are you both so upset?'

'Else, I'm so relieved you stayed at home!' Mother took off her hat and sank into a chair. 'The most dreadful incident occurred after the service when we came out of church. A group of young soldiers appeared from nowhere, armed with rifles, sticks – anything they could find. As people emerged innocently into the open, the louts attacked us, beat us with their weapons! Mindless energy against everyone and anyone: the old, the frail who wanted no trouble, but to go home.' Mother wiped her brow. 'For the soldier boys it was hilarious entertainment: for us it was terrifying! Hans-Dieter and I were lucky to escape – we dodged cudgels and ran and ran! Else, it was a horrific ordeal, impossible to describe.' She shook her head in disbelief.

'You know, Else,' my young brother murmured, wiping tears away with his sleeve, 'they pushed old ladies on the ground and kicked them, over and over. Why did they do that? No one did anything to the soldiers. Why?'

'Hans-Dieter, they do it because they hate German people as much as Russians do. Father told me that when the German army occupied Poland, our soldiers were often cruel to Polish people. Now they're having their revenge: what we saw today is part of that vengeance. Perhaps it's wrong to judge the Poles with harsh criticism; they have bad memories too. But to hurt innocent people . . .'

'I think the world's an evil place!' Hans-Dieter retorted. 'Russian, Pole, German or any other country, it seems bad people are always stronger than the good. Don't you agree, mother?'

'Yes, my child, I do. After witnessing this terrible incident, I feel with more urgency than ever we must get out of here. Tomorrow I'll take the first step to change this awful situation. Tonight, when Ralfie and Marlenchen are asleep, you Else, Hans-Dieter and I will sit together: I have a plan to discuss with you.'

'What, mother? Can't you tell us now?'

'No, Else; wait till later.'

After we'd eaten our evening meal and the little ones were in bed, the three of us entered the living room, where a homely fire gave off warmth and comfort. Hans-Dieter and I were anxious to know what mother intended to tell us, but had to wait patiently until she was ready to talk. We had no electricity, but the firelight glowed pleasantly enough in the room for us to talk to each other.

I wondered what it was about. Ever since she and Hans-Dieter had returned from church, she'd been withdrawn and silent, deep in thought.

'I have something important to say to you.' She sighed deeply. 'I've devised a plan. It's only an idea: I still have to work out the details. But I want you to tell me what *you both* think. You're sensible, Hans-Dieter; and, as for you, Else, your comments will be of great value to me.'

'Thank you, mother, for having faith in us.'

She didn't reply, but said, 'We should have a Polish commandant in this village. I don't know where he and his staff have their quarters, but intend to find out. Tomorrow, Monday, I'll get up early and ask if he'll see me – I hope he'll agree to do so.'

'Why do you need to see the commandant, mother?' asked Hans-Dieter.

'I want to ask him for authorization to leave Glowitz and Pomerania. I'll tell him we wish to return home to Düsseldorf in the West. We're not locals.'

'Why this sudden idea, mother?' I asked.

'It's not sudden, Else. I've mulled it over since I heard Pomerania was promised to Poland. I realised life here wouldn't be what I wished for my children and myself. We all hope father will come home one day. If we stayed here, he wouldn't know where to find us. His heart would be broken if he returned to Düsseldorf and we weren't there.'

'But mother, do you think we'll get permission to leave?' I asked.

'Else, I can only try; but whatever the outcome, we'll have to abide by the rules. I'm not putting you all in danger. However, I really believe we must attempt to get home without delay.'

'And how do you think we'll get there? There are no trains: the lines have been taken up. Düsseldorf's a long, long way away!' I remembered geography lessons in Stolp grammar school – just a memory now. 'We'd have to cross from north-eastern Germany all the way to the far west, many hundreds of kilometres.'

'I know, my child, but there's only one thing we can do: be prepared to walk.'

'Walk! All that way, mother?' gasped Hans-Dieter. Even he knew it was far away.

'We're almost 800 kilometres from home. Perhaps even more. I've been told that all railtracks have been removed between here and Küstrin and sent to Russia. How far it is between Küstrin and Stargard, I don't know. We may have to continue walking . . . But what does it matter? We're young, including me. You, Else, Hans-Dieter and I have two good legs each. Of course we can walk: everything's possible. But don't let that worry you. Once my request has been granted, we'll plan more.'

'Oh, I do hope it will, mother.'

'So do I, Elslein. Then, when we do leave, we can't take much because', she added smiling, 'we haven't got much.'

'Yes, mother, of course.' I smiled in agreement. I was proud of mother; she was such a brave woman. 'With you leading us, mother, we could walk to America!'

'We'd get very wet if we did!' Hans-Dieter giggled, his old high spirits returning after his earlier traumatic ordeal.

I felt a flood of love overpower me for my special family. How I'd missed them. I'd make sure we'd stay together from now on, no matter what, and never be parted again.

'We'll have to travel light, mother, if we're walking. We can't carry much,' I exclaimed.

'We'll each carry a knapsack with only the essentials needed for the journey. Thank God, it's no longer cold.'

'Yes, mother, let's hope the weather stays fine.'

'Now, before we can complete our plans, we must await the outcome of my meeting with the Polish village commandant.'

'Do you think you'll get that precious permit? Will the commandant tell you his decision right away?' I asked.

'I hope so, Else, because now I've made up my mind, I'm eager to go. But one thing you must be prepared for: the journey won't be easy. Yet I still think that with determination, perseverance and your assistance, Else and Hans-Dieter, we can manage it. What do you think?'

'You can rely on us,' I assured her. You'll receive all the help we can give you.'

Monday, 14 May 1945

When I awoke early on the Monday morning, I could hear mother already up and moving about in her bedroom. I could imagine how she felt. After all, it wasn't every day you came face to face with the village commandant. She was bound to be nervous. So much depended on that meeting and I wished I could have gone with her, but knew that wasn't to be; for now she was better left on her own. She'd come and tell me when she was going – then I could wish her luck.

Later, after mother had left, I washed and dressed Marlenchen, watched Ralf cleaning his teeth and from the corner of my eyes watched how Hans-Dieter laid the breakfast table.

'Well done, Hans-Dieter: you're making a good job of that,' I praised him. 'Let's wait for mother to return. Then we can breakfast together.'

'All right, I don't mind,' answered Hans-Dieter, 'but I don't think Marlenchen can wait. She's started to niggle for her food now. Ralf also wants his porridge. Should we give it to them?'

'Yes, but you and I will wait till mother comes home. All right?'

We waited and when she returned, I saw at once that her interview with the authorities hadn't gone as well as she'd hoped.

'Mother, did you see the commandant?'

'No, Else, he wasn't there; I'll have to try again Wednesday. He should be in his office then.' Another two days' wait. Mother was as impatient as Hans-Dieter and me.

Two days later mother went a second time.

As soon as she returned, Hans-Dieter wanted to bombard her with questions. I looked at him sternly and luckily he took the hint and kept quiet. We waited for mother to speak, but she took her time.

Eventually even I couldn't contain my curiosity any longer.

'Mother,' I said, 'why are you so quiet? We've waited for you to talk to us over breakfast. Ralf and Marlenchen are fed. Please tell us what happened. Did you meet the commandant? Did he turn down your request?'

'He was there, but no, Else, he didn't grant it – he couldn't.'

'Why?' Hans-Dieter and I asked together.

'A permit to leave Pomerania can only be issued at the head office in Stolp.'

I shook my head. 'So what happens now?'

'I'm thinking about that. You'll both know my decision in a while.'

Mother had breakfast and then went upstairs. She stayed in her room for some time. When eventually she joined us, she was a different person – relaxed, cheerful and had, obviously, found the answer to a difficult dilemma.

'Children,' she announced, 'I want you all, including the little ones, to come to the living room. Of course this mostly concerns you, Else and Hans-Dieter. You two will have a big responsibility.'

'What is it? Do tell us.'

'I've decided to go to Stolp,' mother said.

'To Stolp? You? On your own?' I asked, somewhat surprised.

'Yes, Else, on my own. If we want to go home, we need a permit; for that I must go to Stolp. You, Else and Hans-Dieter, are the most important people in this venture. I must be able to rely on you both a hundred percent. There may be times when Else has to hide away, either in the pigeon loft or in the attic. Then, Hans-Dieter, you have to be extra strong – and brave. Do you think you can be courageous?'

'Yes, mother, you know I can. I'm old enough and strong.'

'If Polish soldiers visit the farm, you *must* make them believe there are only the three of you and that you're quite alone in the house for a short time. Can you?'

'Of course I can do that.'

'Also, Hans-Dieter, while I'm away, you can't go out to play. Do you understand?'

'Yes, mother, you can rely on me.'

'My child, you're very grown-up. I'm proud of you and your father will also be when he comes home and finds you had to take his place.'

'When will you go, mother?' I asked.

'Early tomorrow morning. I may be gone five days. Perhaps I can make it in four: I'll return as soon as I possibly can.'

Thursday, 17 May 1945

'Elslein, wake up. It's early morning; you don't have to get up yet, but I'm ready to be on my way to Stolp.'

I stirred. 'Else, are you listening to me?' mother repeated, shaking me once more.

Still half asleep, I fought to open my eyes. I rubbed them, sat up in bed and was suddenly wide awake. Dawn was just breaking and in the first daylight, I saw mother standing by my bed. Oh, how I wished she didn't have to go. Such a long way – so much danger! It wouldn't be so bad if I was with her. But her walking alone all the way to Stolp worried me dreadfully.

I tried to hold to hold back my threatening tears. 'Please, please take great care and come back as soon as you can.'

'Of course I will, my darling child. Once I've accomplished the purpose of my journey, nothing will keep me from rushing home to you, my four dearest people, as quickly as my legs will bring me.'

'We'll be waiting.'

Mother crossed the room to pick up her coat and handbag, but returned and sat on the edge of the bed.

'It's about six or seven hours' walk, without stopping to rest or any diversions, and as long as the roads are in good condition – which I doubt. Some say they're still blocked by carts and wagons of refugees, together with locals escaping from the area before the Poles take over. Then I might be stopped by the army every so often. But if I'm lucky, I might even arrive in Stolp late this afternoon. Someone may give me a lift on a farm cart. Still, I think I'll be too late to do anything today – everything will be closed. But first thing tomorrow morning I'll present myself at the office of administration, where I hope I can attain that precious permit to allow us to leave Pomerania. Once it's in my hand, I'll turn around immediately and begin my long walk back to Glowitz.'

Once more mother gently stroked my hair and planted a kiss on my forehead. 'Take care, Else. Please be mindful that danger's never far away. Hans-Dieter's a sensible boy; I can trust him to do his best.'

'I know, mother. Now go . . . take care . . . try not to worry about us.'

One more hug, another kiss, a wave from the door, and mother was gone.

Dear God! I prayed. *Please look after her. What our mother's doing for us is so courageous. She's such a brave person; please let her be successful and unharmed in accomplishing her mission. Bring her home safely: we need her.*

We tried to have as normal a day as possible. Hans-Dieter took Ralfie upstairs to tidy up the toy cupboard, which they'd discovered soon after we'd arrived on the farm. Marlenchen toddled about getting under my feet and touching everything within her reach. I also took her upstairs and asked Hans-Dieter to find something to keep her occupied.

The day went by uneventfully and no soldiers came to bother us; but late afternoon, quite unexpectedly, Frau Ruch called to see that all was well with us. Our thoughts were with our mother all through the day and when we said our evening prayer, we prayed for her safety.

Thursday went by and Friday came: mother's second day away. We anxiously awaited her return. There wasn't a minute in the day that we didn't follow her path in our minds or talk about her. Where could she be now? Had she arrived safely in Stolp? *Would she be successful in obtaining that all-important, valuable permit?* But we could find no answers to our questions, no way to communicate with her. That day too passed uneventfully and nothing untoward happened to cause us anxiety.

Once a group of Polish soldiers stopped in the entrance to our yard. They stood there smoking and laughing, and then, to our relief, went on their way. The night was also peaceful and we were able to sleep undisturbed in our beds.

The next day was Saturday. Surely mother would come home that day, but who could tell? We could only wait. The house was spotless and mother would be pleased we'd managed so well.

And so it went on day after day. There was nothing we could do; we had to be patient and hope all was well with our mother.

On the morning of the sixth day, still no mother, and I was secretly seriously worried. Would she ever return? Had something happened to her? Had she been captured as I was, or abused so badly by soldiers she was too ill to walk? She didn't have our little Marlene with her for her safety as before. The full horror of responsibility, not only for myself but for my three siblings, was starting to sink in. Was I capable of looking after them permanently, of saving them from the occupying forces? Could I on my own take them on that long, long journey back to Düsseldorf? I baulked at how horrendous that expedition could be. Yet there must have been other orphaned children who'd somehow managed to survive. I pushed those thoughts out of my mind – mother had just been held up.

Wednesday, 23 May 1945

On the seventh day Hans-Dieter and Ralf were busy on the farm. They wanted to tidy the barn once more, so they said, and I let them be. They needed to occupy themselves and I knew I could trust my big brother to keep an eye on his little one.

I played with Marlenchen. Upstairs, in the toy cupboard, we found some coloured wooden bricks and she tried to copy me and build a tower. When they fell down, the little girl shrieked with excitement and we repeated it again and again.

Suddenly I heard footsteps on the yard gravel. Soldiers? I grabbed Marlene and was ready to run to the attic. But then a shout from Hans-Dieter and Ralfie: 'Mother, mother you're home! Else, mother's back! We've waited for days!'

Out of the window I saw them hugging her and prancing around. Their gladness at her return made them delirious.

I rushed outside, Marlenchen on my arm, and stood there, watching the happy reunion of mother and her boys. With a voice choked with emotion, I said, 'Welcome home, dearest mother,' and promptly burst into tears.

'Don't cry, Else. I'm safe now and unharmed. Come, children. Let's go indoors. I have a lot to tell you; but first I must take off my coat and sit down: I'm mighty weary.'

Hans-Dieter and Ralf stood in front of her. I knelt at her feet and buried my face into her lap. 'Mother, dearest mother, I'm so glad you're home. I constantly feared for your safety.'

Later, with coffee in her hand, mother told us how frustrated she'd been. Again and again she was turned away from the office of administration and told to return the following day. When she asked how long she might have to wait for a permit, there was no answer, just a shrug of shoulders. Only one German girl worked in the office, but she had no answer. Sunday of course it was shut. And when she started for home, the weather was bad.

'All's well, Elslein, and now I'm here, back with you. I know you're burning to ask me a question, so fire away!'

'Mother,' I asked, 'please tell us – did you get a permit for us to leave Pomerania?'

All our eyes were on mother. She looked at the three of us, hugging our little sister, sitting on her lap. Slowly I saw a smile spread over her face and joyfully she cried, 'Yes, children! Yes, I got it! It's our most precious possession. We must guard it, because it's our passport to freedom and home.'

'When can we go?' Hans-Dieter asked. 'Tell us when it will be.'

'Soon, my child. Very soon. But we have a long journey before us and must prepare for it. We have to plan carefully, get provisions and advice, find a safe route. Be patient, children. We'll go. Our days in Pomerania are numbered: Düsseldorf and home await us!'

Chapter 38

Tree-Lined Road

30 May 1945

'Else, listen to me,' mother called from the kitchen. 'This evening, when the little ones are in bed, you, Hans-Dieter and I will sit round the table and make plans.'

'How exciting!' I exclaimed. 'It will bring our trip much closer and make it real!'

'Yes, Else, it will. We've spoken about it, but now it's near, we must plan every detail most carefully. I need suggestions, and Hans-Dieter, you must also be included in our discussion.'

The evening had turned chilly and mother lit a fire, making the room cosy.

She gathered paper, pencils and a map: 'Now let's work out a rough route.'

'Mother, must we walk all the way? What about trains to Stettin?'

'I don't know, Else. We must see what we encounter, gather information as we walk. People talk and we'll keep our ears open.'

'I'll be your scout,' Hans-Dieter announced, 'like Old Shatterhand in my books.'

'Exactly, Hans-Dieter. That will be most useful. Next we need a list of things to take and a way to carry them.'

'We all have knapsacks,' Hans-Dieter said. 'Even Ralf. I'm strong and it will be easy!'

Mother praised Hans-Dieter and promised she'd consider his suggestions.

'Of course Marlenchen must ride in the pram together with as much food as we can get for the journey. I've no pushchair for her and she can't walk any distance. Ralf can sit at the end when his legs tire. You must be fit, Else. With such a long journey behind you you're used to walking.'

'Yes, I am. I've done plenty of it during the last few weeks.'

'And your legs, Hans-Dieter – they're strong,' mother said. 'You're a young man and will manage the walk just as well as I can, don't you agree?'

'Yes, mother,' was his reply, 'but do tell us *when* we're going?'

'You're impatient, my lad,' mother laughed, ruffling his hair. 'Now listen. I've decided that if we work together, we'll aim at next Wednesday, as early in the morning as possible. I want to avoid attention to our leaving. It's best we just disappear.'

'But mother, people will wonder what's happened to us, won't they?'

'Yes, Else, they probably will. But for now we have more important things to discuss. We're soon coming into June. Days will be warmer, the sun stronger and nights shorter. Mind you, children, it's chilly out there tonight – just three weeks from midsummer! But it will be a pleasant walk, don't you think, Else?'

'Yes, mother.'

'We can stop whenever we're tired and treat the journey as a holiday – a hiking holiday – as we used to do with father before the war.'

'Oh mother, how well I remember those outings. What fun they were: picnics in fields, sitting in tall grass, warm sun shining down on us, paddling in the cool water of a shallow stream – you and father as well. Perhaps one day those happy times will return.' A big sigh escaped from deep inside me for a time long past.

Mother laid her arm on my shoulder. 'Don't let sad thoughts depress you. Just remember that at the end of our journey we'll be home in our own apartment with our own furniture and belongings – if our house on Neckar Street is still standing.'

'Mother, what about your friends?' I asked. 'Don't you want to say goodbye to them?'

'Dear child, there are few left. Either they're dead, or have disappeared in search of safety. Some, like you, were taken by the Russians; others left before the enemy arrived.'

'But you'll take your leave from Aunt Katrin? She'll be sad to lose us.'

'And so will I, Else. I can't imagine us meeting again. Her future's more uncertain than ours. Who knows what plans the Poles have for the Glowitz people? So many rumours, and what's the truth? In retaliation for Germany's crimes against the Polish, will every German be evicted, so Polish nationals can resettle Pomerania as their new homeland?'

'That's terrible, mother! Where are our people supposed to go?' I asked.

Mother shrugged. 'But you see now why it's so important for us to go as soon as possible?'

'Yes, mother,' we replied.

'When we leave here, will we be refugees?' asked Hans-Dieter.

'No, son,' mother answered. 'Refugees flee their homes to seek safety from persecution or political unrest. That's not us. We have a home to go to, so we're *not* refugees.'

'Oh, it's so exciting!' Hans-Dieter exclaimed, 'I can't wait to go. I'll be sad to leave my friends, but when I get back to Düsseldorf I'll soon find new ones.'

'And you, Else?' mother asked.

'Well, mother, I have few friends now. Gisela – my best friend – is dead. Sylvia von Voeltheim? Last I heard she was in Berlin. And now? As for schoolfriends, I've no idea where they are or what has become of them. I miss school: it's ages since I went. Perhaps, when we get home, I can return to my old Flora School, if it's still standing. What do you think, mother?'

She shook her head. 'Let's wait and see when we're home.'

'Even if I lose a year, I'll soon catch up with extra homework. I want to do well.'

'I know, Elslein, and I'm sure you will, but one step at a time. Don't think too far ahead. We'll leave and start the journey, and, God willing, survive it and reach home.'

The next day our preparations started. Mother assigned Hans-Dieter and me to return things not belonging to us to their rightful place; she, Marlene and Ralf walked to get more provisions from the farmer – anything he could spare. She'd been successful before and hoped her charm would acquire them again. We needed food to tide us over the first few days. After that we'd have to scrounge, beg or help ourselves from abandoned fields and gardens.

Wednesday, 6 June 1945

The long-awaited day of our departure arrived. I'd been awake for hours; in fact I felt I'd hardly slept. A few minutes before, the landing clock had struck two, yet I was wide awake, ready to get up. Was mother still asleep? Perhaps she'd also found it impossible to rest?

I'd decided to start a new diary. I missed my old one, a dear friend that had been with me since the beginning of the war. Somehow I'd lost it in the upheaval of the Russian army's arrival. Now I had only an old exercise book, but it would do, for want of anything better. At least I could record our journey home to Düsseldorf. I'd jot down our route: who knew – if we survived, I might one day tell my tale of a once-in-a-lifetime journey.

I'd knock gently on mother's door and if she was asleep and didn't react, I'd return to bed.

But she was awake and called me into her room.

'Else, why are you up so early? It's still night-time. Try to sleep.'

'I can't, mother. My mind's in a whirl. I'm so anxious to be on our way.'

'Come, Elslein, lie beside me. Try to rest just another hour: we need our strength. Then we'll both get up, have a *good* cup of coffee (I have a little just for this morning), and we'll both rouse Hans-Dieter and the little ones.'

I drifted back to sleep, in the comfort of mother's arms, but awoke with a start as, later, her hand touched my shoulder.

'Else, wake up: now it *is* time to get out of bed. We won't linger. I want to be away while it's still dark. Wash and dress quickly; then see how your brothers are managing. I'll care for Marlenchen.'

'What's for breakfast, mother?' I asked.

'I've prepared porridge, with water only, but there's a small jug of milk on the table and sugar in the basin. Divide it between the four of you.'

'But, mother, you can't go without; it's important we all have something – including you!'

I wrote in my diary:

> It's amazing how quickly we're ready. There's urgency in our action, showing how eager we are to get on our way. I was so busy rushing around, checking the rooms one last time, that the meaning of our imminent departure was nearly lost on me. Suddenly reality has hit me. Very soon we'll leave Glowitz and Pomerania for ever; and perhaps, over time, every unpleasant, ugly moment

we've endured during the past weeks and months will fade. A tremendous feeling of freedom overwhelms me. I dance for joy, and exuberantly run from one to the other of my dear family, hug and whirl them around. But mother puts a stop to my high-spirited performance.

'Enough, Else!' she admonishes me. 'We must be on our way.'

Marlene's in her pram, sitting high with most of our provisions stored underneath her mattress. She's safely strapped into her harness, or she'll topple out!

Ralf, proudly carrying his own little bag with blanket and change of clothing, stands beside me, holding fast to my hand.

Dieter's knapsack looks heavy. 'Whatever are you carrying, Hans-Dieter,' mother enquires, as she ties a large saucepan onto the side of the pram. 'I asked you to take only what's necessary. I hope you've remembered that. And have you packed your blanket?'

'Yes, I have!' Hans-Dieter answers. 'I can carry my bag easily.'

Suddenly I remember something. 'Mother, give me a minute please.'

'Don't be long, Else. We really must be on our way.'

'I won't!'

I come downstairs. Mother stops what she's doing and looks at me, dumbfounded. 'Else, what are you wearing? You intend to walk in your best silk dress? How suitable is that for a journey? It's not a party – you look absurd! Go upstairs immediately and change into something suitable. Take your dress if you wish; pack it into your knapsack – it's light enough – or leave it behind; that's up to you.'

I know better than to argue with mother. She's lenient in many ways but when she objects, we must obey without argument.

At last we were ready to leave. It was 4.30 a.m. and mother hurried us along. The first signs of dawn were visible in the east and, minute by minute the sky grew lighter. We walked out of the farmyard for the last time, through the white iron gates, shutting them firmly behind us. Mother led the way with Marlene in her pram, Hans-Dieter by her side, his precious possession, a Tyrolian hat, firmly on his head, a pair of sturdy boots on his feet, and his knapsack, looking far too heavy, on his back.

I followed, holding Ralfie's hand. 'I'm a big boy now,' he said. 'I'm going to march all the way to Düsseldorf. It's a long way, isn't it?'

'Yes, my darling, it is – a very long way. But don't worry, Ralf; we'll manage it. If we have to, we'll help each other. It's a wonderful outing for us with many things to see. You and Hans-Dieter will learn a great deal: all very useful when you go to school.'

A cheerful little group, we set off on our great adventure.

Round the corner and down a slope we went, looking for the last time at Aunt Friedel's shop, now empty and rundown. I'd always liked Aunt Friedel and her husband, Uncle Ernst, and loved to visit their small village shop.

Where were they now? One day they were there; then, without warning, they'd disappeared – like so many others. Now the villagers would say the same of us. I remembered the fuss they'd made of me in the forest – they'd risked everything to smuggle me home.

At the bottom of the slope I'd stood among a group of women, herded together and watched over by Russian soldiers – their aim to march us to Stolp, and further. How many were now in labour camps somewhere deep inside Russia? How many still alive? What joy to think I'd managed to escape! The thought of their fate sent shudders through my body.

Mother guessed what was going through my mind. 'Else, don't think back,' she said. 'Look forward to your future, and perhaps some good will come out of the suffering you endured. It will help you grow up, teach you perceptiveness and tolerance towards humanity.'

'Yes, mother, but it's not easy to forget.'

As we reached the high street at the end of the slope, I looked for the last time at the ancient arch and driveway leading to the estate. Never again would we walk through that arch: those days, and the Puttkamer family lay in the past. But we would not forget them.

We turned right. I'd lived in Glowitz for three years, every winter the same. In my mind the snows lay deep and our young ghosts hurtled downhill on our toboggans. Village children's laughter echoed down the street, however bitter the weather.

We passed the bank, now empty, windows shattered, doors on broken hinges thumping against the wall. What would become of it? Would it be a bank again? Past the dead mayor's residence, his lovely house empty and neglected. A ghostly bang still hung in the air – the shot that ended his life.

As we reached the bottom of the hill, we crossed the former railway line. I couldn't help myself: my eyes wandered along it. There, hidden from view, stood the little hut where a drunken Russian soldier had wanted to violate me. I shuddered. I now knew what would have happened had I not managed to escape.

Forget it, Else. Put it to the back of your mind. Those days are gone and I hope never to return to this place.

A schoolfriend had once lived in the now derelict station house. Her father, the station master, a kind, friendly man, had allowed us to let the barriers down when a train approached. Where were they now? I hoped her family had reached safety.

The road to Stolp that ran through the small village of Klenzin further along the former railway line was a typical Pomeranian tree-lined road, trees close together on either side – like most of the roads we'd marched on with our Russian captors. Once a well-known landmark in Pomerania and well tended by local people, the roads were now littered with debris. Deep potholes – a legacy of heavy tanks – made walking difficult for mother as she pushed the heavy pram.

The sun shone hot from a cloudless sky – too hot – as we trekked along, seeking shade under the ancient trees. Long and straight, shimmering with a heat mirage, the road disappeared into the distance, into an unknown future. It took me away for ever from Glowitz and childhood and innocence.

On and on we walked. Marlene, sitting in her pram, grew miserable and wanted to get out. That wasn't always possible – her little legs couldn't keep up with us, and we had to push on. Ralf and Hans-Dieter were older and made of sterner stuff. Ralf could rest at times on the bottom of the pram, but my tough young brother Hans-Dieter ploughed on with never a long face or a grumble.

'Mother, do you think we'll get as far as Stolp this evening?' asked Hans-Dieter.

'No, son,'she answered. 'That's too far, but soon we'll come to a farm, which I saw on my way home. It's just before a village called Zedlin. When I went to get our permit, I stopped there and asked the farmer if we could stay a night in his barn and he agreed. Not long now and we'll be there.'

'Good!' Hans-Dieter exclaimed. 'My legs are tired and want a rest.' But then he added, 'I'm not!'

When at last we reached the farm, mother told us to wait outside while she went to tell the farmer we'd arrived. He was expecting us and pointed in the direction of a barn where we could spend the night. Mother beckoned us and we gladly followed her. The farmer's wife had also seen us and came over with a small jug of milk and a bag of potatoes.

'Something towards your evening meal, Frau Hopp. Please take care when you light a fire: the hay in the barn's very dry and could easily burn it down.'

'We'll be careful,' mother assured her. 'Please don't worry.'

We settled in. Hans-Dieter and I, with Ralf's help, made a cosy bedspace for the five of us; mother lit a fire on rough earth to cook potatoes in their skins. We'd enjoyed them like that many times with a sprinkling of salt and a small blob of butter. That day we had to forget the butter, but it wasn't necessary. We were very hungry and our simple meal tasted delicious. For a short while Marlene was allowed to run and stretch her little legs, but she soon tired and, after a drink of warm fresh milk supplied by the farmer, settled down in her snug haybed.

Dieter and Ralf were allowed to stay up a little longer, both eager to explore the farm. They asked if they could see the two carthorses in their stable, and the farmer, who loved children, gave them each an apple to feed to the huge animals.

But then it was the boys' turn to settle. Mother sent them for a quick wash under the yard pump. 'This water's icy!' Hans-Dieter grumbled. 'Mother, can't you heat some for us?'

'Dieter, you surprise me,' she answered. 'A tough lad like you? Be an example to your brother; he complains less than you do.'

'Can we stop here another day?' my big brother asked when he returned. 'It's nice and my legs are *so* tired!'

'No, son, that's not possible. Early tomorrow we must be on our way. As you well know, we've a long way before us. Your legs will be ready to carry you after a night's rest. Remember, the more you walk, the tougher and stronger they'll get. In a few days, they won't ache any more.'

Mother was invited to join the farmer and his wife for a little chat and an exchange of views after the children and I had settled for the night. She told us next morning that the farmer had given her a lot of good advice, discussing in detail the quickest route to Stargard, where we might perhaps be able to catch a train for Stettin, or even Berlin.

Thursday, 7 June 1945

Next morning we awoke early, eager to be away. Mother had prepared a special breakfast for us. She announced we needed it to build up our day's strength.

There was a boiled egg for each of us that the farmer's wife had given her. From her knapsack she took a loaf of bread and a few slices of smoked ham, which she divided among us. It was a feast fit for a king!

After we'd eaten and removed all traces of our presence from the barn, we were ready to go.

As we were leaving, the farmer came across to wish us a safe journey. They'd pray for us, he said, and hoped we'd find our Düsseldorf home undamaged. He shook mother's hand and presented her with a large salami sausage. 'Here you are, Frau Hopp; you'll find it useful on your journey.'

As mother thanked him, his wife joined us. In her hand was a small rag doll, which she gave to Marlene, and a bag of apples for Hans-Dieter and Ralf. She gave me a little box, lined with hay, which contained five brown new-laid eggs. 'There,' she said with pride, 'you all have something to remember us by.'

Mother was deeply touched; she knew how scarce food was for everyone, but the farmer wouldn't hear of a refusal. So she accepted the precious gifts. Marlene, who had been very quiet, now gurgled, 'Mama, a baby, my baby! I must take her home too!'

We waved to the farmer and his wife at the farmyard gate – two very kind people, generous in their hospitality.

'Well, children,' mother smiled brightly at the four of us, 'we're on the road again. The weather's lovely and walking should be easy after our good sleep.'

'Which way are we walking today, mother?' I asked.

'Well, we won't stay in Stolp when we get there; just look for the road to Schlawe, which I hope we'll reach by midday.'

Eventually we entered Stolp. To our horror, the damage done to that beautiful city during the ferocious fighting only a few weeks before was heartbreaking. As I looked at the many places I knew, some burned to the ground, memories came crowding back, threatening to overwhelm me. I'd spent happy times at school among my many friends, but what had become of them? I thought of the Schröter family, their daughter Anneliese, and Herr Schröter in his sinister black SS uniform. I'd never liked him – he'd frightened me when I'd boarded with them. *That uniform will be no good to him now. Are they still alive?* I thought of my grilling when the Russians thought my family were Nazis; perhaps the Schröters had managed to escape in time.

The beautiful avenue, flanked by graceful lime trees and beeches, with elegant shops on the right, hotels and restaurants on the left, was no more. Every building was destroyed and the centre of the road piled high with rubble. Daily I'd walked that street from the railway station to the city on my way to school. 'Look, mother, even Café Reinhardt's gone. Do you remember the day you treated me to coffee and delicious cream cake?'

'Yes, Else, sadly those days are gone. Perhaps they'll come back one day – who knows?'

'Mother, can we not stay awhile and look around? I'd love to know if that magnificent building, the town hall, has survived. Also the grandiose department store. I loved the old-fashioned lift with iron gates – such fun to ride up and down – although the attendant wasn't amused!'

But we had to walk on; I knew we'd never again return to that lovely part of Pomerania. Who knew – perhaps one day the city would rise again to become proud Little Paris?

Walking quickly, we soon left Stolp and were on the way to Schlawe.

'Where from there?' Hans-Dieter asked.

'We'll pass Schlawe, and then look for a pleasant, peaceful spot for lunch.'

'And after that, Mother?' I wanted to know.

'The next town will be Koslin. I don't know if we can manage to get that far, but we'll find a suitable place for the night. There should be a farm or cottage to give us shelter.'

Marlene was very happy with her doll. I smiled at her talking to it like a real baby. Hans-Dieter and Ralf amused themselves, finding interesting objects in ditches by the wayside. Many people, fleeing from the Russian advance, had earlier discarded surplus luggage that delighted the two boys, but mother was adamant that nothing should be picked up. 'They don't belong to us,' she said. 'Leave them. We have enough!'

Outside Schlawe we found a pretty setting among some trees and stopped for lunch.

Mother had saved potatoes from the previous evening and, together with a slice of ham,they made a nourishing meal. Water had to quench our thirst, but a rest from walking was welcome. The boys ran about investigating their surroundings, while Marlene toddled along on unsteady little legs, delighted with her freedom.

But after a while mother urged us to go. 'It's time to walk on. The day's young but we must get within sight of Koslin.'

Mother noticed a deserted, tumbledown cottage in a field, a small distance from the road. She and Hans-Dieter went to investigate and returned, saying it was badly ruined and far too dirty to live in. But mother, ever the optimist, declared we could clean it sufficiently with some effort to accommodate us just for the night. There was well water and mother, with her magic touch, soon had a fire burning brightly.

'What can we have for supper?' asked Hans-Dieter anxiously. 'I'm so hungry.'

'So am I!' added Ralf.

'Don't worry, children. I won't let you starve. I've planned to make soup. You, Hans-Dieter, and Ralf fill my shopping bag with as many nettles as you can; be quick about it!'

'But mother, they'll sting us!'

'You've gloves in your knapsacks – they'll stop the nettles stinging. Now go. If you're as hungry as you say, you'll hurry!'

'Mother, what can I do,' I asked, watching her put our water-filled saucepan on the fire.

'In the pram find a turnip, a few carrots and some potatoes. Peel and add them to the pot. Then cut off five slices of salami sausage to add to the vegetables. After that, please see how the boys are managing.'

'All right. If they've found enough nettles, I'll wash them ready to add to the veg. I've never tasted nettle soup. What does it taste like?'

'I remember my mother cooking it during the last war when I was little. We also had hard times and had to be inventive. I survived, and so will you.'

Soon the boys returned with nettles in their bag. 'Is that enough, mother?' Hans-Dieter asked.

Mother laughed. 'Yes, you've done well. Our meal will be ready soon.'

And it was! It tasted good with plenty to go round for all of us.

After our meal, mother asked Hans-Dieter to find something to sweep the floor. 'A branch will do – better than nothing, as long as it rids the floor of all this dirt.'

'I'll go and look!'

'Oh dear,' muttered mother, running her hands through her hair and staring at the mess. 'How will we manage day after day? It's tragic to put you through all this. It makes me despair. I fear, when we reach home – *if* we reach it – we'll be so dirty and unkempt no one will want to know us.'

Mother's so distressed, I thought, *yet there's little cheer to lighten her load. Perhaps a night's sleep will make her more positive. Today's only our second day, and we have hundreds of kilometres before us. Will she survive it? She's had a lot to contend with.*

In a hut adjacent to the cottage, Hans-Dieter discovered an old but solid wooden door. When he showed mother, she told him to brush it down with straw from a pile in the corner.

Later he and Ralf, wrapped in their blankets, shared the door to sleep on.

Marlenchen had her pram mattress and mother and me? We took some of the straw; slightly damp, but needs must.

The boys and our little girl were soon asleep. It took longer for mother and me to nod off. We couldn't relax: too many worries crowded our minds and prevented us from sleeping.

After a chat, I said, 'Goodnight, mother. Try to rest easily. Thank you for all you do for us. We're a responsibility. I wish I could do more to lighten your load.'

'Bless you, child. Your help is everything. Where would I be without you?'

Friday, 8 June 1945

How glad I was when at last the night was over. I was cold and my whole body ached. I looked across at mother, but she'd gone. Then I heard her moving about outside. Was she stoking the fire? She must have longed for a cup of coffee, but there was none.

I tried to be cheerful. 'Morning, mother. Are you well? Did you have any rest?'

'Oh, Else, I wish I could say I did. No, my night was uncomfortable and freezing cold. I was longing for morning. Anyway, I've had a thorough wash. Cold water! It made me shudder, but revived me and I feel a lot better. Go and try it, Else. You'll soon know what I mean.'

'Is there any food left for breakfast?'

'Not much, but sufficient for one meal. I know how hungry the boys will be, and Marlene – that little girl would be satisfied with dry bread, but I still have a little butter for her.'

'Yes, mother, and I'll share my portion with you. Don't pretend you're not hungry; you especially must have food inside you. You're our captain and your crew needs you!'

As I sat by the fire, drinking a cup of boiling water and chewing a dry piece of bread, I asked mother how far she hoped we'd walk.

'Else, I've studied the map from the Glowitz farm – thank goodness we have it! We'd be very lost without it.' She looked up. 'I've decided to avoid the town of Koslin and take country roads to Belgard instead. I hope we can get there by late afternoon.'

'Why do you wish to avoid the towns, mother?'

'I think country roads will take us through small villages selling provisions: we need some urgently. I must get milk for Ralf and Marlene; also you and Hans-Dieter must have a proper drink.'

'And you, mother,' I reminded her.

'But I wish to avoid populated areas where there might be soldiers. They'd stare at us and ask about our route. We also need a place to stop for a day or two – where I can heat some water. I need to wash our clothes. It's a blessing Marlenchen's dry: it saves a lot of hard work.'

'I'll help you, mother; you know that.'

'Bless you, child. I hope we'll find another kind farmer who'll offer us the use of his barn. Then, when we've reorganised our belongings and obtained food for the next few days, we'll walk with renewed resolve and determination to reach Stargrad.'

'Yes, mother, and perhaps there'll be a train to take us to Berlin and the West. That would be wonderful!'

'It certainly would, Elslein. Let's wait and see.'

Our walk that day was long and wearying. At midday mother divided among the children the small amount of remaining food. The fields we walked through were barren and, anyway, most vegetables were not ready for picking. I was incredibly hungry but knew mother must feel the same.

Suddenly we saw a large farm taking shape in the distance.

'Look, mother! Would that do? We could ask if we might stay a night or two?'

'Yes, Else, I'll go. It's a quiet place, sleepy and unspoilt. Stay here with Hans-Dieter and Marlene. I'll take Ralf: a little lad might soften the farmer's heart.'

Mother rapped on the door repeatedly till it was eventually opened by an old lady, dressed completely in black.

'Yes?' she squinted at mother and little Ralf. 'What do you want? Who are you?'

Mother explained and asked for shelter as politely as she could. The farmer – perhaps her son – joined the old lady and after a lengthy discussion agreed to let us stay in a disused stable away from the rest of the farm. There was plenty of dry clean straw, more than sufficient for our needs. In the yard a pump would give us fresh water and there was space to build a fire.

When mother asked to buy food for her family, the farmer promised to see what they could spare and asked her to come back later. But when she returned, he was less willing to sell any food; he didn't want payment in reichsmark.

'What can we do with it?' he asked. 'That money's useless. Soon we'll only have Polish zloty. If you want food for your children, pay with something other than money.'

'What do you want?' mother asked.

'Anything of value; you must have something? Jewellery, rings, watches . . . but not money – it's no good to us.'

Mother returned, dejected.

'Else, stay with the children, I'll join you shortly.'

She took her coat and sat in a corner of the barn. With her nail-scissors she unstitched part of the seam and removed a tiny clothbag, containing one of her precious rings. I saw what mother was doing but didn't comment. She put the ring on her finger, gently kissed it and whispered, 'Forgive me, Willy. I need to do this – your ring will help us survive.'

Then she took a large bag, beckoned me to join her and together we returned to the farmhouse.

Mother's ring earned us many provisions. The old lady was thrilled and ordered her son to give us all the food we could carry, including a large jug of fresh milk.

'Come back, before you leave,' she called after my mother. 'We'll give you plenty to take on your way.'

Chapter 39

Unseeing Eyes

Tuesday, 12 June 1945

We stayed on that farm three days and four nights. The weather was kind, although it was cold at night, with a heavy dew each morning that covered fields and meadows and dripped from bushes and trees like raindrops. Yet once the sun warmed the earth, every drop soon disappeared.

Rested, we felt ready to walk again. We'd tidied our belongings and mother had washed our dirty clothes and dried them, spread over bushes or fresh patches of grass. The farmer brought us more provisions as he'd promised and these, added to our earlier supplies, gave us plenty for our journey. Of course, the ring mother had given in payment was far more valuable than any amount of food we received in return. But we were glad, for now at least, we didn't have to go hungry.

When I awoke that last morning, I was surprised to see mother washed, dressed, and preparing our breakfast.

She saw I was awake, and smiled and greeted me. 'Good Morning, Else. Did you sleep well?'

'Yes, mother, but I'm hungry. Can we eat soon?'

'Yes, dear, as soon as you're ready we can eat. Tell me, do you know what date it is today? I've lost all sense of time.'

'Today's Tuesday 12 June, the day we're leaving for Stargard, isn't it?'

'Yes, it is. Wake the boys and send them to wash under the pump; that will soon drive sleep from their eyes. After they've put on their clothes, I want them to stow their blankets in their knapsacks. Will you see to Marlenchen, give her a wash and help her dress? Then, when all's done, we'll have breakfast and get on our way.'

'How far's it to Stargard?' Hans-Dieter asked. 'Will you ask the farmer, mother?'

'If I see him, I will, but however far it is we must go there. Don't let's panic – we'll reach it; if not today, then tomorrow.'

The day was overcast and grey. No sunshine, but at least it was another day without rain. There was a chill in the air; unlike June weather. We were glad of our overcoats and, walking briskly, they kept us warm.

We waved to the farmer, working in the yard, but the old lady was nowhere to be seen.

We passed many villages on our route; here and there, an isolated farm, surrounded by fields. There were small copses, densely wooded, offering cool shade to grazing animals during hot summer days. Most of the fields lay neglected and barren, with only a few showing tended summer crops.

When we tired, we sat at the roadside, refreshing ourselves with drinks of cool water and milk for the young ones.

Late afternoon we saw houses on the horizon and tall chimneys belching smoke. Could that be Stargard? Only one way to find out – we had to ask someone.

A man on a bicycle stopped, seeing us hesitate, and asked if we were lost.

'Not really lost,' mother replied. 'We wondered if the town ahead could be Stargard?'

'No, Madam, that's Belgard. Stargard's much further. Tell me why you wish to go there? There was a lot of fighting in the town; even now, there's much unrest. I'd strongly advise against your going there with your children, unless it's absolutely unavoidable.'

'We need to go to Berlin,' mother answered. 'We were told trains went from there.'

'No, madam, no trains go to Berlin. How would they get there? They couldn't cross the Oder River – all the bridges are down. Trains go only as far as this side of Stettin, but that's not suitable if you want to go to Berlin. Must you go there? Berlin's in a bad way; there's still fighting and active resistance in the centre. Do you live there? The city's in chaos; who knows what awaits you if you go there!'

'We need to go to the West; Düsseldorf's where we live, so we must go through Berlin.'

'You may be right, but not through the city. Make your way to Küstrin. There's supposed to be a pontoon bridge to cross the Oder. You'll be in the Russian sector again, so take care. From Küstrin, walk south of Berlin, through Potsdam to Brandenburg. Keep to the outskirts – it's the safest way.'

'Thank you for your advice; I'm most grateful.' mother turned to go, but then paused. 'Can I ask you one more question? We can't go much further today. You don't know of a place we can shelter for the night? The children are very tired now.'

The man smiled. 'Come with me. My house is big enough for all of you for one night. It's not grand, but you'll be made welcome. My wife and I have one spare room, but it's large and you'll find it warm and comfortable.'

'Oh, thank you. You're so kind!' Mother was relieved. 'I hate imposing on you and your wife. Will she mind?'

'It's no trouble. By the way, my name's Arno Helmer.' He leaned over his handlebars to shake mother's hand. 'And my wife's name is Martha. Come now; it's only a short way home.'

Mother was deeply touched to receive such kindness. How obliging people could be! Perhaps the children – or mother's incredible courage – touched their hearts. It boosted our morale and provided an incentive to carry on when spirits were low and the long journey threatened to overwhelm us.

When we arrived at Arno Helmer's house, he introduced us to his wife. Martha's greeting was friendly, her welcome genuine. 'My dear lady, you're walking alone with your children? Where are you going?'

Mother introduced us. She explained that we wanted to reach western Germany and, as the railway tracks had been removed by the Russians, we had to walk.

'You're very brave, Frau Hopp,' stated Frau Helmer. 'I wish you a most successful return to your home. But meanwhile, please prepare a meal for your children: I offer you the use of my kitchen.'

The two ladies, mother and Frau Helmer, delighted in each other's company. They had a lot to talk about and it was good to see mother conversing with someone her own age.

It was an early night for us youngsters. The two boys were worn out. They'd walked since early morning and Marlene, having had a slice of bread dipped in hot milk with a little sugar, was happy to sleep. She'd also walked a few times during the day. Her little legs were weak and mother worried that by sitting in the pram too long she'd lose their use. We encouraged her to walk as much as possible, if only for a few minutes at a time.

Mother spent the evening in the company of Herr and Frau Helmer. She'd tell me in the morning any important information I should also know.

We had a wonderfully comfortable night in a real bed, cuddled up tight, lying toe to toe. We didn't mind. That big bed easily accommodated the five of us and, eventually, after a lot of twisting and turning, amidst fits of giggles, we all settled down.

Wednesday, 13 June 1945

Very early next morning we said goodbye to our generous hosts and again continued our long journey. Mr Helmer advised mother on the most suitable route: to the river Warthe and later to Küstrin. There he said was a pontoon bridge over which we could cross the river Oder.

The world was quiet, and at such an early hour it was still cold. We shivered and jumped up and down to warm ourselves.

'Come, children. Let's stride out,' mother chivvied us along. 'While we march, we won't feel cold; the sky promises a lovely day. Soon the sun will come out and warm us.'

'You know, mother,' Hans-Dieter said, 'I'm getting used to sleeping in different places. It's fun, isn't it?'

'Well, Hans-Dieter,' mother answered, 'it may be fun for you but for my part I wish this journey was over. I'm longing to get home to Düsseldorf.'

'So am I,' I added. 'I can't get there soon enough. My shoes are falling apart; they won't last much longer, and then I'll have to walk barefoot.'

As the day wore on, we'd still not reached the town of Driesen on the river Netze. Hans-Dieter started to grumble and Ralf joined in; Marlene wanted to get out and walk. She'd grizzled on and off all day. Finally mother lost her temper.

'Come, mother,' I said. 'Let's try to find shelter for the night.'

'Yes, child, I think that's what we have to do. But it won't be easy. The land's sparsely populated and all houses we've passed look neglected and uncared for. If we see a place that looks promising, we must knock and ask for a resting place. Perhaps we'll be lucky again.'

Once more we approached an isolated farm and asked the farmer if we could spend a night in his barn. Once more mother built a fire where it was safe, and again she cooked potatoes in their skin, which we ate for our evening meal. We seemed to live on potatoes in their skin – what a blessing we all liked them!

Friday, 15 June 1945

The country roads we walked were mostly devoid of people; often we felt as if we were the only living beings on earth, and it was a strange and eerie feeling. It took two long days of walking before we reached the town of Driesen. Now we were back in the Russian zone. There were no frontiers as such: one minute we were in the Polish sector and then, quite suddenly, we'd enter the Russian zone. As yet, on our walk, we'd seen only a few soldiers passing us, mostly on motorcycles. It had sent shivers down my spine and once again I experienced the awful fear that tied my inside in knots. But the soldiers didn't molest us. They smiled and waved. Any fear we might have felt had been groundless.

We went down to the river's edge and watched the gentle waters flowing by. It wasn't a large river, but fishing boats, upended, lay on a narrow strip of beach. Dotted here and there were fishermen's huts and one of them had a wide-open door.

Dieter and I ran to look inside. It was fairly clean and almost empty: fishing tackle, rods and nets were stored in a corner.

'I think, children, this is where we'll spend the night. It will do us fine and I doubt anyone would object to us being here. Hans-Dieter, remember you and Ralf mustn't touch any equipment. It belongs to someone else – please respect that.'

Mother sent the boys off to find driftwood, and told them to be quick. She, in the meantime, searched for a place to build a fire.

The boys soon returned, carrying plenty of wood, more than was needed.

'Well done, you two, 'mother called out. 'Now take the potatoes from the bucket, go down to the river and thoroughly wash them. I'll cook them in their skin with a slice of salami and we'll have a tasty, satisfying evening meal.'

Saturday, 16 June 1945

That day we made an early start. We wanted to try to reach Küstrin if possible.

My mind was in turmoil. We were walking along the river Netze, and twice Russian jeeps and lorries had passed, driving in the opposite direction towards southern Germany. Soldiers leant over the tailboards, shouting and singing, drinking from bottles and waving them in the air. They shouted to us as they passed, 'Woman, Germany finished; war finished; everything finished!'

'Mother, what do they mean? The war's been over for some weeks now.'

'I know, child,' mother answered me. 'The fighting here must have gone on longer than in our part of Pomerania. Thank God we've been spared; we must hope the destruction and bloodshed have at last come to an end.'

On our way along the river we could see much evidence of wilful damage.

'There's been a lot of fighting here,' mother declared. 'Look, Else. Every house standing has been wrecked. The rest are razed to the ground.'

'And only tree stumps are left. Everything's destroyed.' I looked around. 'Where have the people gone? Instead of rejoicing, the streets are completely empty.'

'I think, Else, this must have been the site of a fierce battle.'

I wrote in my diary:

> We creep on in silent shock. The landscape's desolate and debris-strewn, around us a revolting stench of decay and rotting flesh. Wagons, tipped over, lie on their sides in mud with horses still attached, legs in the air, bodies bloated. Flies everywhere, and we swat them. Scattered over the scarred battlefield are corpses of dead soldiers, all of them German. Who will bury them? Large birds fly overhead. Will the men ever be given a resting place, or will they become the feast of vultures and scavengers? The Russian dead have been removed for burial by their comrades, while any German soldier who survived the carnage would have been taken prisoner and marched away to God knows where. Bomb craters are everywhere. I dare not venture near for fear of what I might find. This battle could only have taken place a short while ago. In Glowitz the war was declared over at the beginning of May, but here it appears to have lingered on and on.

> 'Watch the children, Else,' mother whispers. 'Keep them away from the worst of this scene of horror.' She squeezes Ralf into the pram beside Marlene and pulls the hood over them. Hans-Dieter stands beside me, his face white, eyes glazed. Yet he can't look away . . .he's mesmerized by the horror of it all. I take his hand. Come away, little brother. Don't look any more

> The tragedy makes me weep. Tears of sadness roll freely down my cheeks, each a droplet of sorrow for an unknown father or son. Father, dear father, is this also *your* fate?

> Yet there, in front of me, I see a German soldier lad, so young; probably about sixteen. He lies in the grass at the side of the road. As Hans-Dieter has fled for the protection of the pram, I stare down at him: he reminds me of the three women I'd been made to look at. His eyes are open; a surprised look contorts his face. With unseeing eyes he stares up at me, pleading. Death came too suddenly for him: he was unprepared for it.

I notice his boots, still attached to his legs, and want them. He wants me to have them . . .

'Else, come away.' Mother's at my side.

'Mother, his boots – to replace my broken, worn-out shoes. Can you remove them?' I croak.

'Else, no!' She stares down in horror; then looks at my feet. She hesitates and then bends down. I see it takes all her courage to touch him, all her strength to pull them from the stiff legs. I want to help her, but can't move. I look from his huge staring eyes to my poor mother, my dear mother, struggling away for my sake. Bitter tears run down her face.

They're off – one, then the other. I try on a boot. It's too large. I must find something to make it fit – I remember a petticoat I stuffed in my knapsack. I take it out, sitting beside my dead friend – what's his name? I tear it into strips; press each tightly into the boots; stand up and try them again. 'Look, mother. They fit beautifully.'

Poor soldier boy! Too young to die so far from home.

'Mother, is there an address in his pocket? We could contact his family. Tell them what happened to their son. Please, mother, please?'

Mother looks at me with disbelief. Without speaking she bends down again, and from the soldier boy's breast pocket withdraws a small wallet. I put out my hand, but she puts it into her bag. 'Later,' she murmurs. 'Now let's get away from this gruesome place.'

I glance again at the sad eyes and whisper a prayer for his soul and thanks for his gift. A young life frozen in death for eternity. Then I turn away and follow the others.

We came to the point where the river Netze flowed into the river Warthe. Mother's map showed us that somewhere nearby must be a town called Landsberg. Would some buildings still be standing? And would there again be people who would give us shelter? Fighting here couldn't have taken place many days before. And now we were told the war was over here as well. Could it be true? What a blessing that would be, after all the tragedy.

'If we do find a place to rest,' mother said to me, 'we can stay only one night. I don't like it here. We must try to cross the rivers Warthe and Oder and make our way to Küstrin. I'll feel much happier then – this is no place to be.' She wipes her forehead, still stressed by the episode of the young boy. 'Once we're in Küstrin, we'll be on our way to Berlin.'

Suddenly, to our surprise, a large army truck came up behind us and halted at our side. The driver, a Russian soldier, jumped down from his cab and approached mother. She in turn fumbled in her bag for our precious permit. I nervously stepped behind her. In halting

German he asked where we were going, and when she told him we wanted to cross the Oder to Küstrin, he pointed to his lorry and indicated we should get on and that he and his mate were willing to take us there. He made it clear to mother that Küstrin was still a long way away and the terrain we walked through was hazardous to her and the children.

Mother was reluctant and I begged her to refuse, but Ralf and Hans-Dieter were persistent and begged to be allowed to ride with the soldiers. Both men were smart and polite.

Mother looked at her tired children and consented.

We were helped up into the back of the high lorry and, with a little effort, the pram was also lifted in. The soldiers gave us a drink of water and found a square of chocolate for each boy and Marlene. They even offered mother vodka from their bottle but she turned that down with a smile and pointed to our little girl in the pram. I was still nervous of them and kept my distance. They, however, had hardly glanced at me, showing no signs of being interested in me.

When we approached the river Oder we saw another battle-scared town in front of us, which we assumed to be Küstrin. But on that side of the river? We hadn't expected that. Very carefully the soldiers negotiated a pontoon bridge across the river and once we reached the other side, they stopped, jumped down from the cab and opened the tailboard. They lifted mother and the pram down to the ground; then came Ralf, while Hans-Dieter and I clasped hands and both jumped together – we didn't need help.

The driver pointed in the direction of a small village and to a row of houses in particular, all empty and nearly all of them war-damaged and unsuitable to live in. But he wanted us to go there and promised to return later with milk and other food. I noticed for the first time that he furtively leered at me, his eyes trailing up and down my body. It frightened me, and how relieved I was when at last he climbed back into his lorry and drove off on the Berlin road.

'Mother, let's get out of here,' I pleaded. 'Look, there's so much damage; it sends shivers down my spine. Don't let's spend the night here; I don't want the soldiers to return, even if they have food for us.'

Mother looked at me. I knew what she was thinking: which was the best step to take. Hans-Dieter and Ralf were so tired and Marlene was in urgent need of attention.

'Come, children, just a quick walk away from here. It's not nice and we can't guarantee the soldiers will bring us food; we could wait around for nothing. We'll find a place to stay, but you two lads have to walk a little further until we're out of this village. At least we're on the other side of the rivers. They were a huge barrier for us. Now we must aim for Berlin.'

'Mother, why couldn't we stay with the soldiers?' Hans-Dieter asked. 'They'd have taken us.'

'They had to let us off, Hans-Dieter. Soldiers are not allowed civilian passengers: if they were caught they'd have been in trouble. They could only take us over the river – no further. To take us this far was a risk for them.'

'But mother, where *will* we go? If we stay in this hamlet, and they try to find us – but can't – they'll search from house to house in every direction. Who knows what damage they'll cause.'

'Oh, Else, what should we do? I'm at my wits' end,' mother muttered. 'I desperately don't know which way to turn. We must find shelter: if it's in a ruined house, as once before, it has to be. Let's walk now. Who knows, perhaps we might find just what we're looking for around the next corner.'

We walked in silence, mother deep in thought and I, desperately looking around, searching for somewhere suitable to stay the night. And then I saw it! A small undamaged house away from the road. It was inviting us to come nearer.

'Mother, would you like me to knock on the door?' I asked. 'I could enquire if there's a spare room to shelter us?'

'No, Else,' mother answered, 'I'll go myself and take Ralf. You stay with the pram and Hans-Dieter. I won't be long. I don't want you begging on my behalf. If the people can't put us up, I'll ask for a little food and drink of milk for Marlenchen and Ralf. Wait here!'

Mother and Ralf went down an untended garden path to the front door. They knocked sharply, hoping to be heard by the occupants. At first there was no response, but when mother knocked again, two young women opened the door a crack. We saw them talking and mother pointing at us. One woman disappeared inside but soon returned, beckoning mother to follow. We waited, and in a few minutes she reappeared, smiling, a sure sign she'd been successful.

'Can we stay?' I asked.

'Yes, Else we can. Follow me. I have a lot to tell you. There's a small garden house, very smart with sufficient room for us all. It's perfect – we'll be most comfortable.'

Mother hadn't exaggerated. The annex adjoining the main building had everything we needed. It was also private and self-contained. In the kitchen was a gas cooker and sink with running water. The bedroom had a huge double bed and sofa in the corner, and a second settee in the sitting room gave us ample room to sleep in comfort.

One of the young women knocked and entered, carrying a box with all kinds of foods and a jug of fresh milk. 'For your evening meal, Frau Hopp. Tomorrow, we'll bring you potatoes and a cabbage.'

Mother blossomed: she was speechless but so happy. I hadn't seen her like that for some days. The box contained the food we needed so urgently: a loaf of bread, butter a generous piece of smoked ham and, to mother's greatest joy, a small jar of real coffee beans.

'Where does all this food come from, mother?' I asked, getting more and more curious. 'What *is* this house?'

Mother tried to explain. 'Three young women are living here and, as far as I can gather, they're under the protection of three Russian officers. Most evenings, the girls tell me, the officers come from Berlin and spend the night here.'

'With the girls, mother?'

She nodded, 'Yes, Else, with the girls. You know what I mean: you've learned enough in the last few months. I suppose it's a question of survival for the young women, and in return for their services they get food, drink and everything they need – and to spare. Whatever they want, they only have to ask.'

'Perhaps they like it that way, mother; the lesser of other evils.'

'Also, in the evenings soldiers from Berlin drink and socialize here. Apparently the old 'Red Light' District of Berlin's ruined. There's nowhere for the soldiers, so they come here.'

'Well, *I* don't want to see them mother.'

'I understand, child, but they want company and know they can find it here.'

'But mother, what about me? Must I stay in hiding? I don't want anything to do with them: the thought of having to go with them makes me shiver – terrifies me. I feel sick just thinking about it. No, mother, I can't go through that again. War's over now; surely rape must also stop?'

'The girls have assured me, Else, you need not be afraid. You're quite safe, but they do suggest you keep out of the way when the soldiers – not the officers – come in the evenings. They arrive unannounced some evenings: other nights they stay away.'

I shook my head. 'All right, I'll be careful. I just hope the women *can* protect me.'

I could talk to mother of my private fears and anxieties; she'd answer truthfully and without hesitation any question I asked, however personal or intimate. Mother treated me as an adult: I'd shed the mantle of innocent childhood for ever, and it seemed from here on nothing, however abhorrent or loathsome, would shock me.

'But anyway, mother, we'll soon be gone again, won't we?'

'Yes, dear, we won't stay too long. But wherever we go, while we're in Russian territory, we must be on our guard.'

We stayed five nights and four days. Marlene was in heaven, out of her pram and running about, exercising her little legs. Hans-Dieter and Ralf were allowed to play in the gardens. The three women had no objections; and, with warm, sunny weather, both lads had a wonderful time exploring their new surroundings.

For dinner that first evening mother cooked potatoes and cabbage with ham, and when it was ready, we sat round a real kitchen table and enjoyed that simple meal. It tasted so good: after our frugal diet, nothing could have been more delicious.

Wednesday, 20 June 1945

Mother called me into the small lounge where she sat by an open window, catching a few rays of morning sunshine.

'Yes, mother?'

'Else, I want to talk to you. I think tomorrow we should leave this pleasant place. We've been here long enough to restore our energy; I'm restless and want to move on to Berlin.'

'Is it far, mother?'

'It's a fair way. We can't do it in one day, but that's unimportant; every step will bring us closer.' From a drawer mother took her precious map, which she unfolded on the table to show me the distance. 'If the sun shines, it will be good for travelling. We'll take the main road – make walking quicker. I Hope there won't be too much traffic.'

She pointed out various villages and towns we had to pass en route; but I could see it would be impossible to accomplish our journey to Berlin in one day.

'Mother, that poor map's looking very tattered. Still, we'd be lost without it. Show me the detail once more; I want to build a picture in my mind.'

'See here, Else. The first village we reach is Seelow, not too far from here. Then a long trek through uninhabited territory. Possibly marshland. I can't be certain, but the area around here is known for that. Wetlands start south-east of Berlin, and from there it's not far to the Spreewald. The river Spree runs through the Spreewald and branches off in many directions. There are no through roads: all traffic's conducted on waterways.'

'That's interesting, mother. I'd love to go there. Can we?'

'No, child, not this time. Perhaps in years to come. Who knows?' She smiled. 'Now let's study the map again. Can you see Müncheberg?'

'Yes.'

'Well, if we could get as far as there, it would be perfect. But somehow I doubt it. It appears to be too far, but we can try. We've enough food and drink to last us a few days.'

'Yes, and we might, with luck, find shops to supplement our provisions.'

'I hope I can still pay with reichsmark,' mother stated. 'If not, more of my precious jewellery will have to go.'

We didn't make it quite as far as Müncheberg that day, but managed to walk a fair distance and by late afternoon were worn out.

'Mother, can we stop soon,' Hans-Dieter complained. 'My legs are dropping off.'

'So are mine,' added little Ralf.

But, out of the blue, appeared a surprise!

An elderly man was cutting grass at the side of the road with a long-handled scythe. He waved to us with a friendly smile, which mother saw as an invitation to walk across and see if he knew of a place we could spend the night.

He lifted his cap and scratched his head.

After a moment he gave mother a toothless grin and announced, 'Ah, lady, I think I can offer you somewhere that may appeal to you and your little family. Over there', he pointed behind him. 'See the allotments?'

'Yes,' answered mother, screwing up her eyes.

'Well, one's mine. There's a garden hut where I keep my tools and where I rest. If you're willing, it will take you and your children over night.'

'It sounds wonderful,' was mother's immediate reaction. 'May I see it?'

'Certainly, lady. Come with me.'

Mother looked, and liked what she saw. And that's where we spent the night – rough, but adequate and quite sufficient for a makeshift night-shelter. We were far too tired to be fussy. By now we'd learned to sleep wherever we laid our heads.

Friday, 22 June 1945

Next morning it rained! The sky was grey and dark clouds hung low, almost touching the earth. Not a day on which to walk muddy country roads, towards Berlin. Hans-Dieter moaned, Ralf grumbled, Marlene cried and mother lost her temper.

I stepped in. 'Now listen,' I ordered the boys. 'No one can change the weather. Perhaps the sun will shine soon; until then we must occupy ourselves by tidying this hut. It's dusty with cobwebs everywhere. Now let's get rid of them. Is that clear?'

'Yes, Else,' chorused both boys.

Peace reigned, and after a while the owner, carrying a jug of fresh milk, knocked on the door.

'Here you are, lady. Thought your children might like a drink of milk, fresh from this morning's milking – wish I had more to offer you but sadly we're all short of food.'

'I understand. Thank you so much.'

Suddenly the sun did come out. It warmed and dried the earth and mother decided the day was still young enough for us to be on our way.

'How far will we walk this afternoon?' Hans-Dieter asked.

'We're all rested and daylight will be with us for some time yet. Let's see if we can reach Berlin by nightfall.'

While we were walking, mother talked about the beautiful city of Berlin she remembered from many years previously.

'Wait and see what an amazing place it is! There's the Brandenburg Gate and many museums, parks and gardens, wide tree-lined avenues – the most famous being the Unter den Linden. You must see for yourself: they're impossible to describe.

'But wasn't Berlin bombed?' I asked.

'No, child. How? Too far from England. the city's defences wouldn't have allowed enemy aircraft to enter Berlin's airspace.'

'But I thought the girls said –'

'Ah, the soldiers were talking about the suburbs; that's different.'

We were entering the suburbs of Berlin and there were signs of the most terrible devastation. I said nothing, although my thoughts ran in a different direction from mother's.

'Tell me, mother, when were you last in Berlin?'

'Let me see, Else . . . I think it was in 1934. You were only a little girl and I was expecting Hans-Dieter. We lived in Gerresheim, near Grandma and Grandad, when your father was accepted at the Engineering Academy in Zehlendorf here in Berlin. He stayed there twelve months and I visited him during that time, while Grandma looked after you.'

'I expect you enjoyed that, mother.'

'Oh yes, child. It was wonderful.'

As we continued, more and more destruction appeared the nearer the city centre we went. Mother was silent – it seemed she'd lost the power of speech; she was in shock. And then, on a rise in the road, we looked down on what used to be the city of Berlin. What confronted us? A place of ruination, with not a house or building unscathed, and the smoke of numerous smouldering fires covered the city like a dense brown fog as far as the eyes could see.

Unnerving silence lay over everything. Could this really be Berlin, our glamorous German capital?

'Is that where we're going, mother?' I whispered.

'Yes, darling, that's where we're going,' she said gruffly. 'We'll ask someone how to find the Potsdam road. No signposts, but people *must* know the right direction. I can't imagine where they live among this devastation, but somehow they still exist – God only knows how.'

I couldn't understand my mother. She'd been shocked and speechless only a short while ago, but now was again full of steely determination.

'Come, children. Let's forge ahead! We must find our way through this shocking graveyard and labyrinth of ruined buildings. The quicker we get out of here, the better. This is no place for us . . . this is *hell!*'

I tried to understand how she must feel, and my heart ached for her with deep sympathy. Mother had imagined the beautiful city still to be as she remembered it. But her illusion was shattered, like so many other things she'd had to come to terms with.

'Mother, please can we stop,' Hans-Dieter pleaded. 'I'm so tired and my legs ache.'

'And I'm hungry, Mama,' added Ralf. 'Can we eat soon?'

I led my two little brothers to the side of the road, where I knelt and took them in my arms.

'Now listen, you must be good today. Mother's sad. She doesn't quite understand what's happened to this world. She'll find a place where we can stop. We still have a little food left and perhaps we can get more. Please be patient, you two. Mother depends on us to be strong: I can't be, on my own. Do you understand?'

'Yes, Else we do, don't we, Ralf?'

'Yes, Hans-Dieter,' Ralf replied, 'but I'm still hungry.'

I smiled and thought to myself, *Poor little devil, he tries so hard to keep up with his elder brother.*

'Now you two, run back to mother and stay with her. We're soon entering Berlin and must remain close together. Everything's strange here and we don't want to lose each other.'

Dear God, I prayed silently, please help us to get out of this mess. I know we aren't the only ones. We all must fight to survive: it's not easy – but your help in this matter would be much appreciated.

Mother stood and gazed around. I saw the fear and horror in her thoughts reflected in her face and knew she was battling to decide what would be best to do. She desperately needed guidance, but there was no one in sight.

'Else,' she said, 'where should we go? Which way? I don't know where we are. The place is in ruins; fighting here must have been brutal. It's a miracle if anyone lived through it. Let's go on – there must surely be someone who can tell us the way to Potsdam.'

We came to what must have been a market square. There we saw humanity again: women scurrying like ants among the ruins.

'They're salvaging bricks, which they clean with hammers and chisels to reuse at a later date,' remarked a passer-by, as we watched. 'Everything has its uses. They call these women working in the ruins "rubble women" – heroes, every one! All over Germany they're rebuilding our shattered homeland. I do hope they erect a monument in their honour here in Berlin!'

'Where do these women live, mother?' I asked. 'So many of them, yet the houses are in ruins.'

'I know no more than you do, child.'

Shrugging her shoulders, she looked deflated and lost. My heart went out to her.

Chapter 40

Please Take This Piece of Paper

Friday, 22 June 1945

We skirted the city centre of Berlin until we reached Potsdam, one of the suburbs.

Suddenly in front of us was a wide-open space, a former park that might have belonged to the estate of a castle built for the emperor Frederick the Great in the early eighteenth century. Formerly, according to mother, there'd been a vast area of beautiful parkland and lakes here surrounded by well-tended lawns. Now trees and bushes were no more – cut down during the bitter winter and used for firewood. Flower beds trampled, the grass, no longer lush and green, brown and dried up. It was easy to believe nothing here could ever be put right again. But although the gardens were destroyed, they were crowded with people like us, travelling, trying to get home, wherever that was: the homeless, floating driftwood in no-man's-land.

There were wounded men, most likely ex-soldiers, but out of uniform and thanking God they were still among the living. Some had a spot where they could lie down alone, undisturbed, not wanting to be part of the crowd that swarmed about them. Only the children, absorbed in their own little worlds, had no cares as they shrieked and laughed and played games as only children know how.

Suddenly there was a hush – a bell was ringing a small distance away and everyone listened. Excitement gripped the mass of people as we heard the words *food*, *soup* and *kitchen*.

Mother stood staring, utterly bewildered.

A woman ran towards us. 'Come, woman!' she shouted. 'There's food available. That large building over there,' she pointed. 'That's where we get a meal. But we must be quick! The queue will be long and if you don't hurry, there'll be nothing left.'

With a speed I didn't know mother had in her, she gathered us together and, running, we followed her towards the long, long queue that stetched far down the street.

The building in front of us was, amazingly, undamaged. A huge building with many windows and a number of floors.

We joined the queue, which crawled so slowly. It took enormous patience to wait, while tummies rumbled noisily. We were a long way back. Hans-Dieter and Ralf got impatient and had to be reprimanded in mother's stern voice. 'Hush! Do you want to lose our place in the queue and go without supper?'

Two ladies in Red Cross uniform walked along the queue of waiting people. One was from the German Red Cross but the other must have been foreign. Her uniform was dark blue with various medals pinned to her blouse. They appeared to be searching for mothers with children, whom they called out of the line-up and pointed in the direction of the entrance door. Mother pushed Ralf and the pram to the outside, where they could be seen. Eventually they came level with us and, to our immense relief, chose us to leave the long queue and enter the building.

At the door we were met by a second nurse, who directed us through a long corridor, at the end of which, a large door stood open.

'That's where you go,' she told mother. 'At the food hall someone will guide you further.'

The hall was enormous: dozens of tables with long benches either side. Mother was shown where we could sit, a little distance from the main crowd.

'Stay with the little ones, mother, while Hans-Dieter and I see about food.'

'Thank you, Else.' She relaxed. 'I'm glad to sit down. The pram gets heavier to push the further we walk. Thank you for your help. You're both treasures!'

'Come, Hans-Dieter. Let's see what we can get.'

At the front of the hall a number of ladies handed out bowls of hot stew and chunks of freshly baked black bread.

'What do you need?' I was asked.

'We're five in the family,' I answered. 'My brother and I can take three portions now and come back for the other two.'

That's what we did, and when the five of us were seated at the table, the short prayer we said before we ate came from the depth of our hearts.

We also had a warm drink. Nurses walked around with jugs of milk for the children and pots of coffee substitute for grown-ups.

Mother slightly wrinkled her nose.

I looked at her and shook my head. 'Drink it, mother. It's better than nothing. Don't let people see what you think of substitute.'

'I know, Else. I'm not ungrateful. What we had this evening was delicious and most acceptable – an unexpected blessing in fact. We must be thankful for that.'

Marlene and Ralf were very tired and with little tummies full, both visibly sagged.

When a nurse came near and smiled at our two sleeping little ones, mother felt she could ask if she knew somewhere we could spend the night.

'Oh, yes,' she said. 'When you're ready, follow me.'

We walked along the corridor and up two flights of stairs – Hans-Dieter and mother lifted the pram, and I carried Marlene. 'Take the pram into the room I have in mind for you. You'll be safe if you keep your room locked.'

On the second floor was another passage with doors on either side. Nurse opened one with a key, which she handed to mother. Before us was a little room with bunk beds against the wall.

'You can sleep here. There will be more people needing sleeping places, but lock your door from the inside. You can return it in the morning. Don't leave any valuables unattended. Washrooms and toilets are down the corridor – don't go all at once. Either you or your daughter must stay behind.'

'How can I thank you?' mother said, a lump in her throat. 'We had warm food and drink this evening; now a bed for the night: truly a gift from heaven.'

'Don't mention it. It's what we're here for. Now I must go; I've many duties to perform.'

'Before you go, please tell me,' mother asked, 'what was this building?'

'The Royal Academy of Music and its renowned patron was the emperor himself.'

That night our little family of five had every reason to be happy. Mother's sense of humour returned and she amused us with a string of innocent little jokes.

What made that evening extra special, apart from our tummies being full of good nourishing food, was that we had a *real bed* to spend the night in and a room to ourselves, which we could lock for safety – no one to molest us. What more could we want? Only to close our eyes and sleep: we were all utterly exhausted. Sometimes, during the night, as if from a distance, I heard footsteps and voices in the corridor. Once or twice someone tried to open the door, but without success; yet all the sounds seemed far away and didn't present a threat.

Mother had Marlene's pram by her side; the little girl had almost outgrown it. It was all right for her to sit in but it had become far too small for sleeping.

'I ought to discard it,' said mother at first. 'Often it's more of a hindrance than a help. On the other hand, it has carried our possessions for the want of something better, and she still can't walk far. I'll hang on to it as long as necessary. It's become a good friend, helping out when needed.'

Saturday, 23 June 1945

Sadly we could stay only one night. During the day the building was closed and no one was allowed inside. Our breakfast the following morning was nourishing and substantial. There was porridge, bread and margarine with jam, a glass of milk for the boys and Marlene, and coffee substitute (with milk, but no sugar) for mother and me. It was a generous meal, and we hid the leftover bread in the pram to take with us. When mother handed back the key, she was told to return in the evening for a hot meal and bed for the night.

Mother and I talked it over, but both decided to remain in Potsdam no longer. The weather was warm and sunny, the sky blue and our feet were itching to continue on our way towards Brandenburg. It might be very hot by midday and we might need to rest somewhere in the shade. When mother asked the distance between Potsdam and Brandenburg she was told it was about 35 kilometres on country roads and a little less walking along the highway.

'What should we do, Else: highway or country roads?' mother asked.

'I'd prefer the country villages. There may be busy traffic on the main road and in the

Russian zone we could encounter military vehicles. I'm still wary – I don't trust them one bit. Also, mother, we might find a shop or farm to sell us fresh provisions. Anyway, does it matter if we can't make Brandenburg by this evening? It just means we need a night shelter again.'

'Very well, child. We'll do what you say.'

Bypassing Brandenburg, we walked through villages untouched by bombing or fighting. There was silence everywhere, with just occasional sounds of farmyard animals or a farmer carrying out his duties. Although the Russian army also occupied that part of Germany, we could see no soldiers. The land was peaceful, with few houses: meadows either side of the road gave uninterrupted vistas into the distance. Rapeseed had been sown here and there, and the plants already showed bright yellow flowers – a beautiful sight. We traipsed through countryside totally unspoilt and very tranquil. Once mother asked a farmer if she could purchase provisions. She wasn't turned away and was pleased to obtain potatoes, milk and a large home-made loaf, baked with very dark flour. We continued towards Magdeburg, although we knew it was impossible to get there before nightfall.

Hans-Dieter and Ralf had run ahead and suddenly came racing towards us.

'Mother, there's a lake in the distance. Come and look! We can see it over the meadows. It's not far. We could swim in the water!'

'Please?' added Ralfie. 'We're so hot!'

'All right, boys. Let's aim for it, then,' mother urged us on, 'I hope it's not too far; we'll just have to walk faster.'

We did and reached the distant lake before the sun went down. It was large, the water as smooth and clear as a mirror, unruffled in the evening sunshine.

'Oh mother, this is wonderful!' I exclaimed. 'Look at the conifer trees close to the water's edge. They'd make a marvellous shelter and the weather's good; couldn't we stay here a day or two?'

'Well, we do have our blankets and the ground's dry,' answered mother. 'We'll ask the boys, though I know what they'll answer! But let's consult them anyway; it will please them.'

Mother built a fire safely away from the trees. The boys found wood and fir cones, which burned brightly and gave off a sweet aroma. I took potatoes to the water's edge to wash in clear, pure water, ready for mother to boil them. That evening we had no butter or meat, but were hungry and the food tasted delicious and filled our stomachs.

After we'd eaten and rested, mother and I prepared a place to sleep under the trees, while Hans-Dieter and Ralf splashed in the warm water at the edge of the lake. At least it was easy to wash the boys and Marlene; and when that was done, I left mother on guard while I ran down to the water, stripped and with the thrill of getting clean again, dived in up to my neck. Oh it was *wonderful*! The clear, cool water invigorated both body and mind.

'Come in, mother; you'll love it. Our towels are wet, but they'll do. We can hang them over a bush to dry.'

'Yes, darling, I'll look forward to a dip as soon as you get out.'

After that activity, we soon settled down. The children fell asleep within minutes. Stars above were as bright as shiny coins spread out on black velvet and the moon showed only a slither.

'It's a new moon, Elslein,' mother whispered. 'I hope the weather will stay fine.'

'Mother, can you tell when we might arrive in Düsseldorf?'

'Well, it depends how fast we travel. You want to stay here an extra day? Perhaps not such a good idea, for we have a long way to go yet. I'd like to get out of the Russian zone and into the American sector. So much safer there. Tomorrow morning we'll look at our old map, and then decide together what to do. Now – rest. Good night, child. Sleep well and God bless you.'

'Good night, mother. God bless, and *thank you!'*

Sunday, 24 June 1945

In my diary I wrote:

> It's morning. I'm awake early, after a comfortable sleep in my makeshift bed. Last night, before I closed my eyes, I gazed at millions of stars on that black backdrop, but now, though it must still be early, they're not as bright and the sky's tinged with grey. Dawn hasn't yet arrived and no birds have awoken to begin their morning chorus. Behind me, in the east, a pink flush spreads over a cloudless horizon – the first sign of early sunrise and the promise of another fine day.
>
> I glance at mother, sleeping with little Marlene in her arm and Ralf and Hans-Dieter snuggled close to her. All four look so peaceful in their slumber. Mother's face is serene, with not a care in the world. Yet daily, on our journey, she fights for our survival, a battle against all odds, which she's determined to win. She has one aim: to keep us alive and together until the day we reach home. Our mother's heroic, a wonderful, wonderful woman! Mostly she's cheerful, always ready with an encouraging word. If one of us grumbles or moans about being tired or hungry, she'll tell us not to give in and remind us of our reward at the end of the journey . . .
>
> A dense mist covers the lake, obscuring any view of the opposite bank. Yet as soon as the sun comes out, the rays will burn it away.
>
> I know mother wants to carry on today, but it's lovely here. Ralf and Hans-Dieter enjoy the freedom to run about as children do and jump into this clean, crystal-clear water.
>
> When mother wakes, I'll ask her what she thinks is best – it's Sunday after all.
>
> It would be nice to stop another day. But then again, it depends on food.

We won't have enough to see us through until tomorrow and the children's nourishment is vital. I can also see we should go on, even if it's only as far as the outskirts of Magdeburg. That can't be too far to walk. We need to go where there are people, so we can obtain food and drink and perhaps proper shelter for the night. This is not a holiday, however tempting – we have a target to reach and that's Düsseldorf, come what may.

Mother and the three children were still sleeping peacefully and I didn't have the heart to wake them. Yet the morning was too beautiful to sleep away. Then I saw mother's eyes open and watching me.

''Morning, mother,' I whispered. 'Have you slept well?'

'Yes, Else, I had a refreshing sleep, sound and dreamless. I've watched you for a few minutes. You were deep in thought. Is that your diary? What were you writing?'

'Not much, mother, but now I'm thinking how much I'd like to brew us a cup of real coffee! With it I'd serve a freshly baked crusty roll, real butter and a slice of smoked ham, just as you like it. That's what I'd like to give you, mother, and one day I will!'

'Well, that's very tempting, but as we don't have those luxuries, we must be satisfied with what we have – and at the moment that's not much.'

'Do you think our food will last another day?'

'No, Else, I don't. We can't stay till tomorrow, but let's remain here this morning and leave about lunchtime. What do you think?'

'Yes, mother, that's a compromise.'

'Then we must buy food as soon as we see a farm. We don't want charity and I don't want people to think we're begging. As soon as we find a suitable place, we'll stop again.'

'Fine, mother, just as you suggest.'

Meanwhile Hans-Dieter and Ralf had woken up and run down to the lake. They splashed about in the warm water with light-hearted exuberance and shrieks of laughter, their hunger forgotten for a while. But it wouldn't be long before their tummies demanded food.

'Come, Else. Let's see what's left under the mattress in Marlenchen's pram.'

There wasn't much – I found ten uncooked potatoes, a small piece of salami sausage, a few oatflakes that also needed cooking, no milk, no sugar and a little salt. Boiled potatoes wouldn't taste special but when you're really hungry you can't be fussy.

'Is that all there is?' asked mother. 'Not enough for the children, let alone us.'

'Mother, cook all the potatoes and we'll eat them with a sprinkle of salt. We've done it often before. Give Marlene a small piece of sausage; that will keep her happy for a while.'

'Yes,' mother replied, 'but we must change our plans: we can't go hungry. As soon as the children have eaten, we must be on our way to Magdeburg. We'll walk as far as we need to get provisions. When that's done, we can plan further.'

There were just enough potatoes – three for each boy, two little ones for Marlene and one each for mother and me. Not quite sufficient, but better than nothing.

After everything was packed away, our camp tidied and litter free, I went to the water's edge once more and gazed into the distance. Nothing spoilt the view: an uninterrupted vista of the tranquil lake, surrounded by luscious, green meadows. The surface was smooth as a mirror, and empty but for two swans gliding peacefully near the opposite bank, and a family of ducks and ducklings, one behind the other, following in their wake. After our months of turmoil, the peace was therapeutic, and it saddened me to leave such a place.

'Come, Else!' mother jolted me out of my reverie. 'Time we were on our way.'

'Coming, mother,' I answered. I picked up my knapsack, checked nothing was left behind, took Ralf's hand and off we marched, singing as we went. It was vital to keep the children's spirits up, for there was no knowing what we'd find round any corner – another battlefield? Another massacre? Unsavoury soldiers? Famine?

'Now we're the wandering minstrels,' mother said, laughing. 'The louder we sing, the quicker we'll walk.' Our pretence cheered mother and me up. 'Only the birds can hear us – and they're welcome to sing along with us!'

But we found nowhere to buy even basic food. Twice mother knocked on doors, yet each time they were shut in her face. She was most distressed, and I could do nothing to cheer her.

In a small town, practically undamaged by fighting, we at last found a tiny village shop open. It displayed various kinds of vegetables outside: potatoes, carrots and onions; a lady who nodded at us was replenishing the boxes.

'Good afternoon.' Mother surveyed the array of produce; she was nearly drooling, 'I need to buy provisions for my family.'

The shopkeeper ushered her inside. 'Happy to serve you. I have most things.'

'There are various things I need for my children, but first, do you accept reichsmark?' she asked anxiously.

'Yes, that's no problem,' the shopkeeper replied. 'At the moment they have greater value than the Russian rouble. Now tell me what you'd like?'

'Oh, my list is long,' mother replied. 'First there's milk. Can you spare two litres? Then bread: two loaves if you can let me have them; and sugar – whatever you have.'

The shopkeeper also offered a generous portion of smoked sausage – unrecognisable as such, but acceptable nonetheless. A few more items besides, including a small packet of coffee substitute. After mother settled what she owed, a delighted little family went on its way towards Magdeburg with renewed vigour and a spring in its step.

On a farm outside the small town of Ziecar, we were offered shelter in a barn. What a treat for us all to have a generous meal, after which we settled down to a warm night's sleep.

Monday, 25 June 1945

Next morning, as soon as I was awake, I looked at the calendar I'd made before we started our journey, and realised that by the next day we'd have been travelling for nineteen days. It was hard to believe how quickly the days had flown – we'd certainly covered quite a stretch of our journey, but it was still a long way to Düsseldorf and we had yet to cross the dangerous East–West border.

I stepped down from my bed on a strawbale and opened the barn door. It was still early, but the morning was invitingly peaceful; to stay under my blanket would have been sacrilege. There were signs of another lovely day. The sun, now rising steeply, was a huge fireball surrounded by a cloudless azure-blue sky. A cock, sitting on top of a dunghill, crowed happily into the new dawn.

The animals had been awake some time: cows had been milked and taken to fresh pastures, the gently grunting pigs had already been fed and a soft neighing of horses in the stables was a reminder to their groom that they too wanted to be free.

I shook the boys, who grumbled, wanting to stay rolled up in their blankets. But, oh no, big sister wouldn't tolerate nonsense; not on such a marvellous day as that.

Mother was awake but quiet.

'Mother, what is it?' I asked. 'Are you ill?'

'No, Else, not ill; but I feel *so* weary. It will take all my willpower to get moving.'

'Leave things to me, mother. The boys can wash under the pump on their own. I'll see to Marlene, and you – if you feel able – can prepare a little breakfast. Don't bother about me; a slice of bread's all I need: I'm really not hungry.'

'Don't say that, child! You can't walk on an empty stomach. Eat a little.'

'Mother, I will if you do.'

A knock on the barn door announced the farmer with fresh milk. 'That, Frau Hopp, will be good for you.'

'Thank you,' mother said as she carefully took the jug. 'We'll all benefit from a drink of milk; especially the children.'

'Another thing,Frau Hopp – this morning I have to take the cart to Möckern, a small town near Magdeburg to conduct business. You're all welcome to travel with me. It's a long drive and will save you walking so far.'

'Oh Sir, how kind you are; we're most grateful for your offer. We'll not keep you waiting.' Mother's voice suddenly sounded stronger and more cheerful. She was delighted to be offered the gift of a ride to Möckern. She watched the farmer depart across the yard and said, 'Just imagine, children. A ride on a horsedrawn cart all the way without having to use our legs! When we reach Möckern, we'll be almost in Magdeburg – a day or more's walk. Wonderful, wonderful! I feel better just thinking of it.'

I was still concerned about her, however: she wasn't her usual active self. 'Mother, are you sure you're not ill?'

'*No, Else!* I'm simply weary. Please don't worry: it's unnecessary.'

After some food, we tidied the barn and packed away our belongings; then sat and waited for the farmer to call us.

The ride was slow and tediously long. And the cart was uncomfortable – we could feel every bump in the road and it made our bones rattle. Marlene did well though: she had a soft ride in her pram, well cushioned by her mattress and other bits and pieces.

However it was a treat to be driven through unspoilt countryside. Here and there were signs of fighting, but now the land was at peace. There was no motor traffic, just now and then a lonesome person on a bicycle. The silence was wonderful, as the world appeared to be sleeping – or recuperating from the chaos of previous months.

Occasionally we passed tiny hamlets with ancient cottages huddled together, where people waved to us and we cheerfully waved back. In a small town called Loburg, we stopped and the farmer produced a large packet of sandwiches his wife had prepared for us all.

'Mother!' Hans-Dieter shouted. 'This feels like a proper holiday. We're riding along instead of walking, and now we even have a picnic! Isn't it excellent?'

'Yes, my boy,' mother replied, 'it's certainly been a treat for us.'

The day wore on and the children got restless.

'Listen, Hans-Dieter and Ralf, let's have a pretend game. Imagine we're in school and I'm your teacher.'

'You, Else, our teacher? That's very funny. What are you going to teach us?'

'I'll teach you . . . German spelling, biology and a little general knowledge. We won't mention history, but will have geography instead.'

'What about me?' asked Ralf. 'I've not been to school so won't know the answers.'

'Don't worry, my lad; I know exactly what to ask you.'

I tried to make it exciting; the boys behaved and time flew by.

As we came to the end of the day's lessons, I saw in the distance the entrance to a town.

'That's Möckern,' said the farmer. 'We'll soon be at our destination.'

When we came nearer, a large estate appeared on our right – parkland and meadows, cattle grazing in a paddock, horses watching us and young foals running in circles, enjoying life.

'What a delightful place!' exclaimed mother. 'It reminds me of Pomerania and Glowitz Manor.'

'Yes, Frau Hopp. The owners are good friends of mine. There's plenty of space and I want to ask them to give you shelter for a few nights. I think, Frau Hopp, you urgently need rest. Leave it to me: I'll see what I can do.'

Tears welled up in mother's eyes – so unusual, a sign of her tiredness. 'Thank you,' she answered. 'Please convey to your friends we'd gratefully accept their hospitality, were it offered.'

The farmer drove his cart onto the estate, alighted and entered a large farmhouse while we waited. Mother and I admired the handsome building, snow-white with black beams criss-crossing the front and sides. The many windows in front of the house reflected the sun as it dropped lower towards the horizon.

Our tired horse munched softly on a nosebag of oats as it adjusted its stance on the cobbles.

Eventually a lady rushed out of the house. 'Frau Hopp!' she called. 'I'm Frau Hofmann. Welcome into my home. I hear you've walked all the way from Pomerania – so many kilometres! My friend says you're very weary. Please stay for a few days to rest to regain your strength.'

'Thank you for your offer, Frau Hofmann,' mother replied, exhaustion in every word.

'Don't mention it; we have plenty of room, for as yet our sons and daughter haven't returned. Both boys are soldiers; last time we heard, they were retreating from the Russians. Now *the Russians* are here, but where our boys are, we don't know.'

'And your daughter?'

'We heard at one time she was nursing in a military hospital in Königsberg. We don't know if she's dead or alive. Of course, she could have been taken prisoner.' Frau Hofmann mused for a moment, and then realising her guests were watching her, expectantly, continued, 'But I don't know why we're standing here talking. Let's go inside and I'll show you where you can sleep.'

Mother was overwhelmed. So much kindness from a stranger was hard to believe. Yet that wasn't the first time we'd experienced it.

We followed Frau Hofmann. First she showed us a bedroom with a large double bed big enough to accommodate three; also a single bed under a window, very suitable for Hans-Dieter.

'And what's your name?' Frau Hofmann turned to me.

'Else,' I answered. 'I'm fifteen, so I help my mother with the boys and baby sister.'

'Then follow me, Else. I have a little room just for you.'

It was lovely, that little room: very tiny with space for a single bed, and was just right for me, but I offered it to mother. I could sleep with Ralf and Marlene, and she'd have more peace on her own.

But she wouldn't hear of it. 'No, Else, the three of us will be most comfortable. Stop worrying: there's nothing wrong with me. After a day or two, I'll be myself again. But now I must ask Frau Hofmann if I may prepare a meal in her kitchen. We'll have potatoes, mashed with a little milk. Also some small turnips and carrots. A delicious evening meal, and tonight we'll sleep without feeling hungry.'

Our evening meal was simple but tasty. Even the boys and our little girl tucked in and had enough for the next day as well.

Later mother sat in the parlour talking to Frau Hofmann. The two ladies seemed to like each other and it seemed Frau Hofmann was glad of mother's company.

The day ended with a glorious sunset as the sky slowly deepened to violet, with Venus shining like a jewel on velvet. It was the best part of the day. While we were riding on the cart, the heat had been oppressively humid; now there was a gentle breeze and it occurred to me that the two boys and little Marlene would benefit from a stroll along a quiet country lane.

Although it was very quiet when we arrived, this didn't last. Hans-Dieter and Ralf had so much pent-up energy to expend before bedtime that they were like two animals freed from a cage.

The farmer who'd brought us here had started his long journey home some time before. I hoped mother had thanked him well, for it was he who'd guided us to that lovely place.

That night I went to bed at peace with the world.

Monday, 2 July 1945

The days on the farm were relaxing and mother benefited from the peaceful atmosphere. Her energy had been drained by the constant worry of how to feed the five of us, and the never-ending trek along dusty roads had taken its toll. Frau Hofmann was a charming lady who spoiled mother in every way, insisting she rest undisturbed in the private garden.

After some days, I squatted beside mother and asked if I could talk to her.

'Certainly, Else. What is it?'

'Mother, I don't know how to say this, but I think we should soon be moving on. We've rested for a few days and you look much better, but I'm longing to get home to Düsseldorf. This journey's never ending, but once we're in Helmstedt, Frau Hofmann said, we should be able to continue by train.'

'You're right, Else. Yes, we can't stay her for ever. Today's Monday, 2 July. Let's leave tomorrow. All right? We'll pack our belongings and tidy our rooms, so we can be on the road early, straight after breakfast. How does that sound?'

'Sounds good.'

'Mr Hofmann has shown me the route on his map; first through Möckern and then into Magdeburg. The town has, apparently, suffered a lot of damage and the ruins are a shocking sight. There's a temporary footbridge over the river Elbe we must cross to leave Magdeburg.'

'And after that?' I asked.

'He mentioned a town called Eisleben. I don't know if we can get that far in one day – probably not. But once we're there, we'll soon enter the forest that leads us to Helmstedt.'

'What's so special about Helmstedt, mother?'

'It's a frontier town. The Russian sector ends there and the American zone begins. We'll soon see for ourselves what's so special about the place. Now, Else, I'd better tell Frau Hofmann we'll leave tomorrow.'

The boys and I looked forward to getting back on the road. I had visions of reaching Helmstedt soon. That to me was like arriving in the Promised Land – no more Russians, plenty of food, perhaps a bath and clean clothes but, most of all, no more walking. Trains to take us to Düsseldorf and to all corners of western Germany should be available and one of those would take us home.

Mother decided to spend the last evening with Herr and Frau Hofmann. After I'd given the boys and Marlene their evening meal, I put the little one to bed and then asked Hans-Dieter and Ralf to help me repack our knapsacks. By now we owned precious little; our packs had become so much lighter, but it didn't matter, for soon we'd be home. Until then what we had would have to last.

Frau Hofmann was surprised and sad we were leaving so soon. She and mother had become firm friends; they exchanged addresses and promised to stay in touch.

'Who knows,' mother said, 'perhaps one day, when times are better, we may meet again.'

'I look forward to that, Helene,' answered Frau Hofmann. 'The few days with you have been truly special.'

'And so they have for us. Our grateful thanks to you and your husband.'

Mr Hofmann offered to take us through Möckern to the outskirts of Magdeburg. 'It will shorten your journey. Once you're through Magdeburg and across the Elbe, you should reach Eisleben by tomorrow evening. Skirt the town, and later you'll see a large farm on your right, standing back from the road – you can't miss it. The people there are friends of ours. I'll give you a note to hand to them and I'm sure you'll not be refused shelter.'

'Thank you, Heinrich. You and Johanna have treated us with great kindness, and I'll never forget it. I'll write to you once we're home. I hope my letter reaches you.'

Next morning we all awoke early – we'd decided that as soon as breakfast was over we'd be on our way.

The boys and I went down to the kitchen to say goodbye to Frau Hofmann and thank her for her kindness. Her parting present was a bag of assorted fruit from her orchard.

Herr Hofmann called out to mother, 'Lene, can you be ready to leave in half an hour?'

'Yes, Heinrich, we're almost ready now.'

Frau Hofmann came into the yard to see us off as we climbed onto the cart, pram and all.

Mother sat next to Herr Hofmann in front, with the four of us settled in the back. The weather was still good but very humid. 'I think the day will end with a gigantic thunderstorm,' he voiced our thoughts. 'We get them this time of the year. But don't worry, Lene, the sun will shine again tomorrow.'

Dark clouds hung low in the sky, but we prayed the rain would delay till we reached our destination.

Soon we were through Möckern. Now it was only a few kilometres to Magdeburg.

At the entrance to the town, Herr Hofmann stopped. 'Lene, this is as far as I can take you. I must branch off to another village here to conduct business. Straight on you'll come to the river – I hope the bridge has been repaired. If you're lost, ask someone for the Eisleben road; it's not difficult to find. Please give my regards to our friends – they'll help you.'

'Thank you, Heinrich. I'll think of you and Johanna with great affection. You've been most kind to us.'

'Lene, to have met you all is a privilege. God bless you. I pray you get home safely.'

He jumped onto his wagon, picked up his whip and flicked it in the air; his horse responded immediately and off they went. And so we entered Magdeburg, another badly destroyed town. Much of the rubble had been cleared, however, and the roads were passable. Life seemed to be carrying on with some kind of normality. A few Russian soldiers stood on street corners here and there, but ignored us.

Lunchtime came and we were all hungry. Mother asked someone if there was any grassland where we could eat our midday snack. Yes, there was a park, not much left, but good enough for our purpose. The woman guided us there and we found a quiet spot where we ate lunch.

'Else,' mother reminded me, 'we can't stay too long; there's some distance to walk if we want to reach Eisleben.'

To our horror, when we left Magdeburg, a long column of German soldiers marched towards us – if it could be called marching. They dragged their feet in utter weariness, some hardly able to shuffle. A number of them had been wounded and their bloody bandages, covering various bodyparts, were filthy and badly in need of changing. In front, at the rear and in the centre of the column, Russian guards marched with rifles at the ready, a heartbreaking sight.

'Frau,' one of the soldiers whispered, 'please take this piece of paper . . . my home address. Tell my wife I'm alive but have been taken prisoner.'

'And the same for me?' said another. The request was repeated again and again until a guard noticed and ran to see what they were doing.

Davai! he shouted, *Davai, davai!* And taking a truncheon from his belt, he hit mercilessly and indiscriminately at heads and bodies. The other Russian soldiers were furious and joined in, their rage awesome. Was it fear of losing control that made them go berserk? We wished we could help but could only stand and watch in silence. The long column shuffled past and we waited until they slowly disappeared into the distance.

'Mother,' I croaked, struggling to find my voice, 'where are they going? Berlin and on to Russia?'

'Possibly, my child. Many of those poor men will never see their homeland again.'

Chapter 41

Stoi! Stop!

Tuesday, 3 July 1945

We imagined that once we reached the outskirts of Magdeburg, it would be an easy walk to Eisleben. But we were wrong. Outside the city were fields on either side of the road far into the distance.

'Mother,' I said, 'surely it can't be that far. I can't see a house, certainly no farm. Are we on the right road?'

'I'm sure we are. I was told it was the only way to the forest, so we must carry on. We need to find shelter for the night, reason enough not to give in.'

Marlene and Ralf had fallen asleep, Ralf like a little dormouse huddled at the bottom of the pram. A slight-but-persistent drizzle had set in with a foreboding, heavy grey sky for the rest of the day. Luckily mother had a waterproof sheet in the pram; spread over Marlene and Ralf it would, at least, keep the two youngest dry. Hans-Dieter was tired and getting wet, poor lad. He badly needed a rest, but in a few minutes his energy revived and he started telling jokes.

'Dieter,' I said, 'you're a plucky lad: you've hardly complained since we started this trek and you're always cheerful. Mother and I are proud of you!'

Then Ralf woke up, damp, cold and hungry – real tears started to flow.

'Come Ralfie,' I said, 'be brave like Hans-Dieter. Soon we'll be at the farm. Just a little longer. Please don't cry; we're all hungry and tired. I tell you what: let's have a game. We'll look out for a large white farmhouse and the first to shout *there it is*, will be the winner and receive a prize.'

'What prize?' asked Hans-Dieter and Ralf in unison. 'We haven't any prizes.'

'All right, let's pretend.'

'Hans-Dieter, if you could choose, what would you most want for a prize?' asked mother.

Dieter made up his mind immediately. 'I'd like to win a large bar of chocolate to myself – to eat all at once.'

'Then you'd have an awful tummy ache and be sick.'

'But it would be worth it,' replied Hans-Dieter.

'And you, Ralf. What would you like?'

'Don't know . . . Suppose, a whole bag of sweets would be yummy, but mother says they're bad for my teeth.'

'I know what would be right for you – you could have an orange.'

'An orange, Else? What's an orange?'

'Don't you know anything?' piped in Hans-Dieter. 'You've eaten oranges before. It's a long time ago, but you *should* remember.'

'It's a fruit, Ralfie, from distant lands. It tastes delicious, but before you can eat it, you peel it. The flesh is juicy and sweet. Perhaps soon there'll be oranges in the shops; then you can have as many as you like.'

'What can Marlenchen have?' asked Ralf.

'I think we'll give her a banana. She'll like that; it's good for little girls.'

'I've never seen a banana.'

'It's another fruit. Like a small, yellow cucumber – you know what that is, Ralf?'

'Of course I do!'

'Well, we haven't seen bananas for years. They come from faraway countries and grow in large bunches on tall trees. Before they're ripe, they're green, but turn yellow as they ripen. Their flesh is creamy and sweet, and when I was little, Ralfie, mother would give me one for breakfast.'

'Good,' Ralf said. 'If Marlene has a banana and I have an orange, I could give her half my orange for half her banana; then we'd both have something new. What do you think, mother?'

'A wonderful idea!'

Our little discussion had passed the time away. We were very wet now. The gentle drizzle had become a hefty downpour and, apart from dripping trees lining the road, there was no shelter anywhere. Except for Ralf and Marlene under their waterproof, we looked like waifs pulled out of a pond.

Mother saw the farmhouse first, looming out of the mist. 'Look, children. There it is! The farm we're looking for. Not far now.'

'What if they turn us away, mother?' a possibility that put fear into me.

'Else, don't think like that. I have Frau Hofmann's letter; it should help.'

We knocked at the door, mother presented her letter of introduction, and we were made welcome. There was a large room on the ground floor.

'You can stay here, Frau Hopp, with your children. There are ample sleeping facilities for all of you: bathroom and toilet next door. Does that suit your requirements?'

'It's magnificent,' answered mother. 'Thank you for your generosity.'

The lady was Frau van Moerbeek, of Dutch origin.

What a luxurious feeling to dry ourselves on fluffy clean towels!

Mother wanted to go into the kitchen to prepare a meal, but Frau van Moerbeek said, 'Frau Hopp, I've cooked plenty this evening, far more than we can eat. Please share the food with us; the children need a warm meal before bed.'

Mother was grateful and so was I, but we were so exhausted we only picked at that wholesome, tasty food. Marlene and Ralf were fretful and mother hurried them into bed. 'They're totally worn out, poor mites. Look at Hans-Dieter – he's almost asleep on his feet. Just a quick wash tonight, face and hands, and into bed; they'll be out in minutes.'

'Such a strain you're under, Frau Hopp. Even the children notice: they're too young to express their feelings verbally, but the worries and anxieties are there.'

'Yes,' mother said, 'I appreciate your understanding.'

'We want you to get back into the west safely. The room you occupy has been used for the same purpose many times. Just after Russia took over, crowds fled eastern Germany for the west. No one stopped the flow of people; it appeared the Russians didn't care. But then it became a mass exodus and the occupying forces decided to put a halt to it.'

'What happened then?'

'If you and your daughter join us when the children are asleep, we'll tell you. This is the most dangerous part of your journey. We want to give you advice, and hope it will help you.'

'We'd be grateful for any advice. I thank Mr and Frau Hofmann for leading us to you.'

The children were soon sound asleep and mother and I made our way to the drawing room, where Frau van Moerbeek waited. Her husband was present and looking grave. That discussion was more serious than mother anticipated. Sitting opposite her, I was stunned to see how incredibly tired she looked, with dark rings I'd never seen before under her eyes.

Please, dear Lord, don't let her be ill. I help her as much as I can – I only hope it's enough, I prayed silently.

Thinking about mother so intensively, I missed much of Mr van Moerbeek's conversation. I had to pay attention. Apparently for months a stream of people had walked to the frontier through the forest.

'Is the frontier far from here?' I asked.

'No, Else, just at the end of the forest path that used to go all the way into the next town. It was a good route and news of it spread fast. One day the Russians decided to put a stop to it. Very early one morning, they arrived with equipment and materials: barbed wire, sturdy wooden poles and sacks of cement. They started building a fence surrounding the whole woodland area, kilometres and kilometres in both directions. No one could either go into or come out of the wood.

'At first, soldiers stood guard the whole length of the fence. Locals were told that anyone trying to enter the woodland area would be shot without warning.

'As our fields adjoin the edge of the forest, I noticed small gaps here and there, where a person could slide through. I watched the sentries patrolling back and forth and timed them: slowly a pattern emerged.'

'Were you able to help some people?' I asked.

'Yes, Else, but we won't discuss what's past.' He ran stressed fingers through his hair. 'Frau Hopp, let me come back to you and your family. I see you have a pram – I'm afraid you'll have to leave it behind. As for your belongings, discard everything you don't need; take only what's absolutely necessary.'

Mother and I glanced at each other. Though we had little, it would be a hard decision.

'There's one main path through the wood, which you must ignore. You have to walk through the undergrowth and be extremely quiet. It won't be easy with the little ones, but, Frau Hopp, you have to silence them somehow. That's vital. At the end of the wood's the steep, high grassy bank where small prickly bushes have rooted. It's not far from where you enter the woodland to the steep bank. At the top's a busy road that leads to Helmstead, and with luck the noise of traffic – mostly military – may hide any noise you make. At the bottom of the bank another fence has been erected. It's not too tall and, by helping each other, it shouldn't be too difficult to overcome that hurdle. But once you're through it at the bottom of the slope, be quick. There you're entirely exposed, and as you near the top, one of you must shout for help . . .' He paused to work out if he'd forgotten any important information. Finally he said, 'How do you feel about it now, Frau Hopp? I think I've given you as much advice as I'm able to.'

'Thank you so much. I don't feel too good about it: I fear for my children. But what can we do? We've come so far; there's no turning back . . . When's the best time to leave?'

'As early as possible: before sunrise. That's when the sentries are tired and want to be in bed. They think they have nothing to fear and are less vigilant. But you and Else must be alert *at all times*. Never, for a moment, be careless.' He rose. 'Go with God: may he protect you!'

'Thank you both for your generosity,' said mother, rising too. 'And may God also protect *you* in all the risks you undertake so regularly. If you let me have your address, I'll write to you once we've returned to Düsseldorf. I've promised the same to Johanna and Heinrich, two wonderful people who also treated us with great kindness.'

When we returned to our bedroom from the van Moerbeek's drawing room, mother instantly went to the little chair by the window, sat down and burst into tears. She cried bitterly, all her pent-up emotions welling up to the surface.

'Mother, whatever's the matter? Why are you crying? Please don't: there's no need.'

'Elslein, my darling, I've let you down badly. All this is my fault. I should have had more sense than to take you four children – because that's what you are – and drag you halfway through Germany. Now look at the state we're in,' she continued, desperation in her voice. 'We're here only due to the kindness of the van Moerbeeks and are almost in Russian hands again. Else, can't you see? We're virtually back where we started!'

'But mother,' I answered, 'it's not that bad. Look at us; we're all in good health, thanks to you. Don't lose heart, now we're so near our final hurdle.'

'Nothing you say, Else, can make me feel better. I despair: I'm quite lost.'

'Mother, you're tired and weary in mind as well as body. Have faith. Our guardian angel will protect us; he has so far. We rely on you. The last few months have been difficult; don't give up now.'

'Elslein, what would I do without you? You're so young to share every responsibility with me. Without you our venture would have failed long ago, no doubt about it.'

'Well, don't be disheartened. I'm not giving up now. Come and lie down. Try to sleep for a while. When Mr van Moerbeek calls us, just after 4 a.m., we'll be ready to follow him. Would you like a cup of coffee?'

'You mean coffee substitute? No, I don't want it. I hate it!'

Now mother was being unreasonable, so without saying more, I guided her to bed, tucked her up and, trying to keep quiet, began to sort out our belongings.

I was excited. I couldn't wait for the hours to pass – I wanted to be over the border. It was still raining, beating against the window. Perhaps that weather was sent by God to help us escape. There was danger ahead, but I was ready to face it.

Wednesday, 4 July 1945

After everything was sorted and each little knapsack packed, waiting to be picked up, I sat down and closed my eyes. I must have dozed. I woke with a start and wondered how long I'd slept. Was it minutes, or an hour or two? Outside it was pitch-black and still raining, perhaps not quite as heavily as earlier, but still coming down in a steady downpour.

Suddenly I heard a gentle knock on our door. 'Frau Hopp, are you awake?'

I opened it and was met by Herr van Moerbeek.

'Is it time to get ready?' I asked, 'Mother and the little ones are asleep. But if you're waiting to go, we can be off in minutes.'

'I can give you half an hour – no longer,' the farmer replied. 'We must be at the forest fence before daylight. The rain has stopped, but it's very muddy underfoot. Wear as many clothes as possible to keep yourselves warm and dry. You can always discard them later.'

I woke mother: she'd slept soundly for some time and it took a while for her to come to her senses. The boys were easy. They realised what was happening and knew there was no time to hang about. Ralf was too slow for Hans-Dieter and an argument broke out, which had to be stopped before it ended in tears. Marlene hated being disturbed. She wanted to continue sleeping; and because I wouldn't let her, she threw a tantrum.

'Now, quiet!' I shouted. 'Do you think this is fun for mother and me? We've talked about this and you know what's happening. In a short while Herr van Moerbeek will take us to the forest; and from that moment, until we tell you otherwise, there'll be NO TALKING. Not a sound. Understand?'

'Yes, Else,' Hans-Dieter and Ralf murmured together.

Excited, our nerves on edge, we tidied up as best we could, and were ready in less than half an hour; now we just had to wait for Herr van Moerbeek to call us.

It was a damp, dismal morning away from the shelter of the farmhouse. Black clouds threatened more rain and the wind was vicious as it blew across the open fields. Once we were outside the building, there was utter darkness and the ground was so soggy our feet sank up to the ankles in mud.

We were led behind the house, across the farmyard and along a narrow footpath bordering a field, ending at the edge of the forest. It loomed dark and sinister in the distance. In the east glimmered a faint lightening of sky, the start of dawn. Gradually our eyes became accustomed to the darkness surrounding us and we could distinguish the shape of trees at the entrance to the wood. Everyone trekked in complete silence; the boys and even our little girl seemed to realise its importance. With Marlene on my arm, my knapsack on my back and Ralfie tightly clasping my hand, I stumbled along. Mother held tight to Hans-Dieter for her own sake; she carried her own knapsack and Marlenchen's bag. We'd left the pram behind.

Suddenly, at the edge of the woodland, we made out a small gap in the fence, which had been concealed and could be identified only on close inspection. The farmer stopped.

'Here I must leave you,' whispered Herr van Moerbeek. 'You must go on and I have to return. Goodbye, Frau Hopp.' He squeezed mother's hand warmly. 'I hope all goes well for you. Our thoughts will be with you and we wish you a safe journey home.'

We'd already been given all the necessary instructions, so what we did next was in our own hands. Very quietly we crawled through the gap. I went through first with Marlene, and Ralfie followed, keeping close to me. Then it was Hans-Dieter's turn. Mother handed me her knapsack and bag and followed last, closing the gap behind her as well as she was able. Instantly the trees hid us. Mother put her finger to her mouth, indicating we had to be silent.

She gathered Ralf and Hans-Dieter in her arms and whispered,'Now we must be extra careful – not a sound. You mustn't speak. Understand? For our safety no one must know we're here. Let's go now; keep straight and, in a short while, we'll find the steep bank which we must climb as quickly as we can – and if we can reach the top, with a lot of luck, we should be free!'

The farmer had already melted into the darkness, and we were on our own. Although it wasn't raining, the forest was very wet. Trees dripped, and the early morning stillness amplified the 'plop, plop' sound of the raindrops. No birds sang – all was silent.

We crept through the undergrowth. Marlene grew heavy and I lost all feeling in my arm, yet knew I had to hold on. We saw no silhouettes of sentries; neither did we hear that guttural sound of Russian voices. Deeper, ever deeper into the heart of the forest we stumbled. In a small clearing we paused for a rest, quietly, huddling together. We had to stand: it was too wet, impossible to sit down. Our feet were sodden and we had nothing extra to wear for protection.

After a few minutes, we ploughed on.

'Come, children. It won't be long till the end of the wood. Let's hope we'll avoid the border guards.' I thought to myself, *To be caught now would be unthinkable*.

Then suddenly, out of the darkness, loomed a high, steep grassy bank, bordered by a low but dangerous, ugly, barbed-wire fence. I stared in horror. The bank was so high and the wet grass dreadfully slippery. Was what lay before us achievable? After all that – would it be possible to reach the top?

'We must climb over,' whispered mother. 'For God's sake, keep quiet! Don't hesitate – *just do it!* Else and I will help you.'

'Hans-Dieter, you first. Mind that wire above your head,' I said, hiding my fear. 'I'll go next; mother, hold Marlenchen. I'll take her as soon as I'm through. Hans-Dieter, stay where you are. Don't start climbing: wait until we're all over . . . we *must* stay together. Ralfie, don't cry – Mama will come, we won't leave her behind; just stand still; I'll lift you over, now.'

For a minute there was chaos. Clothing and bags caught on barbs, legs scratched. I hoped the children would remain brave and not cry out. Could we be so lucky? I wondered.

As mother climbed over the fence, we saw, to our horror, two soldiers approaching. Their silhouettes were small, as they were some distance away and might not have seen us – yet . . . For moments, there was panic and confusion; we hesitated . . . We were on the wrong side of the fence to hide in the forest, and it was difficult enough fighting the lethal barbs this time; if we returned, someone might get stuck. WHAT TO DO? To go back, or risk being killed?

Suddenly we came to life! Mother and I exchanged glances. It was now or never – and with our lives literally at stake – probably never!

'Dieter, quick! Climb ahead as fast as you can,' urged mother. 'When you get to the top, shout "HELP!" as loudly as possible. We're right behind you!' She struggled to gather the bags. 'Else, quick. Hurry! Take care of Marlene. I have Ralf – we're coming.'

But so were the Russians – closer and closer. They'd seen us and were starting to run: '*Stoi!* Stop!' they yelled, again and again. We ignored the command: for us there was one thought – climb to the top of the slope and out of danger. We were utterly exposed to the Russian guns. Would they really shoot us? Bang! A bullet whizzed over our heads. Our situation seemed hopeless. My heart beat in my throat. Bang! Bang! Fear was a living thing – it captured our bodies and took control. We *had* to make it. *Please God, don't desert us now!* A spate of shots echoed across the forest: thunderous noise, and birds flapped away. Had any of us been hit? Mother? Ralfie? I dared not glance down behind me, below my feet. *Don't let us be caught: not now . . . not the very last minute . . .*

Dieter had scrambled over the top and I could clearly hear him shouting for help. If they didn't hear him, they'd hear the gunfire – but human instinct was to take shelter, not rescue us.

The treacherous grassy bank was desperately wet and slippery, and far steeper even than it appeared. We were climbing one step forward and sliding two back. Hands and knees, grasp at a tuft, but away it came in my hand. A stone rattled down on mother. I was so near, our little girl heavy on my arm; she clutched my coat and buried her head, while mother clung on to Ralfie behind me. I heard her panting heavily and knew she was close. Slowly we inched nearer and nearer the top – it seemed to stretch on for ever, a formidable wall of black grass. More shots rang out, one zinging past my ear. *Guardian angel, save us! They must be level with us.*

'Hurry, Else!' mother croaked, gasping for breath.

Realising she was failing, I turned and hauled up Ralf with my spare hand. And, as one, he and I also shrieked 'HELP!' as loudly as we could. He was climbing really well beside me, fear making his hands and feet work like a little machine.

And then, on the crest – *two men reached down to us.* 'Hold on, quick!' shouted one of them in American English; it was obvious what he wanted. He grabbed Ralf's little arms, swinging him up and out of my grasp.

'Gimme the kid!' The other soldier reached out and took Marlene. She disappeared, but instantly the man returned. 'Quick, don't look back! We gotcha! You're safe now.' I knew enough English to understand him. 'Here!' I grabbed a hand and he tugged at me.

But the two Russian border guards were now by the fence at the base of the bank, directly below us. They shouted desperately and fired bullets into the air in a most threatening manner – if not to hit us and our rescuers, then definitely to summon support. But they were too late.

'Hey, guys! Hold your fire!' the first American soldier was also shouting and pointing a huge automatic weapon down at them. The diversion was enough: I reached safety and rolled over the top into the long grass; they could harm us no more – us children. *But where was mother?*

'Mother!' I screamed.

My rescuer returned to the edge.

Last to struggle over the brow was mother. She paused, gazed at us, saw we were all there and then, without a sound, collapsed into unconsciousness.

While the Russians were still shouting and shooting, the American soldiers picked mother up and carried her over to a wagon. Gently they laid her on a sofa bed and covered her with a soft blanket.

Hans-Dieter tugged at my jacket. 'Else, can I talk now?' he whispered.

'Yes, little brother, you can. We're safe now: we can all talk. Nothing bad will happen to us any more.'

'And can I talk too?' little Ralf wanted to know.

'Yes you can, but quietly. Mother's not well.'

'Else,' Hans-Dieter asked, 'are the soldiers Americans?'

'Yes, Hans-Dieter, they are. But at the moment they're attending to mother, who's ill. Later, you may talk to them.'

'But I can't speak American. Will they understand me?'

'I don't know, Hans-Dieter. You have to wait and see.'

Mother must have regained consciousness, because I thought I could hear her crying. We were still standing on the road, waiting. All noise had ceased from the bottom of the bank, so presumably the guards had admitted defeat. I didn't dare look over the bank to see. We wanted to be with our mother, but no one took any notice of us.

Eventually the door of the trailer opened, a soldier looked out and waved us over. 'Your mom's awake; she's sure asking for you!'

Using my school English, I could understand what he was saying, and pushed my brothers in front of me. We walked towards him, hesitantly and shyly and then entered that smart, silver wagon, overcome by what met our eyes. Inside it was light, clean and warm. We were speechless. The soldier handed us towels to dry our faces and wet hair. *What must they think of us?* I thought. *To them we must look like rag-dolls pulled from a pond.*

'Come on in,' another soldier beckoned. 'Ya mother's fine – happy to see ya.' He turned to me: 'You understand English, kid?' I nodded. 'She's ill, needs looking after. We must get you all to camp.'

'Please, what's wrong with her?' I asked.

'She's doggone tired – needs ter rest. Where ya going?'

'Home. Düsseldorf.'

'Düsseldorf?' The soldiers whistled. 'Gee! You sure have a long way to go, but you're outta danger now: rest easy. Ya'll be looked after. Got it?'

I smiled: I'd got it. As we waited for something to happen, we relaxed with them.

I'd been holding mother's hand. She was too weak to talk, but words were not needed. She'd led us to safety, at last.

After a while, I looked around for my little ones. One soldier, whom I hadn't noticed before, was sitting in a corner with Marlene on his lap, feeding her with chocolate and what he called 'cookies'. Ralf and Hans-Dieter were sitting at a table drinking milk and eating a large sausage in a piece of white bread.

'Look, Else,' Hans-Dieter called out, 'look, I have a "hot dog"!'

'Hans-Dieter, what are you saying?'

'Well, that's what the soldiers call it – a "hot dog".'

That must be American, I thought. Perhaps Americans speak their own language.

They poured mother and me a beaker of coffee, real coffee, not substitute, all we'd had to drink for such a long time.

'Luxury!' Mother uttered with a smile back on her face. *'Now* I believe we're safe – Thank you, God.'

I looked at the soldiers and asked in halting school English, 'Is it true? We're really safe?'

They smiled, 'Yeah, you sure are! You're way out of the reach of any Russians. They ain't gonna harm you no more.'

'Thank you,' I whispered. 'Thank you.' Then, after a pause: 'What now?'

'Rest awhile, jis' relax. Soon transport will come and take ya all to Helmstedt. There ya'll be looked after real good and ya mom cared fer. Don't worry.'

While I sat by her, mother had drifted back to sleep. She was very pale. Now and then she moaned as if ugly dreams were haunting her. My English wasn't good enough to converse much with the soldiers but I understood sufficient to answer a few questions.

'Miss,' one of them spoke in clearer English, 'your mother's very ill. She needs a doctor urgently. Very soon we'll take you to Helmstedt. It's a catchment area for people like you guys. They've fled from the east and managed to break into the west. They're waiting for permission to travel to different parts of Germany.'

'We have a permit. How long do we have to stay there?' I asked.

'Depends,' answered the soldier. 'First your mom's health must improve. She'll be cared for, but you mustn't worry her. When you see her, be cheerful; that'll help her recovery.'

Another soldier asked about our home. I told him it was a town called Düsseldorf in West Germany, on the river Rhine. He nodded and wrote it down.

'So you were evacuated? And that was where?'

'A village called Glowitz. The nearest town's Stolp.'

'And Stolp is?' He scratched his head.

'We travelled from Pomerania, Sir – Pomerania – Polish soldiers took over from the Russians.'

'Pomerania?' Another soldier joined us. 'Ain't that near the Baltic Sea – way north-east? Gee, ain't that some long way!'

'How many kilometres did you travel? And how long did that take you?' The first soldier asked.

And when I told him four weeks and many, many kilometres and mostly on foot, they both looked truly stunned.

'My, what a journey that was,' he commented. 'That's incredible! Hey, man. Did you hear that?' he called to his other comrade. 'All them kilometres they travelled! On foot?' he turned to me again. And when I nodded, he added, 'No wonder their mom's so darned ill. That long journey with four youngsters to care for! Now ya talking courage!'

I watched their astonishment as they crowded round to gaze at us with new respectful eyes. Yes, that was what we'd accomplished. *You American soldiers in your luxury trailer* and smart uniforms have no idea what hardship and suffering the German people have had to endure. But, like my games teacher used to say, we German women are tough: we'll survive. It's our determination that'll see us through to the end.

But mother was ill. I could see the Americans trying to make her comfortable and was grateful to them. However they were talking too fast for me to understand.

One of the soldiers looked at me and said, 'Little Miss, we've radioed for a Red Cross wagon to take you to a camp in Helmstedt. There your mother can have medical care, and you four guys also need looking after. You're sure dirty and bedraggled.' He touched the sleeve of my jacket to emphasise what he meant. 'Yeah – bathtubs and clean clothes: that'll make you human again! Then, good tasty food and a proper bed.'

'Food! Bed, Else!' Hans-Dieter understood those words. 'Yeah!' He copied the American lingo.

I smiled. *Yes, by tomorrow, the world will look a brighter place*, I thought.

'I hear your brother call out "Else",' the soldier continued. 'Guess that's your name?'

'Yes, it is,' I answered, but just as I was about to introduce my two brothers and little sister, I heard a vehicle come to a stop outside the trailer. 'Is that our transport,' I asked?

'Sure is,' one soldier answered, as he opened the door to look out. 'Guess ya on your way, agin. Come on you young'uns; climb in the back: we'll bring your mother. She'll have to lie down – there's a cot ready for her.'

They handed us our knapsacks and then helped mother, who was unable to stand unaided.

It all happened so quickly that we hardly had time to thank the Good Samaritans who'd saved our lives, before the engine roared into life and we were off, not really knowing where to.

Through a small window above mother's stretcher I could see the road was busy, carrying mostly military traffic. There was also a continuous line of pedestrians walking in one direction only – west. Was it towards the town? Many pushed prams; others had bicycles; some were pulling small handcarts, laden with personal belongings.

All the time we were travelling, I watched mother. She was very ill. Her eyes were closed and I wondered if she was sleeping. But the bumpy journey wasn't helping.

'Mother,' I said, 'can you hear me? Look, I have Marlenchen on my lap and Ralf and Hans-Dieter by my side. We're all worried about you and the little ones don't understand. Can you open your eyes and speak to them? Just a few words – just to reassure them?'

Mother didn't respond. It was so unusual, and her lethargy worried me terribly. I wished I knew what I could do to make her better. Perhaps the professionals would have an answer.

Out of the window I saw we were in a built-up area. Helmstedt? We drove on. Not here then.

Almost out of town, we came to a halt outside large iron gates. They reminded me of the entrance to Stolp prison. Immediately I was filled with fear as terror overwhelmed me.

Surely, it can't happen again? I thought. *The Americans have treated us kindly . . . till now. Why would they want to imprison us? Because we're Germans?*

The gates opened as if by invisible hands and the ambulance drove into a large courtyard. Many people milled about us, mostly women and children. They looked contented enough – didn't they? But as we climbed down from the van, they hardly glanced at us.

Two Red Cross nurses approached. They wanted us to go with them, but I was not having that. Oh no, not without mother! I had to know what would happen to her: NO ONE had the right to keep us separated. We were not prisoners, and I was very angry. In German I let the nurses know how I felt. They stared at me. Then I saw two men from the ambulance carry mother on a stretcher into a building in front of us.

'Where do you take our mother?' I cried out in English with desperation in my voice. 'We must be with her. She will miss us: then she will not get better.'

'Your mother needs nursing,' I was told in German. 'She'll receive the best care possible. You can see her every day and, as soon as she's well, you'll be together again. Now, come with me,' the nurse concluded, firmly, 'you all need looking after too, don't you?'

It was a relief to understand and be understood. So what could we do? We had to follow. We were allocated a room and a woman showed us where to shower. But before that, she took us into a large hall where we were each handed a pile of clothing – not new, but all in good condition.

'Try them on,' the woman said. 'If they don't fit, let me know and I'll change them.' Then she looked at me, shrewdly, and asked how old I was.

'I'm fifteen and will be sixteen in September.'

'Will you be able to look after your brothers and little sister?' she asked.

'Of course! I always do. We must be together: mother would be upset if we were separated.'

Then we all had a glorious shower; luckily for us the shower room was empty: the two boys went in one cubicle, while Marlenchen and I were in another. Oh, it was heavenly! I washed my hair and then my sister's and, as I did so, noticed dirt and grime running down our bodies in rivulets. I could have stayed under that shower for ever, but we needed food and then I had to find mother.

My two brothers were marvellous. They saw to themselves and when they came out of their cubicle, dressed in an assortment of clothes, they were a comical sight. I laughed. 'Who's this?' I asked. 'Two lads, scrubbed clean with shining faces? Who could they be?'

'Else, it was wonderful,' Hans-Dieter assured me. 'We haven't felt so clean for a long time.'

How happy we were, all of a sudden. If only mother could be with us, but we'd see her immediately we were allowed.

Another nurse took us to a large room where a wholesome meal awaited us. However, Ralfie and Marlene were so tired, they could hardly lift their spoons.

'Dieter,' I said, 'will you stay with the little ones while I try to find mother As soon as I know where she's well looked after, I'll join you. Then, when we've had a rest, we'll visit her together.'

'OK, Else,' Hans-Dieter answered, 'you go.'

'OK?' I asked. 'What does that mean?'

'I don't know; that's what American soldiers say all the time. It's good, isn't it? I like to say it: OK, OK, OK!'

We went to the room that had been allocated to us. First a toilet for Ralf and Marlene, then bed and a good long sleep. Hans-Dieter promised to remain, while I searched for the sickbay.

After losing my way a couple of times, I was directed to her room. A nurse was with her and told me I could stay only a few minutes.

'Please tell me, Nurse, what's wrong with our mother?'

'She's exhausted: her illness is mental, not physical. She has the most terrible nightmares. Your mother must have suffered dreadfully. She keeps calling out, "Else, my child, my child; has something terrible happened to you?" Is that you?' I nodded. 'When you speak to her, talk of pleasant things . . . mention home. You say you come from Düsseldorf? Talk about it – draw her into the conversation.'

'Yes I will, Nurse. I do hope she'll get better soon, so we *can* go home.'

'You'll get there – eventually – but you must be patient.'

Saturday, 14 July 1945

We stayed ten days in Helmstedt. Mother had expert care and every day I saw her health improve. As often as we were allowed, we visited her. Then, to our great joy, on the sixth day we found her dressed and walking about.

'Mother, mother; you're better!' The boys ran to hug her, both talking at the same time.

'Children, slowly: you're crushing me. Let's sit down and have a peaceful conversation.'

'Mother!' I said, after calming everyone down. 'Look at you. You *are* much better. It's amazing to see you out of bed and dressed. Perhaps, in another couple of days, you can join us in our room. We've missed you!'

'And I've missed being with you, my children. I can't understand what happened; one minute I was well and then, suddenly, I felt utterly exhausted. It's as if I couldn't cope any more.'

'Mother, the worry was too much. You fought your battles trying to keep us alive and in the process suffered the most. But let's forget it. Soon we'll be back in Düsseldorf. Just think of that . . . can you imagine what it will feel like to be home again?'

'Elslein, my girl, I do; I do! I'll be with you soon – the sooner, the better.'

'Yes, we all wish that.'

'Ralfie, come to me; also you Hans-Dieter and, of course, we mustn't forget our little girl. Tell me, how are you all? Have you behaved yourselves and done what Else asked?'

'Yes, mama, we tried to be good and we've had fun, but it would have been much better if you'd been with us.' Ralf put his little arms around her neck and hugged her.

'And how did you pass your days?' mother asked, smiling happily.

'We had plenty to do; we managed fine. Went for walks everyday; sometimes into town, but there's not much to see. In the other direction are woodlands and fields: much more pleasant. A lady in the next room lent us a pushchair. Marlenchen's too heavy to be carried now.'

'My dearest child, with you in charge I have no need to worry. When father comes home from wherever he is, we'll have so much to tell him and he'll be proud of his grown-up daughter and two sensible sons. And his little girl.' She hugged Marlene. 'Always so good.'

'You know, mother, if your health continues to improve we might soon leave Helmstedt. Where do we go from here?'

'Our next stop will be Braunschweig, but we have to wait for transport. We're not the only ones being transferred. Nurse said I'll be assessed by a doctor who specializes in my disorder. If he declares me fit to travel, we'll get permission to make the train journey . . . all the way to Düsseldorf! No more walking for us!'

'Yippee!' shouted Ralf. 'I love trains: they go fast. We'll like that, Hans-Dieter, won't we?'

'Yes, Ralf,' answered big brother. 'Let's wait till mother can travel; then we'll be off.'

Now, we were well into July. The weather was very hot – a forerunner of violent storms. Summer thunderstorms were not unusual in Germany. We'd frequently had them in Düsseldorf: they remained on one side of the river for hours until they lost their power and fizzled out. Heavy rainshowers accompanied them, even hail sometimes, with stones as large as tennis balls.

At last, towards mid-July, mother was called to Reception. She was told we were to assemble the following day and be taken by military road transport to a camp in Braunschweig.

Once again we packed our knapsacks, and this time they were a little heavier with the clothes that had been given to us, for which we were grateful. My army boots had been replaced by a pair of sandals. Marlene also had sandals, while Hans-Dieter and Ralf wore canvas shoes, which they declared to be 'OK!'

Monday, 16 July 1945

On a dull, overcast day we said goodbye to Helmstedt – another milestone – for the last lap of our journey home.

There must have been about twenty people waiting for the 'three-ton-truck' to Braunschweig. In the back, behind the cab, benches had been fitted either side: bare wooden seats, not comfortable, but preferable to standing or squatting on the floor. Mother sat in front with the two drivers. We were sheltered from the chilly airstream by a tarpaulin, stretched over the rear of the lorry. It also hid our view, but sounds of traffic and our slow speed told us the road was busy.

Hans-Dieter and Ralf were excited to be on the move. Marlene, our quiet, contented little girl, sat on my lap smiling at the other women and children and entertained us with funny faces and her warm, friendly personality.

Braunschweig wasn't far, about 40 kilometres, which, at the rate we were moving, should have taken roughly an hour. What would await us there? I listened to the women's talk and gathered some of them had known Braunschweig before the war: an historic town with many old buildings and treasures. Would it be unharmed? Doubtless some destruction, but that could be repaired. After all, the British had chosen it as a gathering post: they had to have facilities . . .

I thought to myself, *What will we find when we arrive? The same ritual as in Helmstedt? Go to reception, answer a multitude of questions, fill out endless forms . . . and only then be allocated a bed space?*

After we arrived, we were shown a shower room and where to eat; then we sat somewhere, anywhere, and wondered about the people: where did they come from and where were they going?

There was no peace. I perched, little sister on my lap, two young brothers at my side. They were silent, confused by the hustle and bustle around us. Mother had disappeared. Earlier I'd seen her with a nurse: off, I assumed, to see a doctor. We had to wait and not move. When she was free, she'd find us.

Chapter 42

Wasteland

Monday, 16 July 1945

When mother returned from her visit to the consultant, she was cheerful and optimistic.

'Children,' she announced, 'it won't be long now till we're on our way again. Just a few days longer. The doctor will see me daily this week and then, I hope, he'll discharge me.'

'Mother, what sort of treatment does he give you?' I asked.

'No treatment really, Else. I just sit in a comfortable chair while he asks questions and I answer.'

'What about?'

'Everything since the Russians invaded Pomerania back in March. Also your capture and imprisonment and how you escaped.'

'Why is that of interest, mother?'

'It is. He's the kind of doctor who specializes in illnesses of the mind.'

'I never knew such doctors existed. It must be new.'

Mother shrugged. 'He's American but speaks excellent German. And most importantly, I think he'll cure me. I needed to talk through the miseries of our hardship from my soul, and that's such a relief.'

'"Treatments of the mind"? Quite amazing!'

'Else, I don't care. I know I feel better: that's all that matters.'

'Good, mother; wonderful!''

'Dearest, go into town and find the railway station. People say everything's in ruins but there must be a way through. Please?'

'Yes, certainly. Hans-Dieter can come with me. OK, Hans-Dieter?'

'OK, Else; that's great. Just me . . . not Ralf?'

'Yes, just you and me.'

Braunschweig, 'a historic town guarding treasures that have for centuries stood the test of time', those women had said. But no! What we saw as we entered what I presumed was the heart of the town made me gasp in horror – devastation, which must have resulted in thousands of lives lost and thousands more made homeless. Like so many towns, Braunschweig, its heart torn out, lay bleeding, mortally wounded. So much destruction! Street fighting and bombing had left a cruel legacy: could it really be rebuilt to its former glory? Certainly not patched up quickly. Hans-Dieter and I, holding hands for mutual support in the face of such desolation, stared around in silence at that architectural graveyard. The tragedy of war against civilians hit us here more than anywhere. If that was so destroyed, what about our beloved Düsseldorf? A shiver of dread struck me. Had mother envisaged the possibility that everything we'd known might no longer exist?

It was not difficult to pick our way to the railway station. By some miracle it was still useable; lines unbroken – not twisted, ripped up snakes of steel, as some we'd passed were. So presumably there were trains, though how many and how often, I couldn't tell. A constant stream of people, old and young, wound their way through the entrance. They carried belongings in suitcases, on handcarts, or any other form of transport with wheels that might lighten their loads.

'Else, if all these people want to get on the trains, will there be room for us?'

'Dieter, we're not leaving just yet. Perhaps in a few days' time, there won't be so many. Let's wait and see.'

'Wait and see, wait and see – BUT WHAT IF?' Those last three words echoed in my brain, but for the sake of my darling family, that's where they had to stay. To keep everyone's spirits up, we all just had to 'wait and see'. It was no good planting more seeds of fear in their minds than they already had.

Now we'd found the station, there was little left to see of that once-beautiful old city. We were shocked to see how shattered everything was, as we stared at the ruins of former noble structures, now just piles of rubble, some like naked skeletons, walls papered and fireplaces intact, yet floorless; gaping windows staring blindly into the streets.

We also saw many soldiers in khaki uniforms around us. When I asked a woman who they were, she said they were British.

I didn't realise we'd now reached the British sector. How far did it stretch? Yet *another* force invading our beloved country . . . I sighed. Russian, Polish, American – now British. So what were they like? I wondered. These British – how would they treat us? Should I be nervous of them? The Americans seemed fine and spoke a similar language. Did British forces also occupy Düsseldorf?

'Come, Hans-Dieter. Let's return to camp. It may be crowded and noisy but at least we're all together and our bed space is roomy and clean.'

'Yes, Else, and the food's good, isn't it? You know, I feel quite hungry now.'

'So do I. Come. Let's hurry back.' Nothing was said about the awful things we'd seen.

Friday, 20 July 1945

Three more days we had to be patient. Then, on the fourth, mother returned from her consultation in a jubilant mood.

'Children,' she called out. 'Listen, I've been discharged: now, we *can* go home. This afternoon I'll try to get our travel warrant to Düsseldorf. When I have it, we can leave!'

'Mother,' I asked, 'you sure you're well enough to start travelling? Where's our next stop?'

'Yes, Else, I'm fine; stop worrying – and our next stop will be Hannover.'

'And then?' I asked.

'That child, I don't know . . . yet.'

Soon after breakfast we packed our meagre belongings. A short while before, we'd had plenty of everything: now we were left with almost nothing. We missed Marlene's pram. Oh yes, we had our lives and thanked God for that, but we'd paid a price for them, often and dearly.

Now, we were ready to move.

I lagged behind for a moment and prayed a short, silent prayer: *Dear God. Please, look after mother and let her remain well. I'll do my best to help where I can, but I know her determination will drive her on. At what cost? Amen.*

So, on a sunny morning in late July, we were on our way to Braunschweig railway station. No one could tell us if trains were running to Hannover. Timetables were non-existent, so we had to take a chance.

The station was appallingly crowded – it seemed every German was participating in a mass exodus.

And then we too joined that motley crowd, people clustered together in family groups around their precious possessions.

We waited two hours, but no train. Then, as we were about to give up hope, a tannoy announcement said a train to Hamburg via Hannover was approaching. Suddenly the whole platform was alert, as the jostling and shoving reached danger level. Anxious people shouted, while frightened children cried; we were pushed to the edge of the line and had to be careful not to fall onto the track.

Slowly, hissing steam and throwing up swirls of smoke, the train pulled into the station.

Dear God, how can we possibly get on it? I thought. What confronted us was truly shocking. Each carriage was already full to bursting point. Men clung to the roofs, stood on bumpers, and hung onto doors and windows. The danger was beyond belief. Inside the carriages they were so crammed together it was a miracle they could breathe. And more and more tried to board.

'No, Else!' Mother declared, 'We'll stay put. I won't even attempt to take the children on the train. We'll wait! Perhaps a less-crowded train will come. We're in no hurry and safety for my family's too important to me.'

The train left and the residual crowd dispersed. Some people remained, while others left the station; where to, we had no idea.

'Mama,' Ralf whispered, 'I need a toilet: don't want to go on my own.'

'Of course, darling. We'll go together.'

Mother and Ralf were gone for some time. Hans-Dieter and I chatted: we were disappointed at letting the train go, though of course we agreed with mother's decision. Suddenly I began to wonder what had happened to her, when I saw them in the distance talking to a station official.

They eventually returned, eager to recount what had been discussed. 'Oh, I have something exciting to tell you. Listen!'

Mother led us to a corner where we squatted on the ground. She spoke conspiratorially: 'The stationmaster says there's a train on a siding at the end of the platform. It's scheduled to leave for Hamburg via Hannover tomorrow morning . . . there are no more trains leaving today. He also said he'd unlock a carriage and let some families with children spend the night in it. He's promised to try to find some basic food and drink, especially for the children.'

'That's kind of him. When can we board it?'

'He'll call us,' mother answered. 'Meanwhile we'll sit here and wait. *Don't* talk about our news, Hans-Dieter. Nor you, Ralf. We don't want a riot on our hands, do we?'

We didn't wait long before the stationmaster guided us and some other families to the siding. 'Food and drink will arrive later. Please be patient.'

He unlocked a second-class compartment carriage. The seats were upholstered: we'd sleep in comfort.

True to his word, food arrived in the late afternoon.

We spent a fairly comfortable night. The carriage was spacious and we were fortunate to have a compartment to ourselves. Some children fretted during the hours of darkness; poor little mites, all so unsettled. My fitful sleep was interrupted by babies crying – I couldn't rest: the day's events had disturbed me to such an extent that no matter how I tried, sleep wouldn't come.

Once or twice mother spoke to me. She was also unable to relax, so we lay awake and wondered what the next day would bring.

Sunday, 22 July 1945

Morning came at last, but we had no way of telling what time it was – neither mother nor I had had a watch since the Russians had stolen ours, and there was no clock nearby. We waited and waited, and the children became restless. One carriage door was unlocked, so I decided to take the boys and Marlene for a walk in the fresh morning air. There was little to see: just a neglected, untidy landscape. We walked the length of the train, away from people who once more had gathered on the opposite platform. But they spotted us and frantically waved across. Any minute I expected them to storm the train, so I hurried the children back, locking our doors from the inside. If only the stationmaster would come, surely he'd demand order and decent behaviour. When would the train be ready to leave? But no one came to stoke the boiler. At that rate we'd still be here by evening.

Hours went by, but no official came near us. Our food was gone and the children were fretful. It was distressing simply to sit and wait, but what could we do? We needed that train to take us to Hannover: patience was called for and so be it. Mother and I tried to keep Marlene entertained, but it was more difficult to occupy the boys.

To stimulate their minds mother and I thought up quizzes, and who could answer first became a noisy challenge. The boys enjoyed it; but after a while mother and I were worn out. Because of the boys' enthusiasm, we almost missed the arrival of the stoker and mate.

Dieter, of course, wanted to run and see what was going on: Ralf also, but mother wouldn't let them leave the compartment.

'Stay here,' she ordered. 'If the stationmaster spots you running about, he may order us off the train.'

'Mother, it's exciting. I want to drive trains when I grow up: I need to see how they work.'

'And I want to be a train driver too', said Ralf, 'and travel the world: that's what I want.'

'So you will, my boy, but now you stay here. I hope, before long, this train will go.'

'Mother, I could take Hans-Dieter to find some food. The stationmaster may know where.'

'Please don't be long,' mother said anxiously. 'I worry when you're not here.'

'We'll be back soon, mother.'

Off we went, Hans-Dieter and I, across the railtracks and on to the platform.

Already a crowd had gathered, all waiting to board the train. Luckily the one on the siding, except for the carriage the families occupied, was empty. Even with so many people on the platform there should be room for all.

'Look, Else,' Hans-Dieter pointed. 'There's a railway worker. Let's ask him if he knows where we can get food.'

He told us of a bakery directly outside the station that might have bread. But he warned us to hurry – bread in shops never lasted long.

As fast as we could, we left the station and, outside, on a corner, we spotted the bakery. Something was being sold because a long queue had formed outside.

'Dieter, take this money,' I said, handing him a wad of reichsmark. 'When we get to the shop, don't talk to me. Pretend we're strangers – buy what you can get and so will I.'

'All right, I'll keep my mouth shut. From now on, I don't know you.'

We both managed to purchase an assortment of dark bread, not the best quality, but it was food, a vital commodity.

Sadly there was nothing to drink. I'd spotted a water tap: if I could find a bottle or two, we could quench our thirst.

Mother was delighted with our purchases. Special praise went to my brother, who'd cannily bought whatever he could.

'How is it you managed to get so much, Hans-Dieter?' I asked, 'You've more than I have.'

'I told the woman I have many brothers and sisters, and our mother's unwell. We have to travel to Hannover: and all of us are starving.'

Hours passed and we wondered why the train had still not left the station. While Hans-Dieter and I had been shopping, the train had left the siding, to mother's concern, and was now stationary on the platform. Why were we waiting? I needed to find out, and it didn't take long. A train coming from Hamburg had broken down, blocking the track somewhere near Hannover. We had another long wait before the line was cleared. Being Sunday, it could take hours.

A cheer went up when, at last, the train grunted and groaned, clanked, chugged and hissed, and slowly began to move. It was already late afternoon, and the distance from Braunschweig to Hannover was just over 100 kilometres: we should arrive before darkness.

I gazed out of the window at a terrible wasteland, stretching as far as the horizon. 'Mother, how will it ever be possible to restore Germany? There's hardly a building undamaged – how people exist under these conditions is a mystery.'

'I also ask myself that question, and can't help wondering what we'll find when we eventually reach home.' Had mother read my private thoughts?

Every now and then our train stopped; nowhere in particular and not at a station – it simply stopped. Then after a while it chugged on again. Darkness was fast approaching when at last we reached the outskirts of Hannover. Slowly the train pulled into a badly damaged station. Amid a lot of pushing and shouting, people alighted, my little family among them. For some time the strange surroundings baffled us and mother and I felt disorientated.

'Mother,' I said, 'stay here. I'll tell an official – if I find one – that we want to travel to Düsseldorf and ask how to get there.'

I found the information I was seeking, but it wasn't encouraging: 'A goods train coming from Hamburg will travel to Münster in Westphalia. It takes coal to Hamburg, returning empty to be reloaded. It will pause here. If we wish, we can travel on it as far as Osnabrück or Münster. From there we may find a train to Duisburg.' I hesitated. 'But, mother, surely we can't travel in a coal wagon? That's going too far!'

'Mmm . . .' mused mother, 'let's discuss it. Here we are in Hannover: we want to get to Düsseldorf as quickly as possible. Our only opportunity's a goods train carrying coal that travels empty to Münster. Now tell me: do we wait here, hoping eventually a train will take us there in comfort? Or should we say "What the heck!" and travel the fairly short distance in a goods wagon? What's your opinion?'

'I suggest we go in whatever comes first. If it's a coal train, that's fine,' I said. 'Münster must have somewhere for us to wash coal dust off our hands and faces. Hans-Dieter, do you agree?'

'Yes, Else. I want to get going. I'm tired of hanging around.'

The decision was made.

We waited; and when the goods train arrived, many passengers who'd been on the platform piled into empty wagons, not caring what they'd previously contained.

Dieter and I were the first to climb into one and were able to claim a corner; then we helped mother and the little ones up. That gave us a small amount of privacy and we clung to it as other passengers piled in after us. They also had children, some of them very small – tiny little mites distressed and very fretful. I could see how anxious the mothers were, not knowing how to calm their babies. Mother asked where they were going. They said Munster.

She looked around the large carriage. 'Let's hope it doesn't rain. There's no roof and we'd be drenched. Not only that, but with thick coal dust, what would we look like?' There was nowhere to sit, just hard, cold metal flooring. Mother was still doubtful. 'Else, I hope we've done the right thing, getting on this train. It's dark and we're still not moving. It may be summer, but the nights are chilly and none of us has any covering whatsoever.'

'Mother, let's see how fast this train travels – when it eventually leaves – and how often it stops on the way. Anyway, at this rate, we could still be here in the morning!'

But while we contemplated our plight, the train gave an incredible jerk, throwing us all off balance. A smaller one followed, and then we were on our way. We huddled into the corner away from the cold airstream. But it was uncomfortable and Ralfie and Marlene whimpered, miserable and upset. We tried to console them, but it wasn't easy. Sitting shivering, as the train rumbled through the night, I realised how, well fed and clothed, we'd left Pomerania, but now, close to home, were practically destitute. We had nothing of our own. Even mother's precious jewellery, carefully sewn into the hem of her coat, was gone; and her coat was gone too!

I must have dozed, hunched up as near to the side as possible, because I awoke with a start, completely disorientated, stiff and frozen. Ralfie was asleep on my lap, and now and then a sob escaped from deep inside him: his dreams were disturbing and he was crying in his sleep.

Dieter, curled in a tight ball, was a tenacious lad, who accepted everything life threw in his path; his cheerfulness and good humour never left him.

As we travelled through the night, the stars shone brightly in a blue-black sky and once a shooting star slid across the horizon. I made three wishes and hoped they'd be granted. They were simple but important. The first was to complete the journey; the second, that we'd find our house still standing; and the third, that we'd arrive home in good health with strength to face all the further difficulties we might have to confront.

I catnapped on and off, and eventually awakening after a restless slumber saw above us the first signs of early dawn heralding a brand-new day. I could already make out shadowy shapes: mother and Marlene in the corner; Hans-Dieter in deep sleep, still in a tight ball. Ralf, on my lap, relaxed and sleeping soundly. He'd become so heavy that I had little feeling in my arms.

Minute by minute, darkness gave way to daylight. And then, what a sight confronted my eyes! Black faces made unrecognizable by the streaky coal dust, which, during the night, had whirled around the goods wagon and settled on us all. The fine particles also made us cough every now and then.

Monday, 23 July 1945

Gently I took Ralf from my lap and crawled over to where mother still slept.

'Mother,' I whispered, so as not to wake anyone. 'Mother, it's morning. The train's slowing down; I think we're passing through the suburbs of a town – where I don't know.'

She yawned. 'How are you? I'm still sleepy, while you're wide awake, bright and breezy – and looking charming with your black-streaked face!' She tried to move. 'I'm stiff and aching: I'll never stand, let alone walk.'

'Mother, I've been thinking. Suppose, wherever the train stops next, we get off, find a washroom and, when we're cleaner, find something to eat? We're all hungry.'

It was light enough to see through a chink between the large sliding doors that the train was approaching a station. Then I saw a large sign attached to the roof – 'Osnabrück'.

'Osnabrück! Please let's get off here. Surely we'll be able to get a train from here to Duisburg or even Düsseldorf. Please, mother!'

'Very well, Else. I don't think any others want to leave this train, but that's up to them.'

The train shunted noisily to a stop. We seized our meagre belongings and, stiff and aching, dropped down onto the platform. What a sorry sight we were!

'Else, what now?' mother asked. 'Have you any suggestions?'

'Let's think. There, a few steps away, is a seat. You and the children sit down, while I find where we can get assistance from the Red Cross or some official in charge.'

'Yes, yes, Else, do what you have to; we'll wait here.'

Hans-Dieter and Ralf with yawning dirty faces stayed with mother, Marlene sound asleep in her arms.

Mother and I exchanged looks and smiles. What a ridiculous situation we were in. The smiles became giggles, and soon we doubled up with helpless laughter. How good it was to laugh! Till now we'd had little to laugh about, but the absurd situation we found ourselves in released mirth and tears of hilarity that flowed down our dirty faces, making us look worse than before. While we were sharing in that wonderful merriment, the train had moved off. We never noticed it depart. I took a deep breath to pull myself together: time to do what I could for my family.

At the end of the platform I saw a station porter returning from seeing off the goods-train. Perhaps he could give me some information. I hurried towards him and he stared at me in amazement.

'Good morning,' I said, politely.

'And the same to you, young lady.'

I asked him where we could wash. 'You see we're covered in coal dust,' I added.

'I do see!' he replied, grinning. 'Not your normal look, then?'

I was about to deny it, when I realised he was joking.

'Certainly, Fraulein. No problem. By the station entrance, are two cloakrooms: gents and ladies. Not glamorous, but they'll serve your purpose.'

'Thank you, Sir. Just what we need.'

He nodded, still smiling. Then as I turned to run back, he called out, 'Wait, girl. I haven't finished. Next to the cloakrooms is a small café where you should get food and drink – you look as though you need something to stem your hunger and thirst.'

'Thanks,' I said, returning to offer him my hand, which, after inspecting it, he refused. 'May I ask you one more question, please?'

'More? Fire away. What else?'

'Can you tell me how to get from here to Düsseldorf?'

'Ah! Not difficult. A train leaves at midday, arriving in Duisburg eighty minutes later. Change there. It should be fairly easy to get a connection to Düsseldorf. Are those *all* your questions, young lady?'

'Yes, Sir; thank you for your help.'

He'd walked with me until he was in sight of mother and the children, also streaked. His body heaved with a series of silent chortles. 'Your family? You've made my day: a company of zebras!' Eventually, having absorbed enough of the sorry scene, he took off his hat and wiped his forehead. 'Well, my dear – I wish you and your mottled family a safe arrival in Düsseldorf.' And with that he returned to his office.

Chapter 43

Dancing on the Pavement

Monday, 23 July 1945

Waiting for the train to leave Osnabrück, I took my battered notebook and wrote:

> We were told the train would leave at midday: now it's 3 p.m. and we're still sitting, waiting for it to move. We'll never get to Duisburg today. The long wait's stretching our patience – so near, yet so far. It's difficult to remain calm and cheerful; even among ourselves we start to bicker. Yet there's nothing we can do except sit and wait. The boys are getting impatient, their energy, for so long held in check, has burst to the surface. Even Marlenchen, usually so placid, indicates extremely loudly that she wants to get out.

> Luckily we have a second-class compartment: upholstered seats and ample room for the five of us. The third-class compartments have wooden benches, hard and very uncomfortable. We appreciate the luxury of soft upholstery.

> When I asked a porter if he knew when this train would leave, he shrugged his shoulders and remarked that, regretfully, he couldn't say.

> Probably the truth, but nevertheless very annoying indeed!

'Mother,' I asked, 'when we reach Duisburg, might we still get a train to Düsseldorf today?'

'That depends on when we leave. I hope it's soon, but who can tell? Duisburg's a large town, and trains to Düsseldorf should run frequently; but in these uncertain times one never knows.'

'And then, mother, how do we get from the station to our house on Neckar Street?'

'Darling, that's no problem. Trams stop outside the station at frequent intervals: we'll catch the number eight to Hamm.'

'Oh mother, isn't it exciting? We'll be home soon! Did you really doubt we'd complete this long journey?'

'Yes, Else, many times. I know that, without your support, I'd never have managed it.'

'Thank you, mother, but I've done nothing special.' I smiled at the praise, however. Then after a while I said, 'I wonder how Düsseldorf has changed? Do you fear a lot of of it might be destroyed? We've seen desolation everywhere and I can't believe it will be any different in Düsseldorf.'

'Else, I can't imagine our city in ruins. Surely Adolf Hitler wouldn't have allowed our beautiful hometown to be flattened? He'd have defended it somehow.'

Mother seemed to be lost in a world of make-believe. In her mind she saw Düsseldorf as it used to be, undamaged and as splendid as ever. It saddened me to realise that soon she might be as devastated as she was in Berlin – somehow she found reality difficult to grasp.

I couldn't bring myself to shatter her illusions, so kept silent. Soon we'd see the reality for ourselves, and I hoped what met us on our arrival won't be so traumatic that the shock completely overwhelmed us . . .

Suddenly a shudder ran through the train. Something was happening! Could it be we were moving at last? Out of the compartment window I could see the stationmaster rushing alongside the carriages, closing any open doors. And then, a tremendous jerk, followed by a hesitant start and, glory be, we were finally on our way. A quick glance at the station clock: 5.15 p.m. – five and a quarter hours late leaving.

'We're moving!' shouted Hans-Dieter and Ralf together, and even our baby sister clapped her tiny hands together, while shouting, 'Mama, puffer-train off!'

What a wonderful feeling!

We tried to ignore the view from the window of a landscape not only ruined, but totally neglected. The train crawled, and its slowness brought more impatience and irritability. Now and then it stopped for no apparent reason, and each time we came to a halt more people were waiting to get on.

It passed through Münster station without stopping. That was the industrial heart of Westphalia, but there was little industry to see. Where were the smoking chimneys, formerly the sign of that ever-busy region? Those that remained stood silhouetted, black and smokeless, against a slowly darkening evening sky.

The train didn't stop at Essen, a large town I once knew well. Mother's cousin lived there before the war and we occasionally visited her. They were pleasant outings, made more exciting if mother and Aunt Grete took us to one of the beautiful parks that had made the town famous. We'd sit outside the restaurant and, as a special treat, Hans-Dieter and I were allowed to choose a scrumptious slice of cake and glass of lemonade, while mother and Aunt enjoyed their small pots of real coffee and a slice of their favourite cake – in mother's case the usual Black Forest gateau).

How long ago it all seemed. I longed to know what had happened to my aunt and to Uncle Arno? Were they still alive?

As the train pulled out of the station, the landscape was more devastated. I realized most of the towns and cities in Germany were like that. Industrial areas bore the brunt of heavy fighting and bombing, and consequently, few buildings remained undamaged.

What would face us on our arrival in Düsseldorf? These were my anxious thoughts, but I kept them to myself, because once we reached our destination, the answers would be revealed.

Tuesday, 24 July

When, at last, the train drew into Duisburg station and halted at the platform, I glimpsed the station clock hanging from a beam. It said 6.25 p.m. Now we had to disembark and find the train to Düsseldorf.

'Would you go, Else?' Mother struggled to get up; she was still not completely fit.

'Yes, mother. I'll find someone. Come on, Hans-Dieter. We need to stretch our legs.'

'Sure, Else.'

We didn't have far to go before a conductor came past. When I asked him about trains to Düsseldorf, he said one would leave the station just after 7 p.m. from platform three. He also explained how to get there.

'Tell your mother to go straight to the platform. You need to find a seat as soon as the train arrives, as there are many passengers at this time of day. By 8 p.m. everyone must be off the streets. Our curfew in Duisburg is very strict; it may be in Düsseldorf too.'

Curfew? What's a curfew? I'd never heard the word before. I had to ask mother; perhaps she'd know. But first we had to get to platform three. At present the station was quiet – so different from Braunschweig, where people had fought to get on a train, hanging from windows and doors, and sitting on bumpers and carriage roofs, with no regard for others.

Here in Duisburg the situation was far more civilized. Perhaps it would also be so in Düsseldorf?

No train waited on platform three. We found a bench to sit on, and hoped we wouldn't wait long for the last lap of our journey. Düsseldorf seemed within reach, yet in reality . . .

We waited in silence, as there was little to talk about. Every time I looked at mother she was deep in thought, and I didn't want to intrude. What was going through her mind? She appeared worried. Perhaps it terrified her to imagine what we might find in Neckar Street. Would we have a home to go to?

'Mother, I'm hungry,' Hans-Dieter announced.

'And so am I,' added Ralf.

'I'm sorry, children – I doubt it's possible to get food at this time of day. Once the train leaves, it won't take long. You boys have been so good; please be patient a while longer.'

'Yes, mother,' the boys nodded. But their tummies rumbled. We hadn't had a proper meal for days.

'Just think, children, one hour and we'll nearly be home. Düsseldorf station's much larger. Perhaps the restaurant's open. If so, we'll have a treat, splash out on a substantial meal.'

Oh mother, I thought. *What dreams! I hope you won't be disappointed. It will be a miracle if the restaurant's still functioning.*

Aside to her, I said, 'Let's hope our house is still habitable, mother – we've been away a long time. Suppose someone else is living there now? What would we do then?'

'Elslein, we'll get over that hurdle when we come to it. I've a strong feeling the building's fine and that we'll find our apartment just as we left it. But time will tell.'

I'd been watching the hands of the station clock. How slowly they moved! Now it was 7.20 p.m. and still no train. Mother was talking to two ladies travelling to Cologne. It helped to pass the time for her, but for the children and me, the waiting was unbearable.

I took out my diary again, and scribbled my thoughts:

> Waiting . . . waiting . . . the whole long trek across Germany has been a series of slow trudges and long, long waits, with each chance of moving on being firmly in the hands of God. For certainly no one, official or otherwise, has really known when – or even if – there would actually be a link to the next step of the journey. And those steps have been so small, the pace of a toddler. From one town to another on foot . . . by cart or lorry if we were lucky. From one camp to another, and now from one train to the next. How many stages have there already been?
>
> All those endless roads we'd trudged on for days and weeks – with swollen, blistered, weary feet, hoping every night to find food and some sort of shelter, hoping to avoid the authorities and trouble, yet longing for someone to come to our aid . . . and they had. Farmers and strangers, locals in dire need of sustenance for their own survival had shared their last crusts with us. Crusts of dry bread, a few potatoes – bare rations day after day. Because of the children? I wonder how mother and I would have fared on our own? It was the sad and hungry faces of Ralfie and little Marlene and the bravery of my dear Hans-Dieter that softened people's hearts.
>
> As I look at them now, I can understand it. Three young children who should be out playing as I did at their age, knowing that when mother calls, a hearty tea and warm, soft bed beckon. Even during the war years we'd lived on nourishing produce from Glowitz Manor farm, either prepared in those vast kitchens or on our own little stove. Now we're reduced to scraps, tiny snacks wherever we can track them down. See how thin they are, my darling siblings, their stomachs rumbling with hunger. Yet people tell us the war's over, finished! I see little sign of it – no decent food has passed these children's lips for days. They're still waiting, sitting silently on a hard bench without a single complaint among them. Whatever mother says they believe. They have utter faith in her that, within a short while, all their dreams will come true and they'll be home, dining on milk and honey, and live happily ever after. That's how all fairy tales end, don't they?
>
> I've tried hard to go along with mother's beliefs – or pretences – that all will be well just as soon as we get to Düsseldorf. But if I'm honest, there's a horrible feeling in the pit of my stomach, which is not simply hunger, but also exhaustion and fear.

Exhaustion because, even though I'm weary, I've tried to be strong for everyone, especially since mother's illness, struggling to take the strain, to bear the brunt in moments of action, or, as now, the stress of inaction, keeping everyone's spirits up, passing endless hours occupying little restless minds. I'm not sure how much longer I can go on like this . . .

And fear – fear that . . . dare I say it? The fairy tale WE have dreamed of, our happy ending: a safe, solid-walled, familiar house in Düsseldorf. Will, or could, our dreams possibly end so easily? Or will we finish up homeless like so many others, refugees for months, years, and this time without a destination, no place to aim for? No relatives still alive to help us. Nothing. Just more and more WAITING . . .

Just then there was an announcement: 'The next train arriving on platform three should leave Duisburg at 7.35 and arrive in Düsseldorf at about 8.20.'

'There! You see, mother. We'll get to Düsseldorf today!' I must overcome my previous morbid thoughts and rally some strength from somewhere, if just for the sake of my darling patient family. 'Oh, isn't it exciting! I have butterflies in my tummy and don't know whether to laugh or cry.'

'My darling daughter!' Mother laughed a high nervous laugh. 'I know how you feel. I think we can all be proud of our achievement. I still can't believe we've done it.'

'Yes, mother, today's *Tuesday, 24 July*, and the day we left Glowitz was *Wednesday, 6 June 1945*. Such a long, long journey and it's because of you and you alone that we will, at last, reach home safely.'

'No, Else; you were always there to help me.'

'What about me and Ralf, mother?' asked Hans-Dieter. 'We tried to help, but Else's grown up and can do much more. We did try. And so did Marlene – she's not cried once on the platform.'

'I know, my boy. You, Ralf, Marlene – all heroes. Thank you.'

'Tell me, mother,' I whispered, 'how do you really feel now our journey's almost over?'

'Elslein, glory be! Thanks to God for guarding us all the way. But now I'm so weary of travelling and will be mighty glad when our wandering days are truly over.'

We boarded the train and settled once more. No second-class compartment this time: we had to endure hard, uncomfortable wooden seats to Düsseldorf. And the train was crowded, with most people continuing to Cologne. Passengers made room for us and wanted to know where we'd come from, plying us with questions. I didn't wish to get involved, but it was good to see mother joining in a lively discussion. For too long she'd put up with childish chatter from Marlene and Ralf, interspersed with occasional intelligent conversation with me and Hans-Dieter.

The conductor blew his whistle and the train started to move. I tried to look out of the dirty, soot-streaked window, hoping I'd recognize familiar places, but it was no easy task. Terrible devastation lay everywhere – from Krefeld on towards Düsseldorf, nothing but ruins. It beggared belief how anyone could have survived such carnage . . .

Soon the outlying suburbs of Düsseldorf drew nearer. I recognized a few landmarks, and by now felt excitement rising and my heart beating at twice its usual rate. I looked at mother and knew she felt the same. *Dear Lord, please let's find we still have a home.*

The train was now hurrying us towards Düsseldorf's main station, but I kept silent. Words failed me as fear rose within. What exactly I was afraid of, I couldn't say; yet I trembled and a lump swelled in my throat. I had to struggle not to cry.

The boys also sensed something extraordinary was happening to our family. Silently they too looked out of the window as minute by minute the train sped nearer our destination. What would they make of it?

'Dieter, do you remember Düsseldorf? I'm not sure you will, Ralf. You were too young. And Marlene, you've never been here – welcome to your hometown!'

They smiled at me, but didn't answer; just turned to stare outside again.

As I gazed out of the window my thoughts were with our dear ones whom we haven't seen for so long. Grandma and Grandad, father's parents in Gerresheim; was their house still standing? Would we find them alive and in good health? We had to visit them soon. Surely trams were running? A number three would take us almost to their front door. How thrilled they'd be to see us standing there.

Grandad Barbier, mother's father, and Aunt Berta, her stepmother – what had become of them? Their house stood so near the river. If there'd been fighting, had theirs also been reduced to rubble?

My best friend, Marlies, and her parents, Herr and Frau Wunder. Were they still living in the house in Erft Street? I longed to see her again. So much time had passed since we were last in touch, and so much had happened in our lives. I wondered – had she been evacuated in the end? Had she also suffered? I hoped not!

But what had happened to me I'd keep to myself. I couldn't talk about that – not even to my best friend.

The train skirted the city, yet little was visible, as the sky was nearly dark. But the suburbs told their own story: a picture of utter destruction. What would we find when we finally arrived?

We passed the suburb of Düsseldorf-Ratingen. In minutes we'd arrive in the centre of Düsseldorf. We sat, silently wrapped in thought. I couldn't believe that train to Düsseldorf really was the last we'd take for, I hoped, a long, long time.

'Mother, we're almost there,' I breathed, as the engine slowed down.

'I know, my child. It's nearly over.'

At a very slow pace the train crawled into the station. The station clock was still in its usual place and showed 8.30. I felt sick with apprehension. I wanted to hold mother's hand but she had Marlene and Ralf – her hands were full. I needed reassurance, a stranger in my hometown.

Then Mother rose to her feet and said, 'Come, children. Let's get our things and go.'

'Mother, as soon as we're on the platform, I'll try to find somewhere to eat and see if the trams are running. If not, I fear we'll have to walk.'

'Walk to Neckar Street?' asked Hans-Dieter, unhappily. 'Mother, that's too far; I'm tired.'

'And so am I,' added his echo.

'If we can find food, and our tummies are full, you'll be surprised how far you can walk, Hans-Dieter,' mother announced. 'All the way back to Glowitz if you had to, isn't that so?'

'Mother, you're joking! I'll *never* go back to Pomerania again. Never!

The train jolted to a halt and let off steam. Mother opened the door and we stepped down. Hans-Dieter was the first to jump. I followed and turned to help Ralf, who was determined to jump down by himself. But the steps were too high, so he accepted a little help from me. Mother was the last down. She handed me our knapsacks, which I piled in the middle of the platform; then she and Marlene joined us. We hugged and huddled together; we kissed and laughed and cried. Our emotions, corked up for so long, now released, made us very excited, whatever was to come.

During that commotion we forgot we were hungry.

'Mother,' I said, picking up a couple of knapsacks, 'let's go downstairs and walk towards the entrance. We may find a café.'

I had to look for yet another station officer for information – the most important question being where we could get some food. Fortunately there was an official at the bottom of the stairs. 'Please, where can we find a restaurant or cafeteria?' I asked.

'My girl,' he answered, 'that's difficult. At this time in the evening the station restaurant's closed, and once you get out of here there's nothing.'

'Nothing at all in this wonderful city?' I asked in surprise.

'Where have you come from, young lady? "Cafeteria", "restaurant"? No, my dear, no such places are available anywhere in this wonderful city of Düsseldorf! Anyway, don't you know there's a curfew? It started at 8 p.m. and won't be lifted till 7 a.m. tomorrow. After eight, no civilian's allowed on the road – no cars, no trams. Nothing at all. If the military police catch you and you don't have a valid excuse, you could end up in prison. They're incredibly strict here; but of course they have to be to curb riots and looting.'

'That's awful.' I stared at him. 'But how can we get home? Are there no taxis?'

The man laughed loudly, holding his sides. 'Taxis? You must be joking, child. Of course there are no taxis! We're very poor, you know – we have nothing any more.'

I stared around desperately. 'But tell me, please – there must be somewhere we can find some food? We haven't eaten for hours; days actually!'

'But I tell you what,' he continued, kindly, surveying our sad little family, standing like waifs in a line in the almost deserted foyer. 'Make your way to the main entrance. On your left is the station restaurant – closed now, as I said. Opposite is a kiosk selling hot sausages in rolls, which remains open later – for people on official business. You might be lucky; only don't set your hopes too high. There aren't many people about and, if business is slack, he may have shut. But it's worth trying. If he's still there, he'll certainly serve you.'

'Thank you, Sir,' I answered. 'That's a great help!'

I dashed back to mother and the children: 'Make for the entrance, Mother; I'll run ahead and see what I can find.'

Please God, let him be open. If we can't get food here, any food at all, then I don't know what to do. I ran and ran, and reached the kiosk, totally out of breath. There, thank God, was the man wiping down his counter. If only he had some food left. It didn't have to be anything special – just a dry roll each would have been excellent. We really were starving.

Seeing me rushing towards him, he called out, 'Slow down, lady. Can I help?'

'Oh yes,' I answered, gasping. Once I got my breath back and could talk normally, I put my request to him.

The man inspected me closely from top to toe. 'Tell me, where have you come from?'

'My mother and I, we – together with my two brothers and small sister – have come from Pomerania near the Baltic Sea.'

'Goodness! How did you get here?' He stared; then rummaged under the counter.

'We walked most of the way; occasionally we took a cart – in Braunschweig we got on a goods train. It had carried coal, so we were terribly dirty when we got off.'

'Do you live in Düsseldorf?' asked the man.

'Yes, we live – lived – near the harbour.'

'That's a long way to walk. Do you know there's a curfew?'

'Yes, I know. But what can we do? We must get home.'

'Then I wish you luck. Here's a parcel with some morsels to eat. Not much, but it might fill a hole.'

I thanked him and returned to mother, clutching my precious food parcel. When she saw me, her face lit up. She was beaming: she could see I'd been successful.

'Elslein!' she said. 'You're bringing us food? If anyone could get some, it would be you.'

I handed her the parcel, and she opened and shared it among us.

While we were contentedly munching, savouring each mouthful, a porter approached us. 'Madam, how much longer will you all be there?'

'Not long, sir,' answered mother. 'We'll soon be gone, but first we must finish our meal. We got a snack at the kiosk. We're very hungry. It's the first nourishment offered to my children for, for days. When we've finished, we'll go.'

'You know there's a curfew,' the official reminded her.

'So we're told,' she replied, 'but your colleague said it started at 8 p.m. Yet it's now nearly nine. Why are people still walking about and leaving the building, when we can't?'

'That's different,' he said. 'These people have special permits allowing them on the streets until 9 p.m., but not a minute longer.'

'So who are they?' pressed mother.

'Doctors, nurses, shift workers. Also railway workers. The occupying forces give them special permission. But it's not easy to get a permit: the man in the street has to live by the rules.' Then he added, 'Or else!'

'Well,' mother declared, 'it's almost nine; we must also go. Luckily we live in the outskirts of Düsseldorf. That was our last train! Come, Else. Let's pack away the rest of the food to eat later.'

As we stepped outside the station onto the forecourt, we saw in front of us terrible devastation. We expected a degree of bombing and that a few features we'd loved would have disappeared, but what we encountered was a dreadful spectacle. The splendid city we remembered was no more – ruined. And not just a few houses razed to the ground, but every building, as far as the eyes could see, reduced to a gigantic heap of rubble.

Mother, Hans-Dieter and I were stunned into shocked silence.

'Dear God!' exclaimed mother at last. 'Is Düsseldorf like this all over? All those places of centuries past, now just flattened, gone! Luxurious hotels, fashionable department stores and elegant private houses, where are you now?' She voiced what we couldn't believe we were viewing. 'Everything, but everything, is gone!' She stepped forward and turned a full circle. The station alone stood in its former glory. 'It's all so gruesome. No wonder there's a curfew. How terrifying to be out and about overnight in this destroyed city with its bomb craters, its burnt beams sticking into pathways, walls about to collapse at a touch . . . and heap upon heap of rubble.' Despair was in our mother's voice as bitter tears coursed down her cheeks. 'I fear we must be prepared for more horror to confront us nearer home.'

'Mother, please don't cry,' I put an arm around her. 'It's bad now, but it won't stay this way. One day all this will be rebuilt. And just as beautifully as before – perhaps even better. We may have lost the war, but we're Germans: no one, but no one can stop us. German people will rebuild this and every city in our lovely country; everyone still alive will work together. Cities will rise out of the ruins; you wait and see.'

'Elslein, I hope your optimism rubs off on me; but all this is a shock. I'm ashamed to let my emotions get the better of me. Yes my darling, like you I'll face the future with hope.'

'I think it likely that some streets have been cleared, mother. There could be trams in the morning, but not now because of the curfew. It seems we must walk again, so we'd better start in case we get caught.'

'Very well, Else. Let's go,' mother said. 'We're wasting time. Let's make the most of what's left of the twilight. All too soon it will be dark and we have some way to go. Until we get used to the mutilated city, the sights will break our hearts.'

Just as we set out across the wide forecourt a British jeep raced onto it. Tyres screeching, the driver stopped the car directly in front of us. Two British military policemen, looking very formidable in their brown uniforms, glared at us intimidatingly.

Mother clutched Marlene, who buried her head, and Ralf hid partly behind me. Hans-Dieter faced them boldly.

One jumped out and walked towards us. 'Madam, what are you doing out on the street?' he asked. 'Don't you know there's a curfew?'

'Yes sir, I do,' was mother's brave reply, 'but we've just arrived by train. We're tired and need to get home.'

'And where's *home*?' the soldier asked.

'Near the harbour. We live in Neckar Street – if our house is still there.'

'Don't you know? Why? Where have you come from?' he questioned.

'Glowitz near Stolp – we have travel permits.'

He glanced at his colleague. 'Glowitz? Stolp? Where's that?'

'Pomerania. We were evacuated there . . . near the Baltic Sea. It's now Polish. Conditions got bad. We left at the beginning of June and have been on the road ever since . . . walking mostly – almost 1,000 kilometres. Now we're dirty and weary and our only desire is to get home.'

The English military policeman stood there, mouth gaping. He'd obviously understood her.

'You walked all that way, Madam? And your children? That's incredible!'

She nodded. 'As we can't go on the street, soldier, do we have to stay in the station all night?'

He took off his cap and scratched his head. 'People like you are common. They arrive every day but not usually at this time. You've put me in a dilemma – I daren't let you go.' He replaced his cap and scuffed his shoe while he thought. 'I'll risk it! I'll issue you a permit to safeguard you on your way.'

'Thank you,' mother replied gratefully, as he handed her a signed piece of paper. 'Tell me, are street lights working in the city, or will it be plunged into darkness soon?'

'There are a few lights, but not many. One or two have just been repaired on Graf-Adolf Street and some also function on Königs Boulevard. But it's still unpleasant to walk through town after dark. As soon as we leave, you'd better get going; we wish you a safe homecoming.' The policeman jumped back into the jeep and the driver started the engine. It roared off, leaving us alone on the forecourt.

The jeep disappeared around a corner, the sound of its engine fading into the distance as we walked towards the main road. Suddenly an unmistakable noise broke the curfew's silence. There it was again, and coming nearer. And then a jeep slowed to a stop in the road in front of us.

'What now?' mother muttered. 'Just as we get going, someone else is eager to detain us.'

But no, it was the same jeep and the same men who'd stopped us before.

Once more the British soldier jumped out while the driver kept his engine running.

'Lady!' he shouted. 'I need my head examining – we can't just drive off and leave you and your children here. We'll take you as far as Graf-Adolf Square and the Schwanenspiegel Lake, but we really must leave you there. From there you can walk home; it's not too far and we think you can manage it.'

'Thank you so much!' croaked mother. 'We really do appreciate your kindness . . . I hope it won't get you into trouble?' Her voice wasn't steady and she sounded close to tears.

'It's a risk – but a responsible one . . . worth it.'

The five of us just managed to pile into the backseat. It was a tight squeeze, but heaven to be driven. The jeep went at speed through Graf-Adolf Street and in no time came to a stop close to the lake. What had taken minutes in the jeep would have taken us more than an hour by foot.

'You must get out here, madam; we can't take you further.' The soldier smiled. 'But it's not far to your destination.'

Once we'd stepped out of the jeep, it raced around a corner and out of sight.

We stood by the lake, still trying to absorb the incredible ruination of our beloved city. Was it plausible to expect our house still to be standing? And if it wasn't, what then? Where could we go in the curfew? Was there some hall nearby? We'd soon find out. We had to see for ourselves. Who knew? Miracles did occasionally happen, so why shouldn't we encounter one now?

The lake lay dark and silent, without a ripple on the water or a swan in sight. Would they still glide in all their beauty as they used to? Or would they have flown in terror as the bombs fell?

I remembered our boat trips on summer Sunday afternoons, our frolics on the ice in winter. Would those carefree days come back, I wondered? I fervently hoped so, but somehow doubted it.

The unnatural silence surrounding us was unnerving and sent shivers down my spine. I knew mother felt it too, and Hans-Dieter and the little ones sensed our unease.

'Come on, children. Pick up your knapsacks and let's start our last walk. We mustn't linger any longer but try to get home before it's completely dark.

With knapsacks on our backs, I took Ralf's hand, while Hans-Dieter walked beside me. Marlene trotted close to mother. Wearily we trudged on to complete this final stretch of our long journey. Turning the corner into Hammer Street, we saw our beloved river Rhine for the first time in almost four years. The sight was welcoming, for although we'd found our beautiful city destroyed, our river remained as always – dependable and unchanged. Silently it flowed from its source in Switzerland to where it entered the sea in the Netherlands; no one could ever change that: the glorious river was ours.

Seeing our river flowing powerfully before us lifted our spirits, and, with renewed vitality, we continued down Hammer Street, which seemed to stretch for ever into the distance. Beyond the harbour entrance, we saw that the low wall we'd climbed and run along still existed. Goods trains stood on sidings, loaded or waiting for supplies to arrive by ship, ready to take them to other parts of Germany.

As we came nearer and nearer our home, mother became silent, wrapped in her own thoughts. What were they? I didn't ask. Then suddenly it burst out of her. 'Elslein!' she cried. 'I don't know what to do. I'm afraid of what we'll find when we reach our street. Look at the houses opposite. Not one is undamaged, and we expect our house to be still standing unharmed, in one piece? It's impossible!'

'Mother,' I answered, 'don't despair yet: there's always a chance. Anyway, you say there's a solution to every problem, no matter how large it seems. Look at what we have been through!'

At last we reached Wupper Street. A corner house was badly damaged but as I noticed a low wall, a sudden idea occurred to me, a challenge I'd take for mother's sake.

'Mother,' I said, 'why don't you stay here and sit on the wall with Ralf and Marlene? Hans-Dieter and I will run ahead to see what's happened to our street. Please don't move away; we'll only be gone a few minutes. But it's best you're prepared for what we find.'

'Yes, Else, a good idea,' she replied, uncertainly. 'We won't leave here until you return. But please come back soon.' She sat down anxiously, with the two little ones beside her.

'Come, Hans-Dieter,' I said. 'Let's go.'

We both held hands and ran the rest of the way towards the corner of Erft and Neckar Street. The sky was in a late state of twilight with a luminous glow shining through dark clouds that silhouetted everything in front of it. However, as soon as we could see the length of our street, we froze in horror. *Every house on both sides of our once-elegant road was flattened*; all that remained were heaps of charred timbers and dusty rubble.

'Dieter, what should we tell mother? I don't know how to face her.'

'Let's walk down the street, Else. It's dusk now; nothing can be seen clearly. Come on; at least we'll know for sure what kind of damage our home suffered – if we can work out which one it is.'

'Very well, let's go and see.'

We walked along the street, counting doorsteps – in some cases, all that was left. Slowly a ghostly black structure loomed up on our right. We crept nearer, until it was clearly visible in the evening twilight. Unlike the skeleton-walled hollow shells opposite, that structure appeared bold and solid.

'Dieter, look carefully: here are buildings still standing.'

They consisted of three apartment houses, sole survivors in a desolate landscape. Three familiar buildings, *our house being the first of them*! And the flat on the top storey was also intact. Its black windows stared down, silently awaiting our arrival.

I moved closer to the three houses to make sure. I studied the windows – unbroken? Cracked, but not broken. I ran my eyes over the bells at the side of the front door: 'W. Hopp', the name still engraved as it always had been. Beside it was the bell where I'd contacted mother upstairs. 'Number Fifteen' still attached to the front door – *our house*.

'Dieter, it's just as we left it. What a wonderful sight. What a relief.'

'Isn't it amazing! It seems undamaged,' exclaimed my young brother, passing his hand over the brickwork as though checking for cracks. It was as though the sense of touch made it all the more real. Eventually we convinced ourselves that our home stood intact.

Dieter reacted first: 'Come on, Else. We must get back and give mother the wonderful news.'

As we ran back down the street, I danced up and down the pavement steps, as I had done so long ago in a time of innocent childhood. Tiredness gone, my feet had wings.

Before we turned the corner of Erft Street, I couldn't resist glancing over to where Marlies had lived. It looked as though her house was also standing. But now was not the time to get in touch with her – that would have to wait.

Mother, Ralf and Marlenchen were still sitting where we'd left them. As she saw us approaching, mother rose to her feet.

Suddenly I couldn't contain myself any longer. I ran flat out towards her, shouting, 'Mother, it's *standing*! Our house is still in one piece! WE HAVE A HOME!'

Mother lifted Ralf and Marlene off the wall without taking her eyes from us, and the three of them walked towards us.

Dieter was sobbing as he ran into mother's arms. I followed, and mother and I clutched each other, the lump in my throat threatening to choke me, while mother's tears streamed down her face.

We hugged and kissed; we laughed and cried – tears of joy and thankfulness to God that our long trek had reached a happy end.

We thought of our dear father. If only he could be with us and share our joy. Our thoughts fly to you wherever you are! We miss you Vati, come home soon.